Frommer's®

Washington, D.C.
from $80 a Day

12th Edition

by Elise Hartman Ford

Here's what the critics say about Frommer's:

"Amazingly easy to use. Very portable, very complete."
—*Booklist*

"Detailed, accurate, and easy-to-read information for all price ranges."
—*Glamour Magazine*

"Hotel information is close to encyclopedic."
—*Des Moines Sunday Register*

"Frommer's Guides have a way of giving you a real feel for a place."
—*Knight Ridder Newspapers*

WILEY
Wiley Publishing, Inc.

About the Author

Elise Hartman Ford has been a freelance writer in the Washington, D.C., area since 1985. Her writing has appeared in the *Washington Post; Washingtonian* magazine; the London-based *Bradman's North America Guide; The Essential Guide to Business Travel; Ladies' Home Journal;* and other national, regional, and trade publications. In addition to this guide, she is the author of *Frommer's Washington, D.C.; Frommer's Memorable Walks in Washington, D.C.;* and *Unique Meeting, Wedding, and Party Places in Greater Washington.*

Published by:

Wiley Publishing, Inc.

111 River St.
Hoboken, NJ 07030-5744

ISBN 0-7645-4128-5

Editor: Jennifer Moore
Production Editor: Donna Wright
Cartographer: John Decamillis
Photo Editor: Richard Fox
Production by Wiley Indianapolis Composition Services

Front cover photo: Capitol Building, evening
Back cover photo: White House

For information on our other products and services or to obtain technical support, please contact our Customer Care Department within the U.S. at 800/762-2974, outside the U.S. at 317/572-3993 or fax 317/572-4002.

Wiley also publishes its books in a variety of electronic formats. Some content that appears in print may not be available in electronic formats.

Manufactured in the United States of America

5   4   3   2   1

Contents

List of Maps

An Invitation to the Reader

In researching this book, we discovered many wonderful places—hotels, restaurants, shops, and more. We're sure you'll find others. Please tell us about them, so we can share the information with your fellow travelers in upcoming editions. If you were disappointed with a recommendation, we'd love to know that, too. Please write to:

Frommer's Washington, D.C. from $80 a day, 12th Edition
Wiley Publishing, Inc. • 111 River St. • Hoboken, NJ 07030-5744

An Additional Note

Please be advised that travel information is subject to change at any time—and this is especially true of prices. We therefore suggest that you write or call ahead for confirmation when making your travel plans. The authors, editors, and publisher cannot be held responsible for the experiences of readers while traveling. Your safety is important to us, however, so we encourage you to stay alert and be aware of your surroundings. Keep a close eye on cameras, purses, and wallets, all favorite targets of thieves and pickpockets.

Other Great Guides for Your Trip:

Frommer's Memorable Walks in Washington, D.C.
Frommer's Washington, D.C.
Frommer's Portable Washington, D.C.
The Unofficial Guide to Washington, D.C.

Frommer's Star Ratings, Icons & Abbreviations

Every hotel, restaurant, and attraction listing in this guide has been ranked for quality, value, service, amenities, and special features using a **star-rating system.** In country, state, and regional guides, we also rate towns and regions to help you narrow down your choices and budget your time accordingly. Hotels and restaurants are rated on a scale of zero (recommended) to three stars (exceptional). Attractions, shopping, nightlife, towns, and regions are rated according to the following scale: zero stars (recommended), one star (highly recommended), two stars (very highly recommended), and three stars (must-see).

In addition to the star-rating system, we also use **seven feature icons** that point you to the great deals, in-the-know advice, and unique experiences that separate travelers from tourists. Throughout the book, look for:

Finds	Special finds—those places only insiders know about
Fun Fact	Fun facts—details that make travelers more informed and their trips more fun
Kids	Best bets for kids, and advice for the whole family
Moments	Special moments—those experiences that memories are made of
Overrated	Places or experiences not worth your time or money
Tips	Insider tips—great ways to save time and money
Value	Great values—where to get the best deals

The following **abbreviations** are used for credit cards:

AE	American Express	DISC	Discover	V	Visa
DC	Diners Club	MC	MasterCard		

Frommers.com

Now that you have the guidebook to a great trip, visit our website at **www.frommers.com** for travel information on more than 3,000 destinations. With features updated regularly, we give you instant access to the most current trip-planning information available. At Frommers.com, you'll also find the best prices on airfares, accommodations, and car rentals—and you can even book travel online through our travel booking partners. At Frommers.com, you'll also find the following:

- Online updates to our most popular guidebooks
- Vacation sweepstakes and contest giveaways
- Newsletter highlighting the hottest travel trends
- Online travel message boards with featured travel discussions

What's New in Washington, D.C.

Washington, D.C., in the year 2004, continues to grapple with security issues as the city meanwhile carries on as a busy business and tourist destination. You may encounter road blocks, concrete barriers, and police officers directing you around town, as well as metal detectors and more intense scrutiny at most sightseeing attractions.

You will also notice that the capital is a city under construction. This is a good thing, since it augurs prosperity, though it can be unsightly and sometimes inconvenient. Major museums, such as the Phillips Collection, are in the midst of an expansion, and others, like the Corcoran Gallery of Art, are about to embark on a significant expansion. An underground visitors center is nearing completion at the U.S. Capitol, and, by the time you read this, the same may be underway on the grounds of the Washington Monument. Two large hotels are being built in neighborhoods, the waterfront and the Mount Vernon/Shaw area, that only recently would have been unlikely choices; these days, D.C. is developing all over the place.

GETTING HERE If you are hoping to book a flight to D.C. on a discount airline, you probably know about Southwest Airlines, which flies into Baltimore-Washington International Airport, and you may know about the relatively new, low-fare airline, JetBlue, which flies into Washington-Dulles International Airport. But you may not have heard of the latest discount airline on the scene: the Delta Airlines subsidiary, **Song** (℃ **800/359-7664; www.flysong.com**). Song started up service to Dulles Airport in late 2003, with flights to only a handful of cities, including some in the northeast and Florida. Check it out.

GETTING AROUND In mid-2003, the Washington Metropolitan Area Transit Authority (WMATA) lengthened Metrorail's hours of operation on weekends, so that now Metro trains start running at 7am on Saturday and Sunday and stop running at 3am Saturday and Sunday. To fund this expanded service, WMATA increased base fares (for the first time in 8 years) for bus and rail service by 10¢, to $1.20, with $3.60 the maximum you would pay for travel to the furthest destination.

The District and federal governments, and downtown businesses are discussing the creation of a **"Circulator"** shuttle bus system, whose buses would run every 5 minutes along two east-west routes between Union Station and Georgetown and two north-south routes between the D.C. Convention Center and the waterfront in southwest D.C. Similar in service and purpose to the successful Georgetown Shuttle, the Circulator is intended to ease the city's congested streets while providing quick, easy, and cheap (50¢ one-way) access to well-traveled spots around town. Proponents of the system expect residents, tourists, and federal workers to use the buses, which will supplement Metro's rail and bus transportation. If approved, some Circulator buses will have started circulating in 2004.

ACCOMMODATIONS Hotels are few indeed near the National Mall. So the arrival of a brand-new hotel, for the cost-conscious traveler, at that, is welcome news. The **Residence Inn,** near the Mall (at 4th and E sts. SW), is slated to open in the fall of 2004, to coincide with the debut of the nearby Smithsonian National Museum of the American Indian.

DINING The area around the MCI Center, downtown, is popping with new restaurants, most of them in the expensive category. Two exceptions are **Matchbox,** 713 H St., NW (© **202/ 289-4441**) and **Ella's,** 901 F St. NW (© **202/638-3434**). Oddly enough, both eateries are pizza places, with Matchbox offering other entrees and salads, while Ella's pretty much sticks to pizza. Until now, this part of town really didn't have a good pizzeria—now it has two. If you're willing to spend a little more money and you're a lover of French cuisine, you should try to reserve a table at the new **Bistrot D'OC,** 518 10th St. NW (© **202/393- 5444**) whose dishes are inspired by the Languedoc region of France. But best of all is the newest venture of Washington's favorite chef, Jose Andres: **Zaytinya,** 701 9th St. NW (© **202/638-0800;** www.zaytinya.com), a restaurant with a Mediterranean-styled decor and a menu drawn from the cooking of Turkey, Greece, and Lebanon. Because Zaytinya serves mostly tapas, that is, a vast selection of little dishes of food, it's possible to eat here without spending a lot of money. The restaurant is a hit, but it takes reservations for lunch and pre-theater dinner only.

SIGHTSEEING Security concerns continue to keep certain sites closed to public tours and have altered touring procedures at other sites. Unless policies have changed by the time you read this, you will not be able to tour the **White House** or the **Pentagon** as an individual (certain group tours are allowed; read write-ups in chapter 7). The **U.S. Capitol,** at the east end of the Mall (© **202/225-6827**), is open to public tours, but you can no longer go through self-guided, nor can you arrange reserve tickets ahead of time, as you could in the past.

Construction continues on a comprehensive underground **Capitol Visitor Center,** with completion scheduled for 2005. The new visitor center is being created directly beneath the plaza where people traditionally lined up for tours on the east side of the Capitol, which means that you must now stand in line at the southwest corner of the Capitol, the side facing the Mall, at the intersection of 1st Street and Independence Avenue SW.

In December 2003, the **National Air and Space Museum**'s auxiliary gallery opened in Virginia, near Washington-Dulles International Airport; the **Steven F. Udvar-Hazy Center** is free and open to the public, displaying 200 aircraft and 135 space craft. In fall 2004, the Smithsonian's much heralded **National Museum of the American Indian** opens on the National Mall, its three permanent exhibit halls displaying up to 2,000 objects from the museum's 800,000-piece collection. The museum also has a theater and an outdoor performance space. On May 29, 2004, the dedication of the **National World War II Memorial** takes place, on the National Mall.

Throughout 2004, the Smithsonian's **American Art Museum** and **National Portrait Gallery** remain closed for renovation, as does the **FBI Building** and the annex of the **Phillips Collection** (the main building at the Phillips stays open). The **Kennedy Center of the Performing Arts** is going on with all shows, though the place looks like construction-central, as it will for the coming decade while its grand expansion, including a pedestrian plaza, is in production.

The Best of Washington, D.C., on a Budget

Nearly 20 million visitors come to the nation's capital each year plotting itineraries that list Washington, D.C.'s most famous "best" experiences: tours of the presidential memorials, the White House (at least from the outside), the Capitol, the Supreme Court, the Library of Congress, the National Archives, the Smithsonian museums, and other of D.C.'s premier museums. Your own itinerary should include all of these and more. Try to catch one of the free concerts staged nightly at the John F. Kennedy Center for the Performing Arts, and make sure you fit in a delicious meal at one of D.C.'s many good and inexpensive ethnic eateries. Ride the Metro and observe Washingtonians at their most serious; rent a bike and pedal along a path that parallels the Potomac River; stroll one of D.C.'s charming neighborhoods. Discovering the best of Washington has as much to do with experiencing the city's less touted charms as it does with hitting its "hot" spots. This chapter suggests some of the best ways to see the best of Washington.

1 Frommer's Favorite Free & Affordable Washington Experiences

- **Visiting the Lincoln Memorial After Dark.** During the day, hordes of rambunctious schoolchildren may distract you; at night, the experience is infinitely more moving. See chapter 7.
- **Taking a Monument and Memorials Walking Tour.** Have a hearty breakfast, then take the Metro to Foggy Bottom, and when you exit, turn right on 23rd Street NW and follow it to Constitution Avenue NW. Cross the avenue, make a left, walk past Henry Bacon Drive, and follow the signs to the Vietnam and Lincoln Memorials; cross Independence Avenue, and follow the cherry tree–lined Tidal Basin path to the FDR Memorial and further to the Jefferson Memorial; proceed to the new World War II Memorial, if you're here after May 29, 2004,

when it officially debuts; and finish your tour at the Washington Monument. This is a long but beautiful hike; afterward, head up 15th Street NW for a strength-restoring meal at one of the many excellent downtown restaurants. See chapters 6 and 7.

- **Rambling Through Rock Creek Park.** A paved bike/walking path extends 11 miles from the Lincoln Memorial to the Maryland border. You can hop on the trail at many spots throughout the city—it runs past the National Zoo, behind the Omni Shoreham Hotel in Woodley Park, near Dupont Circle, and across from the Watergate/Kennedy Center complex. You can rent a bike from **Big Wheel Bikes** at 1034 33rd St. NW (© **202/337-0254**) in Georgetown, or from

Impressions

My God! What have I done to be condemned to reside in such a city!

—A French diplomat in the early days

Thompson's Boat Center (© 202/333-4861), located on the path across from the Kennedy Center. For a really long bike ride, trek to the Lincoln Memorial, get yourself across the busy stretch that connects the parkway to the Arlington Memorial Bridge, and cross the bridge to the trail on the other side; this path winds 19 miles to Mount Vernon. See chapter 7.

- **Spending the Day in Alexandria.** Just a short distance (by Metro, car, or bike) from the District is George Washington's Virginia hometown. Roam the quaint cobblestone streets, browse charming boutiques and antique stores, visit the 18th-century houses and other historic attractions, and dine in one of Alexandria's fine restaurants. See chapter 10.

- **Weighing in Judgment.** If you're in town when the Supreme Court is in session (Oct to late Apr; call © 202/479-3211 for details), you can observe a case being argued; it's thrilling to see this august institution at work. See chapter 7.

- **Admiring the Library of Congress.** The magnificent Italian Renaissance–style Thomas Jefferson Building of the Library of Congress—filled with murals, mosaics, sculptures, and allegorical paintings—is one of America's most notable architectural achievements. See chapter 7.

- **Attending a Millennium Stage Performance at the Kennedy Center.** Every evening at 6pm, the Kennedy Center presents a free 1-hour concert performed by local, up and coming, or nationally known musicians. This is a

winner. Call © 800/444-1324 or 202/467-4600, or check the website, **www.kennedy-center.org**. See chapter 9.

- **Spending a Morning on the Mall.** Take the Metro to the Smithsonian station early in the morning (about 8:30 is early enough), when the Mall is magical and tourist-free. Walk toward the Capitol Building along Jefferson Drive to the Smithsonian Information Center (the Castle) and stroll through the magnolia-lined parterres of the beautiful Enid A. Haupt Garden. Return to Jefferson Drive, walk further east to the Hirshhorn, ducking in, on your way, for a look at the lovely Ripley Garden, before crossing the street to tour the Hirshhorn's sunken Sculpture Garden. Climb back to street level and cross the Mall to the enchanting National Gallery Sculpture Garden, at 7th Street and Madison Drive. See chapter 7.

- **Debarking at Union Station.** Noted architect Daniel H. Burnham's turn-of-the-20th-century beaux arts railway station is worth a visit even if you're not trying to catch a train. Dawdle and admire its coffered 96-foot-high ceilings, grand arches, and great halls, modeled after the Baths of Diocletian and the Arch of Constantine in Rome. Then shop and eat: The station's 1988 restoration filled the tri-level hall with everything from Ann Taylor and Crabtree & Evelyn to a high-quality food court. See chapters 7 and 8.

- **Enjoying an Artful Evening at the Phillips Collection.** Thursday evenings year-round, from 5 to

8:30pm, you pay $5 to tour the mansion-museum rooms filled with Impressionist, post-Impressionist, and modern art. Your tour ends up in the paneled Music Room, where you'll enjoy jazz, blues, or other musical combinations performed by fine local musicians, topped off by an artful lecture. It's a popular mingling spot for singles (there's a cash bar and sandwich fare). Call ⓒ **202/387-2151** for information. See chapter 7 for complete details on the Phillips Collection; see chapter 9 for more nightlife.

- **Strolling Along Embassy Row.** Head northwest on Massachusetts Avenue from Dupont Circle. It's a gorgeous walk along tree-shaded streets lined with beaux arts mansions. Built by fabulously wealthy magnates during the Gilded Age, most of these palatial precincts are occupied today by foreign embassies. See chapter 7 for more information.

- **People-Watching at Dupont Circle.** One of the few "living" circles, Dupont's is the all-weather hangout for mondo-bizarre biker-couriers, chess players, street musicians, and lovers. Sit on a bench and be astounded by the passing scene. See chapter 4.

- **Cutting a Deal at the Georgetown Flea Market.** Pick up a latte from the nearby Starbucks and spend a pleasant Sunday browsing through the castoffs of wealthy Washingtonians, hand-painted furniture by local artists, and a hodgepodge of antiques and collectibles. Everybody shops here at one time or another, so you never know who you'll see or what you'll find. The market is located at Wisconsin Avenue NW at S Street NW in Georgetown; it's open year-round, Sunday from 9am to 5pm. See chapter 8 for more shopping.

- **Shopping at Eastern Market.** Capitol Hill is home to more than government buildings; it's a community of old town houses, antiques shops, and the veritable institution, Eastern Market. Here, the locals barter and shop on Saturday mornings for fresh produce and baked goods, and on Sunday for flea market bargains. It's located at 7th Street SE, between North Carolina Avenue and C Street SE.

- **Ordering Drinks on the Sky Terrace of the Hotel Washington.** Posher bars exist, but none with this view. The experience is almost a cliche in Washington: When spring arrives, make a date to sit on this outdoor rooftop terrace, sip a gin and tonic, and gaze at the panoramic view of the White House, Treasury Building, and monuments. Open from the end of April through October, for drinks and light fare (ⓒ **202/347-4499**).

- **Chilling to the Sounds of Live Jazz in the Sculpture Garden.** Friday evenings in summer at the National Gallery of Art Sculpture Garden, dip your toes in the fountain pool and chill, as a live jazz group plays a set for you, from 5 to 8pm. The garden's Pavilion Café sells tapas and wine and beer, by the way. See chapter 7.

- **Ice Skating on the Mall.** The National Gallery Sculpture Garden pool turns into an ice skating rink in winter. So visit the Gallery (at 7th St. and Madison Dr.), finishing up at the Sculpture Garden, where you can rent skates and twirl around on the ice, admiring sculptures as you go. Treat yourself to hot chocolate and sandwiches at the Pavilion Café in the garden. See chapter 7.

2 Frommer's Best Budget Hotel Bets

See chapter 5 for complete reviews of all the hotels mentioned below. The "Family-Friendly Hotels" box on p. 87 rounds up the best choices for families traveling with kids.

- **Best Location for Touring Capitol Hill:** The **Capitol Hill Suites,** 200 C St. SE (© **800/424-9165** or 202/543-6000), is the only hotel actually *on* Capitol Hill, which is why a number of congressional members book long-term stays here. You're a block away from the Capitol, Library of Congress, and Supreme Court, and just up the hill from the Mall. See p. 86.

- **Best Location for Visiting the Smithsonian Museums:** The **Hotel Harrington,** 436 11th St. NW (© **800/424-8532** or 202/ 628-8140; www.hotel-harrington. com), lies within easy walking distance of both the White House and the Mall. See p. 91.

- **Best Budget Boutique Hotel:** In the District, the boutique hotel, the **Jurys Normandy Inn,** 2118 Wyoming Ave. NW (© **800/424-3729** or 202/483-1350; www.jurys doyle.com), charges $89 to $185 for rooms that are small but charming, and for service that's personable; extras like an exercise room, a pool, and a restaurant are available at its sister hotel around the corner. See p. 98.

- **Best Lodging If You're on a Shoestring Budget:** The less private the accommodations and the fewer number of bathrooms a property offers, the cheaper its rates. If you don't mind bunking down with strangers, check out **Hostelling International,** 1009 11th St. NW (© **202/737-2333;** www.hiwashingtondc.org), which is well run, centrally located, close to the Metro, and dirt cheap ($29 a night). See p. 93.

- **Best B&B:** I recommend two, each a restored 100+-year-old house in the wonderful, walk-to-restaurants-and-shops neighborhood of Dupont Circle. **Swann House,** 1808 New Hampshire Ave. NW (© **202/265-4414;** www.swann house.com), is remarkably pretty and comfortable, with luxurious accommodations that include whirlpool baths, fine art, working fireplaces, and antique furnishings. My new favorite B&B, **The Inn at Dupont Circle,** 1312 19th St. NW (© **888/467-2100** or 202/467-6777; www.theinnatdupontcircle. com), opened in 2000 and offers gracious common rooms and guest rooms with distinctive features, such as loveseats in alcoves and Persian rugs on shining hardwood floors. See p. 103 and 102.

- **Best Service:** The staff at **Lincoln Suites Downtown,** 1823 L St. NW (© **800/424-2970** or 202/ 223-4320; www.lincolnhotels. com), aims to please, greeting you by name and serving you complimentary homemade cookies and milk each evening. See p. 96.

- **Best for Romance:** Either of the B&Bs mentioned above would be lovely. In the hotel category, downtown's **Henley Park Hotel,** 926 Massachusetts Ave. NW (© **800/ 222-8474** or 202/638-5200; www. henleypark.com), is the hands-down winner. The English-style hotel features luxurious lodgings, plus little bonuses, like afternoon tea, an intimate restaurant, a fun pub, and nearly nightly entertainment (see description, below, for "Best for In-House Entertainment"), so you need never leave the hotel. The rack rates make this a splurge choice, but you can often get lucky with good packages and discounts here, perhaps paying as little as $99 on some summer and weekend nights. See p. 93.

- **Best for Business Travelers Without a Bottomless Expense Account:** The **Four Points Sheraton, Washington, D.C. Downtown,** 1201 K St. NW (© **888/481-7191** or 202/289-7600; www.fourpointswashingtondc.com), is your best bet. With a great central downtown location near the new convention center, weekday rates as low as $99, and perks that include high-speed Internet access in all rooms, an excellent on-site restaurant for business entertaining, and a 24-hour fitness center, this hotel might please even the most jaded business traveler. See p. 90.

- **Best Health Club:** Though the **Hotel Tabard Inn,** 1739 N St. NW (© **202/785-1277;** www.tabardinn.com), doesn't have its own on-site health club, guests get free passes to the nearby YMCA, which offers Universal equipment, basketball, racquetball/handball/volleyball courts, a weight and exercise room, 25-meter indoor heated pool, a jogging track, stair climbers, treadmills, stationary bikes, a steam room, a whirlpool, and more. See p. 101.

- **Best for Travelers with Disabilities:** **Jurys Washington Hotel,** 1500 New Hampshire Ave. NW (© **800/423-6953** or 202/483-6000; www.jurysdoyle.com), has 11 rooms equipped for disabled guests, four with roll-in showers, and wider than normal corridors and entryways. Ramps throughout the hotel allow for easy access to the meeting room, restaurant, and pub. See p. 102.

- **Best Hotel for Feeling at Home Acting the Tourist:** The **Hotel Harrington,** 436 11th St. NW (© **800/424-8532** or 202/628-8140; www.hotel-harrington.com),

may not be anything fancy, but the friendly staff at the front desk is willing to answer questions, and a tour bus stops right outside the front door. See p. 91.

- **Best for In-House Entertainment:** The **Henley Park Hotel,** 926 Massachusetts Ave. NW (© **800/222-8474** or 202/638-5200; www.henleypark.com), is notable for hosting live jazz and dancing weekend nights in its Blue Bar, and a pianist plays there Monday through Wednesday nights. See p. 93.

- **Best Hotel for Running into Locals:** Several D.C. hotels have excellent restaurants and fun bars that draw a regular crowd of inside-the-beltway types. Two of the best, and most affordable, are the **Hotel Tabard Inn,** 1739 N St. NW (© **202/785-1277;** www.tabardinn.com), and the **Jurys Washington Hotel,** 1500 New Hampshire Ave. NW (© **800/423-6953** or 202/483-6000; www.jurysdoyle.com). See p. 101–102.

- **Best Views:** The **Channel Inn,** 650 Water St. SW (© **800/368-5668** or 202/554-2400; www.channelinn.com), overlooks the boat-filled Washington Channel. Be sure to ask for a waterfront room.

- **Best Choice If You've Got Hippie Sensibilities and a Discriminating Palate:** The **Hotel Tabard Inn** (see mentions in other categories above) is decorated in a comfortable but decidedly funky style; fortunately, the well-esteemed restaurant focuses on seasonally fresh American cuisine, so there's nary a wheat germ or square of tofu to be found. See p. 101.

- **Best Lodgings for a Spiritual Experience:** Of course, it doesn't get much more uplifting than the quarters provided in the College of Preachers' building on the hilltop

Site Seeing: The Best Washington Websites

- **www.washingtonpost.com**: This is the *Washington Post*'s site, a most helpful source for up-to-date information on restaurants, attractions, and nightlife (as well as world news).
- **www.washington.org**: The Washington Convention and Tourism Corporation operates this site. It gives a broad overview of what to see and do in D.C. and provides travel updates on security issues. Click on "Visitor Information" for tips on where to stay, dine, shop, and sightsee.
- **www.washingtonian.com**: Sure, you'll find some nice articles from the print magazine of the same name, but there's much more here. "What's Happening" is a monthly guide to what's on at museums, theaters, and other cultural showplaces around town. The magazine really wants you to buy the print edition, though—for sale at bookstores, drugstores, and grocery stores throughout the area.
- **www.fly2dc.com**: In addition to its extensive information about airline travel in and out of Washington (and ground transportation from each airport), this site also offers fun articles about restaurants and things to do in D.C.
- **www.opentable.com**: This site allows you to make reservations at some of the capital's finest restaurants.
- **www.dcaccommodations.com**: This nicely designed site recommends hotels suited for families, women, sightseers, or business travelers.
- **www.hotelsdc.com**: Capitol Reservations, a 20-year-old company, represents more than 100 hotels in the Washington area, each of which has been screened for cleanliness, safety, and other factors. You can book your room online.
- **www.bnbaccom.com**: For those who prefer to stay in a private home, guesthouse, inn, or furnished apartment, this service offers more than 80 options for you to consider.
- **www.si.edu**: This is the Smithsonian Institution's home page, which provides information about visiting Washington and leads you to the individual websites for each Smithsonian museum.
- **www.kennedy-center.org**: Find out what's playing at the Kennedy Center and listen to live broadcasts through the Net.

campus of **Washington National Cathedral,** 3510 Woodley Rd. NW (© **202/537-6383;** www. pecf.org). See p. 107.

3 Frommer's Best Dining Bets on a Budget

See chapter 6 for complete reviews of all the restaurants mentioned below.

- **Best Spot for a Celebration: Café Atlantico,** 405 8th St. NW (© **202/393-0812**), will give you reason to celebrate even if you

didn't arrive with one. The restaurant is pure fun, with charming waiters, seating on three levels, colorful wall-size paintings by Latin and Caribbean artists, fantastic cocktails, and unusual but not

- **www.mountvernon.org**: Click on "Visitor's Guide" for daily attractions at Mount Vernon and a calendar of events, as well as information on dining, shopping, and school programs. For a sneak preview, click on "Mansion Tour" to see images of the master bedroom, dining room, slave memorial, and the Washingtons' tomb.
- **www.nps.gov/nacc**: This National Park Service site includes links to about a dozen memorials and monuments. Among the links: the Washington Monument, Jefferson Memorial, National Mall, Ford's Theatre, FDR Memorial, Lincoln Memorial, and Vietnam Veterans Memorial.
- **www.house.gov**: Once you're in the U.S. House of Representatives site, click on "Visiting D.C." to learn more about touring the Capitol building. From here, click on "The House Chamber," where you can get a view of the chamber where the House meets and learn whether the House is in session. The site also connects you with the Web pages for each of the representatives; you can use this site to e-mail your representative.
- **www.senate.gov**: In the U.S. Senate site, click on "Visitors Center" for an online virtual tour of the Capitol building and information about touring the actual Senate Gallery. It takes a few seconds for the images to download, but it's worth the wait to enjoy the panoramic video tour. Also, find out when the Senate is in session. The site connects you with the Web pages for each of the senators; you can use this site to e-mail your senator.
- **www.whitehouse.gov**: You'll find all sorts of links here, from those for Congressional Tours, to Web pages for each U.S. president, to archived White House documents, to an e-mail page you can use to contact the president or vice president.
- **www.metwashairports.com**: Ground transport, terminal maps, flight status, and airport facilities for Washington Dulles International and Ronald Reagan Washington National airports.
- **www.bwiairport.com**: Ground transport, terminal maps, flight status, and airport facilities for Baltimore–Washington International Airport.
- **www.wmata.com**: Timetables, maps, fares, and more for the Metro buses and subways that serve the Washington, D.C., metro area.

trendy Latin/Caribbean food. Another good choice: **Kinkead's,** 2000 Pennsylvania Ave. NW (© **202/296-7700**), a terrific splurge choice for a special occasion. See p. 128 and 148.

- **Best View: Les Halles,** 1201 Pennsylvania Ave. NW (© **202/347-6848**), whose awning-covered sidewalk in summer becomes enclosed in winter, is a fine spot for viewing the sights along Pennsylvania Avenue all year round. Or consider one of the restaurants at the **Kennedy Center** (at the southern end of New Hampshire Ave. NW, and Rock Creek Pkwy.; © **202/416-8555**): its **Roof Terrace, Hors D'Oeuvrerie,** or **KC Café,** where immense windows provide a sweeping panoramic view of the Potomac River and

Washington landmarks. See p. 124 and 119.

- **Best for Kids: Famous Luigi's Pizzeria Restaurant,** 1132 19th St. NW (© 202/331-7574), serves up some of the best pizza and spaghetti in town, plus the place is loud and indestructible. See p. 132.

- **Best Chinese: Tony Cheng's Seafood Restaurant,** 619 H St. NW (© 202/371-8669), in the heart of Chinatown, is consistently good and a great place for Hunan, spicy Szechuan, and Cantonese specialties. See p. 126.

- **Best French:** For French staples and bistro atmosphere, head to **Bistrot Lepic & Wine Bar,** at 1736 Wisconsin Ave. NW (© 202/333-0111), or **Bistrot du Coin,** 1738 Connecticut Ave. NW (© 202/234-6969). See p. 154 and 140.

- **Best Southern:** At **Vidalia,** 1990 M St. NW (© 202/659-1990), chef Jeff Buben calls his cuisine "provincial American," a euphemism for fancy fare that includes cheese grits and biscuits in cream gravy. See p. 134.

- **Best Mexican: Lauriol Plaza,** 1835 18th St. NW (© 202/387-0035), isn't completely Mexican (it's also Salvadoran and Cuban). But it's all delicious and well priced, and worth standing in line for, since the restaurant does not take reservations.

- **Best Pizza:** At **Pizzeria Paradiso,** 2029 P St. NW (© 202/223-1245), peerless chewy-crusted pies are baked in an oak-burning oven and crowned with delicious toppings; you'll find great salads and sandwiches on fresh-baked focaccia here, too. If you like thick, old-fashioned pizzas, head to **Famous Luigi's Pizzeria Restaurant,** 1132 19th St. NW (© 202/331-7574). See p. 143 and 132.

- **Best Healthy Meal:** At **Legal Sea Foods,** 2020 K St. NW (© 202/496-1111), follow up a cup of light clam chowder (made without butter, cream, or flour) with an entree of grilled fresh fish and vegetables and a superb sorbet for dessert. It's guilt-free dining. See p. 133.

- **Best for a Bad Mood:** At **Al Tiramisu,** 2014 P St. NW (© 202/467-4466), the waiters, the owner, the conviviality, and the Italian food gently coax that smile upon your face. See p. 145.

- **Best Spot for Romance on a Budget: Bistro Français,** 3124-28 M St. NW (© 202/338-3830), is *très romantique,* but you must ask to be seated in the more intimate, candle-lit dining room section. For something exotic, try the **Bombay Club,** 815 Connecticut Ave. NW (© 202/659-3727), where the food is ambrosial and the service royal. Here you can linger over a meal as long as you like, enjoying the mood created by the pianist's music, in a dining room that recalls the days of the British empire. See p. 150 and 131.

- **Best Breakfast:** Stuff yourself at an all-you-can-eat buffet at **Reeves Restaurant & Bakery,** 1306 G St. NW (© 202/628-6350), for just $6.95 daily. See p. 127.

- **Best Brunch:** For something a little different (like drag queens slinking around the room), go to **Perry's,** in Adams-Morgan, at 1811 Columbia Rd. NW (© 202/234-6218), where brunch is $23. For best value, make a beeline to **Old Glory Barbecue,** 3139 M St. NW (© 202/337-3406), and pay $12 ($6.95 for kids 11 and under) for a limitless buffet of waffles, omelets cooked to your liking, muffins, biscuits with sausage gravy, fruit salad, complimentary beverages, and more. Live music is sometimes an added feature. See p. 140 and 152.

- **Best Teas:** Unlike the more formal, British-style afternoon repasts, afternoon tea at **Teaism,** 800 Connecticut Ave. NW (© **202/835-2233**), is a casual affair, charming and relaxed. The Asian "tea list," comprising several dozen varieties, is as lovingly composed as the wine list of the most distinguished French restaurant. The Teaism located at 400 8th St. NW (© 202/638-6010) also serves afternoon tea. See p. 144.

- **Best American Cuisine:** The whimsically decorated **Luna Grill & Diner,** 1301 Connecticut Ave. NW (© **202/835-2280**), serves creatively homey food in a hip setting at fabulous prices. See p. 144.

- **Best Italian:** For traditional (and affordable) classic Italian fare, Roberto Donna's **Il Radicchio,** 223 Pennsylvania Ave. SE (© **202/547-5114**), does the trick. See p. 117.

- **Best Seafood:** At **Johnny's Half Shell,** 2002 P St. NW. (© **202/296-2021**), you simply can't go wrong choosing from the small but exacting menu of fried oysters, wild rockfish, softshell crabs, and the like, all superbly prepared. Or treat yourself to a splurge at **Kinkead's,** 2000 Pennsylvania Ave. NW (© **202/296-7700**), one of the city's best restaurants. See p. 142.

- **Best Southwestern Cuisine:** It doesn't get more exciting than the **Red Sage Border Café,** 605 14th St. NW (© **202/638-4444**), where hot cuisine trends meet traditional Southwestern cookery. See p. 125.

- **Best Place to Spot Your Congressperson:** If you're Mall-bound, slip into the opulent **House of Representatives Restaurant,** Room H118, at the south end of the Capitol (© **202/225-6300**), and grab a cup of that famous bean soup. See p. 118.

- **Best Desserts:** No frou-frou desserts are served at **Café Berlin,** 322 Massachusetts Ave. NE (© **202/543-7656**); these cakes and tortes and pies and strudels are the real thing—as hearty as those house-special wursts and schnitzels. See p. 117.

- **Best Late-Night Dining:** For comfortable, romantic surroundings and delicious French cuisine, try **Bistro Français** (see above), which serves a specially priced $20, three-course menu until 1am nightly. Up all night? Head for **Kramerbooks & Afterwords Café,** 1517 Connecticut Ave. NW (© **202/387-1462**), which stays open around the clock on weekends. See p. 145.

- **Best Outdoor Dining: Raku,** 1900 Q St. NW (© **202/265-RAKU**), occupies a prominent, excellent people-watching corner near Dupont Circle. The scene gets better when, spring through fall, Raku's windowed walls open to its sidewalk cafe. See p. 143.

- **Best Ethiopian Cuisine: Meskerem,** 2434 18th St. NW (© **202/462-4100**), is a good pick in this category, both for setting and for food. See p. 136.

2

Planning an Affordable Trip to Washington, D.C.

In at least one major way, the nation's capital is the frugal traveler's dream destination: Nearly all of the city's tourist attractions, including the monuments, memorials, and museums, are absolutely free. If it weren't for those pesky lodging, eating, and transportation expenses, you'd be coming to town all the time, I'll bet. The fact is, if you are traveling to the capital on a limited budget, you need to plan wisely and in advance.

This chapter aims to help you avoid financial catastrophe, or any other, for that matter, by offering money-saving tips, as well as essential information about what to bring, the weather you can expect, what's going on in D.C. throughout the year, how to get here, how to plan your trip online, and assorted other important points. If you have a question that isn't answered in these pages, you'll find references to a number of helpful sources for additional and timely information.

1 The Washington from $80 a Day Premise

This premise might seem like a pipe dream, but it's not. The idea is this: With good planning and a watchful eye, you can keep your basic daily living costs—accommodations and three meals a day—down to as little as $80. This budget model works best for two adults traveling together who have at least $160 a day to work with and can share a double room (single rooms are much less cost-efficient). This way, if you aim for accommodations priced around $90 or $100 for a double (far easier to achieve on a weekend), you'll be left with about $30 or $35 per person per day for food.

If you want to spend even less on accommodations, I have a couple of suggestions for you. For the most part, however, the basic, "from $80 a day" premise assumes that your preference is for a private room, even if it comes with a shared bathroom, and for decent restaurant fare, rather than fast food at every meal.

The $80 a day premise does not include transportation and entertainment expenses. But don't worry—I've got plenty of suggestions on how to keep those costs down. It helps that the capital is such a walkable city, that so many of its attractions are free, and that various venues stage free performances daily.

This book will serve you well even if you don't need to keep to a strict $80 a day. Follow my advice, and you'll be able to make informed decisions on what to see and do so that, whatever your budget, your money is well spent. Here are some ideas to get you started.

2 72 Money-Saving Tips

Some general advice: Be prepared to consult as many resources as possible, starting with this book, and including the Internet, travel clubs, travel agents, specific airlines and hotels you've earmarked as possibilities from your research, car rental agencies, and so on. Don't assume you've gotten the best value from your first source. Thorough research is time-consuming, but it can save you a ton of money.

PLANNING YOUR TRIP

1. Before you leave, **contact the Washington, D.C. Convention & Tourism Corporation,** 1212 New York Ave. NW, Washington, DC 20005 (℗ **202/789-7000**) and ask them to send you a free copy of the *Washington, D.C., Visitors Guide,* which describes hotels, restaurants, sights, shops, and much more. They'll also be happy to answer specific questions. Their website, **www.washington.org**, posts packages and deals from time to time.

2. **Visit a travel agent** to inquire about airfares, hotels, car rentals, and combination packages. These services are free. Remember that not all travel agents are created equal: Often a budget travel agency will dig up exotic fares a mainstream agent will insist are impossible to get. If you're traveling to Washington from Europe, you can save hundreds or even thousands of dollars by calling several different agencies.

3. **Buy a money-saving package deal.** A travel package that includes your plane tickets and hotel stay for one price might just be the best bargain of all. In some cases, you'll get airfare, accommodations, transportation to and from the airport, plus extras—maybe an afternoon sightseeing tour or restaurant and shopping discount coupons—for

less than the cost of a hotel room alone, had you booked it yourself.

4. If you belong to a travel club, such as AAA, obtain maps and tourist information, and find out about **discounts available to club members.** In fact, if you belong to any club or organization, find out whether your membership entitles you to travel benefits in Washington. (For that matter, families, seniors, travelers with disabilities, gay or lesbian travelers, and students may be entitled to discounts. See "Specialized Travel Resources" on p. 33.) AARP members receive discounts on car rentals, lodging, and cruises. A private club to which you or your corporation belongs may grant reciprocal membership privileges, including reasonably priced lodging and free use of health-club facilities, at a signatory club in Washington. The University Club of the City of Washington, D.C., participates in such an arrangement with 150 clubs worldwide.

5. Keep your eyes peeled for discount coupons. A good place to start is your monthly **American Express** bill, which may include discounts you'll receive at various establishments, sometimes in the Washington area.

6. Order **coupon books,** which offer money-saving vouchers for participating hotels, restaurants, stores, car-rental agencies, and other enterprises. **Entertainment Publications Inc.** publishes yearly editions of coupon-crammed books that offer you great values at restaurants, hotels/motels, car rentals, and so on. More than 150 versions exist, covering major cities and regions in the United States and Canada. You have to pay for Entertainment books, and the price fluctuates from year to year. In 2003, two

separate editions covered Washington, D.C.: the Maryland/Washington, D.C. book, and the Northern Virginia/Washington, D.C. book, each costing $40, plus shipping and handling charges. Call © **800/933-2605** for more information, or log onto www.entertainment.com.

7. Try to **schedule your trip during holidays, off-season, or on weekends,** when room rates are sometimes half the weekday or in-season rates. Peak seasons in Washington correspond roughly to two activities: the sessions of Congress and springtime, starting with the blossoming of the cherry blossoms along the Potomac. Specifically when Congress is in session, from about the second week in September until Thanksgiving, and again from about mid-January through June. Hotels are fairly full with guests whose business ties in with Capitol Hill and with those attending the many meetings and conventions that take place here. You get the best room rates on weekends throughout the year, around holidays, and on weekdays and weekends during the periods of July through the first week of September and late November through January.

GETTING HERE
AIR TRAVEL

8. First things first: **Find out whether a low-fare carrier travels between your city and Washington.** Low-fare airlines are on the rise and offer great deals, especially up and down the East Coast, and west from Chicago. See section 11, "Getting Here," for information about discount airlines and which Washington airports they serve. Which leads to the next tip:

9. **Consider all three airports when you're shopping around.** Fares can be markedly different depending on which airport you fly into—Ronald Reagan Washington National, Washington Dulles International, or Baltimore–Washington International.

10. Search the **Internet** for cheap fares—though it's still best to compare your findings with the research of a dedicated travel agent, if you're lucky enough to have one, especially when you're booking more than just a flight. See section 9 of this chapter, "Planning Your Trip Online," for in-depth coverage of how to save by surfing.

11. It always helps to **be flexible.** If you can purchase your ticket long in advance, don't mind staying over Saturday night, or are willing to travel on a Tuesday, Wednesday, or Thursday after 7pm, you'll pay a fraction of the full fare. Many airlines won't volunteer this information, so be sure to ask.

12. Always **ask specifically for the lowest rate, not just a discount fare.** Yes, reservations and travel agents should take for granted that you want the lowest possible fare—but they don't always do so. And, as with every aspect of your trip, ask about discounts for groups, seniors, children, and students.

13. Keep an eye out for **airfare sales.** Check your newspaper for advertised discounts or call the airlines directly and ask if any promotional rates or special fares are available; whether seniors, children, and students receive reduced rates; and if the airline offers money-saving packages that include such essentials as hotel accommodations, car rentals, and tours with your airfare. Read the Sunday travel sections of the *New York Times* and the *Washington Post*. The *Times* column, "Lowest Air Fares for Popular Routes," highlights bargain airfares, while the *Post's* "What's the Deal?" lists "the week's best travel bargains

around the globe, by land, sea, and air," which means that you can also find out about specials offered by hotels, cruise lines, and travel companies. (Again, for more on this, refer to section 9, "Planning Your Trip Online.")

14. You'll almost never see a sale during the peak summer vacation months of July and August, or during the Thanksgiving or Christmas seasons. If you don't mind traveling on Christmas Day or Thanksgiving Day, itself, however, you might snag a cheaper fare (most people would rather not be on an airplane on the actual holiday). If your schedule is flexible, ask if you can **secure a cheaper fare by staying an extra day or by flying mid-week.** (Many airlines won't volunteer this information.) If you already hold a ticket when a sale breaks, it may even pay to exchange your ticket, which usually incurs a $50 to $75 charge. Note, however, that the lowest-priced fares are often nonrefundable, require advance purchase of 1 to 3 weeks and a certain length of stay, and carry penalties for changing dates of travel.

15. **Consolidators,** also known as bucket shops, are a good place to find low fares, often below even the airlines' discounted rates. Basically, they're just big travel agents that get discounts for buying in bulk and pass some of the savings on to you. Before you pay, however, ask for a confirmation number from the consolidator and then call the airline itself to confirm your seat. Also be aware that consolidator tickets are usually nonrefundable or come with stiff cancellation penalties. One way to choose a consolidator is to check with professional organizations whose members, including consolidators, must satisfy certain solid requirements. For example, the United States Tour Operators Association includes a number of tour operators who also handle consolidator business; all USTOA members are listed on its website at www.ustoa.com. Also, when using a consolidator, try booking your ticket through a travel agent experienced with consolidators and always use a credit card to pay.

Several reliable consolidators are worldwide and available on the Net. **STA Travel** (© **800/781-4040;** www.statravel.com) is now the world's leader in student travel, thanks to their purchase of Council Travel. It also offers good fares for travelers of all ages. **Flights.com** (© **800/TRAV-800;** www.flights.com) started in Europe and has excellent fares worldwide. It also has "local" websites in 12 countries. **FlyCheap** (© **800/FLY-CHEAP;** www.1800flycheap.com) is owned by package-holiday megalith MyTravel and so has especially good access to fares for sunny destinations. **Air Tickets Direct** (© **800/778-3447;** www.airticketsdirect.com) is based in Montreal and leverages the currently weak Canadian dollar for low fares.

16. Book a seat on a **charter flight.** Discounted fares have pared the number available, but they can still be found. Most charter operators advertise and sell their seats through travel agents, thus making these local professionals your best source of information for available flights. Before deciding to take a charter flight, however, check the restrictions on the ticket: You may be asked to purchase a tour package, to pay in advance, to be amenable if the day of departure is changed, to pay a service charge, to fly on an airline you're not familiar with (this is not usually the case), and to pay

harsh penalties if you cancel—but be understanding if the charter doesn't fill up and is canceled up to 10 days before departure. Summer charters fill up more quickly than others and are almost sure to fly, but if you decide on a charter flight, seriously consider cancellation and baggage insurance.

17. Join **frequent-flier clubs.** Accrue enough miles, and you'll be rewarded with free flights and elite status. It's free, and you'll get the best choice of seats, faster response to phone inquiries, and prompter service if your luggage is stolen, your flight is canceled or delayed, or if you want to change your seat. You don't need to fly to build frequent-flier miles—**frequent-flier credit cards** can provide thousands of miles for doing your everyday shopping.

18. Join an online, discount travel club such as **Moment's Notice** (✆ **888/241-3366;** www.moments-notice. com) or **Sears Discount Travel Club** (✆ **800/433-9383,** or 800/255-1487 to join; www.travelers advantage.com), which supply unsold tickets at discounted prices.

19. For many more tips about air travel, including a rundown of the major frequent-flier credit cards, pick up a copy of *Frommer's Fly Safe, Fly Smart* (Wiley Publishing, Inc.).

OTHER TRANSPORTATION

20. If you're traveling from New York City (or another city on the East Coast), you may find that it's cheaper to **take the train or bus.** Because trains and buses take you right into the heart of town, you may save time and money on transportation to and from the airport.

21. **Have a flexible schedule when booking train travel, and always ask for the lowest fare.** When you're offered a fare, always ask if you can do better by traveling at different times or days. You can often save money by traveling at off-peak hours and on weekends (when Amtrak's Metroliner fares are substantially reduced). And don't forget to ask for discounts for kids, seniors, passengers with disabilities, military personnel, or anything else that you think might qualify you for a lower fare.

22. Inquire about **Amtrak Vacations and other money-saving Amtrak packages** that may include hotel accommodations, car rentals, and tours with your train fare.

23. Like the airlines, Amtrak offers several discounted fares; although not all are based on advance purchase, **you have more discount options by reserving early.** The discount fares can be used only on certain days and hours of the day; be sure to find out exactly what restrictions apply. Tickets for children ages 2 to 15 cost half the price of a regular coach fare when the children are accompanied by a fare-paying adult. Go to **www.amtrak.com** and click on "Rail Sale," where you can purchase tickets for one-way designated coach seats at great discounts. Likewise, Amtrak's **Savings and Promotions** section lists ticket discounts to various destinations.

24. Take the bus: **Greyhound** is dirt-cheap, as you can see by going to its website's home page at **www. greyhound.com**, and clicking on "Super Friendly Fares." There, you will see that you can travel as far as 500 miles for $49, and across the continental U.S. for as little as $119.

GETTING AROUND THE CITY BY PUBLIC TRANSPORTATION

25. Eschew motorized transportation altogether, and **hoof it.** Washington's magnificent architecture and

lovely parks, gardens, and green spaces make it an ideal city for walking.

26. Consider **skipping a rental car.** Washington's public transportation system is comprehensive and reliable. In fact, you may find that parking nuisances outweigh the convenience of a car. Use the Metro, which, unlike the subways in some other big cities, is delightfully clean, efficient, safe, and user-friendly. It's also the fastest and cheapest way to get around; buy a **One-Day Rail Pass** and you can travel around the city all day long for only $6. If you're going to be here for several days, you can get an even better deal by paying $20 for the Seven-Day Short Trip Rail Pass, which allows you almost unlimited transportation throughout the week. (Rush hour travel, between 5:30–9:30am and 3–7pm weekdays, may require you to use the Exitfare machine in the station to add money to your fare card if the fare for your route exceeds $2.)

27. **Tourmobile** and **Old Town Trolley Tours** (see chapter 7 for details) stop at many Washington sightseeing attractions. A one-price ticket can save you money getting around town if you plan your itinerary to make the most of it.

28. When you're choosing a place to stay, ask whether the hotel offers **free shuttle service** to the airport, nearby Metro station, or attractions.

29. Getting downtown is easiest, fastest, and cheapest from **Ronald Reagan Washington National Airport.** Moving sidewalks transport you from the gates within the terminal to the terminal's entrance, which connects by climate-controlled pedestrian bridges to the Metro platform. Purchase a $1.20 fare card, hop aboard, and 15 to 20 minutes later, you're downtown.

For now, the Metro is an option at National only. For further information, see "Getting into Town from the Airport," later in this chapter.

CAR RENTALS

As stated above, because Washington is such an easy city to navigate, whether on foot, by Metro, or by taxi, you probably won't need a car. But should your visit require one, you should know that car rental rates vary even more than airline fares. The price you pay will depend on the size of the car, where and when you pick it up and drop it off, the length of the rental period, where and how far you drive it, whether you purchase insurance, and a host of other factors. Follow these guidelines and you may save hundreds of dollars.

30. Call all the major rental firms and **compare rates** before you book (and don't forget to check their websites, which usually have special deals). Even after you've made your reservations, call again and check rates a few days or weeks later—you may stumble upon a cheaper rate. See p. 46 for further details on car rentals.

31. Ask for the **cheapest rate on the smallest car.** If there are only two of you traveling, get a compact. The $5 or more per day you save can add up—and you'll save money on gas and have an easier time parking. If the agent tells you that all the economy cars are booked, this may be a ploy to get you to upgrade; thank them and book with another company.

32. Ask if **weekend rates** are lower than weekday rates—if the rate is the same for pickup Friday morning, for instance, as it is for Thursday night.

33. Book at **weekly rates** when possible—you can save a bundle. Even if you only need the car for 4

days, it may be cheaper to keep it for 5.

34. If you arrive at the rental desk with a valid car reservation with a confirmation number, **the agents are obligated to honor the rate you were quoted**—even if they have to give you an upgrade. A ploy some rental companies use when they're all out of the grade of car you booked (economy cars often get booked up first) is to tell you that for just a few more dollars a day, they'll put you in a "better car." Make them stick to their original quote.

35. Always **return your rental car full of gas.** The prices the rental companies charge you to fill your tank when you don't are well above the already high price per gallon charged at local filling stations. Skip the agencies' offers of refueling packages.

36. Find out if the agency assesses a **drop-off charge** if you don't return the car to the same location where you picked it up. Is it cheaper to pick up the car at the airport compared to a downtown location?

37. Are **special promotional rates** available? If you see an advertised price in your local newspaper, be sure to ask for that specific rate; otherwise you may be charged the standard cost. Terms change constantly, and there's no charge to change or cancel an existing reservation if you find a better deal later.

38. Inquire whether **discounts are available for members of AARP, AAA, frequent-flier programs, or trade unions.** If you belong to any of these organizations, you may be entitled to discounts of up to 30%. There's no charge to join the agencies' own **frequent-renter clubs,** which may also help you rack up discounts.

39. Ask how much tax will be added to the rental bill, including **local taxes and surcharges,** which can vary from location to location, even within the same car rental agency. Don't forget to ask if the company charges for adding an **additional driver's name** to the contract. And find out how many free miles are included in the price. **Free mileage** is often negotiable, depending on the length of your rental.

40. Check out **packages** that include airfare, accommodations, and a rental car with unlimited mileage. Compare these prices with the cost of booking airline tickets and renting a car separately to see if these offers are good deals.

41. **Surfing the Web** can make comparison shopping easier. See section 9, "Planning Your Trip Online," p. 38, to read tips for finding a deal on the Web.

ACCOMMODATIONS

42. **Book early.** The best budget hotels are usually the first to fill up. It's best to reserve them as far in advance as possible to ensure low rates. Your choices may be more limited later on. If you find a rate that seems a particularly good value, book it early. Hotels tend to offer special rates for limited periods, and the rate may not be available at a later date.

43. **Consider all hotels, no matter the rate category.** Almost everyone winds up paying much less than the advertised "rack" rate. Even the best and most expensive hotels may be ready to negotiate and often offer bargain rates at certain times or to guests who are members of certain groups, and you may be eligible. Upscale Washington hotels routinely offer discounted **weekend packages, especially during the summer.**

44. **Don't be afraid to bargain.** Always ask for a lower price than the first one quoted. Most rack rates include

commissions of 10% to 25% or more for travel agents, which many hotels will cut if you make your own reservations and haggle a bit. Ask politely whether a less-expensive room is available than the first one mentioned or whether any special rates apply to you. You might qualify for **corporate, student, military, senior, or other discounts.** Mention membership in AAA, AARP, frequent-flier programs, corporate or military organizations, and trade unions, which might entitle you to special deals as well. The big chains, such as Best Western and Comfort Inn, tend to be good about trying to save you money, but reservation agents often won't volunteer the information; you have to pull it out of them. If you arrive without a reservation (only recommended in the off-season, of course), an especially advantageous time to secure lower rates is late in the afternoon/early evening on your day of arrival, when a hotel's likelihood of filling up with full-price bookings is remote. Naturally the first price they'll hit you with is the highest (the chump rate). Counter with a lower offer. The worst thing they can do is say no.

45. Ask about **rates for families,** who often receive discounts, as much as 50% off on a second room adjoining the parent's room, or perhaps free fare in the hotel's restaurant (many Holiday Inns, like the Holiday Inn Georgetown listed in chapter 5, let kids age 12 and under eat free from children's menus year-round). Every hotel (but not necessarily inns or bed-and-breakfasts) included in chapter 5 allows children under a certain age, usually 12 or 18, to stay free in their parent's room.

46. When booking a room in a chain hotel, **call the hotel's local line, as well as the toll-free number, and see where you get the best deal.** A hotel makes nothing on a room that stays empty. The clerk who runs the place is more likely to know about vacancies and will often grant deep discounts in order to fill up.

47. **Consider a suite.** It sounds like the ultimate splurge, but if you're traveling with another couple or your family, a suite can be a terrific bargain. They're always cheaper than two hotel rooms. If you're traveling with your family or another couple, you can pack more people into a suite (which usually comes with a sofa bed), and thereby reduce your per-person rate. Remember that some places charge for extra guests, some don't.

48. **Book an efficiency.** A room with a kitchenette allows you to prepare your own meals (you supply the groceries). Especially during long stays with families, you're bound to save money on food this way.

49. **Investigate reservation services,** both national and local. These outfits usually work as consolidators, buying up or reserving rooms in bulk, and then dealing them out to customers at a profit. They do garner special deals that range from 10% to 50% off; but remember, these discounts apply to rack rates, that is, the published higher prices. You're sometimes better off dealing directly with a hotel, but if you don't like bargaining, this is certainly a viable option. Most of them offer online reservation services as well. See "Planning You Trip Online," later in this chapter, as well as chapter 5, for the list of national and local reservations services.

50. Consider a stay at a **bed-and-breakfast,** often a less costly and more personal experience.

51. **Negotiate a cyberdeal.** See "Planning Your Trip Online," later in this chapter for complete information on how to land the best rate for lodging.

52. If you're staying for an extended period (5 days or more), ask for a better rate for a **long-term stay;** hotels love a sure thing.

53. **If you're traveling in a group, by all means negotiate your rate as a block.** The desk clerk's eyes will light up when you say you want to book five or ten rooms—and then you can put on the hard sell to get the best deal.

54. Business and leisure visitors who travel a lot should sign up for **frequent-stay programs,** which are akin to the airlines' frequent-flier programs, with free stays, gifts, special privileges, frequent-flier mile credits, and other perks granted by appreciative hotels to loyal customers. The Best Western Downtown–Capitol Hill (listed in chapter 5) offers such a program.

55. **Do as little business as possible through the hotel.** Any service they offer will come with a stiff premium. You can easily find dry cleaners or other services in most areas of Washington. And it's usually cheaper to use your cell phone or a pay phone than to pay inflated telephone surcharges in your hotel room.

56. **Book a property that includes great perks in its rates,** such as continental breakfast, complimentary access to a health club, and free parking. All of these items are noted in our listings in chapter 5.

DINING

57. Plan to **eat your biggest meal at lunch,** when you can often order from the same menus that are considerably more expensive at dinner.

58. **Fixed-price menus, early-bird dinners, and light-fare menus** that are available in late afternoon or late at night are big money savers.

59. If you're traveling with kids, find restaurants that offer **reduced-price children's menus,** or better yet, free meals for children, As mentioned in tip #45, above, many Holiday Inns allow children under age 12 to eat free from a children's menu when accompanied by an adult ordering from the main menu.

60. Plan a **picnic.** Buy the fixings at a local grocery and dine alfresco; Washington abounds with lovely outdoor parks and plazas. And there's no tipping, and no food markup. See chapter 6 for picnic fare suggestions and chapter 7 for great picnic locations.

61. Check out Washington's **low-cost cafeterias and food courts.** Notable among the latter are those at Union Station, the Pavilion at the Old Post Office, and the Shops at Georgetown Park (see chapter 8).

62. Go all out on a big **all-you-can-eat brunch** such as the one offered at Old Glory Barbecue for just $12 per adult and $6.95 per child (see chapter 6 for details on this and other brunch options). You'll save money by combining two meals, enjoy a leisurely dining experience, and probably be so full you'll want only a light evening meal.

63. Many bars in Washington offer fairly extensive **happy-hour buffets.** If you're a light eater or you've had a big lunch, this could suffice for a meal. See the box titled "Cheap Eats: Happy Hours to Write Home About" on p. 266.

64. Do your main munching in **government buildings.** The Capitol, congressional office buildings, Library of Congress, and Supreme Court Building, in particular, offer great deals, with most main courses costing less than $9. The dining rooms and cafeterias are open

weekdays only, mostly for breakfast and lunch, and are generally very crowded with congressional staffers and government employees, so time your meal to be slightly off-peak. See chapter 6 for details.

SIGHTSEEING

65. **Take full advantage of the fact that most of the capital's sightseeing attractions, and many of its best events, are free and open to the public.** Visit the Supreme Court to observe the Supreme Court Justices hearing a case; tour the Washington Monument, the Lincoln Memorial, and all of the other monuments and memorials; go to as many of the Smithsonian museums as you can, but also to the U.S. Holocaust Memorial Museum and the National Gallery of Art. See chapter 7 for information about these and the many other admission-free sites awaiting you.

66. **Plan an itinerary** that takes into account the geographical proximity of the sights you're visiting; this will enable you to save money on transportation, as well as time and energy.

67. Save time and maximize your enjoyment of **Smithsonian museums** by taking the excellent (and free) highlight tours they offer. Families should always call museums ahead to inquire about special (often free) programs for children.

68. Read the attractions listings in chapter 7 closely, and **take note of days and times when admission fees are waived.** For example, though it usually costs $11 (per adult) to tour the Mount Vernon Estate and Gardens, admission is free on the third Monday in February every year, in honor of George Washington's birthday; the Corcoran Gallery of Art does not charge its usual $5 admission all day Monday and after 5pm on Thursday.

69. **In Alexandria, purchase discounted block tickets** for attractions; it's less expensive than buying individual tickets.

NIGHTLIFE

70. Take advantage of the many **free concerts, films, lectures, plays, and other forms of entertainment** staged around town all year-round, but especially in the summer. See chapters 7 and 9 for details, as well as the Friday "Weekend" section of the *Washington Post,* and *City Paper* (a free Washington publication you can often find in stores and restaurants).

71. Purchase **half-price theater, concert, and other same-day performance tickets** at TICKETplace (details in chapter 9). Check out theater listings in chapter 9 for information on available discount tickets for students, seniors, people with disabilities, and others. Some theaters also offer discounted tickets just prior to a performance (for example, Arena Stage's half-price program).

72. **Choose a restaurant that offers entertainment** during the meal (but doesn't charge extra for it), from the refined piano music played at the Bombay Club during dinner, to the captivating flamenco dancing performed every Wednesday night at Jaleo. See chapter 6 for reviews of both of these choices.

3 Visitor Information

Before you leave, contact the **Washington, D.C. Convention and Tourism Corporation,** 1212 New York Ave. NW, Washington, DC 20005 (© **800/422-8644** or 202/789-7000; www.washington.org), and

Destination: Washington, D.C.—Red Alert Checklist

- Have you packed a photo ID? You'll need one to board a plane, of course, but even if you are not flying, you might be asked for a photo ID once you're here. As a result of the September 11, 2001, terrorist attacks, some hotels have started requiring some type of photo ID at check in. Government buildings might also require a photo ID for entry.

- And while we're on the subject of IDs: Did you bring documentation that could entitle you to discounts such as AAA and AARP cards, student IDs, and so on? If you are 65 or older, or have disabilities, you can apply in advance (allow at least 3 weeks) to Metro for an ID card that entitles you to discounted travel on the Metro system; see sections on travelers with disabilities and seniors later in this chapter for more information.

- Have you booked theater and restaurant reservations? If you're hoping to dine at a hot new restaurant or return to an old favorite, or if you're keen on catching a performance scheduled during your stay, why not play it safe by calling in advance? Two weeks is realistic to reserve a table, and you can't book theater tickets too early.

- Have you checked to make sure your favorite attraction is open? Some sites, such as the Pentagon, remain closed indefinitely to public tours, for security reasons. Other attractions, such as the National Portrait Gallery, are closed for renovations. Call ahead for opening and closing hours, and call again on the day you plan to visit an attraction, to confirm that it is open.

- Would you like to avoid the wait of a long line or the ultimate disappointment of missing a tour altogether? A number of sightseeing attractions permit you to reserve a tour slot in advance. The Supreme Court, the Library of Congress, the Washington National Cathedral, and

ask for a free copy of the *Washington, D.C. Visitors Guide,* which details hotels, restaurants, sights, shops, and more, and is updated twice yearly. In the past year or so, the Washington, D.C. Convention and Tourism Corporation has vastly improved its website, and it now includes the latest news and information, including upcoming exhibits at the museums and anticipated closings of tourist attractions. The staff will also be happy to answer specific questions.

For additional information about Washington's most popular tourist spots, check out the National Park Service website, **www.nps.gov/nacc** (the Park Service maintains Washington's monuments, memorials, and other sites), and the Smithsonian Institution's **www.si.edu**.

Also helpful is the *Washington Post* site, **www.washingtonpost.com**, which gives you up-to-the-minute news, weather, visitor information, restaurant reviews, and nightlife insights. Another good source is *Washington Flyer* magazine. You can pick up the magazine for free at the airports, but you may want to browse it online in advance (at **www.fly2dc.com**), since it often covers airport and airline news and profiles upcoming events in Washington—things you might want to know before the Kennedy Center all direct you to your senator or representative's office to request advance reservations for "congressional" tours at each of their sites. (Advance tickets for congressional tours are not necessary to tour an attraction, they just preclude a long wait.) Specify the dates you plan to visit and the number of tickets you need. Your member's allotment of tickets for each site is limited, so there's no guarantee you'll secure them.

The switchboard for the Senate is ☎ **202/224-3121;** for the House switchboard, call ☎ **202/225-3121.** You can also correspond by e-mail; check out the websites www.senate.gov and www.house.gov for e-mail addresses, individual member information, legislative calendars, and much more. Or you can write for information. Address requests to representatives as follows: name of your congressperson, U.S. House of Representatives, Washington, DC 20515; or name of your senator, U.S. Senate, Washington, DC 20510. Don't forget to include the exact dates of your Washington trip.

- If you purchased traveler's checks, have you recorded the check numbers, and stored the documentation separately from the checks?
- Did you pack your camera and an extra set of camera batteries, and purchase enough film? If you packed film in your checked baggage, did you invest in protective pouches to shield film from airport X-rays?
- Do you have a safe, accessible place to store money?
- Did you bring emergency drug prescriptions and extra glasses and/or contact lenses?
- Do you have your credit card PIN?
- If you have an E-ticket, do you have documentation?
- Did you leave a copy of your itinerary with someone at home?

you travel. The site also allows you to subscribe to its free weekly e-mail newsletter for the latest information. The Metropolitan Washington Airports Authority publishes the magazine, which carries a comprehensive flight guide for National and Dulles airports in each issue. If you don't have access to the Internet, you can subscribe to the bimonthly by calling ☎ **202/331-9393;** the rate is $15 for six issues, or $3 for one.

4 Money

Perhaps because so many of Washington's attractions (the Smithsonian museums, the monuments, even nightly concerts at the Kennedy Center) are either free or inexpensive, it may come as a shock to see the high price of lodging or a meal at a fine restaurant.

It makes sense to have some cash on hand to pay for incidentals, but it's not necessary to carry around large sums. After all, even some Metro farecard machines accept credit cards now. See "Money" section in chapter 3 for additional information.

ATMS

ATMs (automated teller machines) are everywhere, from the National Gallery of Art gift shop, to Union Station, to the bank at the corner. ATMs link local banks to a network that most likely includes your bank at home. **Cirrus** (② **800/424-7787;** www.mastercard. com) and **PLUS** (② **800/843-7587;** www.visa.com) are the two most popular networks in the United States; call or check online for ATM locations at your destination. Be sure you know your four-digit PIN before you leave home and be sure to find out your daily withdrawal limit before you depart. You can also get cash advances on your credit card at an ATM. Keep in mind that credit card companies try to protect themselves from theft by limiting the funds one can withdraw away from home. Call your credit card company before you leave and let a rep know where you're going and how much you plan to spend. You'll get the best exchange rate if you withdraw money from an ATM, but keep in mind that many banks impose a fee, usually $1.50 to $2, every time you use a card at an ATM in a different city or bank. On top of this, the bank from which you withdraw cash may charge its own fee.

TRAVELER'S CHECKS

ATMs have made traveler's checks all but obsolete. But if you still prefer the security of traveler's checks over carrying cash (and you don't mind showing identification every time you want to cash one), you can get them at almost any bank, paying a service charge that usually ranges from 1% to 7%. **American Express** offers denominations of $20, $50, $100, $500, and (for cardholders only) $1,000. You can also get **American Express** traveler's checks online at www.americanexpress.com, over the phone by calling ② **800/ 221-7282,** or in person at any American Express Travel Service location.

Visa offers traveler's checks at Citibank locations nationwide, as well as at several other banks. The service charge ranges between 1.5% and 2%; checks come in denominations of $20, $50, $100, $500, and $1,000. Call ② **800/732-1322** for information. **MasterCard** also offers traveler's checks. Call ② **800/223-9920** for a location near you.

AAA members can obtain checks without a fee at most AAA offices. (AAA has a downtown Washington office, open weekdays, 9am–5pm, at 701 15th St. NW, ② **202/331-3000,** not far from the White House.)

CREDIT CARDS

Credit cards are invaluable when traveling. They are a safe way to carry money and provide a convenient record of all your expenses. You can also withdraw cash advances from your credit cards at any bank (though you'll start paying hefty interest on the advance the moment you receive the cash). At most banks, you don't even need to go to a teller; you can get a cash advance at the ATM if you know your PIN. If you've forgotten yours, or didn't even know you had one, call the number on the back of your credit card and ask the bank to send it to you. It usually takes 5 to 7 business days, though some banks will provide the number over the phone if you tell

---

Tips **Small Change**

When you change money, ask for some small bills or loose change. Petty cash will come in handy for tipping and public transportation. Consider keeping the change separate from your larger bills, so it's readily accessible and you'll be less of a target for theft.

them your mother's maiden name or pass some other security clearance.

WHAT TO DO IF YOUR WALLET GETS STOLEN

Be sure to block charges against your account the minute you discover a card has been lost or stolen. Then be sure to file a police report.

Almost every credit card company has an emergency 800-number to call if your card is stolen. They may be able to wire you a cash advance off your credit card immediately, and in many places, they can deliver an emergency credit card in a day or two. The issuing bank's 800-number is usually on the back of your credit card—though, of course, if your card has been stolen, that won't help you unless you recorded the number elsewhere.

Citicorp Visa's U.S. emergency number is ✆ **800/336-8472.** American Express cardholders and traveler's check holders should call ✆ **800/221-7282.** MasterCard holders should call ✆ **800/307-7309.** Otherwise, call the toll-free number directory at ✆ **800/555-1212.**

Odds are that if your wallet is gone, the police won't be able to recover it for you. However, it's still worth informing the authorities. Your credit card company or insurer may require a police report number or record of the theft.

If you choose to carry traveler's checks, be sure to keep a record of their serial numbers separate from your checks. You'll get a refund faster if you know the numbers.

If you need emergency cash over the weekend when all banks and American Express offices are closed, you can have money wired to you from **Western Union** (✆ **800/325-6000;** www.westernunion.com). You must present valid ID to pick up the cash at the Western Union office. However, in most countries, you can pick up a money transfer even if you don't have valid identification, as long as you can answer a test question provided by the sender. Be sure to let the sender know in advance that you don't have ID. If you need to use a test question instead of ID, the sender must take cash to his or her local Western Union office, rather than transferring the money over the phone or online.

5 When to Go

The city's peak seasons generally coincide with two activities: the sessions of Congress and springtime, starting with the appearance of the cherry blossoms along the Potomac. Specifically, when Congress is "in," from about the second week in September until Thanksgiving, and again from about mid-January through June, hotels are full with guests whose business takes them to Capitol Hill or to conferences. Mid-March through June traditionally is the most frenzied season, when families and school groups descend upon the city to see the cherry blossoms and enjoy Washington's sensational spring. This is also the season for protest marches. Hotel rooms are at a premium and airfares tend to be higher.

If crowds turn you off, consider visiting Washington at the end of August/early September, when Congress is still "out," and families return home to get their children back to school, or between Thanksgiving and mid-January, when Congress leaves again and many people are ensconced in their own holiday-at-home celebrations. Hotel rates are cheapest at this time, too, and many hotels offer attractive packages.

If you're thinking of visiting in July and August, be forewarned: The weather is very hot and humid. Many of Washington's performance stages go dark in summer, although outdoor arenas and parks pick up some of the slack by featuring concerts, festivals, parades, and more (see chapter 9 for details about performing arts schedules). And, of course, Independence Day (July 4th) in the capital is a spectacular celebration.

THE WEATHER

Check the *Washington Post*'s website (**www.washingtonpost.com**) or the Washington, D.C. Convention and Tourism Corporation website (**www. washington.org**) for current and projected weather forecasts.

Season by season, here's what you can expect of the weather in Washington:

Fall: This is my favorite season. The weather is often warm during the day—in fact, if you're here in early fall, it may seem entirely *too* warm. But it cools off, even getting a bit crisp, at night. All the greenery that Washington is famous for dons the brilliant colors of fall foliage, and the stream of tourists tapers off.

Winter: People like to say that Washington winters are mild—and

sure, if you're from Minnesota, you'll find Washington warmer, no doubt. But D.C. winters can be unpredictable: bitter cold one day, an ice storm the next, followed by a couple of days of sun and higher temperatures. Pack for all possibilities.

Spring: Spring weather is delightful, and, of course, there are those cherry blossoms. Along with autumn, it's the nicest time to enjoy D.C.'s outdoor attractions, to visit museums in comfort, and to laze away an afternoon or evening at an outdoor cafe. But this is when the city is most crowded with visitors and school groups, and, often, protesters.

Summer: Throngs remain in summer, and anyone who's ever spent August in D.C. will tell you how hot and steamy it can be. Though the buildings are air-conditioned, many of Washington's attractions, like the memorials, monuments, and organized tours, are outdoors and unshaded, and the heat can quickly get to you. Make sure you stop frequently for drinks (vendors are everywhere), and wear a hat and/or sunscreen.

Average Temperatures (°F/C) & Rainfall (in inches) in Washington, D.C.

	Jan	Feb	Mar	Apr	May	June	July	Aug	Sept	Oct	Nov	Dec
Avg. High	44/7	46/8	54/12	66/19	76/24	83/28	87/31	85/29	79/26	68/20	57/14	46/8
Avg. Low	30/–1	29/–2	36/2	46/8	57/14	65/18	69/21	68/20	61/16	50/10	39/4	32/0
Rainfall	3.21	2.63	3.6	2.71	3.82	3.13	3.66	3.44	3.79	3.22	3.03	3.0

WASHINGTON CALENDAR OF EVENTS

Washington's most popular annual events are the Cherry Blossom Festival in spring, the Fourth of July celebration in summer, the Taste of D.C. food fair in the fall, and the lighting of the National Christmas Tree in winter. But there's some sort of special event almost daily. Check **www.washington.org** for the latest schedules.

In the calendar below, I've done my best to accurately list phone numbers for more information, but they seem to change constantly. If the number you try doesn't get you the details you need, call the **Washington, D.C. Convention and Tourism Corporation** at ℂ **202/789-7000.**

Once you're in town, grab a copy of the *Washington Post,* especially the Friday "Weekend" section. The **Smithsonian Information Center,** 1000 Jefferson Dr. SW (ℂ 202/357-2700), is another good source of information.

For annual events in Alexandria, see p. 276.

January

Martin Luther King Jr.'s Birthday. Events include speeches by prominent civil rights leaders and politicians; readings; dance, theater, and choral performances; prayer vigils; a wreath-laying ceremony at the Lincoln Memorial (call ✆ **202/ 619-7222**); and concerts. Many events take place at the Martin Luther King Memorial Library, 901 G St. NW (✆ **202/727-0321**). Third Monday in January.

February

Black History Month. Features numerous events, museum exhibits, and cultural programs celebrating the contributions of African Americans to American life, including a celebration of abolitionist Frederick Douglass's birthday. For details, check the *Washington Post* or call ✆ **202/357-2700.** For additional activities at the Martin Luther King Library, call ✆ **202/727-0321.** All month.

Chinese New Year Celebration. A friendship archway, topped by 300 painted dragons and lighted at night, marks Chinatown's entrance at 7th and H streets NW. The celebration begins the day of the Chinese New Year and continues for 10 or more days, with traditional firecrackers, dragon dancers, and colorful street parades. Some area restaurants offer special menus. For details, call ✆ **202/789-7000.** Early February.

Abraham Lincoln's Birthday. Marked by the laying of a wreath at the Lincoln Memorial and a reading of the Gettysburg Address at noon. Call ✆ **202/619-7222.** February 12.

George Washington's Birthday. Celebratory events staged at the Washington Monument. Call ✆ **202/619-7222** for details. Both presidents' birthdays also bring annual citywide sales. February 22. See chapter 10, "Side Trips from Washington, D.C.," for information about the bigger celebrations held at Mount Vernon and in Old Town Alexandria, on the third Monday in February.

International Tourist Guide Day. A 3½ hour motor coach and 1-hour walking tours of Washington during this 15th annual event, departing from a downtown location, with stops at historic spots throughout the city. Each year's tour embraces a different theme; in 2003, the tours embraced the theme "200 years of black history in the capital." The World Federation of Tourist Guide Associations sponsors International Tourist Guide Day, whose members offer educational tours in major cities throughout the world. In Washington, it's the Guild of Professional Tour Guides that conducts the tours, which are free on this day, though space is limited. Call ✆ **202/298- 9425.** Late February.

March

Women's History Month. Various institutions throughout the city stage celebrations of women's lives and achievements. For the Smithsonian's schedule of events, call ✆ **202/357-2700;** for other events, check the *Washington Post.* All month.

St. Patrick's Day Parade, on Constitution Avenue NW from 7th to 17th streets. A big parade with floats, bagpipes, marching bands, and the wearin' o' the green. For parade information, call ✆ **202/789-7000.** The Sunday before March 17.

Smithsonian Kite Festival. A delightful event if the weather cooperates—an occasion for a trip in itself. Throngs of kite enthusiasts fly their unique creations on the Washington Monument grounds and compete for ribbons and prizes. To compete, just show up with your kite and register between 10am and noon. Call ✆ **202/357-2700** or 202/357-3030 for details. A Saturday in mid- or late March, or early April.

April

Cherry Blossom Events. Washington's best-known annual event: the blossoming of the 3,700 famous Japanese cherry trees by the Tidal Basin in Potomac Park. Festivities include a major parade (marking the end of the festival) with floats, concerts, celebrity guests, and more. There are also special ranger-guided tours departing from the Jefferson Memorial. For information, call ✆ 202/547-1500. See p. 216 for more information about the cherry blossoms. Late March or early April (national news programs monitor the budding).

White House Easter Egg Roll. The biggie for little kids. This year is the White House's 125th Easter Egg Roll (and before that, it took place on the Capitol grounds—until Congress banned it). In past years, entertainment on the White House South Lawn and the Ellipse has included clog dancers, clowns, Ukrainian egg-decorating exhibitions, puppet and magic shows, military drill teams, an egg-rolling contest, and a hunt for 1,000 or so wooden eggs, many of them signed by celebrities, astronauts, or the president. *Note:* Attendance is limited to children ages 3 to 6, who must be accompanied by an adult. Hourly timed tickets are issued at the National Parks Service Ellipse Visitors Pavilion just behind the White House at 15th and E streets NW beginning at 7am. Call ✆ 202/208-1631 for details. Enter at the southeast gate on East Executive Avenue, and arrive early, to make sure you get in, and also to allow for increased security procedures. One such new rule: Strollers are not permitted. Easter Monday between 10am and 2pm.

African-American Family Day at the National Zoo. This tradition extends back to 1889, when the zoo opened. The National Zoo celebrates African-American families the day after Easter with music, dance, Easter egg rolls, and other activities. Free. Easter Monday.

Thomas Jefferson's Birthday. Celebrated at the Jefferson Memorial with wreaths, speeches, and a military ceremony. Call ✆ 202/619-7222 for time and details. April 13.

White House Spring Garden Tours. These beautifully landscaped creations are open to the public for free afternoon tours. Call ✆ 202/208-1631 for details. Two days only, in mid-April.

Shakespeare's Birthday Celebration. Music, theater, children's events, food, and exhibits are all part of the afternoon's hail to the bard at the Folger Shakespeare Library. Call ✆ 202/544-7077. Free admission. Mid-April.

Filmfest DC. This annual international film festival presents as many as 75 works by filmmakers from around the world. Screenings are staged throughout the festival at movie theaters, embassies, and other venues. Tickets are usually $8 per movie and go fast; some events are free. Call ✆ 202/789-7000 or check the website, www.filmfestdc. org. Two weeks in April.

Taste of the Nation. An organization called Share Our Strength (SOS) sponsors this fundraiser, for which 100 major restaurants and many wineries set up tasting booths and offer some of their finest fare. In 2003, the event was staged at the Ritz-Carlton Hotel. For the price of admission, you can do the circuit, sampling everything from barbecue to bouillabaisse. Wine flows freely, and there are dozens of great desserts. The evening also includes a silent auction. Tickets are $125 if purchased in advance, $150 at the door, and 100% of the profits go to feed the hungry. To obtain tickets and information, call ✆ **202/478-6578** or check out www.strength.org. Late April/early May.

Smithsonian Craft Show. Held in the National Building Museum, 401 F St. NW, this juried show features one-of-a-kind limited-edition crafts by more than 100 noted artists from all over the country. There's an entrance fee of about $12 per adult, free for children under 12, each day. For details, call ✆ **202/357-4000** (TDD 202/357-1729). For 4 days in late April.

May

Georgetown Garden Tour. View the remarkable private gardens of one of the city's loveliest neighborhoods. Admission (about $25) includes light refreshments. Some years there are related events such as a flower show at a historic home. Call ✆ **202/789-7000** or browse the website, www.gtowngarden.org for details. Early to mid-May.

Washington National Cathedral Annual Flower Mart. Now in its 65th year, the flower mart takes place on cathedral grounds, featuring displays of flowering plants and herbs, decorating demonstrations, ethnic food booths, children's rides and activities (including an antique carousel), costumed characters, puppet shows, and other entertainment. Admission is free. Call ✆ **202/537-6200** for details. First Friday and Saturday in May.

Memorial Day. At 11am, a wreath-laying ceremony takes place at the Tomb of the Unknowns in Arlington National Cemetery, followed by military band music, a service, and an address by a high-ranking government official (sometimes the president); call ✆ **202/685-2851** for details. There's also a ceremony at 1pm at the Vietnam Veterans

Memorial, including a wreath-laying, speakers, and the playing of taps (✆ **202/619-7222** for details), and activities at the U.S. Navy Memorial (✆ **202/737-2300**). On the Sunday before Memorial Day, the National Symphony Orchestra performs a free concert at 8pm on the West Lawn of the Capitol to officially welcome summer to Washington; call ✆ **202/619-7222** for details.

June

Dupont-Kalorama Museum Walk Day. This is an annual celebration of collections by six museums and historic houses in this charming neighborhood. Free food, music, tours, and crafts demonstrations. Call ✆ **202/667-0441.** Early June.

Shakespeare Theatre Free For All. This free theater festival presents a different Shakespeare play each year for a 2-week run at the Carter Barron Amphitheatre in upper northwest Washington. Tickets are required, but they're free. Call ✆ **202/334-4790.** Evenings in mid-June.

Smithsonian Festival of American Folklife. A major event with traditional American music, crafts, foods, games, concerts, and exhibits, staged the length of the National Mall. All events are free; most events take place outdoors. Call ✆ **202/357-2700,** or check the listings in the *Washington Post* for details. For 5 to 10 days in late June and early July, always including July 4th.

July

Independence Day. There's no better place to be on the Fourth of July than in Washington, D.C. The festivities include a massive National Independence Day Parade down Constitution Avenue, complete with lavish floats, princesses, marching groups, and military bands. There are also celebrity entertainers and concerts. (Most events take place on the Washington Monument grounds.) A morning program in front of the National Archives includes military demonstrations, period music, and a reading of the Declaration of Independence. In the evening, the National Symphony Orchestra plays on the west steps of the Capitol with guest artists (for example, Leontyne Price). And big-name entertainment also precedes the fabulous fireworks display behind the Washington Monument. You can also attend a free 11am organ recital at Washington's National Cathedral. Consult the *Washington Post* or call (C) **202/789-7000** for details. July 4th, all day.

Bastille Day. This Washington tradition honors the French Independence Day with live entertainment and a race by tray-balancing waiters and waitresses from Les Halles Restaurant to the U.S. Capitol and back. Free, *mais bien sur.* Twelfth Street and Pennsylvania Avenue NW. Call (C) **202/296-7200.** July 14.

September

National Frisbee Festival. Washington Monument grounds. See world-class Frisbee champions and their disk-catching dogs at this noncompetitive event. Labor Day weekend.

Labor Day Concert. West Lawn of the Capitol. The National Symphony Orchestra closes its summer season with a free performance at 8pm; call (C) **202/619-7222** for details. Labor Day. (Rain date: Same day and time at Constitution Hall.)

Kennedy Center Open House Arts Festival. A day-long festival of the performing arts, featuring local and national artists on the front plaza and river terrace (which overlooks the Potomac), and throughout the stage halls of the Kennedy Center. Past festivals have featured the likes of Los Lobos, Mary Chapin Carpenter, and Washington Opera soloists. Kids' activities usually include a National Symphony Orchestra "petting zoo,"

where children get to bow, blow, drum, or strum a favorite instrument. Admission is free, although you may have to stand in a long line for the inside performances. Check the *Washington Post* or call (C) **800/444-1324** or 202/467-4600 for details. A Sunday in early to mid-September, noon to 6pm.

Black Family Reunion. Performances, food, and fun are part of this celebration of the African-American family and culture, held on the Mall. Free. Call (C) **202/737-0120.** Mid-September.

Hispanic Heritage Month. Various museums and other institutions host activities celebrating Hispanic culture and traditions. Call (C) **202/789-7000.** Mid-September to mid-October.

Washington National Cathedral's Open House. Celebrates the anniversary of the laying of the foundation stone in 1907. Events include demonstrations of stone carving and other crafts utilized in building the cathedral; carillon and organ demonstrations; and performances by dancers, choirs, strolling musicians, jugglers, and puppeteers. This is the only time visitors are allowed to ascend to the top of the central tower to see the bells; it's a tremendous climb, but you'll be rewarded with a spectacular view. For details, call (C) **202/537-6200.** A Saturday in late September or early October.

October

Taste of D.C. Festival. Pennsylvania Avenue, between 9th and 14th streets NW. Dozens of Washington's restaurants offer food tastings, along with live entertainment, dancing, storytellers, and games. Admission is free; food and drink tickets are sold in bundles, usually $6 for 5 tickets, or $25 for 25 tickets. Call (C) **202/789-7000** for details. For 3 days, including Columbus Day weekend.

> **Tips** **Quick ID**
>
> Tie a colorful ribbon or piece of yarn around your luggage handle, or slap a distinctive sticker on the side of your bag. This makes it less likely that someone will mistakenly appropriate it. And if your luggage gets lost, it will be easier to find.

White House Fall Garden Tours. For 2 days, visitors have an opportunity to see the famed Rose Garden and South Lawn. Admission is free. A military band provides music. For details, call ✆ **202/208-1631.** Mid-October.

Marine Corps Marathon. More than 16,000 runners compete in this 26.2-mile race (the fourth-largest marathon in the United States). It begins at the Marine Corps Memorial (the Iwo Jima statue) and passes major monuments. Call ✆ **800/ RUN-USMC** or 703/784-2225 for details. Anyone can enter; register online at www.marinemarathon. com. Fourth Sunday in October.

Halloween. There's no official celebration, but costumed revels seem to get bigger every year. Giant block parties take place in the Dupont Circle area and Georgetown. Check the *Washington Post* for special parties and activities. October 31.

November

Veterans Day. The nation's war dead are honored with a wreath-laying ceremony at 11am at the Tomb of the Unknowns in Arlington National Cemetery followed by a memorial service. The president of the United States or a very high-ranking government personage officiates. Military music is provided by a military band. Call ✆ **202/685-2951** for information. At the Vietnam Veterans Memorial (✆ **202/619-7222**), observances include speakers, wreath placement, a color guard, and the playing of taps. November 11.

December

Christmas Pageant of Peace/ National Tree Lighting. At the northern end of the Ellipse, the president lights the national Christmas tree to the accompaniment of orchestral and choral music. The lighting inaugurates the 4-week Pageant of Peace, a tremendous holiday celebration with seasonal music, caroling, a nativity scene, 50 state trees, and a burning yule log. Call ✆ **202/208-1631** for details. A select Wednesday or Thursday in early December at 5pm.

6 Travel Insurance

Check your existing insurance policies and credit-card coverage before you buy travel insurance. You may already be covered for lost luggage, cancelled tickets, or medical expenses. The cost of travel insurance varies widely, depending on the cost and length of your trip, your age, health, and the type of trip you're taking.

TRIP-CANCELLATION INSURANCE Trip-cancellation insurance helps you get your money back if you have to back out of a trip, if you have to go home early, or if your travel supplier goes bankrupt. Allowed reasons for cancellation can range from sickness to natural disasters to the State Department declaring your destination unsafe for travel. (Insurers usually won't cover vague fears, though, as many travelers discovered who tried to cancel their trips in October 2001 because they were wary of flying.) In this unstable world, trip-cancellation insurance is a good buy if you're getting tickets well in advance—who knows what the state of the world, or of your airline, will be in 9 months? Insurance policy details vary, so read the fine print—and especially make sure that your airline or cruise line is on the list of carriers covered in case of bankruptcy. For information, contact one of the following insurers: **Access America** (© 866/807-3982; www. accessamerica.com); **Travel Guard International** (© 800/826-4919; www.travelguard.com); **Travel Insured International** (© 800/243-3174; www.travelinsured.com); and **Travelex Insurance Services** (© 888/457-46022; www.travelex-insurance.com).

MEDICAL INSURANCE Most health insurance policies cover you if you get sick away from home—but check, particularly if you're insured by an HMO. If you require additional medical insurance, try **MEDEX International** (© 800/527-0218 or 410/453-6300; www.medexassist.com) or **Travel Assistance International** (© 800/821-2828; www.travel assistance.com; for general information on services, call the company's Worldwide Assistance Services, Inc., at © 800/777-8710).

LOST-LUGGAGE INSURANCE On domestic flights, checked baggage is covered up to $2,500 per ticketed passenger. On international flights (including U.S. portions of international trips), baggage is limited to approximately $9.07 per pound, up to approximately $635 per checked bag. If you plan to check items more valuable than the standard liability, see if your valuables are covered by your homeowner's policy, get baggage insurance as part of your comprehensive travel-insurance package, or buy Travel Guard's (© 800/826-4919) "Bag-Trak" product, a 24-hour bag tracking service that locates lost luggage and sends it directly to you. The best thing about this kind of insurance, if you travel a lot, is that the insurance covers you for a year, not just for one trip. Don't buy insurance at the airport, as it's usually overpriced. Be sure to take any valuables or irreplaceable items with you in your carry-on luggage, as many valuables (including books, money, and electronics) aren't covered by airline policies.

If your luggage is lost, immediately file a lost-luggage claim at the airport, detailing the luggage contents. For most airlines, you must report delayed, damaged, or lost baggage within 4 hours of arrival. The airlines are required to deliver luggage, once found, directly to your house or destination free of charge.

7 Health & Safety

WHAT TO DO IF YOU GET SICK AWAY FROM HOME

In most cases, your existing health plan will provide the coverage you need. But double-check; you may want to buy **travel medical insurance** instead. (See the section on insurance, above.) Bring your insurance ID card with you when you travel.

If you suffer from a chronic illness, consult your doctor before your departure. For conditions like epilepsy, diabetes, or heart problems, wear a **Medic Alert Identification Tag** (© 800/825-3785; www.medicalert. org), which will immediately alert doctors to your condition and give them access to your records through Medic Alert's 24-hour hotline.

Pack **prescription medications** in your carry-on luggage, and carry prescription medications in their original containers, with pharmacy labels—otherwise they won't make it through airport security. Also bring along copies of your prescriptions in case you lose your pills or run out. Don't forget an extra pair of contact lenses or prescription glasses. Carry the generic name of prescription medicines, in case a local pharmacist is unfamiliar with the brand name.

If you get sick, consider asking your hotel concierge to recommend a local doctor—even his or her own. You can also try the emergency room at a local hospital; many have walk-in clinics for emergency cases that are not life-threatening. (See the entry for "Hospitals" in "Fast Facts: Washington, D.C.," on p. 82.)

STAYING SAFE

The first thing you want to do is get on the Internet and access the Washington Convention and Visitor Corporation's website, www.washington.org, which publishes travel updates, often on a daily basis. The travel updates alert you to the general state of affairs in D.C. and to new security and touring procedures around town, and refer you to other sections of its website for information about restaurants, hotels, and attractions.

In the years following the September 11, 2001, terrorist attack on the Pentagon, the federal and D.C. governments, along with agencies such as the National Park Service, have continued to work together to increase security,

not just at airports, but around the city, including government buildings, tourist attractions, and the subway. You will notice vehicle barriers in place at a wider radius around the Capitol building and the White House, and new vehicle barriers and better lighting installed at the Washington Monument and at the Lincoln and Jefferson memorials. E Street, south of the White House, and certain streets near the Capitol are closed to car traffic. Self-guided tours of the Capitol are no longer possible, and public guided tours are less comprehensive than they used to be. Greater numbers of police and security officers are on duty around and inside government buildings, the monuments, and the Metro. By the time you read this, 24-hour video surveillance cameras, long in use at the Capitol and the White House, may be in place in public at the Washington Monument, and at the Jefferson, Lincoln, Franklin Delano Roosevelt, Vietnam Veterans, and Korean War memorials.

Just because there are so many police around, you shouldn't let your guard down. Washington, like any urban area, has a criminal element, so it's important, generally, to stay alert and take normal safety precautions.

Ask your hotel front-desk staff or the city's tourist office if you're in doubt about which neighborhoods are safe.

For more safety tips, see "General Safety Suggestions," in chapter 3.

8 Specialized Travel Resources

TRAVELERS WITH DISABILITIES

Washington, D.C., is one of the most accessible cities in the world for travelers with disabilities. The best overall source of information about accessibility at specific Washington hotels, restaurants, shopping malls, and attractions is the nonprofit organization **Access Information.** You can read the information (including restaurant

reviews) online at www.disabilityguide. org, or order a free copy of the *Washington, DC Access Guide* by calling ☎ **301/528-8664,** or by writing to Access Information, 21618 Slidell Rd., Boyds, MD 20841.

The **Washington Metropolitan Transit Authority** publishes accessibility information on its website **www. wmata.com**, or you can call ☎ **202/ 962-1245** with questions about Metro services for travelers with disabilities, including how to obtain a Disabled ID card that entitles you to discounted fares. (Make sure that you call at least 3 weeks ahead to allow enough time to obtain an ID card.) For up-to-date information about how Metro is operating on the day you're using it, for instance, to verify that the elevators are operating at the stations you'll be traveling to, call ℂ **202/962-6464.**

Each Metro station is equipped with an elevator (complete with Braille number plates) to train platforms, and rail cars are fully accessible. Metro has installed 24-inch sections of punctuated rubber tiles leading up to the granite-lined platform edge to warn visually impaired Metro riders that they're nearing the tracks. Unfortunately, a 1- to 3-inch gap between the train platform and the subway car makes it difficult for those in powered wheelchairs to board the train. Train operators make station and on-board announcements of train destinations and stops. Most of the District's Metrobuses have wheelchair lifts and kneel at the curb (the number will increase as time goes on). The TTY number for Metro information is ℂ **202/638-3780.**

Regular **Tourmobile** trams (p. 17) are accessible to visitors with disabilities. The company also operates special vans for immobile travelers, complete with wheelchair lifts. Tourmobile recommends that you call a day ahead to ensure that the van is available for you when you arrive. For information, call ℂ **703/979-0690,** or go to www.tourmobile.com.

All **Smithsonian museum buildings** are accessible to wheelchair visitors. A comprehensive free publication called "Smithsonian Access" lists all services available to visitors with disabilities, including parking, building access, sign-language interpreters, and more. To obtain a copy, call ℂ **202/ 357-2700** or TTY 202/357-1729, or find the information online, at

www.si.edu/opa/accessibility. You can also use the TTY number to get information on all Smithsonian museums and events.

The **Lincoln, Jefferson, and Vietnam memorials** and the **Washington Monument** are each equipped to accommodate visitors with disabilities and keep wheelchairs on the premises. There's limited parking for visitors with disabilities on the south side of the Lincoln Memorial. Call ahead to other sightseeing attractions for accessibility information and special services: ℂ **202/426-6842.**

Call your senator or representative to arrange wheelchair-accessible tours of **the Capitol;** they can also arrange special tours for the blind or deaf. For further information, call ℂ **202/224-4048.**

Union Station, the Shops at National Place, the Pavilion at the Old Post Office, and Georgetown Park Mall are **well-equipped shopping spots** for visitors with disabilities.

Washington theaters are handily equipped. Among the most accessible are the following three.

The **John F. Kennedy Center for the Performing Arts** provides headphones to hearing-impaired patrons at no charge. A wireless, infrared listening-enhancement system is available in all theaters. Some performances offer sign language and audio description. A public TTY is located at the Information Center in the Hall of States. Large-print programs are available at every performance; a limited number of Braille programs are available from the house manager. All theaters in the complex are wheelchair accessible. To reserve a wheelchair, call ℂ **202/416-8340.** For other questions regarding patrons with disabilities, including information about half-priced tickets (you will need to submit a letter from your doctor stating that your disability is permanent), access the center's website, www.kennedy-center.org, or call the Office for Accessibility (℗ **202/416-8727.** The TTY number is (℗ **202/416-8728.**

The **Arena Stage** ((℗ **202/488-3300;** www.arenastage.org) offers audio description and sign interpretation at designated performances as well as infrared and audio loop assisted-listening devices for the hearing impaired, plus program books in Braille and large print. The TTY box office line is (℗ **202/484-0247.** You can also call ahead to reserve handicapped parking spaces for a performance.

The **National Theatre** is wheelchair accessible and features special performances of its shows for visually and hearing-impaired theatergoers. To obtain amplified-sound earphones for narration, simply ask an usher before the performance (you'll need to provide an ID). The National also offers a limited number of half-price tickets to patrons with disabilities, who have obtained a Special Patron card from the theater, or who can provide a letter from a doctor certifying disability; seating is in the orchestra section and you may receive no more than two half-price tickets. For details, call (℗ **202/628-6161,** or go the website, www.nationaltheatre.org.

Many travel agencies offer customized tours and itineraries for travelers with disabilities. **Flying Wheels Travel** ((℗ **507/451-5005;** www.flyingwheelstravel.com) offers escorted tours and cruises that emphasize sports and private tours in minivans with lifts. **Accessible Journeys** ((℗ **800/846-4537** or 610/521-0339; www.disabilitytravel.com) caters specifically to slow walkers and wheelchair travelers and their families and friends.

Organizations that offer assistance to disabled travelers include the **Moss Rehab Hospital** (www.mossresourcenet.org), which provides a library of accessible-travel resources online; the **Society for Accessible Travel and Hospitality** ((℗ **212/447-7284;** www.sath.org; annual membership fees: $45

adults, $30 seniors and students), which offers a wealth of travel resources for all types of disabilities and informed recommendations on destinations, access guides, travel agents, tour operators, vehicle rentals, and companion services; and the **American Foundation for the Blind** ((℗ **800/232-5463;** www.afb.org), which provides information on traveling with Seeing Eye dogs.

For more information specifically targeted to travelers with disabilities, the community website **iCan** (www.icanonline.net/channels/travel/index.cfm) has destination guides and several regular columns on accessible travel. Also check out the quarterly magazine *Emerging Horizons* ($14.95 per year, $19.95 outside the U.S.; www.emerginghorizons.com); **Twin Peaks Press** ((℗ **360/694-2462;** http://disabilitybookshop.virtualave.net/blist84.htm), offering travel-related books for travelers with special needs; and *Open World Magazine,* published by the Society for Accessible Travel and Hospitality (see above; subscription: $18 per year, $35 outside the U.S.).

GAY & LESBIAN TRAVELERS

Washington, D.C., has a strong gay and lesbian community, and clearly welcomes gay and lesbian visitors, as evidenced by the fact that the Washington Convention and Tourism Corporation includes on its website, www.washington.org, a link to information for gay and lesbian tourists: click on "Pride in DC," which appears on the site's home page. You can also order the WCTC's publication, "The Gay, Lesbian, Bisexual and Transgender Travelers Guide to Washington, D.C.," by calling (℗ **202/789-7000.**

While in Washington, you'll want to get your hands on the *Washington Blade,* a comprehensive weekly newspaper distributed free at many locations in the District. Every issue provides an extensive events calendar and a list of hundreds of resources, such as crisis centers, health facilities, switchboards, political groups, religious organizations, social clubs, and student activities; it puts you in touch with everything from groups of lesbian bird-watchers to the Asian Gay Men's Network. Gay restaurants and clubs are, of course, also listed and advertised. You can subscribe to the *Blade* for $85 a year, check out **www.washingtonblade.com**, or pick up a free copy at Olsson's Books/Records, 1307 19th St. NW; Borders, 18th and L streets; and Kramerbooks, 1517 Connecticut Ave. NW, at Dupont Circle. Call the *Blade* office at © **202/797-7000** for other locations.

Washington's gay bookstore, **Lambda Rising,** 1625 Connecticut Ave. NW (© **202/462-6969**), also informally serves as an information center for the gay community, which centers in the Dupont Circle neighborhood.

The International Gay & Lesbian Travel Association (IGLTA) (© **800/448-8550** or 954/776-2626; www.iglta.org) is the trade association for the gay and lesbian travel industry, and offers an online directory of gay- and lesbian-friendly travel businesses; go to their website and click on "Members."

Many agencies offer tours and travel itineraries specifically for gay and lesbian travelers. **Above and Beyond Tours** (© **800/397-2681;** www.abovebeyondtours.com) is the exclusive gay and lesbian tour operator for United Airlines. **Now, Voyager** (© **800/255-6951;** www.nowvoyager.com) is a well-known San Francisco–based gay-owned-and-operated travel service.

The following travel guides are available at most travel bookstores and gay and lesbian bookstores: *Out and About* (© **800/929-2268** or 415/644-8044; www.outandabout.com), which offers guidebooks and a newsletter 10 times a year packed with solid information on the global gay and lesbian scene; *Spartacus International Gay Guide* and *Odysseus,* both good, annual English-language guidebooks focused on gay men; the *Damron* guides, with separate, annual books for gay men and lesbians; and *Gay Travel A to Z: The World of Gay & Lesbian Travel Options at Your Fingertips* by Marianne Ferrari (Ferrari Publications, Box 35575, Phoenix, AZ 85069), a very good gay and lesbian guidebook series.

SENIOR TRAVEL

Mention the fact that you're a senior citizen when you make your travel reservations. Although all of the major U.S. airlines except America West have cancelled their senior discount and coupon book programs, many hotels still offer discounts for seniors. In most cities, people over the age of 60 qualify for reduced admission to theaters, museums, and other attractions, as well as discounted fares on public transportation.

Washington, like most cities, offers discounted admission to seniors at theaters, at those few museums that charge for entry, and for discounted travel on the Metro, although the designated "senior" age differs slightly from place to place. For instance, discount eligibility requires that you must be 60 or older at Arena Stage, older than 62 at the Phillips Collection, and 65 or older for the Metro. Some places, such as Arena Stage, take you at your word that you qualify for a discount, so you may order your tickets over the phone, without showing proof of your age. To obtain discounted fare cards to ride the Metro, you must first apply for a Senior ID card, well in advance of your trip; call © **202/962-2136** for more information.

Members of **AARP** (formerly known as the American Association of Retired Persons), 601 E St. NW, Washington, DC 20049 (© **800/424-3410** or 202/434-2277; www.aarp.org), get discounts on hotels, airfares, and car rentals. AARP offers members a wide range of benefits, including *AARP The Magazine* and a monthly newsletter. Anyone over 50 can join.

The Alliance for Retired Americans, 8403 Colesville Rd., Suite 1200, Silver Spring, MD 20910 (© **301/578-8422;** www.retiredamericans.org), offers a newsletter six times a year and discounts on hotel and auto rentals; annual dues are $13 per person or couple. *Note:* Members of the former National Council of Senior Citizens receive automatic membership in the Alliance.

Many reliable agencies and organizations target the 50-plus market. **Elderhostel** (© **877/426-8056;** www.elderhostel.org) arranges study programs for those aged 55 and over (and a spouse or companion of any age) in the U.S. and in more than 80 countries around the world. Most courses last 5 to 7 days in the U.S. (2–4 weeks abroad), and many include airfare, accommodations in university dormitories or modest inns, meals, and tuition. Recommended publications offering travel resources and discounts for seniors include: the quarterly magazine *Travel 50 & Beyond* (www.travel50andbeyond.com); *Travel Unlimited: Uncommon Adventures for the Mature Traveler* (Avalon); *101 Tips for Mature Travelers,* available from Grand Circle Travel (© **800/221-2610** or 617/350-7500; www.gct.com); *The 50+ Traveler's Guidebook* (St. Martin's Press); and *Unbelievably Good Deals and Great Adventures That You Absolutely Can't Get Unless You're Over 50* (McGraw Hill).

FAMILY TRAVEL

Field trips during the school year and family vacations during the summer keep Washington, D.C., crawling with kids all year long. More than any other city, perhaps, Washington is crammed with historic buildings, arts and science museums, parks, and recreational sites to interest young and old alike. Some museums, like the National Museum of Natural History and the Daughters of the American Revolution (DAR) Museum, have hands-on exhibits for children. Many more sponsor regular, usually free, family oriented events, such as the Corcoran Gallery of Art's "Family Days" and the Folger Shakespeare Library's seasonal activities. It's worth calling or checking websites in advance for schedules from the attractions you're thinking of visiting (see chapter 7 for attractions and activities that appear with a "Kids" icon in the title, to indicate they are especially recommended for children). The fact that so many attractions are free is a boon to the family budget.

Hotels, more and more, are doing their part to make family trips affordable, too. At many lodgings, children under a certain age (usually 12) sleep free in the same room with their parents (I've noted these policies in all the listings in chapter 5). Hotel weekend packages often offer special family rates. See the "Family-Friendly Hotels" box on p. 87 for a rundown of the hotels that are most welcoming to young travelers.

Restaurants throughout the Washington area are growing increasingly family friendly as well. Many provide kids' menus or charge less for children's portions. The best news, though, is that families are welcome at all sorts of restaurants these days and need no longer stick only to burger joints. See the "Family-Friendly Restaurants" box on p. 130 for a list of places kids will especially love.

Washington, D.C., is easy to navigate with children. The Metro covers the city and it's safe. Children under 4 ride free.

Once you arrive, get your hands on a copy of the most recent *Washington Post* "Weekend" section, published each Friday. The section covers all possible happenings in the city, with a weekly feature, "Saturday's Child," and a column, "Carousel," devoted to children's activities.

You can find good family-oriented vacation advice on the Internet from sites like the **Family Travel Network** (www.familytravelnetwork.com); **Family Travel Forum** (© 888/383-6786; www.familytravelforum.com), whose motto is "Have Family, Still Travel," and offers helpful information and travel discounts for families planning trips; and **Family Travel Files** (www.thefamilytravelfiles.com), which offers an online magazine and a directory of off-the-beaten-path tours and tour operators for families.

Also look for two books: *How to Take Great Trips with Your Kids* (The Harvard Common Press) is full of good general advice that can apply to travel anywhere; and *Frommer's Washington, D.C., with Kids.*

STUDENT TRAVEL

When it comes to theater and museum admission discounts in Washington, students rule. The one caveat: You must have a valid ID, although your current school ID should be good enough. For benefits that extend beyond reduced admission to D.C. attractions, you may want to consider obtaining an International Student Identity Card (ISIC).

STA Travel (© 800/781-4040; www.statravel.com) is the largest student travel agency in the world, catering especially to young travelers, although their bargain-basement prices are available to people of all ages. From STA, you can purchase the $22 ISIC, good for cut rates on rail passes, plane tickets, and other discounts. It also provides you with basic health and life insurance, and a 24-hour help line. If you're no longer a student but are still under 26, you can get a **GO 25 card** from the same people, which entitles you to insurance and some discounts (but not on museum admissions). In Washington, STA has an office in Georgetown, at 3301 M St. NW (© **202/337-6464**). (*Note:* In 2002, STA Travel bought competitors **Council Travel** and **USIT Campus** after they went bankrupt. It's still operating some offices under the Council name, but it's owned by STA.)

In Canada, **Travel CUTS** (© **800/667-2887** or 416/614-2887; www.travelcuts.com), offers similar services. Irish students should turn to **USIT** (© **01/602-1600**; www.usitnow.ie).

Studentuniverse.com (www.studentuniverse.com) is an online student travel agency in partnership with Orbitz.com. that consistently offers great discounts on airfares to students and faculty.

The Hanging Out Guides (www.frommers.com/hangingout), published by Frommer's, is the top student travel series for today's students, covering everything from adrenaline sports to the hottest club and music scenes.

9 Planning Your Trip Online

SURFING FOR AIRFARES

The "big three" online travel agencies, **Expedia.com, Travelocity.com,** and **Orbitz.com** sell most of the air tickets bought on the Internet. (Canadian travelers should try expedia.ca and Travelocity.ca; U.K. residents can go for expedia.co.uk and opodo.co.uk.) Each has different business deals with the airlines and may offer different fares on the same flights, so it's wise to shop around. Expedia and Travelocity will also send you **e-mail notification** when a cheap fare becomes available to your favorite destination. Of the smaller travel agency websites, **SideStep** (www.sidestep.com) has gotten the best reviews from Frommer's authors. It's a browser add-on that purports to "search 140 sites at once," but in reality only beats competitors' fares as often as other sites do.

Also remember to check **airline websites,** especially those for low-fare carriers such as Southwest, JetBlue, and AirTran, whose fares are sometimes misreported or simply missing from travel agency websites. (Sidestep, it should be noted, *does* include the discount airlines in its search.) Even with major airlines, you can often shave a few bucks from a fare by booking directly through the airline and avoiding a travel agency's transaction fee. But you'll get these discounts only by **booking online:** Most airlines now offer online-only fares that even their phone agents know nothing about. For the websites of airlines that fly to and from your destination, go to "Getting Here," later in this chapter.

Great **last-minute deals** are available through free weekly e-mail services provided directly by the airlines. Most of these are announced on Tuesday or Wednesday and must be purchased online. Most are only valid for travel that weekend, but some (such as Southwest's) can be booked weeks or months in advance. Sign up for weekly e-mail alerts at airline websites or check megasites that compile comprehensive lists of last-minute specials, such as **Smarter Living** (smarterliving.com). For last-minute trips, **site59.com** in the U.S. and **lastminute.com** in Europe often have better deals than the major-label sites. The *Washington Post* also tracks last minute deals on the "Travel" page of its website, **www.washingtonpost. com.** Updated every Wednesday, the list covers airline specials for the coming weekend, on flights at all three Washington airports. You'll find other special offers, with more lead time, posted on this page, as well.

If you're willing to give up some control over your flight details, use an **opaque fare service** like **Priceline** (www.priceline.com; www.priceline. co.uk for Europeans) or **Hotwire** (www.hotwire.com). Both offer rock-bottom prices in exchange for travel on a "mystery airline" at a mysterious time of day, often with a mysterious change of planes en route. The mystery airlines are all major, well-known carriers—and the possibility of being sent from Philadelphia to Chicago via Tampa is remote; the airlines' routing computers have gotten a lot better than they used to be. But your chances of getting a 6am or 11pm flight are pretty high. Hotwire tells you flight prices before you buy; Priceline usually has better deals than Hotwire, but you have to play their "name our price" game. If you're new at this, the helpful folks at **BiddingForTravel** (www.biddingfortravel.com) do a good job of demystifying Priceline's prices. Priceline and Hotwire are great for flights within North America and between the U.S. and Europe.

For much more about airfares and savvy air-travel tips and advice, pick up a copy of *Frommer's Fly Safe, Fly Smart* (Wiley Publishing, Inc.).

SURFING FOR HOTELS

Of the "big three" sites, **Expedia** may be the best choice, thanks to its long list of special deals. **Travelocity** runs a close second. Hotel specialist sites **hotels.com** and **hoteldiscounts.com** are also reliable. An excellent free, downloadable program, **TravelAxe** (www.travelaxe.net), can help you search multiple hotel sites at once, even ones you may never have heard of.

You should also check out the individual websites of Washington hotels; the two, free online reservation services for Washington hotels: **Capitol Reservations,** www.hotelsdc.com, and **DC Accommodations,** www.dc accommodations.com (see chapter 5 for more information about these services); as well as the website for the **Washington, DC, Convention and**

Frommers.com: The Complete Travel Resource

For an excellent travel-planning resource, we highly recommend **Frommers.com** (www.frommers.com). We're a little biased, of course, but we guarantee that you'll find the travel tips, reviews, monthly vacation giveaways, and online-booking capabilities thoroughly indispensable. Among the special features are our popular **Message Boards,** where Frommer's readers post queries and share advice (sometimes even our authors show up to answer questions); **Frommers.com Newsletter,** for the latest travel bargains and insider travel secrets; and **Frommer's Destinations Section,** where you'll get expert travel tips, hotel and dining recommendations, and advice on the sights to see for more than 3,000 destinations around the globe. When your research is done, the **Online Reservations System** (www.frommers.com/book_a_trip) takes you to Frommer's preferred online partners for booking your vacation at affordable prices.

Tourism Corporation (WCTC), www. washington.org, which includes a hotel booking option. I compared rates offered by Expedia, Capitol Reservations, the WCTC, and the hotel websites for the hotels I had chosen: the downtown Henley Park Hotel, within walking distance of the new DC Convention Center; and the River Inn, in the Foggy Bottom neighborhood, and not far from Georgetown, in one direction, and the White House, in the other. My week-in-advance request for a double room for a weeknight during the usually slower summer season turned up least expensive rates of $119 (with AAA discount) or $125 (without the AAA discount) using the hotel's own website, for the Henley Park Hotel; and $89 using the hotel's own website for the River Inn. Surprisingly, Expedia posted the most expensive rates for both properties: $159 for the Henley Park Hotel and $129 for the River Inn. What I'd recommend is to use this book to help you figure out your desired neighborhood and hotel, and then try all sources until you find the best rate for your most preferred lodging.

Priceline and Hotwire are even better for hotels than for airfares; with both, you're allowed to pick the neighborhood and quality level of your hotel before offering up your money. *Note:* Hotwire overrates its hotels by one star—what Hotwire calls a four-star is a three-star anywhere else.

SURFING FOR RENTAL CARS

For booking rental cars online, the best deals are usually found at rental-car company websites, although all the major online travel agencies also offer rental-car reservations services. Priceline and Hotwire work well for rental cars, too; the only "mystery" is which major rental company you get, and for most travelers the difference between Hertz, Avis, and Budget is negligible.

10 The 21st-Century Traveler

INTERNET ACCESS AWAY FROM HOME

Travelers have any number of ways to check their e-mail and access the Internet on the road. Of course, using your own laptop—or even a PDA (personal digital assistant) or electronic organizer with a modem—gives you the most flexibility. But even if you don't have a computer, you can still access your e-mail and even your office computer from cybercafes.

WITHOUT YOUR OWN COMPUTER

It's hard nowadays to find a city that *doesn't* have a few cybercafes. Although there's no definitive directory for cybercafes—these are independent businesses, after all—three places to start looking are at **www.cybercaptive.com**, **www.necafeguide.com**, and **www.cybercafe.com**.

Aside from formal cybercafes, most **youth hostels** nowadays have at least one computer you can get to the Internet on. And most **public libraries** across the world offer Internet access free or for a small charge. Avoid **hotel business centers,** which often charge exorbitant rates.

All three of Washington's airports have **Internet kiosks** scattered throughout their gates. These kiosks, which you'll also see in shopping malls, hotel lobbies, and tourist information offices around the world, give you basic Web access for a per-minute fee that's usually higher than cybercafe prices. The kiosks' clunkiness and high price means they should be avoided whenever possible.

To retrieve your e-mail, ask your **Internet Service Provider (ISP)** if it has a Web-based interface tied to your existing e-mail account. If your ISP doesn't have such an interface, you can use the free **mail2web** service (www.mail2web.com) to view (but not reply to) your home e-mail. For more flexibility, you may want to open a free, Web-based e-mail account with **Yahoo! Mail** (http://mail.yahoo.com). (Microsoft's Hotmail is another popular option, but Hotmail has severe spam problems.) Your home ISP may be able to forward your e-mail to the Web-based account automatically.

If you need to access files on your office computer, look into a service called **GoToMyPC** (www.gotomypc.com). The service provides a Web-based interface for you to access and manipulate a distant PC from anywhere—even a cybercafe—provided your "target" PC is on and has an always-on connection to the Internet (such as with Road Runner cable). The service offers top-quality security, but if you're worried about hackers, use your own laptop rather than a cybercafe to access the GoToMyPC system.

WITH YOUR OWN COMPUTER

Major Internet Service Providers (ISP) have **local access numbers** around the world, allowing you to go online by simply placing a local call. Check your ISP's website or call its toll-free number and ask how you can use your current account away from home, and how much it will cost.

If you're traveling outside the reach of your ISP, the **iPass** network has dial-up numbers in most of the world's countries. You'll have to sign up with an iPass provider, who will then tell you how to set up your computer for your destination(s). For a list of iPass providers, go to www.ipass.com click on "Reseller Locator." Under "Select a Country" pick the country that you're coming from, and under "Who is this service for?" pick "Individual". One solid provider is **i2roam** (www.i2roam.com; ℂ **866/874-0495** or 920/233-5863).

Wherever you go, bring a **connection kit** of the right power and phone adapters, a spare phone cord, and a spare Ethernet network cable. Electricity in Washington is standard 110-volt power; European appliances will require a voltage transformer.

Most business-class hotels throughout the world offer dataports for laptop modems, and many now offer high-speed Internet access using an

Ethernet network cable. You'll have to bring your own cables either way, so **call your hotel in advance** to find out what the options are.

Many business-class hotels in the U.S. also offer a form of computer-free Web browsing through the room TV set. We've successfully checked Yahoo! Mail and Hotmail on these systems.

If you have an 802.11b/**Wi-fi** card for your computer, several commercial companies have made wireless service available in airports, hotel lobbies, and coffee shops, primarily in the U.S. **T-Mobile Hotspot** (www.t-mobile. com/hotspot) serves up wireless connections at more than 1,000 Starbucks coffee shops nationwide. **Boingo** (www. boingo.com) and **Wayport** (www. wayport.com) have set up networks in airports and high-class hotel lobbies. IPass providers (see above) also give you access to a few hundred wireless hotel lobby setups. Best of all, you don't need to be staying at the Four Seasons to use the hotel's network; just set yourself up on a nice couch in the lobby. Unfortunately, the companies' pricing policies are byzantine, with a variety of monthly, per-connection, and per-minute plans.

Community-minded individuals have also set up **free wireless networks** in major cities around the world. These networks are spotty, but you get what you (don't) pay for. Each network has a home page explaining how to set up your computer for their particular system; start your explorations at www.personaltelco.net/index.cgi/WirelessCommunities.

USING A CELLPHONE ACROSS THE U.S.

Just because your cellphone works at home doesn't mean it'll work elsewhere in the country (thanks to our nation's fragmented cellphone system), although it's a good bet that your phone will work here in D.C. But take a look at your wireless company's coverage map on its website before heading out.

If you're not from the U.S., you'll be appalled at the poor reach of our **GSM (Global System for Mobiles) wireless network,** which is used by much of the rest of the world (see below). Your phone will probably work in most major U.S. cities; it definitely won't work in many rural areas. (To see where GSM phones work in the U.S., check out www.t-mobile.com/coverage/national_popup.asp.) And you may or may not be able to send SMS (text messaging) home. Assume nothing—call your wireless provider and get the full scoop. In a worst-case scenario, you can always rent a phone; **InTouch USA** (℃ **800/872-7626;** www.intouch-global.com) delivers to hotels. Washington Dulles International Airport has a **Rent-a-Cellular kiosk,** if you're flying into that airport.

11 Getting Here

BY PLANE

Domestic airlines with scheduled flights into all three of Washington, D.C.'s airports, Washington Dulles International (Dulles), Ronald Reagan Washington National (National), and Baltimore–Washington International (BWI), include **American** (℃ 800/433-7300; www.aa.com), **Continental** (℃ 800/525-0280; www.continental.com), **Delta** (℃ 800/221-1212; www.delta.com), **Northwest** (℃ 800/225-2525; www.nwa.com), **United** (℃ 800/241-6522; www.united.com), and **US Airways** (℃ 800/428-4322; www.usairways.com).

For a list of international airlines with scheduled flights into all three area airports, see chapter 3, "For International Visitors."

Washington, D.C., Metropolitan Area

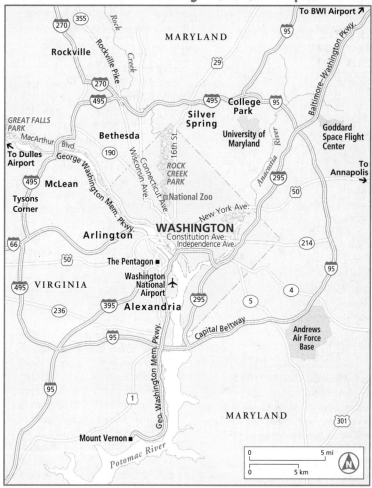

Low-fare airlines seem to be most successful and dependable these days. The newest one to arrive is Delta Airline's subsidiary **Song Airlines** (© 800/359-7664; www.flysong.com), which debuted in 2003, with service starting to Dulles in late summer of 2003. Aiming to compete with Southwest Airlines and JetBlue, Song's destinations will include cities in the Northeast and Florida. If you can do without frills, find out whether Song or any of the following low-fare airlines fly from your city to Washington: **Delta Express** (© 800/325-5205; www.flydlx.com), **AirTran** (© 800/247-8726; www. airtran.com), **Southwest Airlines** (© 800/435-9792; www.southwest. com), **Frontier** (© 800/432-1359; www.frontierairlines.com), **JetBlue** (© 800/538-2583; www.jetblue.com), and **American Trans Air** (**ATA;** © 800/435-9282; www.ata.com). Delta Express flies into Dulles; AirTran flies into Dulles and BWI; Southwest flies into BWI; Frontier flies into

National and BWI; JetBlue flies into Dulles; and American Trans Air flies into National.

SHUTTLE SERVICE FROM NEW YORK, BOSTON & CHICAGO

Delta and US Airways continue to dominate the lucrative D.C.–East Coast shuttle service. Between the two of them, the airlines operate hourly or almost hourly shuttle service between Boston's Logan Airport and Washington, and New York's La Guardia Airport and Washington. The **Delta Shuttle** (© 800/933-5935) travels daily between New York and Washington, while the **US Airways Shuttle** (© 800/428-4322) operates daily between Boston and Washington, and New York and Washington. Both airlines fly into and out of Ronald Reagan Washington National Airport. Discount airline, **Southwest** (see details above), offers nearly hourly service daily between BWI and Chicago's Midway Airport, Providence, Hartford, and Nashville.

D.C.'S AREA AIRPORTS

General information follows that should help you determine which airport is your best bet; for details about individual airport services, see "Visitor Information," in chapter 4.

Note: At these three airports, as at all American airports now, only ticketed passengers are permitted to go through security to the gates, which means that if people are meeting you at the airport they will no longer be allowed to greet you at the gate; you should agree beforehand on some other designated rendezvous site. Don't have your party wait just outside the security clearance areas to greet you, since this section gets pretty crowded, and you may have trouble spotting each other; you may not even be sure that you are both at the same security clearance gates. Your best plan is to arrange to rendezvous at the baggage claim area. Monitors always post the designated baggage claim carousel for each arriving flight, so, for the time being, at least, this zone remains the best spot for reunions—even if you haven't checked your luggage. Eventually, airports may provide waiting rooms.

Ronald Reagan Washington National Airport (everyone still calls it simply "National") lies across the Potomac River in Virginia, a few minutes by car, 15 to 20 minutes by Metro from downtown in non-rush-hour traffic. Its proximity to the District and its direct access to the Metro rail system are reasons why you might want to fly into National. The word is, however, that proximity to the District is also what makes flying into and out of National the most inconvenient, because security procedures are more intense and take more time. There's also the matter of the "30-minute rule": Passengers must stay in their seats for the 30 minutes prior to landing at National, and for the 30 minutes after their plane takes off from National.

Approximately 22 major airlines and shuttles serve this airport. Nearly all nonstop flights are to and from cities located within 1,250 miles from Washington. An aviation bill passed in 1999 allows for a few exceptions and, currently, the flights that National offers beyond the 1,250-mile standard fly to and from Denver, Phoenix, Las Vegas, and Seattle.

While Washington's two other airports are in the midst of extensive renovations, National's own vast renovation was completed in 1997, and so the airport is able to offer certain enhancements that may still be in the works at Dulles and BWI: a new terminal; ticket counters that provide access to passengers with disabilities; more than 100 restaurants and shops; more parking space; and climate-controlled pedestrian bridges that connect the terminal directly to the Metro station, whose Blue and Yellow lines stop here.

The Metropolitan Washington Airports Authority oversees both National and Dulles airports, so the main information numbers and websites are the same for the two facilities: For airport information, call ℂ **703/572-2700** (the operator may answer the phone "Washington Dulles Airport Information," but it is still the source for National info) or go to www.met washairports.com. For Metro information, call ℂ **202/637-7000.**

Washington Dulles International Airport (Dulles) lies 26 miles outside the capital, in Chantilly, Virginia, a 35- to 45-minute ride to downtown in non-rush-hour traffic. Of the three airports, Dulles handles more daily flights and its airlines fly to more destinations, about 72 U.S. and 28 foreign cities. And though the airport is not as convenient to the heart of Washington as National, it's more convenient than BWI, thanks to an uncongested airport access road that travels half the distance toward Washington. A decades-long expansion has so far added two new concourses and a parking garage; eventually, the airport will more than double its annual passenger traffic to 55 million, and add a runway, pedestrian walkways, and an underground airport train system that will replace the inconvenient and unwieldy mobile lounges that, for now, transport travelers to and from the main and midfield terminals. Fifteen major domestic, 8 regional, and 20 international carriers use Dulles. The airport's information line and website are the same as National's: ℂ **703/572-2700;** www.metwashairports.com.

Last but not least is **Baltimore–Washington International Airport** (BWI), which is located about 45 minutes from downtown, a few miles outside of Baltimore. One factor especially recommends BWI to travelers: Southwest Airlines, with its bargain fares, commands a major presence here, pulling in more than one-third of BWI's business. BWI destinations

via Southwest total at least 54, and you should find out whether your city is one of them, if you want to save some money. (A couple of other low-fare airlines operate here as well; see the "By Plane" section earlier in this chapter.)

Call ℂ **800/435-9294** for airport information, or point your browser to www.bwiairport.com.

GETTING INTO TOWN FROM THE AIRPORT

Each of the three airports offers the following options for getting into the city. In each case, you follow the signs to "ground transportation" in your airport, and look there for the banners or a staff representative of the service you desire. All three airports could really use better signage, especially since their ground transportation desks always seem to be located quite a distance from the gate at which you arrive. Keep trudging, and follow baggage claim signs, too, since ground transportation operations are always situated near baggage carousels.

Taxi service: For a trip to downtown D.C., you can expect a taxi to cost anywhere from $8 to $15 for the 10- to 15-minute ride from National Airport; $44-plus for the 30- to 40-minute ride from Dulles Airport; and $55 for the 45-minute ride from BWI.

SuperShuttle buses (ℂ **800/258-3826;** www.supershuttle.com) offer shared-ride, door-to-door service between the airport and your destination, whether in the District or in a suburban location. You can't reserve space on the van for a ride from the airport, which means that you probably will have to wait 15 to 30 minutes before boarding, so that your driver can fill his van with other passengers, to make his trip worthwhile. This also means that you're going to be taken to your destination in rather a roundabout way, as the driver drops off other passengers en route. If you arrive after midnight, you can summon a van by calling the toll-free number above from National Airport, © 703/416-7884 from Dulles, and © 888/826-2700 from BWI. The 24-hour service bases its fares on zip code, so, to reach downtown, expect to pay about $10, plus $8 for each additional person, from National; $22, plus $10 per additional person, from Dulles; and $26 to $32, plus $8 per additional person, from BWI. If you're calling the SuperShuttle for a ride from a D.C. area location to one of the airports, you must reserve a spot at least 24 hours in advance.

Limousine service is the most costly of all options, with prices starting at $25 at National, $42 at Dulles, and $70 at BWI, for private car transportation to downtown D.C. For pickup from BWI, call © **202/737-2600;** for pickup from National or Dulles, try **Red Top Executive Sedan** (© **800/296-3300** or 202/882-3300). Consult the yellow pages for more information.

Free hotel/motel shuttles operate from all three airports to certain nearby properties. Best to inquire about such transportation when you book a room at your hotel.

Individual transportation options at each airport are as follows:

FROM RONALD REAGAN WASHINGTON NATIONAL AIRPORT

If you are not too encumbered with luggage, you should take **Metrorail** (© **202/637-7000**) into the city. Metro's Yellow and Blue lines stop at the airport and connect via an enclosed walkway to level two, the concourse level, of the main terminal, adjacent to terminals B and C. If yours is one of the airlines that still uses the "old" terminal A (Midway, Northwest, Alaska, and ATA), you will have a longer walk to reach the Metro station. Signs pointing the way can be confusing; so ask an airport employee if you're headed in the right direction; or, better yet, head out to the curb and hop a shuttle bus to the station, but be sure to ask the driver to

let you know when you've reached the Metro (it may not be obvious, and drivers don't always announce the stops). **Metrobuses** (© **202/637-7000**) also serve the area, should you be going somewhere off the Metro route. But Metrorail is fastest, a 15- to 20-minute non-rush-hour ride to downtown. It is safe, convenient, and cheap, costing $1.20 during non-rush hours, $1.50 during rush hour.

If you're renting a car from on-site **car-rental agencies, Avis** (© 703/419-5815), **Budget** (© 703/419-1021), **Dollar** (© 703/519-8701), **Hertz** (© 703/419-6300), or **National** (© 703/419-1032), go to level two, the concourse level, follow the pedestrian walkway to the parking garage, find garage A, and descend one flight. You can also take the complimentary Airport Shuttle (look for the sign posted at the curb outside the terminal) to parking garage A. If you've rented from off-premises agencies **Alamo** (© 703/684-0086), **Enterprise** (© 703/553-7744), or **Thrifty** (© 703/838-6895), head outside the baggage claim area of your terminal, and catch the shuttle bus marked for your agency. See appendix B at the back of this book for toll-free numbers and websites.

To get downtown by car, follow the signs out of the airport for the George Washington Parkway. Stay on the GW Parkway until you see signs for I-395 north to Washington. Take the I-395 north exit to the 12th Street exit, which puts you at 12th Street and Constitution Avenue NW; ask your hotel for directions from that point. Or, take the more scenic route, always staying to the left on the GW Parkway as you follow the signs for Memorial Bridge; you'll be driving alongside the Potomac River, with the monuments in view across the river; then, as you cross over Memorial Bridge, you're greeted by the Lincoln Memorial. Stay left coming over the bridge, swoop around to the left of the Memorial, take a left on 23rd Street

NW, a right on Constitution Avenue, and then left again on 15th Street NW (the Washington Monument will be to your right), if you want to be in the heart of downtown.

FROM WASHINGTON DULLES INTERNATIONAL AIRPORT The **Washington Flyer Express Bus** runs between Dulles and the West Falls Church Metro station, where you can board a train for D.C. Buses to the West Falls Church Metro station run daily, every 30 minutes, and cost $8 one way. (By the way, **"Washington Flyer"** is also the name under which the taxi service operates at Dulles.)

More convenient is the fairly new **Metrobus** service that runs between Dulles and the L'Enfant Plaza Metro station, located near Capitol Hill and within walking distance of the National Mall and Smithsonian museums. The bus departs hourly, daily, costs only $2, and takes about 45 to 50 minutes.

If you are renting a car at Dulles, head down the ramp near your baggage claim area, and walk outside to the curb to look for your rental car's shuttle bus stop. The buses come by every 5 minutes or so en route to nearby rental lots. These include **Alamo** (© 703/260-0182), **Avis** (© 703/661-3505), **Budget** (© 703/437-9373), **Dollar** (© 703/661-6630), **Enterprise** (© 703/661-8800), **Hertz** (© 703/471-6020), **National** (© 703/471-5278), and **Thrifty** (© 703/481-3599). See appendix B at the back of this book for these companies' toll-free numbers and websites.

To reach downtown Washington from Dulles by car, exit the airport and stay on the Dulles Access Road, which leads right into I-66 east. Follow I-66 east to exit 73, Rosslyn/Key Bridge. Ask your hotel for directions from this point.

FROM BALTIMORE–WASHINGTON INTERNATIONAL AIRPORT BWI offers an Express Metro

Bus service that runs between the Greenbelt Metro station and the airport. In the airport, look for "Public Transit" signs to find the service, which operates daily, departs every 40 minutes, and costs $2. At the Greenbelt Metro station, you purchase a Metro fare card and board a Metro train, which takes you into the city.

You also have the choice of taking either an **Amtrak** (© **800/872-7245**) or a **Maryland Rural Commuter** (**MARC;** © **800/325-7245**) train into the city. Both trains travel between the BWI Railway Station (© **410/672-6167**) and Washington's Union Station (© **202/484-7540**), about a 30-minute ride. Amtrak's service is daily (ticket prices range from $9 to $38 per person, one way, depending on time and train type), while MARC's is weekdays only ($5 per person, one-way). A courtesy shuttle runs every 10 minutes or so between the airport and the train station; stop at the desk near the baggage-claim area to check for the next departure time of both the shuttle bus and the train. Trains depart about once per hour.

BWI opened a brand-new, off-site, car rental facility in late 2003. From the ground transportation area, you board a shuttle bus to transport you to the lot. Rental agencies include **Avis** (© 410/859-1680), **Alamo** (© 410/850-5011), **Budget** (© 410/859-0850), **Dollar** (© 410/859-5600), **Hertz** (© 410/850-7400), **National** (© 410/859-8860), and **Thrifty** (© 410/859-1136). For these companies' toll-free numbers and websites, consult appendix B at the back of this book.

Here's how you reach Washington: Look for signs for I-195 and follow I-195 west until you see signs for Washington and the Baltimore–Washington Parkway (I-295); head south on I-295. Get off I-295 when you see the signs for Route 50/New York Avenue, which leads into the District, via New York

---

Tips   Don't Stow It—Ship It

If ease of travel is your main concern and money is no object, you can ship your luggage with one of the growing number of luggage-service companies that pick up, track, and deliver your luggage (often through couriers such as Federal Express) with minimum hassle for you. Traveling luggage-free may be ultra-convenient, but it's not cheap: One-way overnight shipping can cost from $100 to $200, depending on what you're sending. Still, for some people, especially the elderly or the infirm, it's a sensible solution to lugging heavy baggage. Specialists in door-to-door luggage delivery are **Virtual Bellhop** (www.virtualbellhop.com), **SkyCap International** (wwww.skycapinternational.com), and **Luggage Express** (www.usxpluggageexpress.com).

Avenue. Ask your hotel for specific directions from New York Avenue NE.

GETTING THROUGH THE AIRPORT

With the federalization of airport security, security procedures at U.S. airports are more stable and consistent than ever. Generally, you'll be fine if you arrive at the airport **1 hour** before a domestic flight and **2 hours** before an international flight; if you show up late, tell an airline employee and she'll probably whisk you to the front of the line.

Bring a **current, government-issued photo ID** such as a driver's license or passport, and if you've got an E-ticket, print out the **official confirmation page;** you'll need to show your confirmation at the security checkpoint, and your ID at the ticket counter or the gate. (Children under 18 do not need photo IDs for domestic flights, but the adults checking in with them need them. Also keep in mind that teenagers younger than 18 often look older, so it's probably a good idea to have your teenager bring a school photo ID or driver's license, to avoid any hassles.)

Security lines are getting shorter than they were during 2001 and 2002, but some doozies remain. If you have trouble standing for long periods of time, tell an airline employee; the airline will provide a wheelchair. Speed

up security by **not wearing metal objects** such as big belt buckles or clanky earrings. If you've got metallic body parts, a note from your doctor can prevent a long chat with the security screeners. Keep in mind that only **ticketed passengers** are allowed past security, except for folks escorting disabled passengers or children.

Federalization has stabilized **what you can carry on** and **what you can't.** The general rule is that sharp things are out, nail clippers are okay, and food and beverages must be passed through the X-ray machine—but that security screeners can't make you drink from your coffee cup. Bring food in your carry-on rather than checking it, as explosive-detection machines used on checked luggage have been known to mistake food (especially chocolate, for some reason) for bombs. Travelers in the U.S. are allowed one carry-on bag, plus a "personal item" such as a purse, briefcase, or laptop bag. Carry-on hoarders can stuff all sorts of things into a laptop bag; as long as it has a laptop in it, it's still considered a personal item. The Transportation Security Administration (TSA) has issued a list of restricted items; check its website (www.tsa.gov/public/index.jsp) for details.

In 2003, the TSA phased out **gate check-in** at all U.S. airports. Passengers with E-tickets and without checked bags can still beat the ticket-counter lines by using **electronic kiosks** or even **online check-in.** Ask your airline which alternatives are available, and if you're using a kiosk, bring the credit card you used to book the ticket. If you're checking bags, you will still be able to use most airlines' kiosks; again call your airline for up-to-date information. **Curbside check-in** is also a good way to avoid lines, although a few airlines still ban curbside check-in entirely; call before you go.

At press time, the TSA is also recommending that you **not lock your checked luggage** so screeners can search it by hand if necessary. The agency says to use plastic "zip ties" instead, which can be bought at hardware stores and can be easily cut off.

BY CAR

Major highways approach Washington, D.C., from all parts of the country. Specifically, these are I-270, I-95, and I-295 from the north; I-95 and I-395, Route 1, and Route 301 from the south; Route 50/301 and Route 450 from the east; and Route 7, Route 50, I-66, and Route 29/211 from the west.

No matter which road you take, there's a good chance you will have to navigate some portion of the **Capital Beltway** (I-495 and I-95) to gain entry to D.C. The Beltway girds the city, 66 miles around, with 56 interchanges or exits, and is nearly always congested, but especially during weekday morning and evening rush hours, roughly between 7 to 9am and 3 to 7pm. Commuter traffic on the Beltway now rivals that of major L.A. freeways, and drivers can get a little crazy, weaving in and out of traffic.

If you're planning to drive to Washington, get yourself a good map before you do anything else. The **American Automobile Association (AAA; ✆ 800/763-9900** for emergency road service and for connection to the mid-Atlantic office; www.aaa.com) provides its members with maps and detailed Trip-Tiks that give precise directions to a destination, including up-to-date information about areas of construction. AAA also provides towing services should you have car trouble during your trip. If you are driving to a hotel in D.C. or its suburbs, contact the establishment to find out the best route to the hotel's address and other crucial details concerning parking availability and rates. See "Getting Around," in chapter 4, for information about driving in D.C.

The District is 240 miles from New York City, 40 miles from Baltimore, 700 miles from Chicago, nearly 500 miles from Boston, and about 630 miles from Atlanta.

BY TRAIN

Amtrak (✆ 800/USA-RAIL; www.amtrak.com) offers daily service to

Travel in the Age of Bankruptcy

At press time, two major U.S. airlines were struggling in bankruptcy court and most of the rest weren't doing very well either. To protect yourself, **buy your tickets with a credit card,** as the Fair Credit Billing Act guarantees that you can get your money back from the credit card company if a travel supplier goes under (and if you request the refund within 60 days of the bankruptcy). **Travel insurance** can also help, but make sure it covers against "carrier default" for your specific travel provider. And be aware that if a U.S. airline goes bust mid-trip, a 2001 federal law requires other carriers to take you to your destination (albeit on a space-available basis) for a fee of no more than $25, provided you rebook within 60 days of the cancellation.

Flying with Film & Video

Never pack film—developed or undeveloped—in checked bags, as the new, more powerful scanners in U.S. airports can fog film. The film you carry with you can be damaged by scanners as well. X-ray damage is cumulative; the slower the film, and the more times you put it through a scanner, the more likely the damage. Film under 800 ASA is usually safe for up to five scans. If you're taking your film through additional scans, U.S. regulations permit you to demand hand inspections. In international airports, you're at the mercy of airport officials. Highly trafficked attractions are X-raying visitors' bags with increasing frequency.

Most photo supply stores sell protective pouches designed to block damaging X-rays. The pouches fit both film and loaded cameras. They should protect your film in checked baggage, but they also may raise alarms and result in a hand inspection.

An organization called **Film Safety for Traveling on Planes, FSTOP** (② **888/301-2665**; www.f-stop.org), can provide additional tips for traveling with film and equipment.

Carry-on scanners will not damage **videotape** in video cameras, but the magnetic fields emitted by the walk-through security gateways and hand-held inspection wands will. Always place your loaded camcorder on the screening conveyor belt or have it hand-inspected. Be sure your batteries are charged, as you will probably be required to turn the device on to ensure that it's what it appears to be.

Washington from New York, Boston, Chicago, and Los Angeles (you change trains in Chicago). Amtrak also travels daily from points south of Washington, including Raleigh, Charlotte, Atlanta, cities in Florida, and to New Orleans.

Metroliner service—which costs a little more but provides faster transit and roomier, more comfortable seating than regular trains—is available between New York and Washington, D.C., and points in between. *Note:* Metroliner fares are substantially reduced on weekends. The most luxurious way to travel is First Class Club Service, available on all Metroliners as well as some other trains. For a hefty additional fee, passengers enjoy more spacious and refined seating in a private car; complimentary meals and beverage service; and Metropolitan Lounges (in New York, Chicago, Philadelphia, and Washington), where travelers can wait for trains in a comfortable setting while enjoying free snacks and coffee.

Even faster, roomier, and more expensive than Metroliner service are Amtrak's high-speed **Acela** trains. The trains, which travel as fast as 150 miles per hour, navigate the Northeast Corridor, linking Boston, New York, and Washington. Acela Express trains travel between New York and Washington in 2 hours and 43 minutes (about 15 minutes faster than the Metroliner), and between Boston and Washington in about 6 hours and 30 minutes. Acela Regional trains travel between New York and Washington in 3 hours and 40 minutes, and between Boston and Washington in about 8 hours. Amtrak continues to refine the design and production of the Acela cars, which have proved problematic since they were introduced in late 2000. Amtrak hopes eventually to run a total of 19 Acela round-trips daily between New York and Washington, replacing Metroliner service between those two cities.

Amtrak trains arrive at historic **Union Station,** 50 Massachusetts Ave. NE (📞 **202/371-9441;** www.union stationdc.com), a short walk from the Capitol, across the circle from several hotels, and a short cab or Metro ride from downtown. Union Station is a turn-of-the-20th-century beaux arts masterpiece that was magnificently restored in the late 1980s. Offering a three-level marketplace of shops and restaurants, this stunning depot is conveniently located and connects with Metro service. There are always taxis available there. (For more on Union Station, see chapters 4, 7, and 8.)

As noted in tip #23, in section 2, "72 Money-Saving Tips," Amtrak offers several ways to obtain discounted fares. If you are purchasing tickets by phone, be sure to ask about discount fares and special rates for children, seniors, AAA members, or any other discount-eligible group to which you or your party may belong. If you're purchasing tickets online, check out Amtrak's bargain fares service, Rail SALE, which allows you to purchase tickets for one-way designated coach seats at great discounts. This program is only available on **www.amtrak.com** when you charge your tickets by credit card. Also review the "Savings and Promotions" page, which posts various kinds of deals, including those that offer discounted train tickets in conjunction with a museum exhibit. (You don't have to show proof of having attended the exhibit to take advantage of the discount.)

Also inquire about money-saving packages that include hotel accommodations, car rentals, tours, and so on with your train fare. Call 📞 **800/321-8684** for details.

Note: Amtrak requires that passengers 18 and older show a valid photo ID when buying tickets or checking baggage.

BY BUS

Greyhound buses (📞 **800/231-2222;** www.greyhound.com) connect almost the entire United States with Washington, D.C. They arrive at a terminal at 1005 1st St. NE, at L Street (📞 **202/289-5154**). The closest Metro stop is Union Station, 4 blocks away. The bus terminal is in an edgy neighborhood, so if you arrive at night, it's best to take a taxi to your hotel. If you're staying in the suburbs, you should know that Greyhound also has service to Silver Spring, Maryland, and Arlington, Virginia. **Peter Pan Bus Lines** (📞 **800/343-9999;** www.peterpanbus.com) traverses the Northeast corridor, arriving and departing from the Greyhound Bus Terminal (see the above address) in Washington.

12 Recommended Reading

You can put yourself in the mood for a visit to Washington by reading some great novels set in Washington, memoirs and histories by some of the city's more famous residents, and other guidebooks whose topics supplement what you've learned in these pages.

Fiction-lovers might pick up books by Ward Just, including his collection of stories *The Congressman Who Loved Flaubert;* Ann Berne's *A Crime in the Neighborhood;* Marita Golden's *The Edge of Heaven;* Allen Drury's *Advise*

and Consent; or one of the growing number of mysteries whose plot revolves around the capital, such as Margaret Truman's series (*Murder at the Smithsonian, Murder at the Kennedy Center,* and so on), or George Pelecanos's hard-core thrillers that take you to parts of Washington you'll never see as a tourist: *Hell to Pay* and *King Suckerman,* to name just two.

If you're keen on learning more about the history of the nation's capital and about the people who have lived here, try Arthur Schlesinger's *The Birth of the Nation*, F. Cary's *Urban Odyssey*, David Brinkley's *Washington at War*, and Paul Dickson's *On This Spot*, which traces the history of the city by revealing exactly what took place at specific locations—"on this spot"—in years gone by, neighborhood by neighborhood. If you like your history leavened with humor, purchase Christopher Buckley's *Washington Schlepped Here: Walking in the Nation's Capital*, to read as a hilarious companion piece to this guidebook. Buckley's book, published in spring 2003, is an irreverent look at the capital's most famous attractions and characters, all of its anecdotes true. Buckley, a Washington insider whose experience includes speechwriting for Vice President George Bush during the first Reagan administration, has also written a couple of funny, Washington-based novels, *The White House Mess* and *No Way to Treat a First Lady*.

Two memoirs are musts for finding out how the powerful operate in Washington: *Personal History*, by the late Katharine Graham, who for many years was publisher of the *Washington Post*, and *Washington*, by Graham's close friend and colleague, Meg Greenfield, a columnist and editor at the *Washington Post* for more than 30 years.

Finally, to find out more about the architecture of Washington, pick up a copy of the *AIA Guide to the Architecture of Washington, D.C.*, by Christopher Weeks; to discover information about Washington's parks, hiking trails, and other green spaces, look for *Natural Washington* by Richard Berman and Deborah Gerhard; for another humorous read, put your hands on Dave Barry's *Dave Barry Hits Below the Beltway*, and for a book that may send chills up your spine, purchase a copy of *Ghosts: Washington's Most Famous Ghost Stories* by John Alexander.

3

For International Visitors

Since September 11, 2001, the United States has instituted stricter security procedures at airports, seaports, and train stations. These requirements affect all travelers, but especially those traveling to the U.S. from other countries. Read carefully the information in this chapter and check with your closest U.S. embassy or consulate for the most up-to-date guidelines, which continue to evolve.

Once you've arrived in Washington, D.C., however, you will find a city happy to have you, along with the million or so other international visitors who journey to D.C. each year.

1 Preparing for Your Trip

ENTRY REQUIREMENTS

Check at any U.S. embassy or consulate for current information and requirements. You can also obtain a visa application and other information online at the **U.S. State Department**'s website, at **www.travel.state.gov**. In Washington, D.C., the State Department's Visa Services public information phone number is ℭ **202/663-1225.** You'll hear taped instructions, with the option to speak to an officer.

VISAS The U.S. State Department has a **Visa Waiver Program** (VWP) allowing citizens of certain countries to enter the United States without a visa for stays of up to 90 days. At press time these included Andorra, Australia, Austria, Belgium, Brunei, Denmark, Finland, France, Germany, Iceland, Ireland, Italy, Japan, Liechtenstein, Luxembourg, Monaco, the Netherlands, New Zealand, Norway, Portugal, San Marino, Singapore, Slovenia, Spain, Sweden, Switzerland, and the United Kingdom. If you are a citizen of a VWP country, you must have the following items to enter the United States:

1. A valid and machine-readable passport.
2. A round-trip transportation ticket issued on a carrier that has signed an agreement with the United States government to participate in the VWP, and you must arrive in the U.S. aboard such a carrier. An exception is made for citizens of participating VWP countries who apply for entry into the U.S. from Canada or Mexico, at a land border crossing point: in such case, you need not present round-trip transportation tickets, nor must you enter aboard a carrier that has signed an agreement with the U.S. to participate in the Visa Waiver Program.
3. A completed and signed Nonimmigrant Visa Waiver Arrival-Departure Record, form I-94W, waiving the right of review or appeal of an immigration officer's determination about admissibility, or deportation. Forms are available from participating carriers, travel agents, and land-border ports of entry.

Citizens who first enter the United States may also visit Mexico and Canada and return to the United States without a visa, as long as the total visit does not exceed 90 days. Further information is available from any U.S. embassy or consulate. Canadian citizens may enter the United States without visas but are required to show proof of citizenship and a photo ID. Citizens of all other countries must have (1) a valid passport that expires at least 6 months later than the scheduled end of their visit to the United States, and (2) a tourist visa, which may be obtained from any U.S. consulate.

To obtain a tourist visa, here's what you should do:

1. Visit the U.S. State Department's website, http://unitedstatesvisas. gov, for thorough and up-to-date information about the process.

2. Contact your nearest U.S. Embassy or Consulate to find out how to obtain application form DS-156, and, if you are a man between the ages of 16 and 45, supplemental form DS-157. Make an appointment and ask about fees, which are nonrefundable and must be paid prior to your appointment. Procedures can vary among embassies and consulates.

3. Gather required documentation: valid passport; completed and signed applications; 2-by-2-inch-square photo; evidence detailing your financial status, including evidence of funds to cover your expenses in the U.S.; documentation supporting the reason for your trip, as well as binding ties to a residence abroad; proof of payment of fees.

4. Submit your application, passport, and supporting documents to your embassy or consulate, which will review the information and issue the visa.

Note: The visa process often takes much longer than it once did, so be sure to allow at least 3 or 4 weeks.

British subjects can obtain up-to-date passport and visa information by calling the **U.S. Embassy Visa Information Line** (© 09055/444-546), or go to the U.S. Embassy Great Britain website (**www.usembassy.org. uk/cons_web/visa/visaindex.htm**) for information and e-mail contact.

Irish citizens can obtain up-to-date passport and visa information through the **Embassy of USA Dublin,** 42 Elgin Rd., Dublin 4, Ireland (© 353/ 1-668-8777), or by checking the visa website at **www.usembassy.ie**.

Australian citizens can obtain up-to-date passport and visa information by calling the **U.S. Embassy Canberra,** Moonah Place, Yarralumla, ACT 2600 (© 02/6214-5600), or checking the website's visa page (**http://usembassy-australia. state.gov**).

Citizens of **New Zealand** can obtain up-to-date passport and visa information by calling the **U.S. Embassy New Zealand,** 29 Fitzherbert Terr., Thorndon, Wellington, New Zealand (© 644/462-6000), or can get the information directly from the website (**http://usembassy.org.nz**).

DRIVER'S LICENSES Foreign driver's licenses are mostly recognized in the United States, although you may want to get an international driver's license if your home license is not written in English.

PASSPORT INFORMATION

As of October 1, 2003, the U.S. requires that passports be machine readable, which means that the size of the passport and photo, and the arrangement of data fields containing biographical data meet the standards of the International Civil Aviation Organization, Doc 9303, Part 1 Machine Readable Passports.

Safeguard your passport in an inconspicuous, inaccessible place like a money belt. Make a copy of the critical pages, including the passport number, and store it in a safe place, separate from the passport itself. If you lose your passport while in Washington, visit your country's embassy or consulate as soon as possible for a replacement. Passport applications are downloadable from most government Internet sites, including those listed in the text that follows for Canada, the United Kingdom, Ireland, Australia, and New Zealand.

Note that the International Civil Aviation Organization (ICAO) has recommended a policy requiring that *every* individual who travels by air have his or her own passport. In response, many countries are now requiring that children must be issued their own passport to travel internationally, where before those under 16 or so may have been allowed to travel on a parent or guardian's passport.

Procedures, fees, and processing times for obtaining or renewing passports vary, of course, from country to country, and requirements can change as governments incorporate more effective security precautions into their procedures. Best to inquire at the closest passport office in your country. Here is a list of central passport offices for the following English-speaking countries: Canada, the United Kingdom, Ireland, Australia, and New Zealand.

CANADA
Canada has 29 regional passport offices rather than one central office; call the toll-free number ✆ **800/567-6868,** or check the website, **www.passport.gc.ca,** to find out the location nearest you. Send written inquiries to Passport Office, Department of Foreign Affairs and International Trade, Ottawa, ON K1A 0G3.

UNITED KINGDOM
London Passport Office, Globe House, 89 Eccleston Square, London SW1V 1PN (✆ **0870/521-0410; www.ukpa.gov.uk**).

IRELAND
Passport Office, Setanta Centre, Molesworth Street, Dublin 2 (✆ **01/671-1633; www.irlgov.ie/iveagh/services/abroad**).

AUSTRALIA
Australia operates a central Australian Passport Information Phone Service line, ✆ **131 232,** which you may call from anywhere in Australia, or access the website, **www.dfat.gov.au/passports,** for information. The government directs its citizens to one of its 1,700 Australia Post outlets for passport applications and processing; there is no central passport office.

NEW ZEALAND
Department of Internal Affairs, New Zealand Passports, Level 3, Boulcott House, 47 Boulcott St., Wellington (✆ **0800/225-050**). By mail, the address is Department of Internal Affairs, New Zealand Passports, P.O. Box 805, Wellington. For information online, go to **www.govt.nz**.

CUSTOMS
WHAT YOU CAN BRING IN
U.S. Customs and Border Protection, whose duties include regulating every aspect of what our government allows travelers to bring in and take out of the country, is now an agency of the U.S. Department of Homeland Security. Rules are comprehensive, covering everything from the maximum amount of money a foreign tourist is permitted to carry in or take out without having to declare it to Customs ($10,000 in U.S. or foreign currencies), to whether you can bring your cat to the United States (yes, as long as the cat is free of evidence of diseases communicable to humans

when the cat is examined at the U.S. port of entry).

If you have any questions about what you may bring to the U.S., the first thing you should do is contact the Commercial Officer at your nearest U.S. Embassy or Consulate, who can give you the list of U.S. Customs regulations. You can find the address of your closest embassy/consulate on the website, www.state.gov. You can also go directly to the Customs Service website, www.cbp.gov, and click on "Travel." At that site, you will be able to download brochures, read more about regulations, and contact the U.S. Customs Service by e-mail to obtain answers to specific questions.

Upon arrival by plane in the United States, you can expect to complete an arrival/departure form and be interviewed by a U.S. official at the airport. The Customs Service is working to improve its customer service to international travelers at major U.S. airports. Washington Dulles International Airport is one of the 20 or so ports of entry where Customs has "Passenger Service Representatives" in place. If you arrive at Dulles, look for posted photos to help you find a rep, who can then assist you in clearing Customs. Customs has also installed kiosks at certain airports (Dulles should have some by the time you read this), that feature touch-screens that you can use to obtain information about Customs regulations.

Visitors arriving by air, no matter what the port of entry, should cultivate patience and resignation before setting foot on U.S. soil. Getting through immigration control can take as long as 2 hours on some days, especially on summer weekends, so be sure to carry this guidebook or something else to read.

People traveling by air from Canada, Bermuda, and certain countries in the Caribbean can sometimes clear Customs and Immigration at the point of departure, which is much quicker.

Finally, if you have further questions while you're here in Washington, you can always call Customs and Border Protection's customer service number ✆ **202/354-1000** for answers and assistance.

WHAT YOU CAN TAKE HOME

Again, this information will vary from country to country, and in every case, you should determine this information before you leave your own country. Here are the first points of contact for residents of the U.K, Canada, Ireland, Australia, and New Zealand.

U.K. citizens: Contact **HM Customs & Excise,** ✆ **0845 010 9000,** www.open.gov.uk.hmce (then use the alphabetic index to access the Customs and Excise section), for information and the address of the nearest office; from outside the U.K. ✆ 44/208-929-0152.

Canadian citizens: Contact the **Automated Customs Information Service,** ✆ **800/461-9999, www.ccra-adrc.gc.ca**; from outside Canada, call ✆ 506/636-5064.

Irish citizens: Contact the **Customs and Excise Information Office,** ✆ **9010 877 6200, www.revenue.ie**. In Washington, you can contact the Irish Embassy, ✆ **202/462-3939.**

Australian citizens: Contact the **Australian Customs Services,** ✆ **1 300 363 263, www.customs.gov.au**. Outside of Australia, call ✆ **61 (2) 6275 6666.** Australian Customs Services has its own contact in Washington, D.C.: ✆ **202/797-3185.**

New Zealand residents: Contact **New Zealand Customs, (**✆ **08004 28 786, www.customs.govt.nz**. Outside of New Zealand, call ✆ **04-473 6099.**

HEALTH INSURANCE

Although it's not required of travelers, health insurance is highly recommended. Unlike many European countries, the United States does not usually offer free or low-cost medical care to its citizens or visitors. Doctors and hospitals are expensive, and in most cases will require advance payment or proof of coverage before they render their services. Policies can cover everything from the loss or theft of your baggage and trip cancellation to the guarantee of bail in case you're arrested. Good policies will also cover the costs of an accident, repatriation, or death. See "Medical Insurance," in chapter 2 for more information. Packages such as **Europ Assistance** in Europe are sold by automobile clubs and travel agencies at attractive rates. **Worldwide Assistance Services, Inc.** (© 800/777-8710; www.worldwide-assistance.com), is the agent for Europ Assistance in the United States. Worldwide Assistance Services has offices in Washington, D.C., at 1133 15th St. NW, Suite 400, Washington, D.C., 20005; © 202/331-1609.

Though lack of health insurance may prevent you from being admitted to a hospital in nonemergencies, don't worry about being left on a street corner to die: The American way is to fix you now and bill the living daylights out of you later.

INSURANCE FOR BRITISH TRAVELERS Most big travel agents offer their own insurance, and will probably try to sell you their package when you book a holiday. Think before you sign. **Britain's Consumers' Association** recommends that you insist on seeing the policy and reading the fine print before buying travel insurance. **The Association of British Insurers** (© 020/7600-3333; www.abi.org.uk/) represents 400 companies and publishes *Holiday Insurance,* a free (also downloadable) fact-sheet detailing policy provisions and prices. The ABI has also teamed up with the Foreign and Commonwealth Office to provide helpful insurance and other information to travelers; go to **www.fco.gov. uk/knowbeforeyougo**. You might also

shop around for better deals: Try **Columbus Direct** (© **020 7375-0011;** www.columbusdirect.net/).

INSURANCE FOR CANADIAN TRAVELERS Canadians should check with their provincial health plan offices or call **Health Canada** (© **613/ 957-2991; http://hwcweb.hc-sc.gc. ca**) to find out the extent of their coverage and what documentation and receipts they must take home in case they are treated in the United States.

MONEY

CURRENCY The U.S. monetary system is very simple: The most common **bills** are the $1 (colloquially, a "buck"), $5, $10, and $20 denominations. There are also $2 bills (seldom encountered), $50 bills, and $100 bills (the last two are usually not welcome as payment for small purchases). All the paper money was recently redesigned, making the famous faces adorning them disproportionately large. The old-style bills are still legal tender.

There are seven denominations of coins: 1¢ (1 cent, or a penny); 5¢ (5 cents, or a nickel); 10¢ (10 cents, or a dime); 25¢ (25 cents, or a quarter); 50¢ (50 cents, or a half dollar); the gold "Sacagawea" coin worth $1; and, prized by collectors, the rare, older silver dollar.

CURRENCY EXCHANGE It's best to change money before you arrive in the United States, but if you do need to exchange currency, you can go to the currency-exchange desk at any of the three airports, or to one of the following locations: the Thomas Cook currency exchange office (© **202/371-9220**) at Union Station, opposite Gate G on the train concourse; the Sun Trust Bank, 1445 New York Ave. NW (© **202/879-6308**); and at three Riggs Bank locations: 1913 Massachusetts Ave. NW, 1503 Pennsylvania Ave. NW, and 800

17th St. NW (dial ✆ **301/887-6000** to be connected to the individual locations).

TRAVELER'S CHECKS Though traveler's checks are widely accepted, make sure that they're denominated in U.S. dollars, as foreign-currency checks are often difficult to exchange. The three traveler's checks that are most widely recognized—and least likely to be denied—are **Visa, American Express,** and **Thomas Cook.** Be sure to record the numbers of the checks, and keep that information in a separate place in case they get lost or stolen. Most businesses are pretty good about taking traveler's checks, but you're better off cashing them in at a bank (in small amounts, of course) and paying in cash. Remember: You'll need identification, such as a driver's license or passport, to change a traveler's check.

CREDIT CARDS & ATMs Credit cards are the most widely used form of payment in the United States: **Visa** (BarclayCard in Britain), **MasterCard** (EuroCard in Europe, Access in Britain, Chargex in Canada), **American Express, Diners Club,** and **Discover.** Most Washington establishments accept Visa, MasterCard, and American Express, and many also accept Diners Club, Discover, and Carte Blanche. A handful of stores and restaurants do not take credit cards at all, so be sure to ask in advance. Most businesses display a sticker near their entrance to let you know which cards they accept. (*Note:* Businesses may require a minimum purchase, usually around $10, to use a credit card.)

You should bring at least one major credit card. You must have a credit or charge card to rent a car. Hotels and airlines usually require a credit-card imprint as a deposit against expenses, and in an emergency a credit card can be priceless.

You'll find **automated teller machines (ATMs)** on just about every block—at least in almost every town—across the country. Some ATMs will allow you to draw U.S. currency against your bank and credit cards. Check with your bank before leaving home, and remember that you will need your personal identification number (PIN) to do so. Most accept Visa, MasterCard, and American Express, as well as ATM cards from other U.S. banks. Expect to be charged up to $3 per transaction, however, if you're not using your own bank's ATM.

One way around these fees is to ask for cash back at grocery stores that accept ATM cards and don't charge usage fees. Of course, you'll have to purchase something first.

ATM cards with major credit card backing, known as "debit cards," are now a commonly acceptable form of payment in most stores and restaurants. Debit cards draw money directly from your checking account. Some stores enable you to receive "cash back" on your debit-card purchases as well.

SAFETY
GENERAL SAFETY SUGGESTIONS Although tourist areas are generally safe, they are not crime-free. You should always stay alert. Ask your hotel front-desk staff or call the Washington Convention and Tourism Corporation (✆ **202/789-7000**) if you have specific questions about traveling to certain neighborhoods.

Travel Tip

Be sure to keep a copy of all your travel papers separate from your wallet or purse, and leave a copy with someone at home should you need it faxed in an emergency.

Read chapter 4's "The Neighborhoods in Brief" section to get a better idea of where you might feel most comfortable.

Avoid deserted areas, especially at night, and don't go into public parks at night unless there's a concert or similar occasion that will attract a crowd.

Avoid carrying valuables with you on the street, and don't display expensive cameras or electronic equipment. If you're using a map, consult it inconspicuously—or better yet, try to study it before you leave your room. In general, the more you look like a tourist, the more likely someone will try to take advantage of you. If you're walking, pay attention to who is near you as you walk. If you're attending a convention or event where you wear a name tag, remove it before venturing outside. Hold on to your purse, and place your billfold in an inside pocket. In theaters, restaurants, and other public places, keep your possessions in sight.

Remember also that hotels are open to the public, and in a large hotel, security may not be able to screen everyone entering. Always lock your room door.

Be careful crossing streets, especially in the downtown area, especially at rush hour. Though this may seem like obvious and silly advice, it's worth a mention here, as there's been an alarming increase lately in the number of pedestrians being hit by cars and buses. Drivers in a hurry run red lights, turn corners too quickly, and so on, so be sure to take your time and check for oncoming traffic when crossing streets, and to use the crosswalks. If you're from Great Britain, you'll need to pay special attention, looking to your left first, rather than to your right, on two-way streets.

DRIVING SAFETY   Question your rental agency about personal safety and ask for a traveler-safety brochure when you pick up your car. Obtain written directions—or a map with the route clearly marked—from the agency showing how to get to your destination. And, if possible, arrive and depart during daylight hours.

If you drive off a highway and end up in a dodgy-looking neighborhood, leave the area as quickly as possible. If you have an accident, even on the highway, stay in your car with the doors locked until you assess the situation or until the police arrive. If you're bumped from behind on the street or are involved in a minor accident with no injuries, and the situation appears to be suspicious, motion to the other driver to follow you. Never get out of your car in such situations. Go directly to the nearest police precinct, well-lit service station, or 24-hour store. You may want to look into renting a cellphone on a short-term basis. (Many agencies now offer the option of renting a cellular phone for the duration of your car rental; check with the rental agent when you pick up the car.) One recommended wireless rental company is **InTouch USA** (© **800/872-7626;** www.intouchusa.com). (For other sources, see "Using a Cellphone," in chapter 2.)

Park in well-lit and well-traveled areas whenever possible. Always keep your car doors locked, whether the vehicle is attended or unattended. Never leave any packages or valuables in sight. If someone attempts to rob you or steal your car, don't try to resist the thief/carjacker. Report the incident to the police department immediately by calling © **911.**

2 Getting to the United States

Most international flights to the Washington, D.C., area land at Washington Dulles International Airport, with Baltimore–Washington International Airport handling some, and Ronald Reagan Washington National Airport offering service to only one international carrier. Specific information follows.

The one international airline with scheduled flights into Ronald Reagan Washington National Airport is **Air Canada** (ℂ 888/247-2262; www.air canada.ca).

International airlines with scheduled flights into Baltimore–Washington International airport include **Air Canada** (see above), **British Airways** (ℂ 0845/77 333 77 in the U.K., or 800/247-9297; www.british-airways. com), and **Aer Lingus** (ℂ 800/474-7424; www.aerlingus.com).

International airlines with scheduled flights into Washington Dulles International Airport include **Aeroflot** (ℂ 888/340-6400; www. aeroflot.com), **Air Canada** (see above), **Air France** (ℂ 800/321-4538; www.airfrance.com), **ANA Airways** (ℂ 800/235-9262; http://svc.ana.co. jp/eng), **British Airways** (see above), **KLM** (ℂ 800/225-2525; www.klm. com), **Lufthansa** (ℂ 800/645-3880; www.lufthansa.com), **Saudi Arabian Airlines** (ℂ 800/472-8342; www. saudiairlines.com), and **Virgin Atlantic** (ℂ 01293/450 150 in the U.K., or 800/862-8621 in the U.S.; www.virgin-atlantic.com).

AIRLINE DISCOUNTS   The smart traveler can find numerable ways to reduce the price of a plane ticket simply by taking time to shop around. For example, overseas visitors can take advantage of the APEX (Advance Purchase Excursion) reductions offered by all major U.S. and European carriers. For more money-saving airline advice, see "Getting Here," in chapter 2. For the best rates, compare fares and be flexible with the dates and times of travel.

3 Getting Around the United States

BY PLANE   Some large airlines—Northwest, for example—offer travelers on their transatlantic or transpacific flights special discount tickets under the name **Visit USA ("VUSA"),** allowing mostly one-way travel from one U.S. destination to another at very low prices. These discount tickets are not on sale in the United States and must be purchased abroad in conjunction with your international ticket. This system is the best, easiest, and fastest way to see the United States at low cost. You should obtain information well in advance from your travel agent or the office of the airline concerned, since the conditions attached to these discount tickets can be changed without advance notice.

BY TRAIN   International visitors (excluding Canada) can also buy a **USA Railpass.** Amtrak sells six kinds of passes, covering six geographic regions. All of the passes allow for 15 or 30 days of unlimited travel on Amtrak (ℂ **800/USA-RAIL;** www. amtrak.com). The "Northeast," which includes Washington, D.C., in its coverage from Virginia to Montreal, Canada, also offers a 5-day ($149) pass, along with its 15-day ($185–$205), and 30-day ($225–$240) passes. (These are 2003 prices.) USA Railpasses are available through many foreign travel agents. With a foreign passport, you can also buy passes at Amtrak stations and at travel agencies in the United States, including locations in San Francisco, Los Angeles, Chicago, New York, Miami, Boston, and Washington, D.C. Reservations are generally required and should be made for each part of your trip as early as possible.

FAST FACTS: For the International Traveler

Automobile Organizations Auto clubs will supply maps, suggested routes, guidebooks, accident and bail-bond insurance, and emergency road service. The **American Automobile Association (AAA)** is the major auto club (really an organization of regional auto clubs) in the United States. If you belong to an auto club in your home country, inquire about AAA reciprocity before you leave. You may be able to join AAA even if you're not a member of a reciprocal club; to inquire, call the MidAtlantic Region's AAA (© **800/763-9900;** www.aaa.com), which is also the number you would call in the Washington, D.C., area for AAA's emergency road service.

Business Hours Offices are usually open weekdays from 9am to 5pm. Banks are open Monday through Thursday from 9am to 3pm, 9am to 5pm on Friday, and sometimes Saturday mornings. Stores typically open between 9 and 10am and close between 5 and 6pm from Monday through Saturday. Stores in shopping complexes or malls tend to stay open late: until about 9pm on weekdays and weekends, and many malls and larger department stores are open on Sundays.

Currency & Currency Exchange See "Money" under "Preparing for Your Trip," earlier in this chapter.

Electricity Like Canada, the United States uses 110 to 120 volts AC (60 cycles), compared to 220 to 240 volts AC (50 cycles) in most of Europe, Australia, and New Zealand. If your small appliances use 220 to 240 volts, you'll need a 110-volt transformer and a plug adapter with two flat parallel pins to operate them here. Downward converters that change 220–240 volts to 110–120 volts are difficult to find in the United States, so bring one with you.

Embassies & Consulates All embassies are located in the nation's capital, Washington, D.C. On the Internet, you will find a complete listing, with links to each embassy, at www.embassy.org/embassies/index.html.

Here are several embassy addresses: **Australia,** 1601 Massachusetts Ave. NW (© 202/797-3000; www.austemb.org); **Canada,** 501 Pennsylvania Ave. NW (© 202/682-1740; www.canadianembassy.org); **France,** 4101 Reservoir Rd. NW (© 202/944-6000; www.ambafrance-us.org); **Germany,** 4645 Reservoir Rd. NW (© 202/298-4000; www.germany-info.org); **Ireland,** 2234 Massachusetts Ave. NW (© 202/462-3939; www.irelandemb.org); **Japan,** 2520 Massachusetts Ave. NW (© 202/238-6700; www.embjapan.org); the **Netherlands,** 4200 Linnean Ave. NW (© 202/244-5300; www.netherlands-embassy.org); **New Zealand,** 37 Observatory Circle NW (© 202/328-4800; www.nzemb.org); and the **United Kingdom,** 3100 Massachusetts Ave. NW (© 202/588-6500; www.britainusa.com/consular/embassy). You can also obtain the telephone numbers of other embassies and consulates by calling information in Washington, D.C. (© **411** within D.C. and its metropolitan area), or consult the phone book in your hotel room.

Emergencies Call © **911** to report a fire, call the police, or get an ambulance anywhere in the United States. This is a toll-free call. (No coins are required at public telephones.)

If you encounter serious problems, contact the **Traveler's Aid Society International** (© 202/546-1127; www.travelersaid.org), a nationwide, nonprofit, social-service organization geared to helping travelers in difficult straits, from reuniting families separated while traveling, to providing food and/or shelter to people stranded without cash, to emotional counseling. Traveler's Aid operates help desks at Washington Dulles International Airport (© 703/572-8296), Ronald Reagan Washington National Airport (© 703/417-3975), and Union Station (© 202/371-1937).

Gasoline (Petrol) Petrol is known as gasoline (or simply "gas") in the United States, and petrol stations are known as both gas stations and service stations. Gasoline costs about half as much here as it does in Europe (about $1.69 per gallon at press time), and taxes are already included in the printed price. One U.S. gallon equals 3.8 liters or .85 Imperial gallons.

Holidays Banks, government offices, post offices, and many stores, restaurants, and museums are closed on the following legal national holidays: January 1 (New Year's Day), the third Monday in January (Martin Luther King Jr. Day), the third Monday in February (Presidents' Day, Washington's Birthday), the last Monday in May (Memorial Day), July 4 (Independence Day), the first Monday in September (Labor Day), the second Monday in October (Columbus Day), November 11 (Veterans' Day/Armistice Day), the fourth Thursday in November (Thanksgiving Day), and December 25 (Christmas). Also, the Tuesday following the first Monday in November is Election Day and is a federal government holiday in presidential-election years (held every 4 years, so 2004 is an election year).

Language Aid **Meridian International Center** provides language assistance via a telephone bank of volunteers who, together, speak 40 different languages. Best of all, this service is free. Call the Center at © **202/939-5552** or 202/939-5554, Monday through Friday, 9am to 5pm. You may hear a recorded voice asking you to leave a message; you can hit "0" for the operator and explain why you are calling, or leave a message, and someone from Meridian will call you back with the assistance you need. Or you can go to Meridian's website at **www.meridian.org** and e-mail the center from there. Meridian also runs an **information desk at Washington Dulles International Airport** (© 703/572-2536). In addition, most Washington museums, hotels restaurants, and other attractions boast multilingual staff. Many sights, like the White House, the Kennedy Center, the Library of Congress, and the Smithsonian Institution, offer free brochures in several languages; the Smithsonian also welcomes international visitors at its Information Center with a multilingual slide show and audio phones. The city's Metro system provides maps in French, German, Japanese, Korean, and Spanish (obtain them in advance by calling © **202/637-7000**), and the Washington Convention and Tourism Corporation has maps, but no visitors guides, in French, Spanish, Italian, Portuguese, and German; you must call © **202/789-7000** to order a map.

Legal Aid If you are "pulled over" for a minor infraction (such as speeding), never attempt to pay the fine directly to a police officer; this could be construed as attempted bribery, a much more serious crime. Pay fines by mail, or directly into the hands of the clerk of the court. If accused of a more serious offense, say and do nothing before consulting a lawyer. Here the burden is on the state to prove a person's guilt beyond a reasonable doubt, and everyone has the right to remain silent, whether he or she is suspected of a crime or actually arrested. Once arrested, a person can make one telephone call to a party of his or her choice. Call your embassy or consulate.

Liquor Laws The legal age for purchase and consumption of alcoholic beverages is 21; proof of age is required and often requested at bars, nightclubs, and restaurants, so it's always a good idea to bring an ID when you go out. Liquor stores are closed on Sunday. District gourmet grocery stores, mom-and-pop grocery stores, and 7-11 convenience stores often sell beer and wine, even on Sunday.

Do not carry open containers of alcohol in your car or any public area that isn't zoned for alcohol consumption. The police can fine you on the spot. And nothing will ruin your trip faster than getting a citation for DUI (driving under the influence), so don't even think about driving while intoxicated.

Mail Generally found at intersections, mailboxes are blue with a red-and-white stripe and carry the inscription U.S. MAIL. If your mail is addressed to a U.S. destination, don't forget to add the five-digit postal code (or zip code), after the two-letter abbreviation of the state to which the mail is addressed. This is essential for prompt delivery.

At press time, domestic postage rates were 23¢ for a postcard and 37¢ for a letter. For international mail, a first-class letter of up to one ounce costs 80¢ (60¢ to Canada and to Mexico); a first-class postcard costs 70¢ (50¢ to Canada and Mexico); and a preprinted postal aerogramme costs 70¢.

Measurements See the chart on the inside front cover of this book for details on converting metric measurements to U.S. equivalents.

Taxes The United States has no value-added tax (VAT) or other indirect tax at the national level. Every state, county, and city has the right to levy its own local tax on all purchases, including hotel and restaurant checks, airline tickets, and so on.

The sales tax on merchandise is 5.75% in the District, 5% in Maryland, and 4.5% in Virginia. The tax on restaurant meals is 10% in the District, 5% in Maryland, and 4.5% in Virginia.

In the District, you pay 14.5% hotel tax. The hotel tax in Maryland varies by county from 5% to 8%. The hotel tax in Virginia also varies by county, averaging about 9.75%.

Telephone, Telegraph, Telex & Fax The telephone system in the United States is run by private corporations, so rates, especially for long-distance service and operator-assisted calls, can vary widely. Generally, hotel surcharges on long-distance and local calls are astronomical, so you're usually better off using a **public pay telephone,** which you'll find clearly marked in most public buildings and private establishments as well as on the street. Convenience grocery stores and gas stations usually have them. Grocery stores, drugstores (pharmacies), and post offices sell **prepaid calling cards** in denominations up to $50; these can be the least expensive way to call home. Many public phones at airports now accept American Express, MasterCard, and Visa credit cards. **Local calls** made from public pay phones in most locales cost either 25¢ or 35¢. Pay phones do not accept pennies, and few will take anything larger than a quarter.

You may want to look into leasing a cellphone for the duration of your trip.

Most long-distance and international calls can be dialed directly from any phone. **For calls within the United States and to Canada,** dial 1 followed by the area code and the seven-digit number. **For other international calls,** dial 011 followed by the country code, city code, and the telephone number of the person you are calling.

Calls to area codes **800, 888, 866,** and **877** are toll-free. However, calls to numbers in area codes **700** and **900** (chat lines, bulletin boards, "dating" services, and so on) can be very expensive—usually a charge of 95¢ to $3 or more per minute, and they sometimes have minimum charges that can run as high as $15 or more. You must first dial 1, before dialing area codes 800, 888, **866, 877**, 700, and 900.

For **reversed-charge or collect calls,** and for person-to-person calls, dial 0 (zero, not the letter O) followed by the area code and number you want; an operator will then come on the line, and you should specify that you are calling collect, or person-to-person, or both. If your operator-assisted call is international, ask for the overseas operator.

For **local directory assistance** (information), dial 411; for long-distance information, dial 1, then the appropriate area code and 555-1212.

Telegraph and telex services are provided primarily by Western Union. You can bring your telegram into the nearest Western Union office (there are hundreds across the country) or dictate it over the phone (© **800/325-6000**). You can also telegraph money, or have it telegraphed to you, very quickly over the Western Union system, but this service can cost as much as 15% to 20% of the amount sent.

Most hotels have **fax machines** available for guest use (be sure to ask about the charge to use it). Many hotel rooms are even wired for guests' fax machines. A less expensive way to send and receive faxes may be at stores such as Mail Boxes Etc., a national chain of packing service shops. (Look in the Yellow Pages directory under "Packing Services.")

There are two kinds of telephone directories in the United States. The so-called **White Pages** list private households and business subscribers in alphabetical order. The inside front cover lists emergency numbers for police, fire, ambulance, the Coast Guard, poison-control center, crime-victims hot line, and so on. The first few pages will tell you how to make long-distance and international calls, complete with country codes and area codes. Government numbers are usually printed on blue paper within the White Pages. Printed on yellow paper, the so-called **Yellow Pages** list all local services, businesses, industries, and houses of worship according to activity with an index at the front or back. (Drugstores/pharmacies and restaurants are also listed by geographic location.) The Yellow Pages also include city plans or detailed area maps, postal zip codes, and public transportation routes.

Time The continental United States is divided into **four time zones:** eastern standard time (EST), central standard time (CST), mountain standard time (MST), and Pacific standard time (PST). Alaska and Hawaii have their own zones. For example, noon in Washington, D.C. (EST), is 11am in Chicago (CST), 10am in Denver (MST), 9am in Los Angeles (PST), 8am in Anchorage (AST), and 7am in Honolulu (HST).

Daylight savings time is in effect from 1am on the first Sunday in April through 1am on the last Sunday in October, except in Arizona, Hawaii, part of Indiana, and Puerto Rico. Daylight saving time moves the clock 1 hour ahead of standard time. At 1am on the last Sunday in October, clocks are set back 1 hour.

For the correct time, call © 202/844-2525.

Tipping Tipping is so ingrained in the American way of life that the annual income tax of tip-earning service personnel is based on how much they should have received in light of their employers' gross revenues. Accordingly, they may have to pay tax on a tip you didn't actually give them.

Here are some rules of thumb:

In hotels, tip **bellhops** at least $1 per bag ($2–$3 if you have a lot of luggage) and tip the **chamber staff** $1 to $2 per day (more if you've left a disaster area for him or her to clean up, or if you're traveling with kids and/or pets). Tip the **doorman** or **concierge** only if he or she has provided you with some specific service (for example, calling a cab for you or obtaining difficult-to-get theater tickets). Tip the **valet-parking attendant** $1 every time you get your car.

In restaurants, bars, and nightclubs, tip **service staff** 15% to 20% of the check, tip **bartenders** 10% to 15%, tip **checkroom attendants** $1 per garment, and tip **valet-parking attendants** $1 per vehicle. Tipping is not expected in cafeterias and fast-food restaurants.

Tip **cab drivers** 15% of the fare.

As for other service personnel, tip **skycaps** at airports at least $1 per bag ($2–$3 if you have a lot of luggage) and tip **hairdressers** and **barbers** 15% to 20%.

Tipping ushers at movies and theaters, and gas-station attendants, is not expected.

Toilets You won't find public toilets or "restrooms" on the streets in most U.S. cities, but they can be found in hotel lobbies, bars, restaurants, museums, department stores, railway and bus stations, and service stations. Large hotels and fast-food restaurants are probably the best bet for good, clean facilities. If possible, avoid the toilets at parks and beaches, which tend to be dirty; some may be unsafe. Restaurants and bars in heavily visited areas may reserve their restrooms for patrons. Some establishments display a notice indicating this. You can ignore this sign or, better yet, avoid arguments by paying for a cup of coffee or a soft drink, which will qualify you as a patron.

4

Getting to Know Washington, D.C.

After 20 years of living here, I am still getting to know D.C. This is a good thing. The city has so much going on in every category, from culture to commercial, transportation to neighborhood reformation, it can be hard to keep up. The capital doesn't stand still. Nor should you. Read this chapter to learn how to navigate the city, learning as you go.

1 Orientation

On the one hand, Washington, D.C., is an easy place to get to know. It's a small city, where walking will actually get you places, but also with a model public transportation system that travels throughout D.C.'s neighborhoods, and to most tourist spots. A building height restriction creates a landscape in which the lost tourist can get his bearings from tall landmarks—the Capitol, the Washington Monument—that loom into view from different vantage points.

On the other hand, when you do need help, it's hard to find. The city lacks a single, large, comprehensive, and easy-to-find visitor center. Signage to tourist attractions and Metro stations, even street signs, are often missing or frustratingly inadequate. In the wake of September 11, touring procedures at individual sightseeing attractions are constantly changing as new security precautions take effect, and these changes can be disorienting.

The District is always in the process of improving the situation, it seems. But in the meantime, you can turn to the following small visitors and information centers, helpful publications, and information phone lines.

VISITOR INFORMATION
AT THE AIRPORTS

If you are arriving by plane, you may as well think of your airport as a visitor information center, since all three Washington area airports offer all sorts of visitor services. See chapter 2 for specific information about each airport's location, flights, designated place to rendezvous when someone is meeting you at the airport, and transportation options into town.

BALTIMORE–WASHINGTON INTERNATIONAL AIRPORT BWI (© **800/435-9294;** www.bwiairport.com) services include two information desks (© **800/435-9294** for information and paging) located on the upper level near the ticket counters and a Maryland Welcome Center (© **410/691-2878**) at Pier C on the lower level near the international arrival gates; foreign-language assistance in French, Italian, Spanish, and German (you just pick up one of the white courtesy phones located throughout the airport and request assistance); several locations for buying insurance and exchanging currency (© **410/850-0237**); several ATMs (at the entrances to Piers C and D on the upper level and

at the international gates on the lower level); plenty of public phones throughout the airport, including 108 with dataports and some with TDD services and
voice-relay phones; many restrooms, restaurants, shops, and bars; a playroom for
kids; and a small aviation museum.

Other useful phone numbers are lost and found (© **410/859-7387**), police
(© **410/859-7040**), and parking lots and garage (© **410/859-9230**).

RONALD REAGAN WASHINGTON NATIONAL AIRPORT "National"
(© **703/417-8000;** www.mwaa.com/national) has general information desks
and customer service centers (© **703/417-3200** or 703/417-3201) at either
end of the second, or concourse, level. Here you can exchange currency, purchase insurance, and recharge batteries. Ticket counters are on the third level,
baggage claim and ground transportation on the first level. Some pay phones
equipped with dataports are located throughout terminals B and C. An
enclosed passageway connects the main concourse to "historic terminal A,"
where a **Traveler's Aid** desk operates (© **703/417-3972**). You should seek
Traveler's Aid assistance if you need foreign-language or crisis help or to page
someone; a second Traveler's Aid desk (© **703/417-3974**) operates on the baggage-claim level of the main concourse. You'll find ATMs located near the cus-
tomer-service centers on the concourse level and next to the Traveler's Aid desk
on the baggage-claim level. National Airport has more than 100 shops and
restaurants.

Other useful phone numbers are lost and found (© **703/417-8560**), parking
lots and garage (© **703/417-7275**), and police (© **703/417-8560**).

WASHINGTON DULLES INTERNATIONAL AIRPORT Dulles (© **703/
572-2700;** www.mwaa.com/Dulles) is the most chaotic airport at which to
arrive, with an ongoing major renovation and heavy traffic. Most flights arrive
at midfield terminals, where you follow the crowd to the mobile lounges, which
you ride for 7 minutes to the main terminal. In time, the plan is for an underground rail system to replace these lounges. The satellite terminals are actually
rather attractive and offer decent shopping; the main terminal is another story.
You can count on getting help from the Traveler's Aid folks on the baggage claim
(lower) level of the main terminal (© **703/572-8296,** or 703/260-0175 for
TDD service). Phone numbers for other help desks include © **703/572-2536**
or 703/572-2537 for the International Visitors Information desk (located at the
west end of the lower level of the main terminal, near the International Arrivals
area); © **703/572-2963** or 703/572-2969 for general service, foreign currency
exchange, and insurance purchases. There are about 40 eateries, 35 retail shops,
7 currency exchanges, and plentiful ATMs, restrooms, stamp vending machines,
and phones.

Other useful numbers: police © **703/572-2952;** lost and found © **703/572-
2954;** and skycap and wheelchair services © **703/661-8151** or 703/661-6239.
Baggage claim areas are at ground level in the main terminal.

AT THE TRAIN STATION

Historic Union Station (© **202/289-1908;** www.unionstationdc.com), 50
Massachusetts Ave. NE, offers a visitor a pleasant introduction to the capital.
The building is both an architectural beauty and a useful stopping place. Here
you'll find a three-level marketplace of shops and restaurants, direct access to
Metro service (you'll see signs directing you to the Metro's Red Line station even
before you reach the main hall of Union Station), and, when you proceed

through the grand arcade straight out through the station's front doors, a stellar view of the Capitol Building.

The central information desk is in the main hall at the front of the building. You'll find ATMs in the gate area, another near the side doors of the building (near the outdoor escalator to the Metro), and on the lower level, at the end of the Food Court. In the gate area are a Thomas Cook Currency Exchange office (✆ **202/371-9220**) across from gate G, and a Traveler's Aid desk (✆ **202/371-1937**) near the McDonald's and gate L. A number of car-rental agencies operate lots here (see "Getting Around," later in this chapter, for specific names and phone numbers). For security, lost and found, and other help or information, call the main number, which is ✆ **202/371-9441.**

AROUND TOWN

The Washington, D.C., Visitor Information Center (✆ **866/324-7386** or 202/328-4748; www.dcvisit.com) is a small visitors center inside the immense Ronald Reagan International Trade Center Building, at 1300 Pennsylvania Ave. NW. To enter the federal building, you need to show a picture ID. The visitor center lies on the ground floor of the building, a little to your right as you enter from the Wilson Plaza, near the Federal Triangle Metro. From March 15 through Labor Day, the center is open Monday through Friday, 8:30am to 5:30pm and on Saturday from 9am to 4pm; from Labor Day to March 15, the center is open Monday through Friday 9am to 4:30pm.

The **White House Visitor Center,** on the first floor of the Herbert Hoover Building, Department of Commerce, 1450 Pennsylvania Ave. NW (between 14th and 15th sts.; ✆ **202/208-1631,** or 202/456-7041 for recorded information), is open daily (except for Christmas Day, Thanksgiving, and New Year's Day) from 7:30am to 4pm.

The **Smithsonian Information Center,** in the "Castle," 1000 Jefferson Dr. SW (✆ **202/357-2700,** or TTY 202/357-1729; www.si.edu), is open every day but Christmas from 9am to 5:30pm. Call for a free copy of the Smithsonian's "Planning Your Smithsonian Visit," which is full of valuable tips, or stop at the Castle for a copy. A calendar of Smithsonian exhibits and activities for the coming month appears the third Friday of each month in the *Washington Post*'s "Weekend" section.

See chapter 7 for more information about these two centers.

The **American Automobile Association (AAA)** has a large central office near the White House, at 701 15th St. NW, Washington, DC 20005-2111 (✆ **202/331-3000**). Hours are 8:30am to 5:30pm Monday through Friday.

PUBLICATIONS

At the airport, pick up a free copy of **Washington Flyer** magazine (www.fly2dc.com), which is handy as a planning tool (see chapter 2).

Washington has two daily newspapers: the **Washington Post** (www.washington post.com) and the **Washington Times** (www.washingtontimes.com). The Friday "Weekend" section of the *Post* is essential for finding out what's going on, recreation-wise. *City Paper,* published every Thursday and available free at downtown shops and restaurants, covers some of the same material but is a better guide to the club and art gallery scene.

Also on newsstands is **Washingtonian,** a monthly magazine with features, often about the "100 Best" this or that (doctors, restaurants, and so on) in Washington; the magazine also offers a calendar of events, restaurant reviews, and profiles of Washingtonians.

HELPFUL TELEPHONE NUMBERS & WEBSITES

- **National Park Service** (© 202/619-7222; www.nps.gov/nacc). You reach a real person and not a recording when you call the phone number with questions about the monuments, the National Mall, national park lands, and activities taking place at these locations. National Park Service information kiosks are located near the Jefferson, Lincoln, Vietnam Veterans, and Korean War memorials, and at several other locations in the city.
- **Dial-A-Park** (© 202/619-7275). This is a recording of information regarding park-service events and attractions.
- **Dial-A-Museum** (© 202/357-2020; www.si.edu). This recording informs you about the locations of the 14 Washington Smithsonian museums and of their daily activities.

CITY LAYOUT

Pierre Charles L'Enfant designed Washington's great sweeping avenues, which are crossed by numbered and lettered streets. At key intersections he placed spacious circles. Although the circles are adorned with monuments, statuary, and fountains, L'Enfant also intended them to serve as strategic command posts to ward off invaders or marauding mobs. (After what had happened in Paris during the French Revolution—and remember, that was current history at the time—his design views were quite practical.)

The U.S. Capitol marks the center of the city, which is divided into quadrants: **northwest (NW), northeast (NE), southwest (SW),** and **southeast (SE).** Almost all the areas of interest to tourists are in the northwest. If you look at your map, you'll see that some addresses—for instance, the corner of G and 7th streets—appear in all quadrants. Hence you must observe the quadrant designation (NW, NE, SW, or SE) when looking for an address.

MAIN ARTERIES & STREETS   From the Capitol, North Capitol Street and South Capitol Street run north and south, respectively. East Capitol Street divides the city north and south. The area west of the Capitol is not a street at all, but the National Mall, which is bounded on the north by Constitution Avenue and on the south by Independence Avenue.

The primary artery of Washington is **Pennsylvania Avenue,** scene of parades, inaugurations, and other splashy events. Pennsylvania runs northwest in a direct line between the Capitol and the White House—if it weren't for the Treasury Building, the president would have a clear view of the Capitol—before continuing on a northwest angle to Georgetown, where it becomes M Street.

Since May 1995, Pennsylvania Avenue between 15th and 17th streets NW has been closed to cars for security reasons. H Street is now one-way eastbound between 19th and 13th streets NW; I Street is one-way westbound between 11th and 21st streets NW.

Constitution Avenue, paralleled to the south most of the way by Independence Avenue, runs east-west, flanking the Capitol and the Mall. If you hear Washingtonians talk about the "House" side of the Hill, they're referring to the southern half of the Capitol, the side closest to Independence Avenue, and home to Congressional House offices and the House Chamber. Conversely, the Senate side is the northern half of the Capitol, where Senate offices and the Senate Chamber are found, closer to Constitution Avenue.

Washington's longest avenue, **Massachusetts Avenue,** runs parallel to Pennsylvania (a few avenues north). Along the way, you'll find Union Station and then Dupont Circle, which is central to the area known as Embassy Row. Farther out are

Washington, D.C., at a Glance

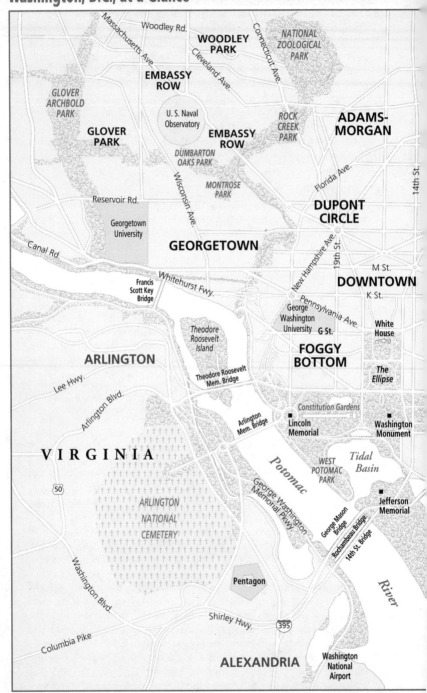

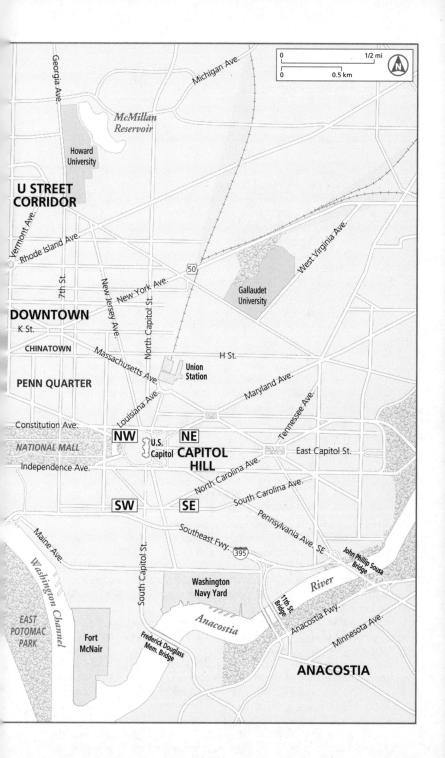

Impressions

It Washington should ever grow to be a great city, the outlook from the Capitol will be unsurpassed in the world. Now at sunset I seemed to look westward far into the heart of the continent from this commanding position.

—Ralph Waldo Emerson

---

the Naval Observatory (the vice president's residence is on the premises), Washington National Cathedral, American University, and, eventually, Maryland.

Connecticut Avenue, which runs more directly north (the other avenues run southeast to northwest), starts at Lafayette Square, intersects Dupont Circle, and eventually takes you to the National Zoo, on to the charming residential neighborhood known as Cleveland Park, and into Chevy Chase, Maryland, where you can pick up the Beltway to head out of town. Downtown Connecticut Avenue, with its posh shops and clusters of restaurants, is a good street to stroll.

Wisconsin Avenue originates in Georgetown; its intersection with M Street forms Georgetown's hub. Antiques shops, trendy boutiques, nightclubs, restaurants, and pubs all vie for attention. Wisconsin Avenue basically parallels Connecticut Avenue; one of the few irritating things about the city's transportation system is that the Metro does not connect these two major arteries in the heart of the city. (Buses do, and, of course, you can always walk or take a taxi from one avenue to the other. Overwhelmingly popular is the Georgetown Metro Connection shuttle, which travels between Georgetown and the Foggy Bottom, Dupont Circle, and Rosslyn Metro stations, and costs $1, or 35¢ with a Metrorail transfer.) Metrorail's first stop on Wisconsin Avenue is in Tenleytown, a residential area. Follow the avenue north, and you land in the affluent Maryland cities of Chevy Chase and Bethesda.

FINDING AN ADDRESS   Once you understand the city's layout, it's easy to find your way around. As you read this, have a map handy.

Each of the four corners of the District of Columbia is exactly the same distance from the Capitol dome. The White House and most government buildings and important monuments are west of the Capitol (in the northwest and southwest quadrants), as are major hotels and tourist facilities.

Numbered streets run north-south, beginning on either side of the Capitol with 1st Street. Lettered streets run east-west and are named alphabetically, beginning with A Street. (Don't look for a B, a J, an X, a Y, or a Z Street, however.) After W Street, street names of two syllables continue in alphabetical order, followed by street names of three syllables; the more syllables in a name, the farther the street is from the Capitol.

Avenues, named for U.S. states, run at angles across the grid pattern and often intersect at traffic circles. For example, New Hampshire, Connecticut, and Massachusetts avenues intersect at Dupont Circle.

With this in mind, you can easily find an address. On lettered streets, the address tells you exactly where to go. For instance, 1776 K St. NW is between 17th and 18th streets (the 1st two digits of 1776 tell you that) in the northwest quadrant (NW). *Note:* I Street is often written Eye Street to prevent confusion with 1st Street.

To find an address on numbered streets, you'll probably have to use your fingers. For instance, 623 8th St. SE is between F and G streets (the 6th and 7th letters of the alphabet; the 1st digit of 623 tells you that) in the southeast quadrant (SE). One thing to remember: You count B as the second letter of the alphabet even though no B Street exists today (Constitution and Independence aves. were the original B sts.), but since there's no J Street, K becomes the 10th letter, L the 11th, and so on.

THE NEIGHBORHOODS IN BRIEF

Capitol Hill Everyone's heard of "the Hill," the area crowned by the Capitol. When people speak of Capitol Hill, they refer to a large section of town, extending from the western side of the Capitol to the D.C. Armory going east, bounded by H Street to the north and the Southwest Freeway to the south. It contains not only the chief symbol of the nation's capital, but the Supreme Court building, the Library of Congress, the Folger Shakespeare Library, Union Station, and the U.S. Botanic Garden. Much of it is a quiet residential neighborhood of tree-lined streets and Victorian homes. There are a number of restaurants in the vicinity and a smattering of hotels, mostly close to Union Station. Keep to the well-lit, well-traveled streets at night, and don't walk alone, since crime occurs more frequently in this neighborhood than in some other parts of town.

The Mall This lovely, tree-lined stretch of open space between Constitution and Independence avenues, extending for 2½ miles from the Capitol to the Lincoln Memorial, is the hub of tourist attractions. It includes most of the Smithsonian Institution museums and many other visitor attractions. The 300-foot-wide Mall is used by natives as well as tourists—joggers, food vendors, kite-flyers, and picnickers among them. As you can imagine, hotels and restaurants are located on the periphery.

Downtown The area roughly between 7th and 22nd streets NW going east to west, and P Street and Pennsylvania Avenue going north to south, is a mix of the Federal Triangle's government office buildings, K Street (Lawyers' Row), Connecticut Avenue restaurants and shopping, historic hotels, the city's poshest small hotels, **Chinatown,** and the White House. You'll also find the historic **Penn Quarter,** a part of downtown that continues to flourish, since the opening of the MCI Center, trendy restaurants, boutique hotels, and art galleries. (Despite a continuing marketing attempt by the city to promote the name "Penn Quarter," no one I know actually refers to this neighborhood by that title—we tend to say "near the MCI Center," instead, and everyone knows where the MCI Center is.) The total downtown area takes in so many blocks and attractions that I've divided discussions of accommodations (chapter 5) and dining (chapter 6) into two sections: "Downtown, 16th Street NW and West," and "Downtown, East of 16th Street NW." 16th Street and the White House form a natural point of separation.

U Street Corridor D.C.'s avant-garde nightlife neighborhood between 12th and 15th streets NW continues to rise from the ashes of nightclubs and theaters frequented decades ago by African Americans. At two renovated establishments, the Lincoln Theater and the Bohemian Caverns jazz club, where Duke Ellington, Louis Armstrong, and Cab Calloway once performed, patrons today can enjoy perform-ances by leading artists. The corridor offers many nightclubs and several restaurants (see chapters 6 and 9 for details). Go here to party, not to sleep—there are no hotels along this stretch.

Adams-Morgan This ever-trendy, multiethnic neighborhood is about the size of a postage stamp, though crammed with boutiques, clubs, and restaurants. Everything is located on either 18th Street NW or Columbia Road NW. You won't find any hotels here, although there are a couple of B&Bs; nearby are the Dupont Circle and Woodley Park neighborhoods, each of which has several hotels (see below). Park-ing during the day is okay, but for-get it at night (although a parking garage did open recently, on 18th St., which helps things a little). But you can easily walk (be alert—the neighborhood is edgy) to Adams-Morgan from the Dupont Circle or Woodley Park Metro stops, or taxi here. Weekend nightlife rivals that of Georgetown and Dupont Circle.

Dupont Circle My favorite part of town, Dupont Circle is fun day or night. It takes its name from the traffic circle minipark, where Mass-achusetts, New Hampshire, and Connecticut avenues collide. Wash-ington's famous **Embassy Row** cen-ters on Dupont Circle, and refers to the parade of grand embassy man-sions lining Massachusetts Avenue and its side streets. The streets extending out from the circle are lively with all-night bookstores, really good restaurants, wonderful art gal-leries and art museums, nightspots, movie theaters, and Washingtonians at their loosest. It is also the hub of D.C.'s gay community. There are plenty of hotels.

Foggy Bottom The area west of the White House and southeast of Georgetown, Foggy Bottom was Washington's early industrial center. Its name comes from the foul fumes emitted in those days by a coal depot and gasworks, but its original name, Funkstown (for owner Jacob Funk), is perhaps even worse. There's noth-ing foul (and not much funky) about the area today. This is a low-key part of town, enlivened by the presence of the Kennedy Center, George Washington University, small and medium-size hotels, and a mix of restaurants on the main drag, Pennsylvania Avenue, and residential side streets.

Georgetown This historic commu-nity dates from colonial times. It was a thriving tobacco port long before the District of Columbia was formed, and one of its attractions, the Old Stone House, dates from pre-Revolutionary days. George-town action centers on M Street and Wisconsin Avenue NW, where you'll find the luxury Four Seasons hotel and less expensive digs, numerous boutiques (see chapter 8 for details), chic restaurants, and popular pubs (lots of nightlife here). But get off the main drags and see the quiet, tree-lined streets of restored colonial row houses; stroll through the beau-tiful gardens of Dumbarton Oaks; and check out the C&O Canal. Georgetown is also home to George-town University. Note that the neighborhood gets pretty raucous on the weekends, which won't appeal to everyone.

Glover Park Mostly a residential neighborhood, this section of town, just above Georgetown and just south of the Washington National Cathedral, is worth mentioning because of the increasing number of good restaurants opening along its main stretch, Wisconsin Avenue NW, and because at least one hotel here offers lower rates than you might expect for its location. Glover Park sits between the campuses of Georgetown and American universities, so there's a large student presence here.

Woodley Park Home to Washington's largest hotel (the Marriott Wardman Park), Woodley Park boasts the National Zoo, many good restaurants, and some antiques stores. Washingtonians are used to seeing conventioneers wandering the neighborhood's pretty residential streets with their name tags still on.

2 Getting Around

Washington is one of the easiest U.S. cities to navigate. Only New York rivals its comprehensive transportation system; but even with their problems, Washington's clean, efficient subways put the Big Apple's underground network to shame. An extensive bus system covers all major D.C. arteries as well, and it's easy to hail a taxi anywhere at any time. But because Washington is of manageable size and marvelous beauty, you may find yourself shunning transportation and choosing to walk.

BY METRORAIL

If you travel by Metrorail during rush hour (Mon–Fri 5:30–9:30am and 3–7pm), you may not be so smitten with the system, since delays can be frequent, lines at fare-card machines long, trains overcrowded, and Washingtonians at their rudest. An increasing ridership is overloading the system, maintenance problems are cropping up, and the Washington Metropolitan Transit Authority (WMATA; **www.wmata.com**) is struggling just to keep pace, much less prevent future crises. Among the solutions are the addition of new trains and the installation of passenger information display boxes on station platforms reporting the number of minutes before the arrival of the next train and any delays or irregularities.

Though it's true that service has deteriorated, Washingtonians were spoiled to begin with. Stations are cool, clean, and attractive. Cars are air-conditioned and comfortable, fitted with upholstered seats; rides are quiet. You can expect to get a seat during off-peak hours (basically weekdays 10am–3pm, weeknights after 7pm, and all day weekends).

Metrorail's system of 83 stations and 103 miles of track includes locations at or near almost every sightseeing attraction and extends to suburban Maryland and northern Virginia. (Construction underway now will add 3 miles and 3 stations by late 2004.) There are five lines in operation—Red, Blue, Orange, Yellow, and Green—with extensions planned for the future. The lines connect at several points, making transfers easy. All but Yellow and Green Line trains stop at Metro Center; all except Red Line trains stop at L'Enfant Plaza; all but Blue

---

Tips Metro Etiquette 101

To avoid risking the ire of commuters, be sure to follow these guidelines: Stand to the right on the escalator so that people in a hurry can get past you on the left; and when you reach the train level, don't puddle at the bottom of the escalator blocking the path of those coming behind you, but move down the platform. Eating, drinking, and smoking are strictly prohibited on the Metro and in stations.

Major Metro Stops

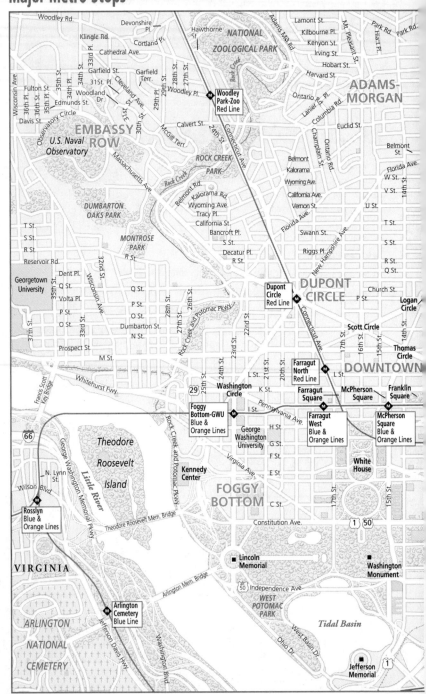

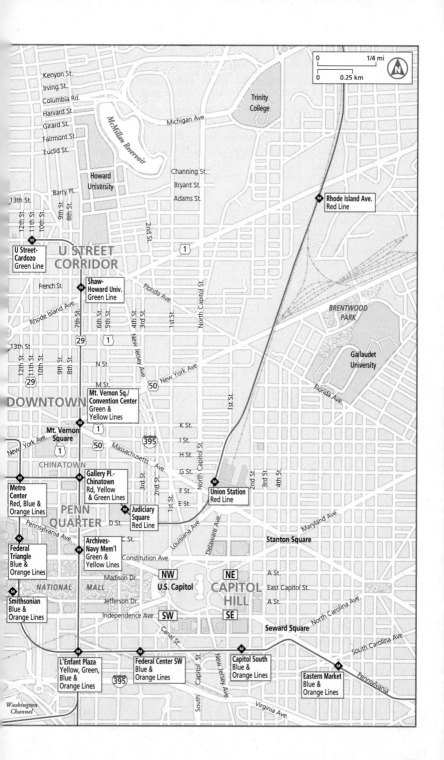

Tips Getting to Georgetown

Metrorail doesn't go to Georgetown but a special shuttle bus, called the Georgetown Metro Connection, links three Metro stations, Rosslyn, Foggy Bottom, and Dupont Circle, to Georgetown. The shuttle travels between the three stations and Georgetown every 10 minutes from 7am to midnight Monday through Thursday, 7am to 2am Friday, 8am to 2am Saturday, and 8am to midnight Sunday. One-way fares cost $1 or 35¢ with a Metrorail transfer.

---

and Orange Line trains stop at Gallery Place/Chinatown. See the color map on the inside cover of this book.

Metro stations are indicated by discreet brown columns bearing the station's name and topped by the letter M. Below the M is a colored stripe or stripes indicating the line or lines that stop there. When entering a Metro station for the first time, go to the kiosk and ask the station manager for a free **"Metro System Pocket Guide."** It contains a map of the system, explains how it works, and lists the closest Metro stops to points of interest. The station manager can also answer questions about routing or purchase of fare cards.

To enter or exit a Metro station, you need a computerized **fare card,** available at vending machines near the entrance. Metro Authority increased fares in July 2003 so now, the minimum fare to enter the system is $1.20, which pays for rides to and from any point within 7 miles of boarding during nonpeak hours; during peak hours (Mon–Fri 5:30–9:30am and 3–7pm), $1.20 takes you only 3 miles. Still, the maximum you will pay to the furthest destination is $3.60. The machines take nickels, dimes, quarters, and bills from $1 to $20; they can return up to $4.95 in change (coins only). If you plan to take several Metrorail trips during your stay, put more value on the farecard to avoid having to purchase a new card each time you ride. Up to two children under 5 can ride free with a paying passenger. Senior citizens (65 and older) and people with disabilities (with valid proof) ride Metrorail and Metrobus for a reduced fare.

Discount passes, called "One-Day Rail passes," cost $6 per person and allow you unlimited passage for the day, after 9:30am weekdays, and all day on Saturday, Sunday, and holidays. You can buy them at most stations; at WMATA headquarters, 600 5th St. NW (© **202/637-7000;** www.wmata.com), and at its sales office at Metro Center, 12th and G streets NW; or at retail stores, like Giant or Safeway grocery stores. Other passes are available—check out the website or call the main number for further information.

When you insert your card in the entrance gate, the time and location are recorded on its magnetic tape, and your card is returned. Don't forget to snatch it up and keep it handy; *you have to reinsert your fare card in the exit gate at your destination,* where the fare will automatically be deducted. The card will be returned if there's any value left on it. If you arrive at a destination and your fare card doesn't have enough value, add what's necessary at the Exitfare machines near the exit gate.

Metrorail opens at 5:30am weekdays and 7am Saturday and Sunday, operating until midnight Sunday through Thursday, and until 3am Friday and Saturday. Call © **202/637-7000,** or visit www.wmata.com, for holiday hours and for information on Metro routes.

BY BUS

The **Metrobus** system encompasses 12,490 stops on its 1,489-square-mile route (it operates on all major D.C. arteries as well as in the Virginia and Maryland suburbs). You'll know the stops by their red, white, and blue signs. However, the signs tell you only what buses pull into a given stop, not where they go. Furthermore, the bus schedules posted at bus stops are often way out of date, so don't rely on them. Instead, for routing information, call ⓒ **202/637-7000.** Calls are taken Monday through Friday from 6am to 10:30pm, weekends and holidays from 8am to 10:30pm. This is the same number you call to request a free map and time schedule, information about parking in Metrobus fringe lots, and for locations and hours of the places where you can purchase bus tokens.

Base fare in the District is $1.20; bus transfers are free and valid for 2 hours from boarding. There may be additional charges for travel into the Maryland and Virginia suburbs. Bus drivers are not equipped to make change, so be sure to carry exact change or tokens. If you'll be in Washington for a while and plan to use the buses a lot, consider buying a 1-week pass ($10), also available at the Metro Center station, 12th and G streets NW, and other outlets.

Most buses operate daily almost around the clock. Service is quite frequent on weekdays, especially during peak hours. On weekends and late at night, service is less frequent.

Up to two children under 5 ride free with a paying passenger on Metrobus, and there are reduced fares for senior citizens (call ⓒ **202/637-7000** for more information) and people with disabilities (call ⓒ **202/962-1245** or 202/962-1100 for more information; see "Travelers with Disabilities," in chapter 2 for transit information for travelers with disabilities). If you should leave something on a bus, a train, or in a station, call Lost and Found at ⓒ **202/962-1195.**

BY CAR

More than half of all visitors to the District arrive by car; but once you get here, my advice is to park your car and either walk or use Metrorail for getting around. If you must drive, be aware that traffic is always thick during the week, parking spaces are often hard to find, and parking lots are ruinously expensive.

Watch out for **traffic circles.** The law states that traffic already in the circle has the right of way. No one pays any attention to this rule, however, which can be frightening (cars zoom into the circle without a glance at the cars already there). The other thing you will notice is that while some circles are easy to figure out (Dupont Circle, for example), others are nerve-wrackingly confusing (Thomas Circle, where 14th St. NW, Vermont Ave. NW, and Massachusetts Ave. NW come together, is to be avoided at all costs).

Sections of certain streets in Washington become **one-way** during rush hour: Rock Creek Parkway, Canal Road, and 17th Street NW are three examples.

ⓒ *Tips* **Transit Tip**

If you're on the subway and plan to continue your travel via Metrobus, pick up a free transfer at the station when you enter the system (not your destination station). Transfer machines are on the mezzanine levels of most stations. With the transfer, you pay 40¢ to board a bus upon exiting your Metrorail station. There are no bus-to-subway transfers.

Other streets during rush hour change the direction of some of their traffic lanes: Connecticut Avenue NW is the main one. In the morning, traffic in four of its six lanes travels south to downtown, and in late afternoon/early evening, downtown traffic in four of its six lanes heads north; between the hours of 9:30am and 3:30pm, traffic in either direction keeps to the normally correct side of the yellow line. Lit-up traffic signs alert you to what's going on, but pay attention. Unless a sign is posted prohibiting it, a right-on-red law is in effect.

To keep up with street closings and construction information, grab the day's *Washington Post,* pull out the Metro section, and turn to page 3, where the column "Metro, In Brief" tells you about potential traffic and routing problems in the District and suburban Maryland and Virginia. The paper also publishes a regular column in the Metro section called "Dr. Gridlock," which addresses traffic questions.

CAR RENTALS

Outside of the city, you'll want a car to get to most attractions in Virginia and Maryland. All the major car-rental companies are represented here, including Alamo, Avis, Budget, Dollar, Enterprise, Hertz, National, and Thrifty. Refer to "Getting Here" in chapter 2 for phone numbers for each of these companies' airport locations. Within the District, car-rental locations include **Avis,** 1722 M St. NW (© 202/467-6585) and 4400 Connecticut Ave. NW (© 202/686-5149); **Budget,** Union Station (© 202/289-5374); **Enterprise,** 3307 M St. NW (© 202/338-0015); **Hertz,** 901 11th St. NW (© 202/628-6174); **National,** Union Station (© 202/842-7454); and **Thrifty,** 12th and K streets NW (© 202/ 371-0485).

Car-rental rates can vary even more than airfares. Taking the time to shop around and asking a few key questions could save you hundreds of dollars:

- Are weekend rates lower than weekday rates? Ask if the rate is the same for pickup Friday morning, for instance, as it is for Thursday night.
- Is the weekly rate cheaper than the daily rate? Even if you need the car for only 4 days, it may be cheaper to keep it for 5.
- Does the agency assess a drop-off charge if you don't return the car to the same location where you picked it up? Is it cheaper to pick up the car at the airport or at a downtown location?
- Are special promotional rates available? If you see an advertised price in your local newspaper, be sure to ask for that specific rate; otherwise, you may be charged the standard cost. Terms change constantly.
- Are discounts available for members of AARP, AAA, frequent-flier programs, or trade unions?
- How much tax will be added to the rental bill? Local tax? State use tax? Local taxes and surcharges can vary from location to location, even within the same car company, which can add quite a bit to your costs.
- What is the cost of adding an additional driver's name to the contract?
- How many free miles are included in the price? Free mileage is often negotiable, depending on the length of your rental.

Some companies offer "refueling packages," in which you pay for an entire tank of gas up front. The price is usually fairly competitive with local gas prices, but you don't get credit for any gas remaining in the tank. If a stop at a gas station on the way to the airport will make you miss your plane, then by all means take advantage of the fuel purchase option. Otherwise, skip it.

As for **insurance,** see chapter 2.

BY TAXI

At the time of this writing, District cabs continue to operate on a zone system instead of using meters, and the cabbies hope to keep it that way. By law, basic rates are posted in each cab. If you take a trip from one point to another within the same zone, you pay just $5 (during non-rush hour) regardless of the distance traveled. So it would cost you $5 to travel a few blocks from the U.S. Capitol to the National Museum of American History, but the same $5 could take you from the Capitol all the way to Dupont Circle. They're both in Zone 1, as are most other tourist attractions: the White House, most of the Smithsonian, the Washington Monument, the FBI, the National Archives, the Supreme Court, the Library of Congress, the Bureau of Engraving and Printing, the Old Post Office, and Ford's Theatre. If your trip takes you into a second zone, the price is $8.40, $9.60 for a third zone, $10.10 for a fourth, and so on. These rates are based on the assumption that you are hailing a cab. If you telephone for a cab, you will be charged an additional $1.50. During rush hour, between 7 and 9:30am and 4 and 6:30pm weekdays, you pay a surcharge of $1 per trip, plus a surcharge of $1 when you telephone for a cab, which brings that surcharge to $2.50

Other charges might apply, as well: There's a $1.50 charge for each additional passenger after the first, so a $5 Zone 1 fare can become $10.50 for a family of four (though one child under 5 can ride free). Surcharges are also added for luggage (from 50¢ to $2 per piece, depending on size). Try **Diamond Cab Company** (© 202/387-6200), **Yellow Cab** (© 202/544-1212), or **Capitol Cab** (© 202/ 546-2400).

The zone system is not used when your destination is an out-of-District address (such as an airport); in that case, the fare is based on mileage—$2.65 for the first half-mile or part thereof and 80¢ for each additional half-mile or part. You can call © 202/331-1671 to find out the rate between any point in D.C. and an address in Virginia or Maryland. Call © 202/645-6018 to inquire about fares within the District. For more information about DC taxicabs than you could ever even guess was available, check out the DC Taxicab Commission's website, www.dctaxi.dc.gov.

It's generally easy to hail a taxi, although even taxis driven by black cabbies often ignore African Americans to pick up white passengers. Unique to the city is the practice of allowing drivers to pick up as many passengers as they can comfortably fit, so expect to share (unrelated parties pay the same as they would if they were not sharing). To register a complaint, note the cab driver's name and cab number and call © 202/645-6010. You will be asked to file a written complaint either by fax (© 202/889-3604) or mail (Commendations/Complaints, District of Columbia Taxicab Commission, 2041 Martin Luther King Jr. Ave. SE, Room 204, Washington, DC 20020).

FAST FACTS: **Washington, D.C.**

American Express   There's an American Express Travel Service office at 1150 Connecticut Ave. NW (© 202/457-1300) and another in upper northwest Washington at 5300 Wisconsin Ave. NW, in the Mazza Gallerie (© 202/ 362-4000).

Area Codes Within the District of Columbia, it's 202. In suburban Virginia, it's 703. In suburban Maryland, it's 301. You must use the area code when dialing any number, even local calls within the District or to nearby Maryland or Virginia suburbs.

Business Hours See "Fast Facts: For the International Traveler," chapter 3.

Car Rentals See "Getting Around," earlier in this chapter.

Climate See "When to Go," in chapter 2.

Congresspersons To locate a senator or congressional representative, call the Capitol switchboard (✆ **202/225-3121**). Point your Web browser to www.senate.gov and www.house.gov to contact individual senators and congressional representatives by e-mail, find out what bills are being worked on, the calendar for the day, and more.

Driving Rules See "Getting Around," earlier in this chapter.

Drugstores **CVS,** Washington's major drugstore chain (with more than 40 stores), has two convenient 24-hour locations: 14th Street and Thomas Circle NW, at Vermont Avenue (✆ **202/628-0720**), and at Dupont Circle (✆ **202/785-1466**), both with round-the-clock pharmacies. Check your phone book for other convenient locations.

Emergencies In any emergency, call ✆ **911.**

Hospitals If you don't require immediate ambulance transportation but still need emergency-room treatment, call one of the following hospitals (and be sure to get directions): **Children's Hospital National Medical Center,** 111 Michigan Ave. NW (✆ **202/884-5000**); **George Washington University Hospital,** 23rd St. NW at Washington Circle (✆ **202/715-4000**); **Georgetown University Medical Center,** 4000 Reservoir Rd. NW (✆ **202/784-2000**); or **Howard University Hospital,** 2041 Georgia Ave. NW (✆ **202/865-6100**).

Hot Lines To reach a 24-hour poison-control hot line, call ✆ **800/222-1222;** to reach a 24-hour crisis line, call ✆ **202/561-7000;** and to reach the drug and alcohol abuse hot line, which operates from 8am to midnight daily, call ✆ **888/294-3572.**

Internet Access Your hotel should be your first stop, since many hotels now offer free Internet access. Away from the hotel, try **Cyberstop Cafe,** 1513 17th St. NW (✆ **202/234-2470**), where you can get a bite to eat while you surf one of 10 computers for $6 per half hour, $8 per hour; the cafe is open from 7am to midnight Monday through Friday, 8am to midnight Saturday and Sunday. In Dupont Circle, the bookstore **Kramerbooks & Afterwords,** 1517 Connecticut Ave. NW (✆ **202/387-1400**), has one computer available for free Internet access, 15 minute-limit.

Legal Aid See "Fast Facts: For the International Traveler," in chapter 3.

Liquor Laws See "Fast Facts: For the International Traveler," in chapter 3.

Maps Free city maps are often available at hotels and throughout town at tourist attractions. You can also contact the **Washington, D.C. Convention and Tourism Corporation,** 1212 New York Ave. NW, Washington, DC 20005 (✆ **202/789-7000**).

Newspapers & Magazines See "Visitor Information," earlier in this chapter.

Police In an emergency, dial © 911. For a nonemergency, call © 202/727-1010.

Safety See "Health & Safety," in chapter 2.

Taxes See "Fast Facts: For the International Traveler," in chapter 3.

Time See "Fast Facts: For the International Traveler," in chapter 3.

Weather Call © 202/936-1212.

5

Accommodations You Can Afford

Since lodging is likely to be your biggest expense in Washington, D.C., my advice to you is this: travel here on a weekend in summer. Rates usually drop substantially at even the best hotels. You may find yourself able to stay at a rather nice hotel for a very low price. I tested this notion by checking the lowest rates posted by the online reservation agency, Expedia, for a Friday in August 2003, at various favorite D.C. hotels (all included in this chapter). Advertised and available were: a suite for $69 at the Capitol Hill Suites, and a double for $79 at the Hilton Garden Inn, $89 at the Jurys Washington Hotel, $98 at the Washington Terrace Hotel, and $109 at the River Inn.

If you're not able or not interested in visiting the capital in the summer, weekends are still your best bet for snagging a good price at a hotel. As a general rule, no matter when you're coming to town, I would always recommend negotiating and checking all sources to find an affordable rate. (See chapter 2, section 1, "72 Money-Saving Tips," the accommodations category, for all possible ways.) Keep in mind that you probably won't be in the position to bargain during cherry blossom season, in late March/early April, and during certain crunch times in Congress, notably mid-September until Thanksgiving. The year 2004 is a presidential election year, as you know, which means that now is not too early to book a hotel room for January 20, 2005, if you're planning on attending the inauguration.

You'll see that I present a wide range of hotel choices in this chapter: student hostels, budget chain motels, intimate bed-and-breakfasts, and moderately priced hotels. All of the accommodations are respectable and clean; I've tried to describe each in terms of its distinctive characteristics.

The chapter organizes accommodations alphabetically within locations. Each description notes a property's highest and lowest rates, usually associated with weekday-versus-weekend or in-season-versus-off-season prices for a room, and room rates are based on double occupancy, unless otherwise noted.

Although I've tried to point out places that advertise good packages, it's important to emphasize that *discounted rates and packages are offered subject to availability.*

As you calculate costs, don't forget tax: In the District, in addition to your hotel rate, you'll pay 14.5% in taxes. The total of state and county taxes on a hotel room is about 9.75% in suburban Virginia and between 5% and 8% in suburban Maryland. And keep in mind that parking can cost a bundle ($15–$25 at most hotels), so inquire about parking rates when you make your reservation, or consider foregoing a car and relying on public transportation.

USING A LOCAL RESERVATIONS SERVICE

If you suffer from information overload and would rather someone else do the research and bargaining, you can always turn to one of the following reputable—and free!—local reservations services. (Refer to appendix B for national chains' toll-free reservation numbers) *Warning:* Always write down your reservation confirmation number and carry it with you! The confirmation number should help guarantee you a room:

- **Capitol Reservations** (© 800/VISIT-DC [800/847-4832] or 202/452-1270; www.hotelsdc.com) will find you a hotel that meets your specific requirements and is within your price range. The 20-year-old service works with about 100 area hotels, all of which have been screened for cleanliness, safe locations, and other desirability factors; you can check rates and book online.
- **Washington D.C. Accommodations** (© 800/554-2220 or 202/289-2220; www.dcaccommodations.com) has been in business for 19 years, and, in addition to finding lodgings, can advise you about transportation and general tourist information and even work out itineraries.
- **U.S.A. Groups** (© 800/872-4777) can help you plan a meeting, convention, or other group function requiring 10 rooms or more; it's a free service representing hotel rooms at almost every hotel in the District and the suburban Virginia-Maryland region, in all price categories.
- **Bed & Breakfast Accommodations Ltd.** (© 877/893-3233 or 413/582-9888; www.bnbaccom.com), in business since 1978, works with more than 80 homes, inns, guesthouses, and unhosted furnished apartments to find visitors lodging. American Express, Diners Club, MasterCard, Visa, and Discover are accepted.

1 Capitol Hill/The Mall

Best Western Downtown—Capitol Hill   This chain hotel has an un-chain-like personality, partly because it's small and partly because its features don't seem cut from a mold. The lobby looks more like a comfortable living room; the reception desk is tiny and staffed by one capable person; rooms have some old-fashioned features, like the cabinet built into a dark-wooden frame that stretches over the top of a bed. Everything is very clean, but not antiseptic.

Besides that, the rates are great and the hotel seems to offer discounts to every possible organization—corporate, government, AARP, AAA, and travel clubs—which explains why the hotel's clientele is an even mix of business people and tourists. Parking is free and a complimentary copy of the *Washington Times* is delivered to your door each morning.

The rooms are attractive, with Impressionist prints on the walls; a 2001 renovation replaced bathroom vanities and floors. Some rooms hold a queen and a twin bed, ideal for small families. Ask for a top- (sixth-) floor room at the back of the house if quiet is essential for you. In 2003, the hotel added a fitness center equipped with a treadmill, stationary bike, and other apparatus. Coming in 2004: complimentary continental breakfast to guests who pay rack rates.

The hotel is located within blocks of the MCI Center, the convention center, Chinatown, Union Station, Capitol Hill, and museums (the Mall is 4 rather long blocks away). One downside is that in spite of its prime location, the hotel lies just enough off the beaten track to warrant special care at night—you won't want to take a stroll through the neighborhood after dark. It's possible that this situation may change with the continuing redevelopment of downtown. A Gray Line tour bus departs for tours from this hotel three times daily.

724 3rd St. NW (between G and H sts.), Washington, DC 20001. ☎ **800/528-1234** or 800/242-4831 or 202/842-4466. Fax 202/842-4831. www.bestwestern.com/downtowncapitolhill. 58 units, 6 with shower only. Mar 1–July 10 and Sept 6–Nov 20 $139–$149 single or double; July 11–Sept 5 $110–$125 single or double; Nov 21–Feb 28 $89–$112 single or double. Extra person $10. Children under 18 stay free in parent's room. AE, DC, DISC, MC, V. Free parking. Metro: Judiciary Square. **Amenities:** Restaurant (American); bar (serving up live entertainment and free eats Mon–Thurs); small fitness center; room service during restaurant hours; same-day laundry/dry cleaning; 2 rooms for those with disabilities. In room: A/C, TV, dataport, coffeemaker, hair dryer, iron.

Bull Moose B&B   A major restoration in 2000 transformed this Victorian town house, formerly known as the Capitol Hill Guest House, from a down-at-the-heels, el cheapo place to bunk, into a bright and inviting inn with attractive furnishings and amenities. Tucked between two parks in a residential neighborhood near the Capitol, the Bull Moose was once a residence for U.S. Senate pages (look for names and comments that some of them carved into the woodwork and desks upstairs). Today's guests tend to be young Hill staffers, scholars doing research at the nearby Library of Congress, and friends and family of those living in the neighborhood.

Guests are invited to use the full kitchen and the inn's "business center" (really the dining room, but it's equipped with fax, phone, printer, and a PC with Internet access). In the cheery parlor, a gourmet continental breakfast is served daily and sherry is available at all hours, along with the day's *New York Times, Financial Times of London,* and other journals.

Bedroom names and decor reflect the owners' interest in Teddy Roosevelt's administration. (The name "Bull Moose" comes from Bull Moose Reform Party, the political party Roosevelt founded and from whose platform he ran for president.) Best rooms are the third floor "Rough Rider" and "Jane Addams" rooms, which have private bathrooms and views of the Capitol dome. The tiny twin-bedded "Upton Sinclair's Jungle" is just large enough for a bedside table complete with a copy of *The Jungle* atop it. The two turreted rooms, the aforementioned Jane Addams and the "Sequoia," have queen beds in the alcoves, plus double beds, along with private bathrooms. Guests staying for a period of time often reserve one of the basement (euphemistically called "the garden level") rooms. These two cozy rooms are rather dim, as you might expect, but they do have narrow windows to let some light in, queen beds, and attractive furnishings; the rooms share a bathroom. The hotel offers the best long-term rates on these rooms.

The Bull Moose offers quiet lodgings, where you might want to take care about the noise you make. No smoking. ☎ **202/547-1050.** www.BullMoose-B-and-B.com. 10 units, 4 with private bathrooms, with shower only. $89–$129 single with shared bathroom; $129–$149 single with private bathroom; $129–$149 double with shared bathroom; $169–$189 double with private bathroom; $189–$209 room for 3 or 4 people with private bathroom. Long-term rates available. Rates include gourmet continental breakfast. AE, DISC, MC, V. Street parking. Metro: Union Station. **Amenities:** Small business center; free use of washer/dryer; use of full kitchen. In room: A/C, no phone.

Capitol Hill Suites ✸ *Kids*   A $3 million renovation completed at this well-run, all-suite property in spring 2000 produced remarkable and lasting results. Bedroom walls are painted cobalt blue, heavy velvet drapes keep out morning sun, lamps and mirrors are from Pottery Barn, desks are long, desk chairs are ergonomically correct, and beds are firm. Bathrooms are tiny, but sparkling.

Kids Family-Friendly Hotels

Capitol Hill Suites (p. 86)   You're on Capitol Hill, within walking distance of the Capitol, Supreme Court, Library of Congress, the Mall, and a Blue line Metro station. Your kids can sleep on the pull-out sofa in the separate living room (ask for a one-bedroom unit and specify that you require one with pull-out sofa). You've got some kitchen facilities, which should help keep costs down on meals, but breakfast is taken care of already, thanks to the complimentary continental breakfast served in the lobby.

One Washington Circle Hotel (p. 104)   A great location in a great neighborhood, bright and airy suites with full kitchens and sofa beds, an outdoor pool, a coin-operated washer and dryer, a good restaurant on the premises—and a hospital across the street in case of emergencies—all for a great price, as low as $99 off season.

George Washington University Inn (p. 103)   You're within walking distance of the Kennedy Center, which has great children's programs, as well as the Metro and Georgetown, when you stay at this hotel. Rooms are spacious and half of the units have a kitchen, always helpful for families.

Hotel Tabard Inn (p. 101)   If you like the homey feel of inns, but worry about bringing your kids for fear they'll break a precious antique, come to the Tabard. It's funky but pleasant and comfortable, with accommodations to suit every request: rooms both with private bathrooms and shared bathrooms, a suite or two, rooms with sitting areas, and one with a kitchen. Rates include continental breakfast and free access to the large YMCA—with a pool—just around the corner. The inn also has a popular, low-key restaurant, and a great lounge area where locals like to hang out. The way the Tabard's dark hallways twist and turn recommend it as a place for playing hide-and-seek, too.

The lobby, which features an enclosed fireplace, leather chairs, and an antique credenza where self-serve coffee is laid out, is inviting enough for lingering. (Sit here long enough and you might spy a congressman or senator—a number of members reserve suites for 100 days at a time.)

The location is another plus: Capitol Hill Suites is the only hotel truly *on* the Hill (on the House side of the Capitol). It stands on a residential street across from the Library of Congress, a short walk from the Capitol and Mall attractions, a food market, and more than 20 restaurants (many of which deliver to the hotel).

The term *suite* denotes the fact that every unit has a kitchenette with coffeemaker, toaster oven, microwave, refrigerator, flatware, and glassware. Most units are efficiencies, with the kitchenette, bed, and sofa all in the same room. The best choices are one-bedroom units, in which the kitchenette and living room are separate from the bedroom. A third option is a "studio double," with two queen beds and a kitchenette, but no living room area. Some rooms in each category have pull-out sofas.

Washington, D.C., Accommodations

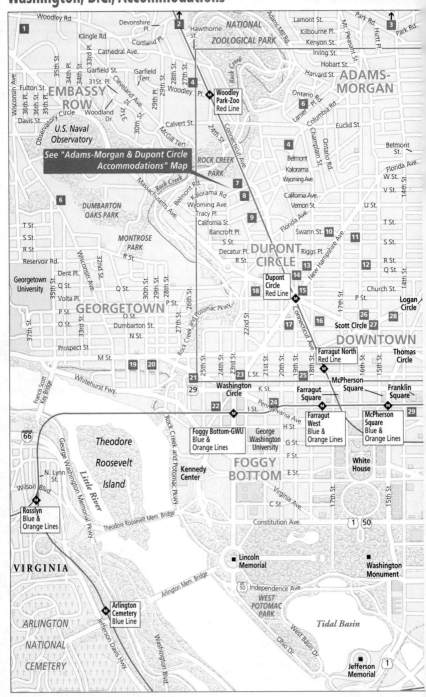

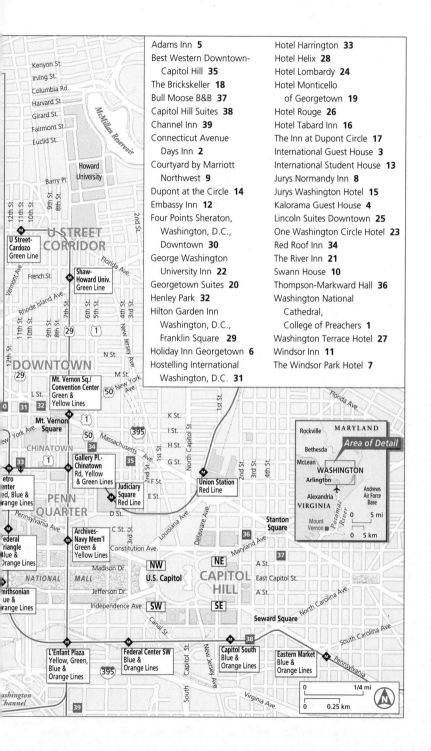

Adams Inn **5**
Best Western Downtown-
 Capitol Hill **35**
The Brickskeller **18**
Bull Moose B&B **37**
Capitol Hill Suites **38**
Channel Inn **39**
Connecticut Avenue
 Days Inn **2**
Courtyard by Marriott
 Northwest **9**
Dupont at the Circle **14**
Embassy Inn **12**
Four Points Sheraton,
 Washington, D.C.,
 Downtown **30**
George Washington
 University Inn **22**
Georgetown Suites **20**
Henley Park **32**
Hilton Garden Inn
 Washington, D.C.,
 Franklin Square **29**
Holiday Inn Georgetown **6**
Hostelling International
 Washington, D.C. **31**

Hotel Harrington **33**
Hotel Helix **28**
Hotel Lombardy **24**
Hotel Monticello
 of Georgetown **19**
Hotel Rouge **26**
Hotel Tabard Inn **16**
The Inn at Dupont Circle **17**
International Guest House **3**
International Student House **13**
Jurys Normandy Inn **8**
Jurys Washington Hotel **15**
Kalorama Guest House **4**
Lincoln Suites Downtown **25**
One Washington Circle Hotel **23**
Red Roof Inn **34**
The River Inn **21**
Swann House **10**
Thompson-Markward Hall **36**
Washington National
 Cathedral,
 College of Preachers **1**
Washington Terrace Hotel **27**
Windsor Inn **11**
The Windsor Park Hotel **7**

Guests, no matter their political leanings, have privileges to dine at the Capitol Hill Club, a members-only club for Republicans, and can charge their meals and drinks to their hotel bill.

200 C St. SE (at 2nd St.), Washington, DC 20003. © 800/424-9165 or 202/543-6000. Fax 202/547-2608. www.capitolhillsuites.com. 152 units. $119–$239 single or double. Weekend and long-term rates may be available. Extra person $20. Rates include continental breakfast and dining privileges at the Capitol Hill Club. Children under 18 stay free in parent's room. AE, DC, DISC, MC, V. Valet parking $24. Metro: Capitol South. **Amenities:** Free use of nearby Washington Sports and Health Club; business services; coin-op washer/dryers; same-day laundry/dry cleaning; 8 rooms for guests with disabilities, all with roll-in showers. *In room:* A/C, TV w/pay movies, 2-line phone w/dataport, fridge, coffeemaker, hair dryer, iron.

2 South of the Mall

Channel Inn This is Washington's only waterfront hotel, located right on the Potomac River. By definition, this means that the hotel is not in the heart of the city. A Metro stop is close by and the Mall and Smithsonian museums are about a mile away—it's an easy walk, but it'll take you through an unremarkable part of Washington that you wouldn't want to traverse at night. Right across the street is one of Washington's best theaters, the Arena Stage (see chapter 9 for details), and right next door is a lively and popular nightclub, Zanzibar on the Waterfront, where you can dance to live music (again, see listing in chapter 9). The Channel Inn caters largely to government employees, but its rates and amenities also recommend it to leisure travelers.

Most rooms offer nice views of the boat-filled Washington Channel and beyond to Virginia; the remainder, unfortunately, overlook the street and pool. The rooms have mahogany furnishings and floral chintz bedspreads and drapes. Some units have high cathedral ceilings; all have balconies. The best rooms are the four suites, all of which face the water; two of these even have sitting rooms separate from the bedrooms.

650 Water St. SW (at 7th St. and Maine Ave.), Washington, DC 20024. © 800/368-5668 or 202/554-2400. Fax 202/863-1164. www.channelinn.com. 100 units. Weekdays $140 single, $145 double; weekends $110 single or double. Suites $150–$190 single or double. Extra person $10. Children under 12 stay free in parent's room. Call toll-free number for best rates. AE, DC, DISC, MC, V. Free parking. Metro: Waterfront. **Amenities:** Restaurant (continental/seafood); coffee shop; bar (with free hors d'oeuvres served at happy hour Mon–Fri and live jazz Tues–Sun); outdoor pool; free access (but no kids) to nearby, fully equipped Waterside Fitness Club; room service during restaurant hours; same-day laundry/dry cleaning, 2 rooms for those with disabilities. *In room:* A/C, TV, dataport, hairdryer, iron.

3 Downtown, East of 16th Street NW

Four Points Sheraton, Washington, D.C. Downtown Value This former Days Inn has been totally transformed into a contemporary property that offers all the latest gizmos, from high-speed Internet access in all the rooms to a 650-square-foot fitness center. A massive renovation undertaken by a new owner essentially gutted the old building, but the location is still as terrific as ever (close to the Convention Center, MCI Center, and downtown). Best of all, the rates are reasonable, and spectacular hotel amenities make this a good choice for both business and leisure visitors.

Five types of rooms are available: units with two double beds, with one queen bed, or with one king bed; junior suites; or one-bedroom suites. In 2003, the hotel put "Heavenly Beds" (a custom-designed, multi-layered, pillow-top mattress) in all of the rooms. Corner rooms (there are only about 10) are a little more spacious than others, which are of standard size. While guest rooms offer city views, the rooftop pool and lounge boasts a sweeping vista of the city that includes the Capitol. Under separate ownership from the hotel is a recommended restaurant, Corduroy.

1201 K St. NW (at 12th St.), Washington, DC 20005. © **888/481-7191** or 202/289-7600. Fax 202/349-2215. www.fourpointswashingtondc.com. 265 units. In season $129–$275 single or double; off-season $89–$245 single or double; from $400 suite. Extra person $20. Children under 18 stay free in parent's room. AE, DC, DISC, MC, V. Parking $24. Metro: McPherson Square or Metro Center. **Amenities:** Restaurant (seasonal American); bar; indoor heated pool on rooftop; fitness center; business center; room service (6am–10pm); same-day laundry/dry cleaning; executive-level rooms; 5 rooms for guests with disabilities, 3 with roll-in showers. *In room:* A/C, TV w/pay movies, 2-line phone w/dataport, minibar, coffeemaker, hair dryer, iron, safe, wireless Internet access.

Hilton Garden Inn, Washington, DC, Franklin Square

Located downtown between H and I streets, the Hilton Garden Inn is across the street from Metro's Blue Line McPherson Square station (and three stops from the Smithsonian museums station) and within walking distance of the White House, the new convention center, and the MCI Center. Rooms are spacious with either king-size or double beds, and are designed for comfort—each room has a cushiony chair with ottoman and a large desk with an ergonomic chair and adjustable lighting. Its location and perks make this 4-year-old hotel a good choice for both business and leisure travelers. The hotel's 20 suites are almost apartment size, with a small pull-out sofa in the living room, and the bathroom separating the bedroom from the living room.

815 14th St. NW (between H and I sts.), Washington, DC 20005. © **800/HILTONS** or 202/783-7800. Fax 202/783-7801. www.washingtondcfranklinsquare.gardeninn.com. 300 units. Weekdays $139–$289 single or double; weekends $109–$179 single or double; $169–$375 suite. Extra person $20. No more than 4 people per room. Children under 18 stay free in parent's room. AE, DC, DISC, MC, V. Parking $22. Metro: McPherson Square. **Amenities:** Restaurant (American); bar with fireplace; small fitness center with indoor pool, Stair-Master, and weight machines; business center; room service (6am–10pm); same-day laundry/dry cleaning; 16 rooms for guests with disabilities, 3 with roll-in showers. *In room:* A/C, TV w/pay movies, 2-line phone w/dataport, fridge, microwave, coffeemaker, hair dryer, iron.

Hotel Harrington ⟨ (*Value*

This is the best hotel deal in this part of town. The family-owned Harrington was built in 1914; Arthur Godfrey once lived here and the Tommy Dorsey and Glenn Miller bands practiced in the ballroom (now a meeting room). Though it's no longer grand, the hotel continues to attract families, groups, and European visitors. Rooms are clean and adequately (if not aesthetically) furnished. Some rooms are nicer than others, so if the hotel's not fully booked and you don't like the first room you see, ask if another is available. The best deals are the family deluxe rooms, which are two rooms separated by an accordion door, one with a queen bed, the other with two single beds, and each with its own bathroom and TV; there is also a refrigerator. Another smart option is the executive king suite, which has a king-size bed, a TV, and a bathroom in one room, and through an open archway, an adjoining sitting room, with a sofa that pulls out into a single bed, a TV, bathroom, refrigerator, and microwave. But keep in mind—this ain't the Ritz. Irons and hair dryers are available at the front desk.

436 11th St. NW (at E St.), Washington, DC 20004. © **800/424-8532** or 202/628-8140. Fax 202/347-3924. www.hotel-harrington.com. 250 units, 15 with shower only. $95–$105 single or double; $135 extra-large room with multiple beds; from $149 for family deluxe room for 2 adults and 2 children; $139 executive king suite. Children 16 and under stay free in parent's room. AE, DC, DISC, MC, V. Parking $10 (lot is 4 blocks from the hotel). Metro: Metro Center. Pets allowed, but must be in cage or on leash at all times. **Amenities:** 2 restaurants (both American); bar; gift shop/tour desk; room service during lunch and dinner; coin-op laundry; same-day laundry/dry cleaning; 6 rooms for those with disabilities. *In room:* A/C, TV.

Hotel Helix ✪   The Helix doesn't so much invite you in, as intrigue you in. Those giant, peacock-blue English lawn chairs and the Magritte-like painting out front are just the beginning. Your steps across a mosaic-tiled vestibule trigger an automatic swoosh of curtains, parting to let you inside the hotel. The small lobby is spare, its main furnishings the illuminated "pods," or podiums with flat computer screens for check in. It's hard to tell who are staff, who are guests, which is intentional—"takes away barriers," says my hotel guide, Danielle. The guest rooms have a minimalist quality to them, too, which is an odd thing to say about a decor that uses such startling colors: cherry-red and royal blue ottomans, striped green settees, bright orange vanities in bathrooms, metallic-sheen walls, lime-green honor bar/armoires. But rooms are uncluttered and roomy, due to a design that puts the platform bed behind sheer drapes in an alcove (in the king deluxe rooms), leaving the two-person settee, a triangular desk, and the 22-inch flat screen TV on its stainless steel stand, out in the open. Deluxe rooms, without alcoves, feel a little less spacious, but otherwise look the same. Roomiest are the suites, with separate bedroom and, in the living room, slate blue sectional sofas. The Helix, like its sister, Hotel Rouge (p. 95), offers "specialty" rooms which play up particular themes, in this case, "Eats" rooms, which include Italian café tables and barstools, and a fully equipped kitchenette; "Bunk" rooms, which have a separate bunk bed area where the TV has a built-in DVD player; and "Zone" rooms, equipped with a plasma screen TV, high-tech stereo system, lava lamp, and lounge chair. Every guest room has a five-disc CD changer, complimentary Internet access at the desk, and Web TV (for a charge).

1430 Rhode Island Ave. NW (between 14th and 15th sts.), Washington, DC 20005. ✆ 866/508-0658 or 202/462-9001. Fax 202/332-3519. www.hotelhelix.com. 178 units. $109–$239 single or double; specialty rooms: add $40 to double rate; suites: add $100 to double rate. Best rates usually on Mon and Tues. Extra person $20. Children under 18 stay free in parent's room. Rates include complimentary continental breakfast and "bubbly hour" (champagne) in evening. AE, DC, DISC, MC, V. Parking $22 plus tax. Pets welcome. Metro: McPherson Square. **Amenities:** Bar/café; exercise room with treadmill, recumbent bike, weight system; room service (during breakfast and dinner hours); same-day laundry/dry cleaning; 9 rooms for guests with disabilities, some with roll-in showers. *In room:* A/C, TV w/pay movies, Nintendo, and Web access (for a fee), 2-line phones w/dataports, minibar, hair dryer, iron, safe, high-speed Internet access, robes.

Red Roof Inn   This popular hotel sits in the heart of Chinatown, within walking distance of many attractions, including the National Building Museum and the MCI Center, and super restaurants and nightlife. The neighborhood is still a little shaky, but looking better all the time: This part of town is undergoing a renaissance.

A thorough renovation of the property completed in 2001 replaced furnishings in every guest room and converted a meeting room into the hotel's Irish Channel restaurant and bar (open daily 7am–1am), where live music plays Thursday through Saturday.

You can choose from rooms with one or two double beds, or one of the "business king" chambers, which are roomier, have king-size beds, and desks and TVs that are larger than those in standard rooms. The 10-story property has only five of these king rooms, and sources tell me that the most popular room in the house is one of these, Room 1025, which is on the top floor and has great city views. Bathrooms throughout have surprisingly generous counter space.

Check out the Red Roof's website for "Red Hot Deals." And another nice money-saving feature: Local phone calls are free.

500 H St. NW, Washington, DC 20001. ✆ 800/733-7663 or 202/289-5959. Fax 202/289-0754. www.redroof.com. 197 units. Peak season $119–$159 single or double; off-peak $89–$119 single or double;

$119–$172 business king year-round. Children under 17 stay free in parent's room. Ask about promotions and check for Internet-only deals. AE, DC, DISC, MC, V. Parking $11. Metro: Gallery Place. Small pets allowed, but only 1 per room. **Amenities:** Restaurant/bar (Irish/Cajun); sunny exercise room with sauna; some business services; coin-op washer/dryers; same-day laundry/dry cleaning service; 8 rooms for those with disabilities, 2 with roll-in shower. *In room:* A/C, TV w/pay movies, dataport, coffeemaker, hair dryer, iron.

SUPER-CHEAP SLEEPS

Hostelling International Washington, D.C.   Situated in a fully renovated eight-story brick building, this hostel offers dorm rooms that sleep 4 to 12 people in each, with two bathrooms (one for males, one for females) on each floor. Accommodations are basic, but the facility includes a huge kitchen where you can cook your own meals (a supermarket is 2 blocks away), a dining room, a comfortable lounge/library, coin-operated washer/dryers, storage lockers, and indoor parking for bicycles. A recent renovation gutted the first and second floors, replacing all beds and mattresses; refurbishing the lounge, lobby, and library; and installing new refrigerators, stoves, counter tops, floors, and everything else in the kitchen. The hostel is entirely accessible to those with disabilities. Internet service is available for a fee, and there's a big-screen TV in the lounge. Continental breakfast is now included.

The staff organizes free special activities for guests—anything from volleyball games to movies to tours of the city. The hostel is 3 blocks from the Metro, and 6 blocks from the Mall. The clientele is monitored, so it's a safe place to take your Girl Scout troop. All age groups are welcome. You have the choice of staying in an all-male, all-female, or a coed dorm. The vast majority of the clientele is international, most between the ages of 18 and 30.

The maximum stay is 28 days, taken altogether or over the course of a year. The hostel provides you with blankets, linens, and pillows; sleeping bags are not allowed. Call as far in advance as possible to reserve. Special rates and deals may be available to interns.

1009 11th St. NW (at K St.), Washington, DC 20001. ☎ **202/737-2333.** Fax 202/737-1508. www. hiwashingtondc.org. 270 beds, sharing about 16 bathrooms. $29, though check the website for various offers. MC, V. Parking at meters and at nearby day lots and locked underground lots for $10–$14, each 24 hr. Metro: Metro Center. **Amenities:** Business services; coin-op washer/dryers; use of a full communal kitchen. *In room:* A/C, no phone.

WORTH A SPLURGE

Henley Park Hotel ✿   This intimate English-style hotel with 119 gargoyles on its facade was originally an apartment house. Built in 1918, the stunning building retains many of its Tudor-style features, including the lobby's exquisite ceiling, archways, and leaded windows. Its design offers a charming counterpoint to that of the newly opened and modern convention center, whose location is "727 steps" away (according to the Henley Park's director of sales). The hotel's popular restaurant, bar, and parlor received face lifts in late 2000, while an ongoing renovation recently replaced wallpaper, linens, and other items in all the guest rooms. Luxurious appointments make this a good choice for upscale romantic weekends, although these lodgings fill up with corporate travelers on weekdays. Rooms are decorated in the English country house mode, with Hepplewhite-, Chippendale-, and Queen Anne–style furnishings, including lovely period beds. Rooms and bathrooms are of standard size. A handful of suites are either one-bedroom or junior (combined living room and bedroom). Look in the Sunday *New York Times* "Travel" section for ads posting low rates.

926 Massachusetts Ave. NW (at 10th St.), Washington, DC 20001. ☎ **800/222-8474** or 202/638-5200. Fax 202/638-6740. www.henleypark.com. 96 units. Weekdays $185–$245 double; summer and weekends

$99–$159 double; suites from $325 weekdays, look for much lower rates on weekends. Extra person $20. Children under 14 stay free in parent's room. AE, DC, DISC, MC, V. Parking $18. Metro: Metro Center, Gallery Place, or Mt. Vernon Square. Call about pet policy. **Amenities:** Restaurant (New American), pub (with pianist Tues–Thurs evenings); afternoon tea (daily 4–6pm); access to a fitness room in the Morrison-Clark Historic Inn across the street; 24-hr. concierge; complimentary weekday-morning sedan service to downtown and Capitol Hill; business services; room service during restaurant hours; same-day laundry/dry cleaning. *In room:* A/C, TV, 2-line speaker phone w/dataport, minibar, coffeemaker, hair dryer, iron, safe, robes.

Washington Terrace Hotel ★   For all intents and purposes, this is a new hotel, the 2002 transformation of the former Doubletree property being so utterly complete. Beautifully landscaped terraces front and back help create a buffer for this urban hotel. The flow of the public spaces leading back to the garden courtyard, and abundant use of earth tones and sandstone in decor, accentuate the hotel's theme of "bringing the outdoors in." This theme resonates in the guest rooms—the light golden wall coverings feature an abstract botanical pattern, and the windows are larger than the hotel norm, delivering lots of natural light. Ask for a room at the front of the hotel for a view of Scott Circle, the park across the street, and the city; request a room at the back for a view of the garden terrace. Best rooms are those on floors six through eight, all of which are spacious suites and have small wet bars, a dining table and sleeper sofa, high-speed Internet access, and larger bathrooms.

Although the Washington Terrace calls itself an "upscale boutique hotel," I think its large size and its practical amenities, like ergonomic chairs in the guest rooms and extensive conference and party facilities, disqualify it. Still, the guest rooms do have a boutiquey feel, thanks to imaginative touches such as granite-topped desks, circular nightstands, and a blueberry toned wall behind the bed (the suites feature other colors: aubergine, nectar, and sienna), contrasting with the light toned coverings on the other walls.

1515 Rhode Island Ave. NW (at Scott Circle), Washington, DC 20005. ℂ **866/984-6835** or 202/232-7000. Fax 202/332-8436. www.washingtonterracehotel.com. 220 units. Weekdays $139–$189 double; weekends $119–$149 double; rates for suites usually run $50 higher than doubles. Extra person $30. Children 16 and under stay free in parent's room. AE, DC, DISC, MC, V. Parking $22. Metro: Dupont Circle or McPherson Square. **Amenities:** Restaurant (contemporary American with Southern flair); bar; fitness center with universal gym, free weights, treadmills, and life cycles; 24-hr. concierge; full-service business center; 24-hr. room service; same-day laundry/dry cleaning; 10 rooms for guests with disabilities, 2 with roll-in showers. *In room:* A/C, TV w/pay movies, 2-line phones w/dataport, minibar, hair dryer, iron, safe, robes, radio/CD player.

4 Downtown, 16th Street NW & West

Embassy Inn   This four-story brick building was rescued from demolition some years back, spruced up, and restored to become a quirky small hotel. Its Federal-style architecture harmonizes with other turn-of-the-20th-century town houses along this block, which was designated a historic district in 1964. Both the Embassy and its sister property, the Windsor (see below), are located near lots of restaurants and just a few streets over from Connecticut Avenue, which forms the center of the lively Dupont Circle neighborhood.

Accommodations are comfortable and clean, though a little peculiar in design: The sink is in the bedroom, not the bathroom; bathrooms have only shower stalls, no tubs; and middle rooms have small windows on the alley. The quietest rooms are on the side or in back, but are rather claustrophobic; the best (and biggest) rooms overlook magnificent 16th Street from a fourth-floor perch that mutes the noise of the neighborhood. The lobby doubles as a parlor, where breakfast is served daily and fresh coffee brews all day; tea, cocoa, and evening sherry are also complimentary. Maps, magazines, brochures, and newspapers are available in the lobby. *Note:* There is no elevator.

1627 16th St. NW (between Q and R sts.), Washington, DC 20009. ② 800/423-9111 or 202/234-7800. Fax 202/234-3309. www.embassyinn.com. 38 units, bathrooms have showers only. Off season $69 single, $79 double, $89 for 2 doubles (only 4 rooms have 2 double beds); peak season $109–$119 single or double, $129 for 2 doubles. Extra person $10. Rates include continental breakfast, evening sherry, and snacks. Children under 14 stay free in parent's room. AE, DC, MC, V. Street parking. Metro: Dupont Circle. *In room:* A/C (certain rooms have individual control, others don't), TV w/pay movies, dataport, hair dryer.

Hotel Rouge ☞ High-energy rock music dances out onto the sidewalk. A red awning extends from the entrance. A guest with sleepy eyes and brilliant blue hair sits diffidently upon the white tufted leather sofa in the small lobby. Attractive, casually dressed patrons come and go, while an older couple roosts at a table just inside the doorway of the adjoining Bar Rouge sipping martinis at 2 in the afternoon. Shades of red are everywhere: in the staff's funky shiny shirts, in the accent pillows on the retro furniture, and in the artwork. This used to be a Quality Hotel: It's come a long way, baby.

The Kimpton Hotel & Restaurant Group, LLC (known for its offbeat but upscale boutique accommodations) has transformed five old D.C. buildings into these cleverly crafted and sexy hotels (see the Helix review on p. 92, for the other Kimpton hotel included in this chapter). In the case of Rouge, this means that your guest room will have deep crimson drapes at the window; a floor-to-ceiling red "pleather" headboard for your comfortable, white-with-red piping duvet-covered bed; and, in the dressing room, an Orange Crush–colored dresser, whose built-in minibar holds all sorts of red items, such as Hot Tamales candies, red wax lips, and Red Bull. Guest rooms in most boutique hotels are notoriously cramped; not so here, where the rooms are spacious enough to easily accommodate several armchairs and a large ottoman (in shades of red and gold), a number of funky little lamps, a huge, mahogany framed mirror leaning against a wall, and a 10-foot-long mahogany desk. The Rouge has no suites but does offer 15 specialty guest rooms, including "Chill Rooms," which have DVD players and Sony PlayStation; "Chat Rooms," which have computer/printers; and "Chow Rooms," which have a microwave and refrigerator. All guest rooms, specialty or otherwise, are equipped for high-speed Internet access. The hotel embraces the theme of adventure, inviting guests to partake of a complimentary Bloody Mary in the lobby on weekends, 10 to 11am. Weeknights, 5 to 6pm, the hotel serves a less frisky refreshment: complimentary wine. If the wine whets your appetite, you can head to the **Bar Rouge** (p. 264), settle into one of the thronelike armchairs and slurp a "Brigitte Bardot Martini" (orange vodka, citron, Grand Marnier, and orange juice), or some other exotic concoction, with a plate of seductive bar food to go with it.

1315 16th St. NW (at Massachusetts Ave. NW and Scott Circle), Washington, DC 20036. ② **800/368-5689** or 202/232-8000. Fax 202/667-9827. www.rougehotel.com. 137 units. Weekdays $159–$219 double; weekends $109–$199 double; add $40 to reserve a specialty room, weekdays or weekends. Best rates available on the website and by calling the 800-number and asking for promotional price. Extra person $20. Rates include complimentary Bloody Marys weekend mornings 10–11am and complimentary wine weeknights 5–6pm. Children under 18 stay free in parent's room. AE, DC, DISC, MC, V. Parking $22. Metro: Dupont Circle. Pets are more than allowed, they're pampered here. **Amenities:** Bar/restaurant (American, with a French twist); modest size fitness center with treadmill and stationary bikes; 24-hr. concierge; business center; room service (7am–11pm); same-day laundry/dry cleaning; 6 rooms for guests with disabilities, 1 with roll-in shower. *In room:* A/C, 27-in. flat-screen TV w/pay movies, 2-line cordless phones w/dataport, minibar, coffeemaker (with Starbucks coffee), hair dryer, iron, free high-speed Internet access, robes, CD player.

Lincoln Suites Downtown ⭐⭐ (Value)   This is a little hotel with a big heart. It tries hard to do right by its guests and, judging from feedback I've received from readers who've stayed here, I would say it succeeds. (Check out the website, where the hotel's can-do personality shines through.) Key elements include the hotel's location, in the heart of downtown, near Metro stops, restaurants, and the White House; a congenial staff; the complimentary milk and homemade cookies served each evening; and daily complimentary continental breakfast in the lobby. Lincoln Suites also has direct access to **Mackey's,** an Irish pub right next door, and to **Recessions,** a restaurant on the lower level serving American/Mediterranean cuisine. **Famous Luigi's Pizzeria Restaurant** ⭐, an Italian restaurant and veritable Washington institution (p. 132), located right around the corner, delivers room service for lunch and dinner.

The all-suite 10-story hotel is quite nice, in a nothing-fancy sort of way. Lots of long-term guests bunk here. Suites are large and comfortable; about 28 offer full kitchens, while the rest have wet bars (mini-refrigerator, microwave, and coffeemaker). An ongoing renovation has slowly but surely overhauled the hotel, replacing all the furniture, appliances, carpeting, and wall coverings. Most recently, the previously cramped lobby was transformed into a hip two-story lobby/lounge.

1823 L St. NW, Washington, DC 20036. ℂ **800/424-2970** or 202/223-4320. Fax 202/293-4977. www.lincoln hotels.com. 99 suites. Weekdays $175–$215; weekends $115–$155. Rates include continental breakfast. Discounts available for long-term stays. Children under 16 stay free in parent's room. AE, DC, DISC, MC, V. Parking $20 (in adjoining garage). Metro: Farragut North or Farragut West. Pets under 25 lb. accepted, 2nd floor only, for $15 a day. **Amenities:** Restaurant (American/Mediterranean); bar (Irish); free passes to the well-equipped Bally's Holiday Spa nearby; 24-hr. front desk/concierge; room service (11am–11pm); coin-op washer/dryers; same-day laundry/dry cleaning; 2 rooms for guests with disabilities, 1 with roll-in shower. *In room:* A/C, TV w/pay movies, dataport, fridge, coffeemaker, hair dryer, iron.

Windsor Inn   Under the same ownership and just a couple of blocks north of the aforementioned Embassy Inn, the Windsor Inn occupies two brick buildings side by side but with separate entrances. The Windsor annex has slightly larger rooms and more charming features, such as the occasional bay window or arched ceiling; the annex and the main building maintain the same comfortable feel of the Embassy. Some of the public areas are done in Art Deco motif. A modest renovation in 2003 replaced windows and TVs throughout and the air conditioners in just the suites. All rooms are neat and comfortable, and a few have sofas or decorative fireplaces. Suites offer the greatest value, are roomy and attractively furnished, and cost less than you'd usually pay in Washington. Lower-level rooms (the smoking floor) face a skylit terrace with lawn furnishings and colorful murals. Readers have reported that this floor is very noisy. The lobby serves as the common room, where continental breakfast, sherry, and other complimentary beverages and snacks are laid out. As at the Embassy, there is no elevator.

1842 16th St. NW (at T St.), Washington, DC 20009. ℂ **800/423-9111** or 202/667-0300. Fax 202/667-4503. www.windsorembassyinns.com. 45 units, 41 rooms have showers only. Off season $69 single, $79 double, $89 for 2 doubles (only 4 rooms have 2 double beds), $129–$159 suites; peak season $109–$119 single or double, $139–$179 suites. Rates include continental breakfast, evening sherry, and snacks. Extra person $10. Children under 14 stay free in parent's room. AE, DC, MC, V. Street parking. Metro: Metro Center. **Amenities:** Use of a common fridge. *In room:* A/C, TV w/pay movies, dataport, hair dryer.

5 Adams-Morgan/North Dupont Circle

Note: The hotels listed here are situated just north of Dupont Circle, more at the mouth of Adams-Morgan than within its actual boundaries.

Adams-Morgan, Dupont Circle & West End Accommodations

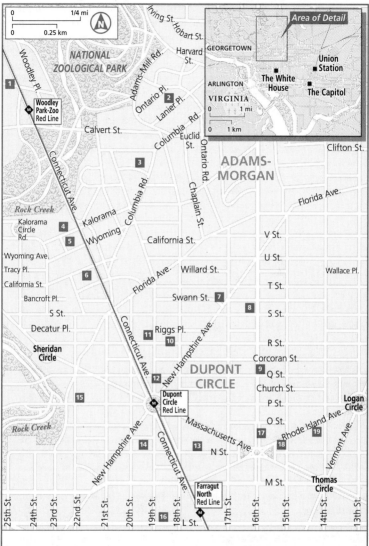

Adams Inn **2**
The Brickskeller **15**
Courtyard by Marriott Northwest **6**
Dupont at the Circle **11**
Embassy Inn **9**
Hotel Helix **19**
Hotel Rouge **17**
Hotel Tabard Inn **13**
The Inn at Dupont Circle **14**

International Student House **10**
Jurys Normandy **5**
Jurys Washington Hotel **12**
Kalorama Guest House **1, 3**
Lincoln Suites Downtown **16**
Swann House **7**
Washington Terrace Hotel **18**
Windsor Inn **8**
The Windsor Park Hotel **4**

Adams Inn   Close to Adams-Morgan restaurants, shops, and a Safeway super-market, the homey Adams Inn occupies 300-year-old brick town houses on a residential tree-lined street. Each has a cozy parlor with decorative fireplace, lots of windows, and books, games, and magazines for guests. A new owner in 2002 updated the look of the inn, changing the decor from Victorian to urban coun-try (if the furniture looks like it came from Pottery Barn or Crate & Barrel, it probably did). Also new are a computer room, where you have free use of a computer with high-speed Internet access, and a breakfast room. The well-kept accommodations have been freshly painted and boast new bedding; some have bay windows or handsome oak paneling. There are no phones or TVs, but you do get a clock radio. The best deal for families or friends traveling together is a lower level two-room suite with a queen-size bed in one room, a double in the other, a couple of sitting areas, and a shared bathroom: starts at $105 for the whole arrangement. Rates include a continental breakfast of breads, cereals, yogurt, and tea and coffee. Guests have use of a common refrigerator, microwave oven, VCR, cable TV, and iron/ironing board. No smoking.

1744 Lanier Place NW (between Calvert St. and Ontario Rd.), Washington, DC 20009. ✆ **800/578-6807** or 202/745-3600. Fax 202/319-7958. www.adamsinn.com. 25 units, 15 with private bathroom, 9 of which have showers only. $75 single with shared bathroom; $85 double with shared bathroom; $85 single with private bathroom; $95 double with private bathroom. Rates include continental breakfast. Extra person $10. Weekly rates available on some rooms. AE, DC, DISC, MC, V. Limited parking $10. Metro: Woodley Park–Zoo (7 blocks away). **Amenities:** Coin-op washer/dryer; TV lounge; use of guest fridge and microwave; free high-speed Internet access. *In room:* A/C; no phone (2 pay phones in the common areas).

Courtyard by Marriott Northwest   This hotel isn't much to look at from the outside, but inside it has a European feel and a well-heeled appearance. Waterford crystal chandeliers hang in the lobby and in the restaurant, and you may hear an Irish lilt from time to time. (The hotel is one of three in Washing-ton owned by Jurys Doyle Hotel Group, an Irish management company.) Guests tend to linger in the comfortable lounge off the lobby, where coffee is available all day.

Guest rooms are very comfortable and bright. Accommodations facing the street on the sixth to ninth floors provide panoramic views. Especially nice are the 15 "executive king" rooms, which are a little larger and are equipped with marble bathrooms, trouser presses, and robes. A refurbishment of all guest rooms is scheduled to be completed by the time you read this.

Look for the best deals in summer, when a "two for breakfast" promotion often runs.

1900 Connecticut Ave. NW (at Leroy Place), Washington, DC 20009. ✆ **888/236-2427** or 202/332-9300. Fax 202/319-1793. www.jurysdoyle.com. 147 units. $99–$245 double. Extra person $15. Children under 18 stay free in parent's room. Ask about discount packages. AE, DC, DISC, MC, V. Parking $20. Metro: Dupont Circle. **Amenities:** Restaurant (American, open for breakfast and dinner); bar; outdoor pool (seasonal); small exer-cise room; business center; room service (5–10pm); coin-operated laundry; same-day laundry and dry clean-ing; 2 rooms for guests with disabilities, both with roll-in showers. *In room:* A/C, TV w/pay movies, 2-line phone w/dataport, coffeemaker, hair dryer, iron, safe.

Jurys Normandy Inn ⭐ *Finds*   This gracious hotel is a gem—a small gem, but a gem nonetheless. Situated in a neighborhood of architecturally impressive embassies, the hotel hosts many embassy-bound guests. You may discover this for yourself on a Tuesday evening, when guests gather in the charming Tea Room to enjoy complimentary wine and cheese served from the antique oak sideboard. This is also where you'll find daily continental breakfast (for about $7), complimentary coffee and tea after 10am, and cookies after 3pm. You can lounge or watch TV in the conservatory, or, in nice weather, you can move outside to the garden patio.

The six-floor Normandy has small but pretty twin and queen guest rooms (all remodeled in 1998), with tapestry-upholstered mahogany and cherry-wood furnishings in 18th-century style, and pretty floral-print bedspreads covering firm beds. Rooms facing Wyoming Avenue overlook the tree-lined street, while other rooms mostly offer views of apartment buildings. The Normandy is an easy walk from both Adams-Morgan and Dupont Circle, where many restaurants and shops await you.

2118 Wyoming Ave. NW (at Connecticut Ave.), Washington, DC 20008. © **800/424-3729** or 202/483-1350. Fax 202/387-8241. www.jurysdoyle.com. 75 units. $89–$185 double. Extra person $10. Children under 12 stay free in parent's room. AE, DC, DISC, MC, V. Parking $20. Metro: Dupont Circle. **Amenities:** Access to the neighboring Courtyard by Marriott Northwest's pool and exercise room; room service at breakfast; coin-op washer/dryers; same-day laundry/dry cleaning (Mon–Sat); 4 rooms for guests with disabilities, 1 with roll-in shower. In room: A/C, TV w/pay movies, 2-line phone w/dataport, fridge, coffeemaker, hair dryer, iron, safe.

Kalorama Guest House   This San Francisco–style B&B has two locations: in Adams-Morgan on Mintwood Place, where a Victorian town house is the main dwelling, with two other houses on the same street providing additional lodging; and in nearby Woodley Park, where two houses on Cathedral Avenue NW offer a total of 19 guest rooms (see "Woodley Park," later in this chapter, for more information about this location).

The cozy common areas and homey guest rooms are furnished with finds from antique stores, flea markets, and auctions. The Mintwood Place town house has a breakfast room with plant-filled windows. There's a garden behind the house with umbrella tables.

Rooms in all the houses generally offer either double or queen-size beds, but the Mintwood Place town house offers larger units in a greater variety of configurations: There's an efficiency apartment with a kitchen, telephone, and TV; one small two-room apartment with a kitchen, cable TV, and telephone; and four suites (2 two-bedroom and 2 "executive" suites, in which the living room and bedroom are together).

All locations serve a complimentary breakfast of juice, coffee, fruit, bagels, croissants, and English muffins. They also give guests access to laundry and ironing facilities, a refrigerator, a seldom-used TV, and a phone (local calls are free; incoming calls are answered around the clock, so people can leave messages for you). It's customary for the innkeepers to put out sherry on Friday and Saturday afternoons, adding lemonade and cookies in summer and tea and cookies in winter. Magazines, games, and current newspapers are available. All of the houses are nonsmoking. At both locations, your fellow guests are likely to be students, Europeans, and conferees.

The Mintwood Place location is near Metro stations, dozens of restaurants, nightspots, and shops. The Cathedral Avenue houses, which are even closer to the Woodley Park–Zoo Metro, offer proximity to Rock Creek Park and the National Zoo.

1854 Mintwood Place NW (between 19th St. and Columbia Rd.), Washington, DC 20009. © **202/667-6369.** Fax 202/319-1262. http://yp.washingtonpost.com/yp/kgh. 30 units, 16 with bathroom, 6 with shower only. $55–$75 double with shared bathroom; $75–$100 double with bathroom; $105–$145 suite or apt. Extra person $5 in doubles, $10 in suites. Rates include continental breakfast. AE, DC, DISC, MC, V. Limited parking $7. Metro: Woodley Park–Zoo or Dupont Circle. Kids 6 and older. **Amenities:** Washer/dryer; common fridge; common TV. In room: A/C, no phone.

The Windsor Park Hotel The Windsor Park isn't as nice as its green-canopied, brass-poled entrance would have you believe, but it's nice enough. Anyway, the setting is lovely: The hotel is situated in a neighborhood of shady, tree-lined streets, chockablock with embassies—that's the Algerian Embassy right next door and the Chinese Embassy across the street.

The Windsor Park offers tidy and simply furnished rooms, with Chippendale and Queen Anne–style furnishings, and bedspreads with matching curtains. You can choose from rooms with two double beds or one queen-size bed. The hotel isn't fancy, but it is satisfactory and safe. Most guests are businesspeople attending conventions at the huge hotels in the area, and tourists. There are no dining facilities, but Adams-Morgan and Dupont Circle restaurants are close by. Soft drinks, coffee, and candy machines are located on the first floor and an extensive continental breakfast is served in the lobby each morning. A small boardroom accommodates groups of 10 to 20. Best rooms are the eight suites, two per floor, which hold a living room and a separate bedroom.

2116 Kalorama Rd. NW (off Connecticut Ave.), Washington, DC 20008. ✆ **800/247-3064** or 202/483-7700. Fax 202/332-4547. www.windsorparkhotel.com. 43 units. $110 single; $120 double; $165 suite (for 4 people). Check website for occasional specials. Rates include continental breakfast. Extra person $10. Children under 12 stay free in parent's room. AE, DC, DISC, MC, V. Metro: Woodley Park–Zoo. **Amenities:** Business services; 2 rooms for those with disabilities. *In room:* A/C, TV, dataport, fridge, hair dryer.

6 Dupont Circle

The Brickskeller The Brickskeller describes itself as a "European-style inn," which is code for "the loo's down the hall." The building is nearly 100 years old, but the inn's been around since 1957, and frankly, you can believe it. A woman sitting behind a desk at the end of a long hall buzzes you in to the building. An ancient elevator takes you upwards.

The guest rooms are large, with a bed dead center, covered with a very white chenille bedspread. There's a big old radiator in one corner and an old-fashioned looking chest of drawers against a wall. A closet, small windows, odd-looking gray-brown carpeting, and that's it. And like I said, the loo's down the hall, eight communal bathrooms for 42 rooms. If you've ever watched one of those black and white 1950's film noir movies, the setting might seem vaguely familiar.

Why do I include the Brickskeller? Because it's clean, safe, and in a good neighborhood. It's cheap, too, although not as cheap as it should be. If you're booking a room here in summer, you'd better ask for a room with an air conditioner—only half of the rooms are air-conditioned (via a window unit). The inn does have two rooms with private bathrooms, TVs, and air conditioning (ask for rooms 305 or 405, the best). Be aware that smoking is allowed in all rooms.

The Brickskeller is better known for its popular saloon (see details in chapter 9), which lies in the basement of the inn and has a separate entrance. In fact, in addition to a clientele of students and professionals, some guests of the inn are beer imbibers from the bar, in no shape to make it home.

1523 22nd St. NW (between P and Q sts.), Washington, DC 20037. ✆ **202/293-1885**. Fax 202/293-0996. 44 units, 42 with shared bathroom, 2 with private bathroom. $44–$54 (with A/C), single with shared bathroom; $73 double with shared bathroom; $73 single with private bathroom; $93 double with private bathroom. AE, DISC, MC, V. Metro: Dupont Circle. **Amenities:** Restaurant/bar; coin-op laundry.

Dupont at the Circle Two Victorian town houses were fused together to form this inn, which is located just off Dupont Circle in a neighborhood of outdoor cafes, bookstores, boutiques, art galleries, and restaurants. Owners Alan and Anexora Skvirsky have restored the houses' original pocket doors, inlaid tile fireplaces, interior window shutters, and plaster moldings, while adding fine antique furnishings throughout, along with wonderful art and photographs, many of which are the work of the Skvirskys's artist daughter.

Depending on the room, you'll find bay windows and stained glass, bedroom alcoves in which beds fit perfectly, high ceilings, a rooftop deck, writing desks, working fireplaces, and all-marble bathrooms with whirlpool tubs. All guest rooms are lovely, and have a queen bed made up with ironed sheets and a snuggly comforter. The handsome first floor parlors include a spot for watching TV or a video from the house collection of 200 films; continental breakfast is served each morning in the dining room. The Dupont also has one room with a kitchenette available on a nightly basis, and one apartment with a full kitchen, TV/VCR, and stacked washer/dryer, that is available for rent on a long-term basis (call for these rates). No smoking.

1604 19th St. NW (at Q St.), Washington, DC 20009. ℭ **888/412-0100** or 202/332-5251. Fax 202/332-3244. www.dupontatthecircle.com. 8 units. From $140 single or double; from $225 suite. Inquire about government rates, AAA and AARP discounts. Extra person $20. Rates include continental breakfast. Limited parking $15. AE, DC, DISC, MC, V. Metro: Dupont Circle. No children under age 13. **Amenities:** In-room massage; common area parlors with TV/VCR. *In room:* A/C, dataport, hair dryer, robes.

Hotel Tabard Inn 🤿 *(Kids)*   If you favor the offbeat and the personal over brand names and cookie-cutter chains, this might be the place for you. The Tabard Inn, named for the hostelry in Chaucer's *Canterbury Tales,* is actually three Victorian town houses that were joined in 1914 and have operated as an inn ever since. Situated on a quiet street of similarly old dwellings, the Tabard is a well-worn, funky hotel that's looked after by a chummy, peace-love-and-understanding sort of staff who clearly cherish the place.

The heart of the ground floor is the dark-paneled lounge, with worn furniture, a wood-burning fireplace, the original beamed ceiling, and bookcases. This is a favorite spot for Washingtonians to come for a drink, especially in winter, or to linger before or after dining in the charming **Tabard Inn restaurant** 🤿 (p. 146).

From the lounge, the inn leads you up and down stairs, along dim corridors, and through nooks and crannies to guest rooms. Can you dig chartreuse? (Ask for room 3.) How about aubergine? (Ask for room 11.) Each is different, but those facing N Street are largest and brightest, and some have bay windows. Furnishings are a mix of antiques and flea-market finds. Perhaps the most eccentric room is the top-floor "penthouse," which has skylights, exposed brick walls, its own kitchen, and a deck accessed by climbing out a window. The inn is not easily accessible to guests with disabilities.

(Moments   **"There's a Small Hotel"**

If you're in Washington on a Sunday night and you're staying at the **Hotel Tabard Inn,** be sure to plant yourself in the paneled parlor by 7:30pm. Even if you're not staying at the Tabard, you might want to get yourself there. From 7:30 to 10:30pm each Sunday, bassist Victor Dvoskin, usually accompanied by a guitarist, plays world-class jazz for free. Order a drink from the bar in the next room, then settle into one of the old chairs or sofas to enjoy the show. "There's a Small Hotel" is the name of a CD released by Dvoskin, in honor of Tabard owners Fritzi Cohen and her late husband, Edward, whose private program, the Capitals Citizens' Exchange, first brought Dvoskin to this country from Russia in 1988.

1739 N St. NW (between 17th and 18th sts.), Washington, DC 20036. ℂ **202/785-1277.** Fax 202/785-6173. www.tabardinn.com. 40 units, 27 with private bathroom, 6 with shower only. $103–$125 double with shared bathroom; $130–$205 double with private bathroom. Extra person $15. Rates include continental breakfast. AE, DC, DISC, MC, V. Limited street parking, plus 2 parking garages on N St. Metro: Dupont Circle. Small and confined pets allowed ($20 fee). **Amenities:** Restaurant (regional American) with lounge (free live jazz Sun evenings); free access to nearby YMCA (with extensive facilities that include indoor pool, indoor track, and racquetball/basketball courts); laundry service; fax, iron, hair dryer, and safe available at front desk. *In room:* A/C, dataport.

The Inn at Dupont Circle ★ *(Finds)*   The Dupont Circle neighborhood has several bed-and-breakfasts with similar-sounding names. The Inn at Dupont Circle is a different establishment than the Dupont at the Circle, above; both are really lovely inns, and near each other on the same street, but on different sides of Dupont Circle, in this charming section of Washington.

Built in 1885, this Victorian town house was renovated and opened to guests in 2000. The innkeepers were careful to preserve its extraordinary features, the 12-foot-high ceilings, bay and Queen Anne stained-glass windows, the white marble floor downstairs, and cherry-pine hardwood floors elsewhere. Guests are welcome to relax in the common areas, the private walled garden, the heated solarium overlooking the garden, and the front salon, where you can play the 1872 Steinway or sip complimentary wine in the afternoon and evening. A full breakfast is offered every morning in the dining room.

The eight guest rooms range from a small room with one twin bed and wicker furniture to a large room with a white iron bed, a non-working marble fireplace, an alcove loveseat that pulls out into a bed for one, original moldings, a Victorian oak armoire, and a Persian rug. The twin-bed room and two queen-bedded rooms share one bathroom; the remaining four guest rooms have private bathrooms. Even the smallest of the rooms is irresistible.

1312 19th St. NW (between Sunderland and N sts.), Washington, DC 20036. ℂ **888/467-2100** or 202/467-6777. Fax 202/293-8819. www.theinnatdupontcircle.com. 8 units, 5 with private bathroom, 3 with shower only. Peak season $89 single, $125 double with shared bathroom, $165–$195 double with private bathroom; off season $89 single, $118 double with shared bathroom, $135–$165 double with private bathroom. (Off season is mid-October to mid-March.) 2-night minimum most weekends. Discounts available for longer stays. Extra person $15. Children under 5 stay free; parents pay for any damage done by children. Rates include full breakfast and late afternoon wine. Limited parking: $15; otherwise street parking or at nearby garages. AE, DC, DISC, MC, V. Metro: Dupont Circle. **Amenities:** Business services; laundry facilities; common fridge. *In room:* A/C, TV, hair dryer.

Jurys Washington Hotel ★ *(Value)*   This hotel gets high marks for convenience (it's located right on Dupont Circle), service, and comfort. Open since 2000, the hotel is favored by business groups especially, who like its reasonable rates. Each of the large rooms is furnished with two double beds with firm mattresses, an armoire with TV, a desk, a wet-bar alcove, and a tiny but attractive bathroom. Decor is Art Deco-ish, with lots of light-wood furniture. All guest rooms offer free, high-speed Internet access. Despite its prime location in a sometimes raucous neighborhood, the hotel's rooms are insulated from the noise. Rooms on higher floors offer the best views of the city and of Dupont Circle. An Irish management company owns this hotel (along with two other properties in Washington), and the comfortable and attractive hotel pub, Biddy Mulligan's, proudly features a bar imported from the Emerald Isle. Its restaurant, **Dupont Grille,** opened in spring 2003, and a welcome addition it is to the hotel and the neighborhood (p. 145). To get the best hotel rates, check the website or call the hotel directly.

1500 New Hampshire Ave. NW (across from Dupont Circle), Washington, DC 20036. (**C**) **800/423-6953** or 202/483-6000. Fax 202/238-3265. www.jurysdoyle.com. 314 units. $99–$245 double; from $600 suite. Extra person $15. Children 17 and under stay free in parent's room. AE, DC, DISC, MC, V. Parking $20. Metro: Dupont Circle. **Amenities:** Restaurant (Irish/American); bar; exercise room; 24-hr. concierge; business center; room service (6:30am–midnight); same-day laundry/dry cleaning; 11 rooms for guests with disabilities, 4 with roll-in showers. *In room:* A/C, TV w/pay movies, 2-line phone w/dataport, minibar, coffeemaker, hair dryer, iron, safe.

WORTH A SPLURGE

Swann House *Finds* At the rate it's going, Swann House may one day be known as "the inn that launched 1,000 marriages," for all of the couples who have become engaged while staying here. ("Three just last weekend, 10 in the past 2 months," says owner Mary Ross, when we spoke several months ago.) This stunning 1883 mansion, poised prominently on a corner 4 blocks north of Dupont Circle, has nine exquisite guest rooms. The coolest unit is the Blue Sky Suite, which has the original rose-tiled working fireplace, a queen-size bed and sofa bed, a sitting room decorated in blue and white toile, a gabled ceiling, and its own roof deck. The most romantic room is probably Il Duomo, with Gothic windows, a cathedral ceiling, a working fireplace, and a turreted bathroom with angel murals, a claw-foot tub and a rain shower head. The Jennifer Green Room has a queen-size four-poster bed, a working fireplace, an oversize marble steam shower, and a private deck overlooking the pool area and garden. The Regent Room also has a private deck overlooking the pool, as well as a king-size bed in front of a carved working fireplace and a whirlpool. There are three suites. You'll want to spend some time on the main floor of the mansion, which has 12-foot ceilings, fluted woodwork, inlaid wood floors, a turreted living room, a columned sitting room, and a sunroom (where breakfast is served) leading through three sets of French doors to the garden and pool. No smoking.

1808 New Hampshire Ave. NW (between S and Swann sts.), Washington, DC 20009. (**C**) **202/265-4414.** Fax 202/265-6755. www.swannhouse.com. 9 units, 3 with shower only. $140–$295 depending on unit and season. 2-night minimum weekends, 3-night minimum holiday weekends. Extended-stay and government rates available. Extra person $35. Rates include expanded continental breakfast. Limited off-street parking $12. AE, MC, V. Metro: Dupont Circle. No children under age 12. **Amenities:** Outdoor pool; access to nearby health club; business services; in-room massage; same-day dry cleaning. *In room:* A/C, TV, phone w/voice mail and dataport, hair dryer.

7 Foggy Bottom

George Washington University Inn *Kids* Rumor has it that this whitewashed brick inn, another former apartment building, used to be a favorite spot for clandestine trysts for high-society types. These days you're more likely to see Kennedy Center performers and visiting professors. The university purchased the hotel (formerly known as the Inn at Foggy Bottom) in 1994 and renovated it. The most recent refurbishment, in 2001, replaced linens, drapes, and the like in the guest rooms.

Rooms are a little larger and corridors are a tad narrower than those in a typical hotel, and each room includes a roomy dressing chamber. More than one-third of the units are one-bedroom suites. These are especially spacious, with living rooms that hold a sleeper sofa and a TV hidden in an armoire (there's another in the bedroom). The suites, plus the 16 efficiencies, have kitchens. The spaciousness and the kitchen facilities make this a popular choice for families and for long-term guests.

This is a fairly safe and lovely neighborhood, within easy walking distance to Georgetown, the Kennedy Center, and downtown. But keep an eye peeled—you have to pass through wrought-iron gates into a kind of cul-de-sac to find the inn.

Off the lobby is the restaurant, **Nectar** (p. 148), which opened in spring 2003. If it's not full, the inn may be willing to offer reduced rates. Mention your affiliation with George Washington University, if you have one, to receive a special "GWU" rate.

824 New Hampshire Ave. NW (between H and I sts.), Washington, DC 20037. Ⓒ **800/426-4455** or 202/337-6620. Fax 202/298-7499. www.gwuinn.com. 95 units. Weekdays $119–$300 double, $139–$320 efficiency, $149–$340 1-bedroom suite; weekends $99–$135 double, $110–$155 efficiency, $125–$170 1-bedroom suite. Children under 12 stay free in parent's room. AE, DC, MC, V. Limited parking $18. Metro: Foggy Bottom. **Amenities:** Restaurant (upscale contemporary American); complimentary passes to nearby fitness center; room service (7am–11pm); coin-op washer/dryers; same-day laundry/dry cleaning; 5 rooms for guests with disabilities, 1 with roll-in shower. *In room:* A/C, TV w/pay movies and Nintendo, 2-line phone w/dataport, fridge, coffeemaker, hair dryer, iron, safe, robes, CD player, microwave, umbrella.

Hotel Lombardy From its handsome walnut-paneled lobby with carved Tudor-style ceilings to its old-fashioned manual elevator (fasten your seat belts—it's going to be a bumpy ride), the 11-story Lombardy offers a lot of character and comfort for the price. Originally built in 1929, it's located about 5 blocks west of the White House. George Washington University's campus is just across Pennsylvania Avenue, so this area remains vibrant long after other downtown neighborhoods have rolled up the sidewalks. Peace Corps, World Bank, and corporate guests make up a large part of the clientele, but other visitors will also appreciate the Lombardy's warm, welcoming ambience and the attentive service of the multilingual staff.

The decor in each spacious room has a unique touch. All are entered via pedimented louver doors, and are furnished with original artwork and Chinese and European antiques. All rooms have large desks, precious dressing rooms, and roomy walk-in closets; new drapes, bedspreads, and carpeting were installed in the spring of 2001. Most of the 36 one-bedroom suites have small kitchens with dining areas. Front rooms overlook Pennsylvania Avenue and the small triangular park across the street, named for President James Monroe. Back rooms are quieter; some overlook the garden of the hotel's next-door neighbor, the Arts Club of Washington, where Monroe once lived.

2019 Pennsylvania Ave. NW (between 20th and 21st sts.), Washington, DC 20006. Ⓒ **800/424-5486** or 202/828-2600. Fax 202/872-0503. www.hotellombardy.com. 127 units. In season $159–$209 double, $179–$209 suites; off season $89–$119 double, $179–$209 suites. Extra person $20. Children under 16 stay free in parent's room. AE, DC, DISC, MC, V. Self-parking $17. Metro: Farragut West or Foggy Bottom. **Amenities:** Restaurant (French); lounge (shares a menu with the restaurant, as well as offering an appetizer menu); fitness center; concierge; room service (6:30am–10pm); same-day laundry/dry cleaning. *In room:* A/C, TV w/pay movies, 2-line phone w/dataport, kitchens (in some rooms), minibar, coffeemaker, hair dryer, iron, robes.

One Washington Circle Hotel 𝐴 *Kids* Built in 1960, this building was converted into a hotel in 1976, making it the city's first all-suite hotel property. The George Washington University purchased the hotel in 2001 (see its other property, the George Washington University Inn, above), closed the place down and totally renovated it, reopening the hotel in 2002. One Washington Circle gleams now, from its double-paned windows to its contemporary new furniture. Five types of suites are available, ranging in size from 390 to 710 square feet. The one-bedroom suites have a sofa bed and dining area; all rooms are spacious and have walk-out balconies, some overlooking the Circle and its centerpiece, the statue of George Washington. But keep in mind that across the Circle is George

Washington University Hospital's emergency room entrance, which is busy with ambulance traffic; even with the installation of those double-paned windows, you may still hear sirens, so ask for a suite on the L Street side if you desire a quieter room. Ninety percent of the suites have full kitchens, including an oven, microwave, and refrigerator.

Clientele is mostly corporate, but families like the outdoor pool, in-house restaurant, prime location near Georgetown and the Metro, and the full kitchen. Call directly to the hotel for best rates and be sure to mention a GWU affiliation if you have one. The well-reviewed **Circle Bistro,** serves bistro food with a Mediterranean influence.

One Washington Circle NW (between 22nd and 23rd sts. NW), Washington, DC 20037. Ⓒ **800/424-9671** or 202/872-1680. Fax 202/887-4989. www.thecirclehotel.com. 151 units. Weekdays $139–$199 smallest suites, $159–$219 largest suites; weekends $119–$179 smallest suites, $139–$199 largest suites. Call hotel to get best rates. Extra person: $20. Children under 12 stay free in parent's room. AE, DC, MC, V. Parking $20. Metro: Foggy Bottom. **Amenities:** Restaurant (traditional bistro with Mediterranean flair); bar; outdoor pool; fitness center; concierge; room service (7am–midnight weekends, 7am–11pm weekdays); coin-op washer/dryers; same-day laundry/dry cleaning; 5 rooms for guests with disabilities, 1 with roll-in shower. *In room:* A/C, TV w/pay movies and Nintendo, 2-line cordless phones, full kitchens (in 90% of suites, w/oven, fridge, microwave), coffeemaker, hair dryer, iron, high-speed Internet access through TV, CD player.

The River Inn ★/★ ✓*Value*   The River Inn lies on a quiet residential street of old town houses, a 5-minute walk from the Kennedy Center, and a 10-minute walk from Georgetown. The inn has always been a sweet little secret, but it got even sweeter in 2003 after a thorough re-design of the hotel's furnishings and overall style. In the guest rooms, tall, milk chocolate–brown leather headboards crown the beds; comfortable armchairs have soft leather footstools; the armoire is ebony; the general color scheme is coppery gold, rust, and brown; and the cool chaise lounge unfolds into a sofa bed. (The architectural design team, Adamstein and Demetriou, is a married couple famous in DC for the many restaurant interiors the two have fashioned—from Austin Grill to Zaytinya.) Suites are spacious and all hold both a bed and the sleeper lounge, a large dressing room, and a separate kitchen equipped with the works, from gas stovetop to pots and pans. All but 28 suites combine the bedroom and living room areas, with a small dining table and chairs in a corner off the kitchen. Those 28 suites are roomy one-bedrooms, with an expansive living room (with sleep sofa) and a separate bedroom that holds a king-size bed and a second TV. Best are the one-bedroom suites on the upper floor that have views of the Potomac River. You can even spy the Washington Monument from some of the rooms, #804 for example.

Many corporate and government guests book long-term stays and benefit from special rates and amenities, such as free parking and complimentary continental breakfast. The River Inn has a modest exercise room and a tiny but rather nice and moderately priced restaurant, **Dish.** A complimentary *Washington Post* is delivered to your door daily.

924 25th St. NW, Washington, DC 20037. Ⓒ **888/874-0100** or 202/337-7600. Fax 202/337-6520. www.theriverinn.com. 126 suites. Weekdays $110–$179 single, $130–$199 double; weekends $99–$159 single, $119–$179 double. Extra person $20. Children under 16 stay free in parent's room. AE, DC, MC, V. Parking $20. Metro: Foggy Bottom. **Amenities:** Restaurant (American w/Southern flair) with bar; small fitness center with treadmill, stair climbers, stationary bike, and other equipment; room service during restaurant hours; coin-op laundry; same-day laundry/dry cleaning; 2 rooms for those with disabilities. *In room:* A/C, TV, 2-line phone w/dataport, kitchen, coffeemaker with coffee beans and grinder, hair dryer, iron, robes.

8 Georgetown/Glover Park

Georgetown Suites   This hotel was designed to meet the needs of business travelers making extended visits, but its casual atmosphere and suites with kitchens work well for families, too. It has two locations, within a block of each other.

The main building, which I prefer, is the one on 30th Street, a quiet residential street that's only steps away from Georgetown's action. This building offers a large lobby for hanging out; it almost feels like a student lounge, with the TV going; games, books, magazines, and daily newspapers scattered across table tops in front of love seats and chairs; and a cappuccino machine on the counter. In the morning, an extensive breakfast, featuring everything from waffles to fresh pastries, is laid out here. By contrast, the property on 29th Street (known as the "Harbor Building") is situated right next to the Whitehurst Freeway, is much noisier, and has a very small lobby (although you can linger outside in the brick courtyard where there are flowering plants and Victorian white wooden benches). Continental breakfast is served here, too, in the lobby.

Accommodations at both locations have living rooms, dining areas, and fully equipped kitchens. About half of the units are studios and half are one-bedroom suites. Glass-topped tables, chrome-framed chairs, and pastel-striped fabrics figure prominently in the decor. The biggest and best suites are the three two-level, two-bedroom town houses attached to the main building. Newly renovated, the town houses have brand-new furnishings, sunken Jacuzzi tubs and double sinks in the bathrooms, TVs with VCRs, CD players, and other deluxe features. These town houses have their own doors on 29th Street, through which you may exit only; to enter a town house, you must go through the hotel, as your key will not unlock the 29th Street door. This building also has two penthouse suites, which have their own terraces overlooking the rooftops of Georgetown.

1111 30th St. NW (just below M St.) and 1000 29th St. NW (at K St.), Washington, DC 20007. © **800/348-7203** or 202/298-1600. Fax 202/333-2019. www.georgetownsuites.com. 220 units. Weekdays $155 studio, $215 1-bedroom suite; weekends $155 studio, $185 1-bedroom suite; penthouse suites from $350; town houses from $425. Rollaways or sleeper sofa $10 extra. Rates include continental breakfast. AE, DC, DISC, MC, V. Limited parking $15. Metro: Foggy Bottom, with a 15-min. walk. **Amenities:** Small exercise room; coin-op laundry; same-day laundry/dry cleaning; 2 rooms for guests with disabilities, both with roll-in showers. *In room:* A/C, TV, 2-line phone w/dataport, full kitchen (with fridge, coffeemaker, microwave, and dishwasher), hair dryer, iron.

Holiday Inn Georgetown   This Holiday Inn does a brisk international business, stemming from its proximity to many embassies and the National Academy of Sciences, visited by scientists from around the world.

If you capture a cheap rate, say $99 to $125, you'll get a fairly good deal: a clean though rather small room with either a king bed and sofa bed, two double beds, or one double bed (all have firm mattresses), and a modest-sized bathroom. The rooms with one double bed are the smallest, so if you end up with one of these, feel free to ask if a larger room is available, since all rooms but the suites are the same price. All four of the suites are one-bedrooms. A renovation of the guest rooms completed in April 2003 gave the decor a sprightly look by replacing bed covers, linens, drapes, and carpeting with new ones in shades of red, blue, and gold. In addition, the rooms now offer Web TV. Bathrooms were last renovated in 2002, replacing tile, wallpaper, mirrors, and other items.

Your kids may stay free in the room with you, and, if they are under 12, they may eat for free when you order a meal.

To get the best rate, try all options and see which one unearths the best price: Call the hotel directly and request a promotional rate, check the hotel's website and bargain travel sites on the Internet, and call the Holiday Inn 800 number. You can get by without a car here, thanks to the daily shuttle service the hotel added in 2003. The free shuttle bus travels regularly between the hotel and the Foggy Bottom Metro station, and will take you anywhere within 2 miles of the hotel. If you're up for a stroll, you're about a 10- to 15-minute walk from the center of Georgetown in one direction, and from the Washington National Cathedral in the other direction.

2101 Wisconsin Ave. NW, Washington, DC 20007. ℭ **800/HOLIDAY** or 202/338-4600. Fax 202/333-6113. www.higeorgetown.com. 296 units. $99–$169 single or double; $129–$249 suites. Extra person $10. Children under 19 stay free in parent's room. Children under 12 eat free. AE, DC, DISC, MC, V. Parking $15. Bus: 30, 32, or 34 travel between Georgetown and downtown; free shuttle travels to Foggy Bottom Metro station and locations within 2-mile radius. **Amenities:** Restaurant (American); bar; exercise room; outdoor pool (summer only); room service during restaurant hours; coin-op washer/dryers, same-day laundry/dry cleaning; 2 rooms for those with disabilities, both with roll-in showers. *In room:* A/C, TV w/pay movies and Nintendo, 2-line phone w/dataport, coffeemaker, hair dryer, iron.

Hotel Monticello of Georgetown ✪ *Value*

This hotel gets a lot of repeat business from both corporate and leisure travelers, who appreciate the intimacy of a small hotel, including personalized service from a staff who greets you by name and protects your privacy. It's also a favorite choice for families celebrating weddings or graduations (both Georgetown and George Washington universities are close by); they sometimes book several suites, or maybe a whole floor. A major renovation in 2000 gutted the whole building and created a more upscale setting (this used to be the Georgetown Dutch Inn). Rooms now bring in much more light, thanks to layout and design changes, better use of windows, and the placement of French doors with frosted glass between rooms. You'll notice that the top sheet on your bed is monogrammed, the sofa in the living room folds out, and those are Hermès bath products in the marble bathrooms.

Accommodations are medium-size one- and two-bedroom apartment-like suites. Six of the suites are studios, in which the living room and bedroom are joined, and nine of them are duplex penthouses with 1½ bathrooms. Every suite has a wet bar with a microwave and refrigerator. The duplex penthouses have full kitchens. In addition to continental breakfast in the morning, fresh fruit, coffee, and herbal tea are available in the lobby all day.

The hotel is in the heart of Georgetown, surrounded by shops and restaurants. The C&O Canal towpath, just down the block, is ideal for jogging and cycling, though you should be wary at night.

1075 Thomas Jefferson St. NW (just below M St.), Washington, DC 20007. ℭ **800/388—2410** or 202/337-0900. Fax 202/333-6526. www.monticellohotel.com. 47 suites. Peak-season weekdays $149–$189, off-peak weekdays $129–$149; weekends, peak- and off-peak season, $109–$129. Call the hotel directly for best rates and to find out penthouse suite rates. Extra person $20. Rates include continental breakfast. Children under 14 stay free in parent's room. Promotional rates and discounts may be available. AE, DC, DISC, MC, V. Limited parking $10. Metro: Foggy Bottom, with a 20-min. walk, or take the Georgetown Shuttle. Bus: 32, 34, or 36 go to all major Washington tourist attractions. **Amenities:** Free access to nearby fitness center; business center; in-room massage; babysitting; same-day laundry/dry cleaning except Sun; 4 rooms for guests with disabilities, 3 with roll-in showers. *In room:* A/C, TV, 2-line phone w/dataport, kitchenette (w/microwave, fridge, and coffeemaker), hair dryer, iron.

Washington National Cathedral ✪

Of the various communal living options listed in this chapter, I consider the National Cathedral's the best. The setting is magnificent: You stay on the 57-acre grounds of the awesome Cathedral, which is surrounded by gardens, a greenhouse, woodlands, and walkways (see chapter 7 for more about the Cathedral as an attraction). The College of Preachers, on the campus of the cathedral, provides the overnight accommodations. The housing, which can accommodate 51 people, is in Tudor-style stone buildings, designed by National Cathedral architect team Frohman, Robb & Little, and erected in 1928. All of the rooms are air-conditioned and handsomely though simply furnished. There are 23 rooms and two suites in the main building, including five with private bathrooms and 20 sharing four hallway bathrooms; three rooms in the connecting guest house that share one huge bathroom and powder room; and four rooms in Woodley House (a separate building), one of which has a private bathroom. The main building holds the "Tower Suite," which has a separate bedroom with queen-size bed, a living room/study, and views of Washington—this is where the presiding Episcopalian bishop stays when in town; another suite with queen-size bed and sitting area; 11 rooms with a single twin bed; and 11 rooms with 2 twin beds. Most have a sink in the room, all have a desk and reading lamp, thick carpeting, and casement leaded glass windows, which can open. Adjacent and connected to the College of Preachers main building is the guest house, which can accommodate up to six people in its three rooms: one queen-bed and two twin-bed rooms. The guest house is on two levels and has a full kitchen, a sitting/dining room with TV and stereo, a huge bathroom and a powder room—this would be the best space for a family. Across the lane is the Woodley House, whose upstairs holds a room with a queen-size bed and twin daybed, with private bathroom; a double-bed room; and a room with two twin beds, which share a bathroom—also recommended for families.

The College of Preachers' main purpose is to teach preaching to students of all denominations from all over the world; it has been operating for more than 70 years. Its lodging is booked on a space-available basis to individuals, families, and small groups, for lodging, meetings, conferences, retreats, and the like. You enter the locked buildings by pressing a number-code on the key pad at the front door. Rooms have no way of being locked, however. If the kitchen is open during your stay, you may have meals in the grand Tudor-style dining room, which features a three-lancet stained glass window and huge fireplace. Breakfast is $11, continental breakfast (weekends only) $8, lunch $14, and dinner $22. You must schedule these meals in advance.

Smoking is not allowed.

The College of Preachers, at the Washington National Cathedral, 3510 Woodley Rd., NW, Washington, DC 20016. ℭ 202/537-6383. Fax 202/537-2235. www.pecf.org. 31 units, 6 with private bathroom. $78 single, $115 double, $150 suite. MC, V. Limited free parking on Cathedral grounds, street parking. Metro: Woodley Park–Zoo (a mile away), 30-series buses on Wisconsin Ave.

9 Woodley Park & Points North

You might consider the Woodley Park location of the **Kalorama Guest House,** at 2700 Cathedral Ave. NW (entrance on 27th St.; ℭ **202/328-0860**), which has 19 units, 12 with private bathrooms. Rates are $55 to $75 for a double with a shared bathroom, $75 to $100 for a double with private bathroom, and include continental breakfast. Limited parking is available for $7, and the Woodley Park–Zoo Metro stop is nearby. See p. 99 for the full listing for the main location of the Kalorama Guest House in Adams-Morgan for more information.

Connecticut Avenue Days Inn   A straight 10- to 15-minute Metro or bus ride up Connecticut Avenue from the heart of town will put you in this residential northwest D.C. neighborhood. Surrounded as it is by apartment and office buildings, shops, houses, and the University of the District of Columbia—with not another hotel in sight—the six-story Days Inn is somewhat of an anomaly. The last major renovation was in 1999, which replaced everything in the hotel, from carpeting to bathroom vanities to bedspreads. Guest rooms are basically of two types, rooms with two double beds or king-size beds and the slightly larger "executive business rooms," which hold a king-size bed and working area, small refrigerator, and microwave. The hotel is a minute's walk from the Red Line of the Metro, which takes you downtown, with stops along the way at the zoo and in neighborhoods like Cleveland Park and Dupont Circle.

Days Inn hotels offer all sorts of deals, honoring special rates for AAA and AARP members, rates for booking last minute and for reserving at least 29 days ahead. Though not always available, these promotions are always worth asking about. You can also look on the hotel's website for postings of special rates.

4400 Connecticut Ave. NW (between Yuma and Albemarle sts.), Washington, DC 20008. © 800/329-7466 or 202/244-5600. Fax 202/244-6794. www.thedaysinn.com/washington06507. 155 units. $89–$149 single or double; $119–$164 single or double executive business rooms. Extra person $10. Children under age 18 stay free in parent's room. Ask about discounts and promotions, and check for Internet rates. AE, DC, DISC, MC, V. Parking $12 plus 12% tax. Metro: Van Ness. **Amenities:** Restaurant (Italian); access to nearby gym (for $10 fee); room service during restaurant hours; dry cleaner next door offers same-day dry cleaning; 4 rooms for those with disabilities. *In room:* A/C, TV w/pay movies, dataport, coffeemaker, hair dryer, iron, safe.

SUPER-CHEAP SLEEPS

International Guest House   East of the Carter Barron Amphitheatre and Rock Creek Park you'll find this guest house, run by the Mennonite Church on a pleasant residential street. Since it opened in 1967, it has accommodated more than 44,000 guests from more than 150 countries—professionals, tourists, educators, and students. Americans are also welcome, but they can stay only 1 week (foreign guests are allowed to stay 2 weeks).

IGH is a friendly place. Guests mingle on the porch (where there's an old-fashioned swing) or in the comfortably furnished living/dining room, which is equipped with a piano and a variety of books and current magazines. There's also a basement lounge with a TV, a Ping-Pong table, a microwave oven, and a refrigerator. Tea and homemade cookies are served nightly at 9pm.

The no-frills rooms (three doubles and two triples, accommodating a total of 12 people at one time) are clean, adequately furnished, and carpeted. Guests share two bathrooms, one for men, one for women. A phone is in the hall. There is no maid service, but fresh bathroom towels are provided daily, bed linens on arrival and once a week.

Bus stops are less than a block away, and a 20-minute ride will take you downtown. The office is closed between 11pm and 7am, during which time the house is locked (this is not a good choice for late-night revelers). Single guests are expected to share a room with another person if the house is full. No smoking; no alcohol. Reserve far in advance.

1441 Kennedy St. NW, Washington, DC 20011. © 202/726-5808. Fax 202/882-2228. 5 units (none with private bathroom). Daily $30, weekly $190 (prices are subject to change). Rates include breakfast and taxes. Children age 6–16 pay half price, age 5 and under free. DISC, MC, V. Limited free parking; plentiful street parking in neighborhood. Bus: S2 or S4 buses go to the Mall and Metro Center. *In room:* A/C, no phone.

10 Suburban Maryland

The close-in Maryland suburbs have fewer hotels and motels than the nearby Virginia suburbs, but the Maryland neighborhoods are more residential and pleasant, which make them preferable, in my view. The properties listed below are in Bethesda, which has become famous for the number (more than 200) and quality of its restaurants, as well as its bars, coffee shops, and, increasingly, nightlife. Everything is within walking distance and it's a good thing, since finding a parking spot in Bethesda is now more difficult than finding one in downtown D.C.

American Inn of Bethesda Two miles south of the Capital Beltway (I-495) and within walking distance of the National Institutes of Health, the Bethesda Naval Hospital (although the motel runs free shuttles to both places), and the Bethesda Metro station, is this small motel, squeezed between taller office and hotel buildings. It's clean and has an outdoor pool and sun deck, which some rooms overlook. A renovation in 2001 replaced wall covering and carpeting in the hallways while a renovation in 2000 put new furniture in guest rooms. Most recently, the motel gutted its bathrooms and installed new sinks, toilets, tubs, wallpaper, lighting, hair dryers, the works.

There are 32 rooms with one double bed, 35 rooms with two double beds, four rooms with a king bed, and three rooms with a queen bed. Rooms with two double beds are largest and some can connect side by side with the next room. Biggest and best is one oversized room that has a queen-size Murphy bed, a queen-size sleep sofa, and a kitchen. All rooms have either a table and chairs or a desk and chair.

Off to the side of the front desk is a small, 24-hour business center that allows you free access to a computer, fax, copier, and e-mail and Internet services. The motel operates a courtesy van that travels to the Metro and nearby locations, such as the National Institutes of Health, weekdays 7:30am to 5pm, and weekends on a pre-arranged, as needed basis.

8130 Wisconsin Ave., Bethesda, MD 20814. © 800/323-7081 or 301/656-9300. Fax 301/656-2907. www. american-inn.com. 76 units. Weekdays $92–$190 single or double; weekends $86–$99 single or double. Corporate, military, government, travel club, group, and senior rates available; also ask about special promotions. Rates include continental breakfast. Extra person $5. Children under 18 stay free in parent's room. AE, DC, DISC, MC, V. Free limited parking. Metro: Bethesda. **Amenities:** Restaurant/bar (Mexican); outdoor pool; access to nearby health club ($5); business center; coin-op laundry; same-day dry cleaning. *In room:* A/C, TV, dataport, hair dryer, iron.

Bethesda Court Hotel ⊀ This polished, attractive property redesigned its lobby in 1999, creating a more welcoming space, and replaced all guest room bed linens, drapes, and carpeting in 2001. Thick white comforters now grace the beds. Designed around a shaded, nicely landscaped inner courtyard, the hotel takes up three floors. Twenty-five units have king-size beds, while each of the remaining units has two double beds. Each room includes a 25-inch TV, a desk and desk lamp, and a small reading chair with its own lamp and ottoman. This is a small, reasonably priced hotel with some deluxe hotel features, including a modest-size fitness room on the second floor with exercise bikes and stair climbers, tea and cookies served nightly in the breakfast room off the lobby, and a rug in the bathroom. A car rental agency (Enterprise) is across the street and the Metro is only a couple of blocks away. Like the American Inn, the Bethesda Court Hotel is 2 miles south of the Beltway, and within walking distance of the National Institutes of Health and the Bethesda Naval Hospital.

7740 Wisconsin Ave., Bethesda, MD 20814. © 800/874-0050 or 301/656-2100. Fax 301/986-0375. www.bethesdacourtwashdc.com. 74 units. Weekdays $159 single or double; weekends $119 single or double. Rates include continental breakfast. Children under 16 stay free in parent's room. AE, DC, DISC, MC, V.

Parking $8.50. Metro: Bethesda. **Amenities:** Fitness center; courtesy limo available 7am–11pm, on a first-come/first-served basis, taking you within a 3-mile radius; coin-op laundry, same-day dry cleaning; 1 room for those with disabilities. *In room:* A/C, TV w/pay movies, 2-line phone w/dataport, fridge, coffeemaker, hair dryer, iron, safe.

11 Suburban Virginia

Hotels and motels abound in the Virginia suburbs of Rosslyn, Arlington, Crystal City, and Alexandria. Here are some choices that are minutes away from the District and easily accessible by Metro.

Motel Fifty Rosslyn   Motel Fifty is located right on Route 50, and so you're going to hear traffic from most of the rooms. But this family-owned-and-operated property is clean, well-run, and friendly. A recent renovation replaced double beds with king-size beds in 10 of the rooms. An extensive continental breakfast is served in the lobby each morning, and free transfer is provided to and from National Airport on request. Many popular restaurants are close by.

1601 Arlington Blvd. (US 50), Arlington, VA 22209. © **800/504-4888** or 703/524-3400. Fax 703/524-0220. 38 units. www.motelfifty.com. Dec–Feb $65–$70; Mar–Nov $75–$80, for up to 4 people. Rates include continental breakfast. AE, DISC, MC, V. Free parking. Metro: Rosslyn. *In room:* A/C, TV.

Quality Inn Iwo Jima *Value*   At this pleasant, red-brick Quality Inn, the guest rooms are attractive and exceptionally comfortable, offering a choice of two double, one or two queen-size, or one king-size bed. Some rooms can connect, which families will appreciate. Though this property is also situated on Route 50, it's set back a bit, which makes all the difference in terms of traffic noise. Tourists and people here on government business make up most of the hotel's clientele. Local calls are free, a nice perk for budget travelers. **MacArthur's Cafe,** a moderately priced restaurant serving American and Italian fare, is decorated with World War II memorabilia. The *Washington Post* is available free in the lobby. The Metro is about 3 blocks away.

1501 Arlington Blvd. (US 50), Arlington, VA 22209. © **800/228-5151** or 703/524-5000. Fax 703/522-5484. www.qualityinniwojima.com. 141 units. High season $99 single, $109 double; off-season $69 single, $79 double. Extra person $10. Children under 18 stay free in parent's room. AE, DC, DISC, MC, V. Free indoor and outdoor parking. Metro: Rosslyn. Pets under 10 lbs. allowed. **Amenities:** Restaurant/bar (Italian/American); indoor heated pool; small fitness room; room service during restaurant hours; coin-op laundry; 12 rooms for those with disabilities. *In room:* A/C, TV w/pay movies, dataport, coffeemaker, hair dryer, iron.

12 Long-Term Stays

A number of the hotels listed in this chapter offer special rates for long-term stays, including the **River Inn** (p. 105), **George Washington University Inn** (p. 103), **Lincoln Suites** (p. 96), and the **Adams Inn** (p. 98). Bed-and-breakfasts often have a designated room or suite set aside for guests who need lodging for a week or longer.

If you don't have the time or inclination to track down acceptable lodging at a good rate, you can have one of Washington's local reservations services, **Capitol Reservations** (© **800/VISIT-DC** or 202/452-1270; www.hotelsdc.com) and **Washington, D.C. Accommodations** (© **800/554-2220** or 202/289-2220; www.dcaccommodations.com), go to bat for you to negotiate a long-term stay at an area hotel or inn. You are probably going to find your cheapest rates in shared lodging, however.

If you're planning on a long-term stay of at least a month, and possibly as long as a couple of years, and you prefer an apartment or house to a hotel, one way to beat the high cost of renting is to share. In a transient city like D.C., roommates come and go. At **Roommates Preferred** (℃ **202/965-4004;** www. roommatespreferred.com), Betsy Neal finds replacements. She keeps in close touch with clients, carefully screens applicants, and tries hard to match up compatible types. She's been doing it successfully for over 2 decades. A personal interview is required; you'll discuss preferences, pets, smoking, lifestyles, and more. Betsy has clients throughout D.C. and in nearby Maryland and Virginia. Rents for listed apartments and houses range from about $350 a month (probably for a house shared by three or four people) on up. The fee is $75, payable when you contact potential roommates. She has sublets from a month to several years. Open weekdays from 10am to 7pm; Saturday from 11am to 3pm.

Finally, if you are a student older than 21, or a young woman between the ages of 18 and 34, you should know about these two options:

International Student House ⭐ *Value*   ISH exists to foster international understanding and promote cross-cultural interaction. For students (over 21) and nationalities, ISH offers an unbeatable package—accommodations (some in a magnificent Tudor building) on a tree-lined street just a few blocks from Dupont Circle, low rates, terrific facilities—all in a relaxed non-institutional atmosphere. English is the official language of the house, so English-speaking guests can expect to share a room with foreign students, to encourage the learning of the language. About 15 of the 90 guests are usually American.

Residents share daily meals (breakfast and dinner) in the wood-paneled dining room, though in nice weather many dine alfresco in the garden. Public areas include an oak-paneled library, a comfortable TV room, and a rec room with Ping-Pong tables, a laundry room, and a lounge. Tea is served Sundays in the dining room. Some activities (nearby embassies often host lectures and musical programs) take place in the exquisite oak-paneled Great Hall, complete with Persian rugs, a grand piano, and a fireplace (copied from the one at Hatfield Hall, a residence of Queen Elizabeth I). Rooms in the Tudor mansion have leaded glass windows, while the newer rooms are more modern with painted concrete walls. Furnishings are modest but functional: bed, desk, chair, dresser, lamp, and bookcase, though phones do have voice mail. Rooms sleep one to four people, with men and women in separate quarters. Guests pay a one-time bed linen charge ($15) and bring their own towels or purchase them on the premises for $10. No maid service—you do your own cleaning. Smoking is allowed outside only.

1825 R St. NW, Washington, DC 20009. ℃ **202/232-4007.** Fax 202/387-4115. www.ishdc.org. 55 units, 5 with private bathroom, showers only. Monthly rates: $770 per person in 4-bed dorm room with shared bathroom, $861–$878 for a shared room with private bathroom, $1,012–$1,056 for a private room with shared bathroom. Daily rates sometimes available at $35–$65. Rates include breakfast and dinner. MC, V. Limited parking $100 a month. Metro: Dupont Circle. **Amenities:** Exercise room with treadmill, stationary bike, and weights; computer room with high-speed Internet connection, printers and connection for laptops; wireless connections available; recreation room w/VCR and table tennis; laundry facilities. *In room:* A/C.

Thompson-Markward Hall   This Capitol Hill accommodation, for women ages 18 to 34 only, was established in 1887. Eleanor Roosevelt dedicated its "new" wing in 1932. It still retains an old-fashioned—one might even say ladylike—ambience. Facilities include a rec room with a color TV and refrigerator, a comfortably furnished living room with a piano and working fireplace, a dining room with white-shuttered windows, a fairly extensive library, a laundry room, a sundeck, and a delightful garden. Guest rooms (mostly singles) are clean, but of the no-frills dormitory variety. Each is simply furnished with a twin bed, dresser, desk, armchair, bookcase, and floor lamp. Closet space is ample, bathrooms are in the hall, and guests provide their own sheets and towels. Female friends can spend the night on a cot in your room for $15, but men are not permitted in the rooms. There is always a waiting list, so reserve as far in advance as possible. Smoking is not permitted in the building. Minimum stay is 2 weeks, maximum 2 years.

235 2nd St. NE (between Maryland Ave. and C St.), Washington, DC 20002. ℂ **202/546-3255.** Fax 202/546-1197. 116 units (none with private bathroom). $308 for 2 weeks, $650 per month. Rates include breakfast and dinner Mon–Sat, brunch Sun. No credit cards. No parking. Metro: Union Station. **Amenities:** Rec room w/TV and fridge; laundry facilities; library. *In room:* A/C.

6

Great Deals on Dining

Washington, D.C., offers all kinds of great deals on dining, and I'm not talking about McDonald's or Burger King. You can choose to eat at a chain or fast food restaurant if you like, but you won't find such places listed in this chapter. No, I'd rather point you to the capital's home-grown, inexpensive eateries, to its restaurants that normally might be beyond your budget, except on vacation, when you're ready to splurge, and to special deals offered by some of Washington's best restaurants at specific times.

Some tips to keep in mind: Don't assume that you won't need a reservation at an inexpensive restaurant. Although most low-budget eateries seat diners on a casual, walk-in basis, some don't. My listings indicate whether a restaurant recommends that you make a reservation; if the listing says nothing on the subject, it means that the establishment does not accept them. For restaurants that do accept reservations, call ahead, especially for Saturday night, which books up especially fast. A number of restaurants are affiliated with an online reservation service called **www.opentable.com**, so

if you've got Internet access, you might reserve your table on the Web.

If you prefer spontaneity and decide to wait until the last minute to make a reservation, expect to dine really early, say 5:30 or 6pm, or really late (by Washington standards, 9:30pm qualifies as late—this is not a late-night town). Or you can sit at the bar and eat, which can be fun, and sometimes more affordable, if you're ordering from a bar menu.

If you're driving (which I would not recommend), call ahead to inquire about valet parking, complimentary or otherwise—on Washington's crowded streets, this service can be a true bonus. Be forewarned, however: when it's not complimentary, valet parking can be prohibitively expensive. Even more costly is parking lot or garage parking. Your other choices, to walk, Metro, or taxi to the restaurant, make more budget sense, and can be just as easy.

I've listed the closest Metro station to each restaurant only when it's within walking distance of a restaurant. If you need bus-routing information, call © 202/637-7000.

MORE ABOUT PRICES

The prices within each review refer to the cost of individual entrees, not the entire meal. You'll notice that the range of entree prices at some establishments, and not just those identified as "Worth a Splurge," start out affordable but top out at astronomical. You may have to be selective and creative to stay within your budget, choosing a menu item from the lower end of the dollar spectrum, sharing an entree, or making lunch your main meal.

Also, as mentioned above, consider the special deals offered by restaurants at specific times. For instance, DC Coast and TenPenh both serve an inexpensive light fare menu at the bar after 2:30pm; Luna Grill offers half-price pastas on Sunday and Monday nights after 5pm; and Bistro Français has a scrumptious three-course early bird/late night menu available nightly 5 to 7pm and 10:30pm to 1am. If you care about food, and you want to experience the Washington restaurant scene, these little maneuverings will be worth it.

1 Restaurants by Cuisine

AMERICAN

Art Gallery Bar & Grille (Downtown West, p. 131)

Ben's Chili Bowl (U Street Corridor, p. 135)

Breadline (Downtown West, p. 132)

Cashion's Eat Place ★★ (Adams-Morgan, p. 138)

The Childe Harold (Dupont Circle, p. 141)

Clyde's of Georgetown (Georgetown, p. 150)

Cup'A Cup'A (Foggy Bottom, p. 147)

Daily Grill ★ (Downtown West, Georgetown, p. 132)

DC Coast ★ (Downtown East, p. 129)

Dupont Grille ★ (Dupont Circle, p. 145)

Felix Restaurant and Lounge ★ (Adams-Morgan, p. 140)

15 Ria ★ (Downtown East, p. 129)

Firefly ★ (Dupont Circle, p. 142)

Garrett's (Georgetown, p. 150)

Kinkead's ★★★ (Foggy Bottom, p. 148)

Kramerbooks & Afterwords Café (Dupont Circle, p. 143)

Le Bon Café (Capitol Hill, p. 118)

Luna Grill & Diner (Dupont Circle, p. 144)

Mendocino Grille and Wine Bar ★ (Georgetown, p. 154

The Monocle ★ (Capitol Hill, p. 120)

Nectar ★★ (Foggy Bottom, p. 148)

Old Ebbitt Grill (Downtown East, p. 124)

Oval Room at Lafayette Square ★★ (Downtown West, p. 134)

Post Pub (Downtown East, p. 125)

Red Sage Border Café ★ (Downtown East, p. 125)

Reeves Restaurant & Bakery ★ (Downtown East, p. 127)

Tabard Inn ★ (Dupont Circle, p. 146)

Vidalia ★★ (Downtown West, p. 134)

ASIAN FUSION

Oodles Noodles (Downtown West, p. 133)

Perry's ★ (Adams-Morgan, p. 140)

Raku (Dupont Circle, p. 143)

Teaism (Dupont Circle, p. 144)

TenPenh ★★ (Downtown East, p. 130)

BARBECUE

Old Glory Barbecue (Georgetown, p. 152)

CHINESE

Ching Ching Cha (Georgetown, p. 153)

City Lights of China (Dupont Circle, p. 141)

Tony Cheng's Seafood Restaurant ★ (Downtown East, p. 126)

DELI

Booeymonger (Georgetown, p. 153)

Dutch Mill Deli (Dupont Circle, Downtown East, p. 127)

ETHIOPIAN

Meskerem (Adams-Morgan, p. 136)

Zed's (Georgetown, p. 152)

FRENCH

Bistro Français ★ (Georgetown, p. 150)

Bistrot D'OC ★★ (Downtown East, p. 127)

Key to Abbreviations: $$$$ = Very Expensive $$$ = Expensive $$ = Moderate $ = Inexpensive

THAI

Bangkok Bistro (Georgetown, p. 149)

Bua (Dupont Circle, p. 141)

Busara (Glover Park, p. 155)

Haad Thai (Downtown East, p. 121)

Sala Thai (Dupont Circle, p. 144)

VIETNAMESE

Miss Saigon (Georgetown, p. 152)

2 Capitol Hill

For information on eating at the Capitol and other government buildings, see the box titled "Dining at Sightseeing Attractions," on p. 118.

Café Berlin *Value* GERMAN   You have to walk past the dessert display on your way to your table at Café Berlin, so forget your diet. These delicious home-made confections are the best reason to come here. The vast spread might include an apple strudel, raspberry Linzer torte, sour-cherry crumb cake, or vanilla-custard cake. Look for items like the *rahm schnitzel,* which is a center cut of veal topped with a light cream and mushroom sauce, or a *wurstplatte* of mixed sausages, among the entrees. Seasonal items highlight asparagus in spring, game in the fall, and so on. Lunch is a great deal: a simple chicken salad on whole wheat sandwich (laced with tasty bits of mandarin orange), the soup of the day, and German potato salad, all for about $8. The owners and chef are German; co-owner Peggy Reed emphasizes that their dishes are "on the light side—except for the beer and desserts." This 18-year-old restaurant occupies two prettily decorated dining rooms on the bottom level of three joined Capitol Hill town-houses, whose front terraces serve as an outdoor cafe in warm weather.

322 Massachusetts Ave. NE. (Ⓒ) 202/543-7656. www.cafeberlindc.com. Reservations recommended. Soups, sandwiches, and salads $6.95–$11 at lunch; main courses $9.95–$23. AE, DC, DISC, MC, V. Mon–Thurs 11:30am–10pm; Fri–Sat 11:30am–11pm; Sun 4–10pm. Metro: Union Station.

Il Radicchio *Value* ITALIAN   What a great idea: Order a replenishable bowl of spaghetti for the table at a set price of $6.50, and each of you chooses your own sauce from a long list, at prices that range from $1.50 to $4. Most are standards, like the puttanesca with black olives, capers, garlic, anchovies, and tomato. My favorite is the radicchio, sausage, red wine, and tomato sauce. It's a great deal.

The kitchen prepares daily specials, like a sautéed fresh trout with sautéed green beans, and garlic and tomato sauce, as well as sandwiches, and an assortment of 14 wood-baked pizzas, with a choice of 26 toppings.

Ingredients are fresh and flavorful, the service quick and solicitous. The restaurant gets a lot of overworked and underpaid Hill staffers, who appreciate Il Radicchio's heartening food and low prices.

223 Pennsylvania Ave. SE. (Ⓒ) 202/547-5114. www.robertodonna.com. Reservations not accepted. Main courses $6.50–$19. AE, DC, DISC, MC, V. Mon–Thurs 11:30am–10pm; Fri–Sat 11:30am–11pm; Sun 5–10pm. Metro: Capitol South.

SUPER-CHEAP EATS

Burrito Brothers TEX-MEX   The Washington area is overflowing with taco joints now, but Burrito Brothers was one of the first. The eateries are small, with a few tables and chairs and stools at a window counter provided as a basic courtesy. But most people order and go with foil-wrapped tortillas crammed with the usual choices of grilled steak, chicken, beef, or pork, combined with beans and salsa. They're quite good for the price. You'll hear a lot of Spanish spoken while you're waiting in line—a good sign. A tip for eating with the least amount of

Dining at Sightseeing Attractions

With so many great places to eat in Washington, I have a hard time recommending those at sightseeing attractions. Most are overpriced and too crowded, even if they are convenient. But a few places stand out, for their admirable cuisine, noteworthy setting, or both.

Two restaurants within the Capitol building itself may be open to the public, with certain conditions: the **House of Representatives Restaurant** (also called the "Members' Dining Room") in Room H118, at the South end of the Capitol (© **202/225-6300**) and the **Senate Dining Room** in Room S110 on the first floor, at the North end of the Capitol (© **202/224-2350**). At the House of Representatives Restaurant, the food is all-American and its prices reasonable: everything from a cup of soup for $1.50, to entree salads for $8.50, to the favorite, crab cake platter, for $19. The Members' Dining Room is open when the House is in session, weekdays 8am to 2:30pm. Tuesday through Thursday lunch (11am–1:45pm), you may dine here only as the guest of a Member. You may dine here unaccompanied by a Member on Monday and Friday, and on any weekday for breakfast, or between 1:45 and 2:30pm. The Senate Dining Room's menu features American cuisine and "comfort food," such as meatloaf, grilled salmon, crab louis (a kind of crab salad), and lots of sandwiches; prices range from $9 to $22. You may dine in the Senate Dining Room weekdays between 1:30 and 2:30pm, as long as you dress appropriately, that is, in jacket and tie for men, no jeans or sloppy appearance for men or women, and you must present a letter from your senator confirming his or her invitation to you. Be sure to call and ask about other requirements.

You are always welcome (after you've gone through security, of course) in the eateries located in the Capitol office buildings across the street from the Capitol. You'll be surrounded by Hill staffers, who head to places like the immense, full-service **Rayburn House Office Building Cafeteria** (© **202/225-7109**), which is in the basement of the building, at 1st

mess: Don't remove the foil, but peel it down as you eat what's inside. Tortilla chips, salsas, tacos, and burritos are all recommended; in fact, the quesadillas are the only thing that's not.

The first Burrito Brothers opened in 1989, and now there are at least seven throughout the greater Washington area, including another on Capitol Hill in the Union Station Food Court (© 202/289-3652); one in Adams-Morgan at 2418 18th St. NW (© 202/265-4048); and one at Dupont Circle at 1718 Connecticut Ave. NW (© 202/332-2308). Days and hours of operation vary by location.

205 Pennsylvania Ave. SE. © 202/543-6835. Tacos, burritos, full plates, and side orders $1.85–$8. MC, V. Mon–Sat 11am–9pm. Metro: Capitol South.

Le Bon Café ★ *Finds* AMERICAN   If you're touring the Capitol Hill area, keep this tiny place in mind. It's open early, serves inexpensive, delicious food, and is frequented by Capitol Hill and Library of Congress staffers, whose conversation is peppered with the names of senators, congresspersons, and bills in Congress. The menu is not extensive, but satisfies, if you can be happy with a sandwich, salad,

Street and Independence Avenue SW. Adjoining the cafeteria is a carry-out that sells pizza and sandwiches. At the **Longworth Building Cafeteria,** Independence Avenue and South Capitol Street SE (© **202/225-0878**), you can grab a bite from a fairly nice food court. By far the best deal for visitors is the **Dirksen Senate Office Building South Buffet Room,** 1st and C streets NE (© **202/224-4249**). For just $11 per adult, $8.50 per child under 10, you can choose from a buffet that includes a carving station and eight other hot entrees; the price covers a nonalcoholic drink and dessert, too. The dining room is often crowded, but accepts reservations for parties of more than five. Other options include the Russell Carryout, in the basement of the Russell Building, and the Cannon Carryout, likewise, in the basement of the Cannon Building. All of these eateries are open weekdays only. The carryouts stay open until late afternoon, while the other dining rooms close at 2:30pm.

In the same neighborhood, two institutions offering great deals and fair views (of famous sights or people) at weekday lunch are the **Library of Congress**'s Cafeteria and its more formal Montpelier Room (© **202/707-8300**), where the lunch options usually cost under $10 per person; and the **Supreme Court**'s Cafeteria (© **202/479-3246**), where you'll likely spy a justice or two enjoying the midday meal.

Among museum restaurants, the ones that shine are the six-story Atrium Cafe in the **National Museum of Natural History** (© **202/357-2700**); the **National Gallery of Art**'s Sculpture Garden Pavilion Café (© **202/289-3360**) and Garden Café (© **202/216-2480**); and the **Phillips Collection**'s snug Café (© **202/387-2151**).

Finally, the **Kennedy Center**'s Roof Terrace Restaurant and the Hors d'Oeuvrerie (© **202/416-8555,** for both) offer theater-goers convenient, gourmet dining in glamorous settings. The Center's Roof Terrace and the KC Café take in dramatic views, since immense windows present a sweeping panorama of the Potomac River and Washington landmarks.

soup, or pastry. I like the smoked turkey club sandwich ("mesquite smoked turkey breast with lettuce, tomato, and bacon on farm bread") and the pumpkin ginger-bread for dessert. My husband, who discovered Le Bon Café, just off Pennsylvania Avenue, near the Library of Congress, enjoys the coffee and scones at breakfast, and lemon oregano chicken (with grilled peppers, onions, and pesto) grilled panini sandwich at lunch. The most expensive item is the grilled salmon Niçoise salad, for $6.95. Seating inside is minimal, with most people grabbing food to go; in pleasant weather, you can sit at outdoor tables.

210 2nd St. SE (at Pennsylvania Ave.). © **202/547-7200.** Breakfast items $1.25–$2.95. Salads/sandwiches/soups $2.45–$6.95. Mon–Fri 7:30am–5pm; Sat–Sun 8:30am–3:30pm. Metro: Capitol South.

WORTH A SPLURGE

La Colline 🎔🎔 FRENCH   This is the perfect spot for that breakfast fundraiser. Hill people like La Colline for its convenience to the Senate side of the Capitol, the great bar, the four private rooms, the high-backed leather booths that allow for discreet conversations, and, last but not least, the food. You'll always get a good meal here. The regular menu offers an extensive list of French standards, including salade Niçoise, terrine of foie gras, and fish—poached, grilled, or sautéed. Almost as long is the list of daily specials—the soft-shell crab is superb here in season, and so is the gratin of crayfish. Trout and salmon are smoked in-house—try them. The wine list concentrates on French and California wines; by-the-glass choices change with the season to complement the menu. Don't let the dessert cart roll past you; the apple pie is a winner, as is the restaurant, which has been in business for 22 years.

400 N. Capitol St. NW. ℭ 202/737-0400. www.restaurant.com/lacolline. Reservations recommended. Breakfast $5–$8.75; lunch main courses $12–$19; dinner main courses $12–$24. AE, DC, MC, V. Mon–Sat 7am–10pm. Metro: Union Station.

The Monocle ♠ *Finds* AMERICAN   A Capitol Hill institution, the Monocle has been around since 1960. This is a men-in-suits place, where the litter of briefcases resting against the too-close-together tables can make for treacherous navigating. But you might want to take a look at whose briefcase it is you're stumbling over, for its proximity to both the Supreme Court and the Capitol guarantees that the Monocle is the haunt of Supreme Court justices and members of Congress. At lunch you'll want to order either the hamburger, which is excellent, the tasty federal salad (field greens and tomatoes tossed with balsamic vinaigrette), the penne pasta with tomato-basil sauce and olives, or the white-bean soup, whenever it's on the menu. At dinner, consider the baked oysters or the pork-rib chop with pommery mustard sauce. Don't bother with the crab cakes. Service is old-style, all-male.

107 D St. NE. ℭ 202/546-4488. Reservations recommended. Lunch main courses $9–$18; dinner main courses $16–$29. AE, DC, MC, V. Mon–Fri 11:30am–midnight. Closed 2 weeks preceding Labor Day. Metro: Union Station.

Montmartre ♠ FRENCH   Montmartre's ambience is warmed by its décor— pale yellow-orange walls, exposed wood ceiling, cozy bar, and old wooden tables. The owners are French, and Montmartre is their little French restaurant offering big French pleasures: chicory salad tossed with crisped bacon and duck-gizzard confit, pistou, potato gratin, confit of guinea hen with Jerusalem artichokes, seared tuna with chopped red pepper and olives, hangar steak served over fingerling potatoes and topped with sautéed shallots and demi-glace sauce, and calves liver sautéed with smothered onions, bok choy, potato puree, and a balsamic vinegar sauce. Desserts, like the Alsatian apple tart, don't disappoint.

327 7th St. SE. ℭ 202/544-1244. Reservations recommended. Lunch main courses $12–$15; dinner main courses $15–$23. AE, DC, DISC, MC, V. Tues–Sun 11:30am–2:30pm; Sun 5:30–9pm; Tues–Thurs 5:30–10pm; Fri–Sat 5:30–10:30pm. Metro: Eastern Market.

3 Downtown, East of 16th Street NW

Andale ♠ MEXICAN   During a visit to the Yucatan peninsula a couple of years ago, chef Allison Swope was so taken with the cuisine of Oaxaca, Mexico, that upon her return to Washington she set about transforming her "robust American" restaurant, The Mark, into the inventive Mexican Andale (*andale* means "let's go!"). The menu features dishes that combine authentic regional Mexican cuisine with fresh and often nontraditional ingredients: sushi grade tuna marinated with achiote, garlic, Mexican oregano, and sour orange juice; *pato al mole Negro oaxaqueno,* which is roasted duck served over Mexican red rice with a nut-based sauce that includes dried chiles, garlic, tomatillos, chocolate, and cinnamon. The leg of lamb, which is roasted in avocado leaves and presented in a soupy sauce of lamb broth, thickened with garbanzo beans, carrots, and potatoes, is a standout. Not to miss: the smoky, spicy salsa picante appetizer and the Mexican-style doughnuts with dipping chocolate for dessert. The bar offers 35 brands of tequila and concocts an excellent margarita.

Avoid being shown to the windowless back room; opt instead for seating in either the storefront window for optimum people-watching (Andale is in the middle of downtown), or in the main dining room, where Mexican artwork now hangs. Great deal: Every Monday after 5pm, you can order a bottle of wine or champagne for half price with the order of an entree. Thursdays, 6:30 to 9:30pm, the restaurant features live music.

401 7th St. NW. (✆) 202/783-3133. www.andaledc.com. Reservations recommended. Lunch main courses $7–$14; dinner main courses $9–$22. AE, DC, DISC, MC, V. Mon–Sat 11:30am–3pm; Mon 5–9pm; Tues–Thurs 5–10pm; Fri–Sat 5–11pm; Mon–Fri bar stays open but no food is served, 3–5pm. Metro: Gallery Place or Archives/Navy Memorial.

Ella's ITALIAN   Like Matchbox (see review below), Ella's brings gourmet pizza to downtown D.C. Until these two restaurants opened, both in spring of 2003, this part of town had every kind of eating establishment except a good pizzeria. Ella helps fill the gap, its menu focused on wood-fired pizzas with toppings like the "soppressata": sausage, shaved fennel, roasted peppers, tomato, and Parmesan. You can also create your own pizza, choosing from at least 31 toppings that range from pinenuts to shrimp, at $1 to $1.50 per topping. Ella's also offers a choice of salads and appetizers. Everything's fresh. I prefer the pizzas and wider selection at Matchbox, but Ella's may suit you better if you're near the International Spy Museum and looking for a pleasant and uncrowded place for a bite—and a drink: Ella's also has a full bar.

901 F St. NW (on 9th St. between F and G sts.). (✆) 202/638-3434. www.ellaspizza.com. Pizzas $8–$12. AE, MC, V. Mon–Sat 11:30am–11pm. Metro: Gallery Place-9th St. exit.

Haad Thai THAI   The Washington area has lots of Thai restaurants, but not many are downtown. Fewer still offer such good food in such pretty quarters. Haad Thai is a short walk from the MCI Center, and surrounding hotels. Plants and a pink and black mural of a Thai beach decorate the dining room. The standards are the best, including *pad thai, panang gai* (chicken sautéed with fresh basil leaves in curry, with peanut sauce), satays, and deep fried snapper with spicy bean sauce. All dishes are flavorful and only mildly spicy; so speak up if you want your food spicier.

1100 New York Ave. NW (entrance on 11th St. NW). (✆) 202/682-1111. Reservations recommended. Lunch main courses $5–$9; dinner main courses $8–$17. AE, DC, MC, V. Mon–Fri 11:30am–2:30pm and 5–10:30pm; Sat noon–10:30pm; Sun 5–10:30pm. Metro: Metro Center.

Jaleo (★) (Finds) SPANISH   In theater season, Jaleo's dining room fills and empties each evening according to the performance schedule of the Shakespeare Theater, right next door. Lunchtime always draws a crowd from nearby office buildings and the Hill. This restaurant, which opened in 1993, may be credited with initiating the tapas craze in Washington. The menu lists about 55 tapas, including a very simple but not-to-be-missed grilled bread layered with a paste of fresh tomatoes and topped with anchovies; savory warm goat cheese served with toast points; a skewer of grilled chorizo sausage atop garlic mashed potatoes; and a delicious mushroom tart served with roasted red-pepper sauce. Paella is among the few heartier entrees (it feeds four). Spanish wines, sangrias, and

Capitol Hill, Downtown & Foggy Bottom Dining

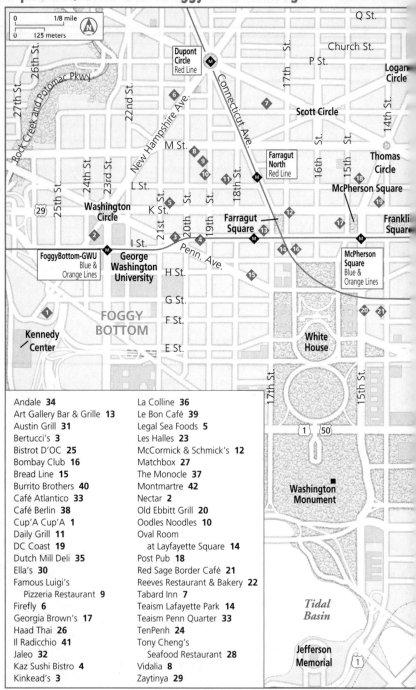

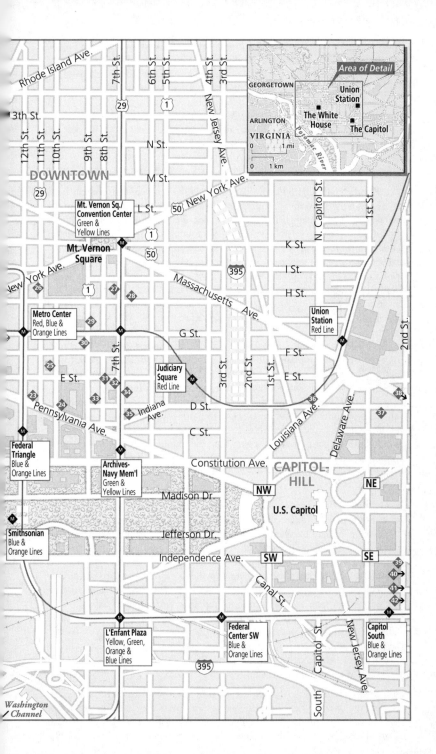

sherries are available by the glass. Finish with a rum-and-butter–soaked apple charlotte in bread pastry or a plate of Spanish cheeses. The casual-chic interior focuses on a large mural of a flamenco dancer inspired by John Singer Sargent's painting *Jaleo*. On Wednesday at 8 and 9pm, flamenco dancers perform.

A second and even prettier Jaleo is located in the suburbs, at 7271 Woodmont Ave., Bethesda, Maryland (☎ 301/913-0003). Though this new branch is within walking distance of my house, I prefer the ambience of the original D.C. location.

480 7th St. NW (at E St.). ☎ 202/628-7949. Reservations accepted until 6:30pm. Lunch main courses $7.50–$11; dinner main courses $11–$28; tapas $3.95–$7.95. AE, DC, DISC, MC, V. Sun–Mon 11:30am–10pm; Tues–Thurs 11:30am–11:30pm; Fri–Sat 11:30am–midnight. Metro: Archives or Gallery Place.

Les Halles FRENCH/STEAK We took our French exchange student here, and guess what she ordered: steak *frites*. I did the same. In fact, everyone in the restaurant was devouring the *onglet* (a boneless French cut hangar steak hard to find outside France), steak au poivre, steak tartare, New York sirloin, and other cuts, all of which come with *frites,* which are a must. (Actually, two diners at our table ordered ravioli and a chicken salad, and boy were they sorry.) The menu isn't all beef, but it is classic French, featuring cassoulet, *confit de canard* (duck confit), escargots, onion soup, *choucroutte garni* (sauerkraut with garnishes), and an irresistible *frisée aux lardons* (a savory salad of chicory studded with hunks of bacon and toast, smeared thickly with Roquefort). Should you spy something on the menu that's not Gallic, ignore it.

Les Halles is big and charmingly French. The banquettes, pressed-tin ceiling, mirrors, wooden floor, and side bar capture the feel of a brasserie. A vast window front overlooks Pennsylvania Avenue and the awning-covered sidewalk cafe, which is enclosed in cold weather and is a superb spot to dine year-round. Every July 14, this is the place to be for the annual Bastille Day race, which Les Halles hosts. (Sometimes the event is held close to Bastille Day, if not on the exact day of celebration; see the "Calendar of Events," in chapter 2, for details.) Les Halles is a favorite hangout for cigar smokers, but the smoking area is well ventilated.

1201 Pennsylvania Ave. NW. ☎ 202/347-6848. www.leshalles.net. Reservations recommended. Lunch main courses $9.50–$26; dinner main courses $11–$26. AE, DC, DISC, MC, V. Daily noon–midnight. Metro: Metro Center or Federal Triangle.

Matchbox ☆ ITALIAN This restaurant occupies three floors of a skinny town house in Chinatown, an odd place to find a pizzeria, maybe, but welcome, nonetheless. Matchbox opened in the spring of 2003 and has been popular from the get-go. The key thing here is the wood-fired brick oven, which bakes the thin pizza crust at temperatures as high as 900 degrees. You can choose a regularly featured pizza, like the "prosciutto white," which is topped with prosciutto, kalamata olives, fresh garlic, ricotta cheese, fresh mozzarella, and extra virgin olive oil; or you can request your own set of toppings, from smoked bacon to artichoke hearts. Matchbox is actually a cut above a pizzeria, for it also serves super salads, appetizers, sandwiches, and entrées, and it has a full bar.

713 H St. NW (between 7th and 8th sts.). ☎ 202/289-4441. www.matchboxdc.com. Pizzas and sandwiches $8–$17; main courses at lunch and dinner $13–$21. AE, MC, V. Mon–Sat 11:30am–10pm. Metro: Gallery Place-Chinatown.

Old Ebbitt Grill AMERICAN You won't find this place listed among the city's best culinary establishments, but you can bet it's included in every tour book. It's an institution. The original Old Ebbitt was established in 1856, at 14th and F streets, around the corner. The Grill moved to this location in 1980, bringing much of the old place with it. Among its artifacts are animal trophies bagged by Teddy Roosevelt, and Alexander Hamilton's wooden bears—one with a secret compartment in which it's said he hid whiskey bottles from his wife. The Old Ebbitt is attractive, with Persian rugs strewn on beautiful oak and marble floors, beveled mirrors, flickering gaslights, etched-glass panels, and paintings of Washington scenes. The long, dark mahogany Old Bar area emphasizes the men's saloon ambience.

Tourists and office people fill the Ebbitt during the day, flirting singles take it over at night. You'll always have to wait for a table if you don't reserve ahead. The waiters are friendly and professional in a programmed sort of way; service could be faster. Menus change daily but always include certain favorites: burgers, trout Parmesan (Virginia trout dipped in egg batter and Parmesan cheese, deep-fried), crab cakes, and oysters (there's an oyster bar). The tastiest dishes are usually the seasonal ones, with the fresh ingredients making the difference.

675 15th St. NW (between F and G sts.). (C) 202/347-4801. Reservations recommended. Breakfast $6.95–$9.95; brunch $5.95–$14; lunch main courses $6.95–$14 (as much as $25 when crab cakes are on the menu); dinner main courses $14–$21 (again, up to $25 for crab cakes); burgers and sandwiches $6.95–$11; raw bar $8.95–$19. AE, DC, DISC, MC, V. Mon–Thurs 7:30am–2am; Fri 7:30am–3am; Sat 8:30am–3am; Sun 9:30am–2am (kitchen closes at 1am nightly; raw bar open every night until midnight). Metro: McPherson Square or Metro Center.

Post Pub AMERICAN   This fits into the comfortable shoe category. Situated between Vermont and 15th streets, across from the offices of the *Washington Post,* the place gets busy at lunch, grows quiet in the afternoon, and picks up again in the evening, but it's never empty. The menu is just what you'd hope for in a pub, listing things like onion rings, sandwiches, and chicken parmigiana, steak, and the occasional fish dish—say haddock. The portions are generous and the food, well, it ain't bad, you know? Old-fashioned black banquettes, booths with coat-hook poles, faux wood paneling, mirrored beer insignias, a jukebox, cigarette machines, and a long bar with tall stools, are the furnishings. Draft beer specials are available 3 to 5pm nightly; happy-hour specials are available from 5 to 8pm nightly and vary: for instance, Friday evenings, "Anything Absolute" is the cry—any drink made with Absolut vodka goes for $3.50.

1422 L St. NW. (C) 202/628-2111. Sandwiches $5.95–$9.25; main courses $7.50–$16. AE, DC, DISC, MC, V. Mon–Fri 11am–midnight; Sat 11am–7 or 8pm. Metro: McPherson Sq.

Red Sage Border Café ✪ AMERICAN/SOUTHWESTERN   Downstairs is the expensive, more formal Grill, upstairs the cowboy-comfortable Border Café and its inexpensive light fare, which, by the way, is available all day, since the café stays open from lunch, into the night. We've liked the sweetish State of the Union chili, which features red beans and bits of bacon; the salmon tacos, for which the salmon has been marinated and grilled; and the hickory-grilled chicken quesadillas. The food is delicious and plentiful, each order accompanied by either coleslaw or cowboy beans. The decor is whimsically Western, with booths held up by horseshoes fashioned into legs and light fixtures designed (according to our waiter) by a descendant of the 19th-century American frontiersman Kit Carson.

Alcoholic drinks add considerably to the cost, naturally. Margarita aficionados should stick with the regular offerings. The occasional two-sip specials aren't different enough to warrant the higher price.

605 14th St. NW (at F St.). (C) 202/638-4444. www.redsage.com. Border Café main courses $6–$15. AE, DISC, MC, V. Mon–Sat 11:30am–11:30pm; Sun 5:30–10pm. Metro: Metro Center.

Tony Cheng's Seafood Restaurant ★ CHINESE/SEAFOOD   Most of the restaurants in Chinatown look seedy, no matter how good the food might be. In the past, I've recommended **Full Kee,** which was exceptional and a favorite of some of the best chefs around town, who would stop there for a bite after their own restaurants had closed for the night. As I write this, Full Kee is undergoing a renovation, but it will have reopened by the time you read this. Let's hope that its appearance has improved but that its food has remained the same. So, check it out, if you like: Full Kee is located at 509 H St. (✆ **202/371-2233**). But back to Tony Cheng's: this is the most presentable of Chinatown's eateries, and also a good choice if you like Cantonese specialties and spicy Szechuan and Hunan cuisine. The restaurant has been here for 27 years and has earned a reputation for its Cantonese roast duck (see it for yourself before ordering, since it is displayed in a case at the back of the restaurant); lobster or Dungeness crab, stir-fried and served with either ginger and scallions or black bean sauce; or Szechuan crispy beef, to name just a few.

619 H St. NW (between 6th and 7th sts.). ✆ 202/371-8669. Reservations recommended. Lunch main courses $8–$14; dinner main courses $10–$32. AE, MC, V. Sun–Thurs 11am–11:30pm; Fri–Sat 11am–midnight. Metro: Gallery Place-Chinatown.

Zaytinya ★★★ GREEK/TURKISH/LEBANESE   Honest, I would have liked Zaytinya even if my waiter, Isa, hadn't told me I had beautiful eyes. Isa also has beautiful eyes, by the way. All right, down to business. Zaytinya, which opened October 2002, is Washington's hottest new restaurant, and if you don't believe me, take it from *Conde Nast Traveler* magazine, whose May 2003 issue named Zaytinya as one of the top 75 new restaurants in the world. Executive chef Jose Andres is behind it all (see reviews of Jaleo, p. 121, where he continues as the executive chef/partner, and of Café Atlantico, p. 128, where he is the creative director). Zaytinya is a big restaurant and it stays busy all the time. The place takes reservations only at lunch and for pretheater dinners, 5 to 6:30pm, which is why the restaurant hands out beeper-discs if there's a long wait for a table. Zaytinya was hopping on the Sunday night we were there, but fortunately we didn't have a wait. Once seated, we received a basket of hot and billowy thin shells of pita bread, along with a saucer of olive oil swirled with pomegranate syrup. Isa guided us through the menu, explaining that the wine list was almost entirely Greek, that Zaytinya is Turkish for "olive oil," and pointing out which mezze dishes he would recommend. Although the dinner menu lists several entrees, what you want to do here is order lots of little dishes. We savored the zucchini-cheese cakes, which came with a caper and yogurt sauce; the carrot-apricot-pine nut fritters, served with pistachio sauce; sardines; a marinated salmon; *fattoush,* or salad of tomatoes and cucumbers mixed with pomegranate reduction, sumac, and olive oil, with crispy pita bread croutons; and shrimp with tomatoes, onions, ouzo, and kefalofraviera cheese. Many of these flavors were new to my palette, but I found everything to be wonderfully delicious. For dessert, we ordered a Turkish coffee chocolate cake, and the more exotic Medjool dates roasted in Vinsanto (a kind of dessert wine), rolled in crushed orange shortbread, with olive oil ice cream. The dates were our favorite. Isa was quite proud of us.

701 9th St. NW (at G St.). ✆ 202/638-0800. www.zaytinya.com. Reservations at lunch and pretheater dinner 5–6:30pm. Mezze items $3.75–$8; main courses at dinner $13–$17. AE, DC, DISC, MC, V. Sun–Mon 11:30am–10pm; Tues–Thurs 11:30am–11:30pm; Fri–Sat 11:30am–midnight. Metro: Gallery Place/Chinatown (9th St. exit).

SUPER-CHEAP EATS

Dutch Mill Deli DELI   Because the Dutch Mill roasts its turkey in-house, look for anything turkey on the menu, in sandwiches, salads, or soup; these are excellent. Also recommended are the ham and roast beef sliced to order, and the fresh desserts and homemade soups, thick french fries, and homemade potato salad. An extensive salad bar offers fresh fruit, greens, and pasta salads, and a hot bar displays about 10 items daily. There's a full bar. At breakfast you can enjoy a stack of pancakes or Belgian waffles here. The Dutch Mill has a few outdoor tables in addition to its first floor room and upstairs bar. The National Archives Building is diagonally across the street.

A second Dutch Mill Deli is located at 1349 Connecticut Ave. NW (© 202/ 293-7331), in the Dupont Circle neighborhood.

639 Indiana Ave. NW (between 6th and 7th sts.). © **202/347-3665.** Main courses $4.75–$5.50; salad-bar/hot-bar selections $4 a pound. AE, DC, MC, V. Mon–Fri 7am–3pm (bar open until 8:30pm). Metro: Archives.

Reeves Restaurant & Bakery ★ AMERICAN   There's no place like Reeves, a Washington institution since 1886, although in a new building since 1992. J. Edgar Hoover used to send a G-man to pick up chicken sandwiches, and Lady Bird Johnson and daughter Lynda Bird worked out the latter's wedding plans over lunch here. It's fronted by a long bakery counter filled with scrumptious pies and cakes. Brass-railed counter seating on both floors uses the original 19th-century wooden stools. The ambience is cheerful, and much of the seating is in cozy booths and banquettes.

Everything is homemade with top-quality ingredients: the turkey, chicken, salads, breads, desserts, even the mayonnaise. At breakfast, you can't beat the all-you-can-eat buffet: scrambled eggs, home fries, French toast, pancakes, dough-nuts, corned-beef hash, grits, bacon, sausage, stewed and fresh fruit, biscuits with sausage gravy, and more. Hot entrees run the gamut from golden-brown Maryland crab cakes to country-fried chicken with mashed potatoes and gravy. Reeves' pies are famous: strawberry, peach, chocolate cream, you name it. No alcoholic beverages are served.

1306 G St. NW. © **202/628-6350.** Main courses and sandwiches starting at $7; buffet breakfast $6.95. MC, V. Mon–Sat 7am–6pm. Metro: Metro Center.

WORTH A SPLURGE

Bistrot D'OC ★★ FRENCH   Spring 2003 was perhaps not the most propitious time for Bernard and Thasanee Grenier to open their French bistro, simply because 10th Street, where the new restaurant is located, was a mess of construction (let's hope everything is back to normal by the time you read this). The torn-up road, however, did not deter fans of the Grenier family, who for 20 years owned the French restaurant, La Miche, in the Maryland suburb of Bethesda. Business was brisk at Bistrot D'OC from the start, and we were among the first to delight in the hangar steak and pommes frites, mussels in cream sauce, bouillebaisse, and a special salad of haricots verts, avocado, and tomato, with a mustard vinaigrette. The cuisine represents the tastes of Bernard's native Languedoc, in southwestern France, and the red and yellow washed walls call to mind the colors found in that part of the country. An extensive wine list includes selections from the Languedoc region.

518 10th St. NW (between E and F sts. NW). © **202/393-5444.** Reservations recommended. Lunch main courses $9.95–$17; dinner main courses $14–$22. AE, DC, DISC, MC, V. Mon–Sat 11:30am–2:30pm; Sat–Sun 11:30am–4:30pm (brunch); Mon–Thurs 5:30–10pm; Fri–Sat 5:30–11:30pm; Sun 4:30–8:30pm. Metro: Metro Center.

Vegetarian Times

You know when a restaurant called Old Glory Barbeque starts to list a "veggie skewer" entree on its menu that vegetarianism has officially entered the mainstream of American eating habits. And it's clear that restaurants are ready to accommodate non-meat-eaters, recognizing that vegetarians like to dine out as much as carnivores. In addition to Old Glory's entree (which, by the way, is a skewer of marinated oak-grilled vegetables with barbecue vinaigrette, for $8.95), here are some other restaurants whose menus cater to vegetarians. See individual listings within this chapter for full descriptions of each establishment.

On the upscale end of the spectrum is **Café Atlantico** (see below), whose Latino dim sum "all you can eat" brunch on Saturday and Sunday, 11:30am to 2:30pm, is a favorite for vegetarians, since the brunch offers a vegetarian tasting menu of close to 20 dishes, from avocado with corn nuts to spinach with pumpkin seeds. The price is $25 per person.

Indian restaurants are always a good bet for vegetarians. The **Bombay Club** (p. 131) offers a full page of nine vegetarian entrees, everything from a mixed-vegetable curry to spinach and lentil dumplings simmered in a yogurt and herb sauce. **Zaytinya** (p. 126), which opened in 2003, is a hit among vegetarians and carnivores alike, for its mouthwatering Greek, Turkish, and Lebanese little dishes: zucchini cheese patties, cucumber and tomato salad, carrot-apricot–pine nut fritters, and other interesting Middle Eastern items. Other ethnic restaurants worth checking out are the inexpensive Italian cafe **Pasta Mia** (p. 136), Ethiopian restaurant **Meskerem** (p. 136), and the **Lebanese Taverna** (p. 156), great options all.

Café Atlantico ★★ *Finds* LATIN AMERICAN   This place rocks all week long, but especially on weekend nights, it's a favorite hot spot in Washington's still-burgeoning downtown. The colorful three-tiered restaurant throbs with Latin, calypso, and reggae music, and everyone is having a fiesta—including, it seems, the waiters. If the place is packed, try to snag a seat at the second-level bar, where you can watch the genial bartender mix the potent drinks for which Café Atlantico is famous: the *caipirinha,* made of limes, sugar, and *cachacha* (sugar-cane liqueur); the *mojito,* a rum and crushed mint cocktail; or the passion-fruit cocktail, a concoction of passion-fruit juice, ginger, and jalapeño mixed with mandarin orange-flavored vodka. But take a gander at the remarkable, award-winning wine list, too—it boasts 110 selections, mostly from South America, with many bottles priced under $30.

Seated at the bar or table, you'll watch as your waiter makes fresh guacamole right before your eyes. As for the main dishes, you can't get a more elaborate meal for the price. Check out the ceviche; duck confit quesadilla with roasted red onions; and seared scallops with coconut crispy rice and ginger, squid, and squid ink oil (though the menu changes, you're sure to find these or their equivalent listed). Tropical side dishes and pungent sauces produce a burst of color on the plate. Feel free to ask your friendly waiter for guidance.

405 8th St. NW. $\copyright$ **202/393-0812.** www.cafeatlanticdc.com. Reservations recommended. Lunch main courses $9–$15; dinner main courses $18–$24; pretheater menu $22 (5–6:30pm); Latino dim sum: you can choose a la carte items, or pay $25 for a vegetarian all you can eat meal, or $35 for a deluxe version (Sat 11:30am–2:30pm). AE, DC, DISC, MC, V. Mon–Fri 11:30am–2:30pm; Sun brunch 11:30am–3pm; Sun–Thurs 5–10pm; Fri–Sat 5–11pm. The bar stays open late on weekends. Metro: Archives–Navy Memorial or Gallery Place/MCI Center.

DC Coast $\star$ AMERICAN   The dining room is sensational: two stories high, with glass-walled balcony, immense oval mirrors hanging over the bar, and a full-bodied stone mermaid poised to greet you at the entrance. Gather at the bar first to feel a part of the loud and trendy scene; while you're there, why not nosh on something from the bar menu, perhaps the crispy fried calamari or maybe a luscious pork spring roll? This continues to be one of the city's most popular restaurants, so call way ahead to book a reservation. Chef Jeff Tunks is famous for his Chinese-style smoked lobster with crispy fried spinach—you'll almost always find it on the menu here. Other entrees that I recommend include the pan-seared sea scallops with braised beef short ribs, and the fish filet encrusted with portobello paste and served with truffled potatoes and porcini broth. Seafood is a big part of the menu, but there are a handful of meat dishes, too. **TenPenh** is another popular Tunks restaurant (p. 130) and by the time you read this, another Tunks eatery, the South American **Ceiba,** will have opened.

1401 K St. NW. $\copyright$ **202/216-5988.** www.dccoast.com. Reservations recommended. Lunch main courses $14–$19; dinner main courses $19–$29; light fare $7–$12. AE, DC, DISC, MC, V. Mon–Fri 11:30am–2:30pm; Mon–Thurs 5:30–10:30pm; Fri–Sat 5:30–11pm (light fare Mon–Thurs 2:30–10:30pm, Fri 2:30–11pm, Sat 5:30–11pm). Metro: McPherson Square.

15 Ria $\star$ AMERICAN   If you're staying at the Washington Terrace, the hotel in which this restaurant is located, you will want to dine here, but even if you're not an overnight guest, the restaurant is a good choice. Fifteen Ria (the acronym for the address: Rhode Island Avenue) serves comfort food, dressed up a little: the burger is on brioche, the Caesar salad alternates layers of romaine with bacon and cherry tomatoes, and the beef short ribs are sweetened with molasses. The restaurant, another newcomer, is becoming known for its nightly specials and for its bar, where drinks are concocted with fresh fruit and juices and the bar menu features some of the best onion rings, popcorn shrimp, and calamari in town. This restaurant also regularly advertises special enticements, like the one offered from July through September of 2003: every party arriving for Sunday brunch with a church program in hand received a complimentary basket of freshly baked pastries and breads—sticky buns, croissants, scones, and muffins—one basket per table.

1515 Rhode Island Ave. NW (at Scott Circle and 15th St.). $\copyright$ **202/742-0015.** Reservations recommended. Lunch main courses $9–$18; dinner main courses $12–$30; light fare $5–$11. AE, DC, DISC, MC, V. Mon–Fri 6:30–11am; Sat–Sun 7–11am; Mon–Fri 11am–2:30pm; light fare weekdays 2:30–5:30pm; Sat–Sun 11:30am–5:30pm; Sun–Thurs 5:30–10:30pm; Fri–Sat 5:30–11:30pm. Metro: Dupont Circle or McPherson Square.

Georgia Brown's $\star$ SOUTHERN   In Washington restaurants, seldom do you find such a racially diverse crowd. The harmony may stem from the waiters, whose obvious rapport results in gracious service, and certainly extends from the open kitchen, where the chef directs his multicultural staff. But in this large, handsome room, whose arched windows overlook McPherson Square, the food might capture all of your attention. A plate of corn bread and biscuits arrives, to be slathered with butter that's been whipped with diced peaches and honey. The menu is heavily Southern, with the emphasis on the Low Country cooking of

Kids   Family-Friendly Restaurants

Nearly every restaurant welcomes families these days, starting, most likely, with the one in your hotel. Chinese restaurants are always a safe bet, and so are these:

Austin Grill (p. 155)   An easygoing, good-service joint, with great background music. Kids will probably want to order from their own menu here, and their drinks arrive in unspillable plastic cups with tops and straws.

Legal Sea Foods (p. 133)   Believe it or not, this seafood restaurant has won awards for its kids' menu. It features the usual macaroni and cheese and hot dogs, but also kids' portions of steamed lobster; fried popcorn shrimp; a small fisherman's platter of shrimp, scallops, and clams; and other items, each of which comes with fresh fruit and a choice of baked potato, mashed potatoes, or french fries. Prices range from $3.95 for the hot dog to $16 for the 1-pound lobster.

Famous Luigi's Pizzeria Restaurant (p. 132)   Introduce your kids to pre-Domino's pizza. Luigi's, which has been around since 1943, serves the real thing: big, thick, ungreasy pizza, with fresh toppings. You sit at tables covered in red-checked cloths that have probably withstood countless spilled drinks and splotches of tomato sauce in their time. The restaurant gets noisy, so chances are that any loud ones in your party will blend right in.

Old Glory Barbecue (p. 152)   A loud, laid-back place where the waiters are friendly without being patronizing. Go early, since the restaurant becomes more of a bar as the evening progresses. There is a children's menu, but you may not need it—the barbecue, burgers, muffins, fries, and desserts are so good that everyone can order from the main menu.

South Carolina and Savannah: collards, grits, and lots of seafood, especially shrimp dishes. The Charleston *perlau* is a stewlike mix of duck, spicy sausage, jumbo shrimp, and rice, topped with toasted crumbs and scallions. It has bite but isn't terribly spicy. For something totally decadent, try the buttermilk batter-fried chicken. Georgia Brown's is famous for its Sunday brunch, lively with the sounds of jazz and conversation, and luscious with the tastes of country sausage, omelets made to order, creamy grits, and many other dishes.

950 15th St. NW. © 202/393-4499. www.gbrowns.com. Reservations recommended. Lunch main courses $7–$20; dinner main courses $15–$23; Sun jazz brunch $24. AE, DC, DISC, MC, V. Mon–Thurs 11:30am–10:30pm; Fri 11:30am–11:30pm; Sat 5:30–11:30pm; Sun 10:30am–2pm (brunch) and 5–10:30pm. Metro: McPherson Square.

TenPenh ★★ ASIAN FUSION   We'd heard that the service was excellent here, and in its early days this proved to be true: Our waiter actually split a glass of wine for me and my friend, when we both wanted a little more, but not an entire additional glass. And then our waiter checked out someone we thought was Rob Lowe in the bar, reporting back to us, alas, that it was not he. But service is not what it used to be, or so it seemed when we dined here recently, and waited quite a while for dinner to arrive. The atmosphere is still lively, however, and the food is still stellar. This is one of those restaurants that has a separate, loungy, hard-to-leave bar, but the dining room itself is inviting, with soft lighting, comfortable booths, and an open kitchen. In this, his second restaurant (DC Coast [p. 129] is his other, and a third, Ceiba, is slated to open in late 2003), Jeff Tunks presents translations of dishes he's discovered in travels throughout Asia: smoked salmon and crisp wonton napoleon (which actually had too much salmon); 5 spice pecan crusted halibut; Chinese style smoked lobster; wok-seared calamari; and dumplings filled with chopped pork and crab. We finished with a trio of crème brûlée, the best of which was the coffee-crème.

1001 Pennsylvania Ave. NW (at 10th St.). ℂ 202/393-4500. www.tenpenh.com. Reservations recommended. Lunch main courses $13–$17; dinner main courses $13–$28. AE, DISC, MC, V. Mon–Fri 11:30am–2:30pm; Mon–Thurs 5:30–10:30pm; Fri–Sat 5:30–11pm. Metro: Archives–Navy Memorial.

4 Downtown, 16th Street NW & West

Art Gallery Bar & Grille MIDDLE EASTERN/AMERICAN   This charming Art Deco eatery is popular with local lawyers, lobbyists, bankers, and government employees. Wall space is used to exhibit works of local artists. In warm weather you can dine alfresco in a canopied cafe with wrought-iron garden furnishings amid planters of greenery.

The owners make everything from scratch: fresh-cooked turkey and chicken, homemade salads, oven-fresh desserts, and more. Daily specials might include anything from a sandwich of grilled chicken breast, avocado, and sprouts on focaccia to kefta (fingers of ground sirloin mixed with parsley, onions, coriander, and scallions) served with hummus, salad, and pita bread. Sandwiches are overstuffed with the deli filling of your choice: pastrami, corned beef, fresh-roasted turkey. Also available are falafel, pizza, burgers, and omelets. Real milk shakes and frozen yogurt are also offered. There's a full bar, and premium wines are offered by the glass. Happy hour is 4 to 8pm, with a DJ playing dance music Friday evenings.

1712 I St. NW. ℂ 202/298-6658. Specialty sandwiches, salads, and burgers $5.95–$11. AE, DC, DISC, MC, V. Mon–Fri 6:30am–9:30pm. Metro: Farragut West or Farragut North.

Bombay Club ℛ *Finds* INDIAN   The Bombay Club is a pleasure, sure to please patrons who know their Indian food as well as those who've never tried it: dishes present an easy introduction to Indian food for the uninitiated, and are sensitive to varying tolerances for spiciness. I'm a wimp in the "heat" department, my husband's the opposite, and we're both happy here.

The spiciest item on the menu is the fiery green chile chicken ("not for the fainthearted," the menu warns—this is the one my husband orders a lot). Most popular are the tandoori salmon and the delicately prepared lobster malabar, that last one is my personal favorite. These two and the other tandoori dishes, like the chicken marinated in a yogurt, ginger, and garlic dressing, are specialties, as is the vegetarian fare—try the black lentils cooked overnight on a slow fire. The Bombay Club is known for its vegetarian offerings (at least nine items are on the menu) and for its Sunday champagne brunch, which offers a buffet of fresh juices, fresh baked breads, and assorted Indian dishes. Patrons are as fond of the service as the cuisine: Waiters seem straight out of *Jewel in the Crown,* attending to your every whim. This is one place where you can linger over a meal as long as you like. Slow-moving ceiling fans and wicker furniture accentuate the colonial British ambience.

815 Connecticut Ave. NW. ℂ **202/659-3727**. www.bombayclubdc.com. Reservations recommended. Main courses $7.50–$19; Sun brunch $19. AE, DC, MC, V. Mon–Fri and Sun brunch 11:30am–2:30pm; Mon–Thurs 6–10:30pm; Fri–Sat 6–11pm; Sun 5:30–9pm. Metro: Farragut West.

Breadline ⓐ AMERICAN   Restaurant critics for the *Washington Post* newspaper and *Washingtonian* magazine love this place, praising Breadline for its bread, baked in every form, from foccacia to knishes to empanadas, and for its many delicious sandwiches, which again range widely: oyster po'boys to grilled cheese. Salads, soups, cookies, and french fries also receive high marks. Breadline is all that. But what the critics don't tell you, and what you should know, is that Breadline is a madhouse at lunchtime—its major meal—and the noise, bustle, and impatience of other diners and some of the staff can prove overwhelming when you're simply trying to read over the menu and make your selection. Also, this is not the place for you if you're a traditionalist. Sometimes all you want is a basic BLT, not a creative interpretation of one. My final complaint is about prices: expect to pay $7 or $8 for your fancy-schmancy sandwich. Dining is inside and out.

1751 Pennsylvania Ave. NW (between 17th and 18th sts.). ℂ **202/822-8900**. Lunch entrées $7–$8.50. AE, MC, V. Mon–Fri 7:30am–3:30pm. Metro: Farragut West.

Daily Grill ⓐ AMERICAN   Talk about retro. In the case of the Daily Grill, retro means revisiting the food favorites of decades past (though the restaurant itself is only a few years old). Step right in and get your Cobb salad, your chicken potpie, your fresh fruit cobbler, your meat and potatoes, made with high quality ingredients (and high caloric value).

It's a big space, with a nice bar at the front and windows on three sides. The winding bar offers an extensive selection: good wines, lots of single malts, tequilas, and small-batch bourbons. The Daily Grill is a favorite lunchtime spot—where else can you order eggs Benedict at noon on a weekday?

Don't know about its chain siblings (mostly located in California), but this Daily Grill rightfully claims a reputation for good service and large portions of grilled meats and fish. (The lunch menu boasts a BLT made with "half a pound of bacon.") You might find it hard to choose from the more than 40 menu items, but favorite orders are the short ribs, the chicken potpie, the meatloaf, and the onion rings.

Another Daily Grill is located in the Georgetown Inn, 1310 Wisconsin Ave. NW (ℂ 202/337-4900).

1200 18th St. NW. ℂ **202/822-5282**. www.dailygrill.com. Reservations recommended. Lunch main courses $8.95–$15; dinner main courses $13–$24. AE, DC, DISC, MC, V. Mon–Thurs 11:30am–11pm; Fri–Sat 11:30am–midnight; Sun 11:30am–3pm (brunch) and 5–10pm. Metro: Farragut North or Dupont Circle.

Famous Luigi's Pizzeria Restaurant ⓚⁱᵈˢ ITALIAN   Before there was Domino's or Pizza Hut or Papa John's, there was Luigi's. Make that *way* before—Luigi's opened in 1943. People who grew up in Washington consider Luigi's an essential part of their childhood. So I took my daughters here one weekday several summers ago, and sure enough, it's remained a favorite place ever since. (They often ask to be taken here on their birthdays.) Whether you go at lunch or dinner, you can expect to be among a sea of office folks. At night, the restaurant's atmosphere changes a little, as office workers come in groups to unwind, have a drink, or get a bite; but this isn't a bar, so it doesn't get rowdy. The menu is long, listing all kinds of pastas, sandwiches, grilled dishes, and pizzas. Come here for a little local color, and to please everyone in the family.

1132 19th St. NW. ℂ **202/331-7574**. www.famousluigis.com. Main courses $5–$17. AE, DC, DISC, MC, V. Mon–Sat 11am–midnight; Sun noon–midnight. Metro: Dupont Circle or Farragut North.

Legal Sea Foods ☆ *Kids* SEAFOOD   This famous family-run Boston-based seafood empire, whose motto is "If it's not fresh, it's not Legal," made its Washington debut in 1995. The softly lit dining room is plush, with terrazzo marble floors and rich cherry-wood paneling. Sporting events, especially Boston games, are aired on a TV over the handsome marble bar/raw bar, and you can usually pick up a copy of the *Boston Globe* near the entrance. As for the food, not only is everything fresh, but it's all from certified-safe waters.

Legal's buttery-rich clam chowder is a classic. Other worthy appetizers include garlicky golden-brown farm-raised mussels au gratin and fluffy pan-fried Maryland lump crab cakes served with mustard sauce and greens tossed with asparagus. You can have one of eight or so varieties of fresh fish grilled or opt for one of Legal's specialty dishes, like the Portuguese fisherman's stew, in which cod, mussels, clams, and chorizo are prepared in a saffron-tomato broth. Top it off with a slice of Boston cream pie. Wine lovers will be happy to know that Legal's wine list has received recognition from *Wine Spectator* magazine; parents will be glad that Legal's award-winning kid's menu offers not just macaroni and cheese, but steamed lobster, popcorn shrimp, and other items, each of which comes with fresh fruit and a choice of baked potato, mashed potatoes, or french fries. At lunch, oyster po' boys and the lobster roll are real treats.

You'll find another Legal Sea Foods at National Airport (© 703/413-9810); a third location is at 704 7th St. NW (© 202/347-0007), across from the MCI Center.

2020 K St. NW. © 202/496-1111. www.legalseafoods.com. Reservations recommended, especially at lunch. Lunch main courses $9–$16; sandwiches $9–$17; dinner main courses $12–$30. AE, DC, DISC, MC, V. Mon–Thurs 11am–10pm; Fri 11am–10:30pm; Sat 4–10:30pm. Metro: Farragut North or Farragut West.

McCormick & Schmick's *Value* SEAFOOD   In this branch of a Pacific Northwest–based restaurant, stained glass in the chandeliers and ceiling evinces a patriotic theme. This huge place seats its patrons in booths, at a 65-foot bar, and at linen-laid tables. The vast, fresh daily menu of more than 30 items offers selections of fresh fish from both nearby and Pacific waters—the more simply prepared, the better. Oyster lovers will choose happily from the half-dozen kinds stocked daily. For good value, look for items like oyster stew and chicken picatta, listed among the pasta and sandwich entrees, and costing in the $6.50 to $12 range. Or head to the bar to enjoy a giant burger, Buffalo chicken wings, Caesar salad, oyster shooters, and mussels, for only $1.95 each, Monday through Friday from 3:30 to 6:30pm and again from 10:30pm to midnight. Friendly bartenders make you feel at home as they concoct "handmade from scratch" mixed drinks with freshly squeezed juices.

A surf-and-turf version of McCormick & Schmick's, the **M&S Grill** is located near the MCI Center, at 13th and F streets NW (© **202/347-1500**).

1652 K St. NW (at the corner of 17th St. NW). © 202/861-2233. Reservations recommended. Main courses $7–$25. AE, DC, DISC, MC, V. Mon–Thurs 11am–11pm; Fri 11am–midnight; Sat 2pm–midnight; Sun 4–10pm. Metro: Farragut North or Farragut West.

SUPER-CHEAP EATS

Oodles Noodles *Value* ASIAN FUSION   Oodles Noodles is one of the original Asian Fusion restaurants in Washington, having opened in 1997. You have more choices now, including the much prettier Teaism (p. 144), and the trendsetting, upscale TenPenh (p. 130). Consider Oodles if you are a famished bargain hunter, since the kitchen serves up plenty of cheap one-dish meals that can satisfy. You can order dumplings, Szechuan *dan dan* noodles (egg noodles), Vietnamese vermicelli, and Thai drunken noodles, among others. Many of the items come in a soup, such as the Shanghai roast pork noodles soup and the Siam noodles soup, which is a spicy sweet-and-sour broth with shrimp, minced chicken, and squid.

But not everything is a noodle. Appetizers include satays, spring onion cakes, curry puffs, and vegetable spring rolls. Curries, teriyaki, and other spicy non-noodle fare round out the menu. I'd recommend the ginger salad and the *nasi goreng* (Indonesian chicken fried rice with chicken satay and egg).

1120 19th St. NW. ℂ 202/293-3138. Reservations recommended for 5 or more at dinner. Main courses $7–$10. AE, DC, MC, V. Mon–Sat 11:30am–3pm; Mon–Thurs 5–10pm; Fri–Sat 5–10:30pm. Metro: Dupont Circle or Farragut North.

WORTH A SPLURGE

Oval Room at Lafayette Square ★★ NEW AMERICAN The Oval Room is a local favorite, another winner for owner Ashok Bajaj, who also owns the Bombay Club (p. 131), across the street, and several other restaurants around town. The Oval Room is a handsome restaurant, with contemporary art hanging on its lettuce-colored walls. Its atmosphere is congenial, not stuffy, no doubt because the bar area separating the restaurant into two distinct rooms sends cheerful sounds in either direction. The quality of the food has always been top-notch: I've liked the seafood Bolognese with sage, ham ribbons, and pappardelle, while my friends enjoyed the New York strip steak with caramelized onions and green peppercorn sauce. In case you haven't figured it out, the Oval Room is a short walk from the White House.

800 Connecticut Ave. NW, at Lafayette Square. ℂ 202/463-8700. www.ovalroom.com. Reservations recommended. Lunch main courses $12–$18; dinner main courses $18–$26; pretheater dinner (5:30–6:45pm) $25. AE, DISC, MC, V. Mon–Fri 11:30am–2:30pm; Mon–Sat 5–10:30pm. Metro: Farragut West.

Vidalia ★★ REGIONAL AMERICAN/SOUTHERN If you're hesitant to dine at a restaurant that's down a flight of steps from the street, your doubts will vanish as soon as you enter Vidalia's tiered dining room. There's a party going on down here. In fact, Vidalia is so popular, you may have to wait a short time in the narrow bar, even if you arrive on time for your reservation. But the bar is fun, too, and gives you a jump-start on getting into the mood of the place.

Executive chef Peter Smith adds Asian and French accents to owner/chef Jeff Buben's regional Southern cuisine. The menu changes frequently, but recommended constants include crisp East Coast lump crab cakes and a fried grits cake with taso ham. Venture from the regular items and you may delight in a timbale of roasted onion and foie gras, sautéed sea scallops with udon cake, or pan-roasted Carolina trout. A signature entree is the scrumptious sautéed shrimp on a mound of creamed grits and caramelized onions in a thyme-and-shrimp cream sauce. Corn bread and biscuits with apple butter are served at every meal. Vidalia is known for its lemon chess pie, which tastes like pure sugar; I prefer the pecan pie. A carefully chosen wine list highlights American vintages.

1990 M St. NW. ℂ 202/659-1990. www.vidaliadc.com. Reservations recommended. Lunch main courses $13–$22; dinner main courses $23–$30. AE, DC, DISC, MC, V. Mon–Fri 11:30am–2:30pm; Sun–Thurs 5:30–10pm; Fri–Sat 5:30–10:30pm. Closed Sun July 4–Labor Day. Metro: Dupont Circle.

5 U Street Corridor

Coppi's *Value* ITALIAN Crowded with neighborhood patrons and hungry club-goers headed for one of the nearby music houses, Coppi's is a narrow room decorated with wooden booths and bicycle memorabilia from Italian bike races. The wood-burning oven turns out a mean pizza, a stiff competitor to that of top-dog Pizzeria Paradiso (p. 143). The crust is chewy, and your choice of toppings includes quality ham, pancetta, cheeses, and vegetables. Coppi's also makes all its pastas and ice cream in-house. Favorite dishes include pastas topped with baby artichoke pesto, bistecca with porcini mushrooms and pine nuts, and fresh ravioli stuffed and sauced with wine-braised beef. You can count on finding an extensive Italian wine list. Service is friendly but can be spotty; if it seems like your waiter has forgotten you, there's a chance that he has, so speak up before too much time passes.

1414 U St. NW. *C* 202/319-7773. Reservations accepted. Main courses $11–$20. AE, DC, DISC, MC, V. Mon–Fri 11:30am–3pm; Sun–Thurs 6–11pm; Fri–Sat 5pm–midnight. Metro: U St.–Cardozo.

SUPER-CHEAP EATS

Ben's Chili Bowl *Finds* AMERICAN   Ben's is a veritable institution, a mom-and-pop place, where everything looks, tastes, and probably even costs the same as when the restaurant opened in 1958. The most expensive item on the menu is the double turkey burger sub, for $6.25. Formica counters, red bar stools, and a jukebox that plays Motown and reggae tunes—that's Ben's. Ben's continues as a gathering place for black Washington and visitors like Bill Cosby, who's a long-time customer (a chili dog is named after him). Everyone's welcome, though, even the late-nighters who come streaming out of nearby nightclubs at 2 or 3 in the morning on the weekend. Of course, the chili, cheese fries, and half-smokes are great, but so are breakfast items. Try the salmon cakes, grits, scrapple, or blueberry pancakes (available during breakfast hours only, 6–11am).

1213 U St. NW. *C* 202/667-0909. www.benschilibowl.com. Reservations not accepted. Main courses $2.48–$6.50. No credit cards. Mon–Thurs 6am–2am; Fri–Sat 6am–4am; Sun noon–8pm. Metro: U St.–Cardozo.

6 Adams-Morgan

La Fourchette FRENCH   The nonsmoking section is upstairs, but even if you don't smoke, you'll want to be downstairs, among the French-speaking clientele and Adams-Morgan regulars. The waiters are suitably crusty and the ambience is as Parisian as you'll get this side of the Atlantic—as is the food. The menu lists escargots, onion soup, bouillabaisse, and mussels Provençal, along with specials like the grilled salmon on spinach mousse and the shrimp Niçoise, ever-so-slightly crusted and sautéed in tomato sauce touched with anchovy. Saturday and Sunday brunch offers French toast, omelets, and the like. A colorful mural covers the high walls; wooden tables and benches push up against bare brick walls. In warm weather, you can sit outside at tables set up on the sidewalk.

2429 18th St. NW. *C* 202/332-3077. Reservations recommended on weekends. Main courses $12–$24. AE, DC, MC, V. Mon–Thurs 11:30am–10:30pm; Fri 11:30am–11pm; Sat 11am–11pm; Sun 10am–10pm.

Lauriol Plaza *Ꮶ* MEXICAN/SPANISH/LATIN AMERICAN   This place is gigantic—it seats 330—but it's immensely popular, so you may still have to wait for a table. Lauriol Plaza looks like a factory from the outside, but inside it's stunning. You have a choice of sitting at sidewalk tables, on the rooftop deck, or in the two-tiered dining room with its large mural of a Spanish fiesta on one wall and windows covering another. We had good, though warm, margaritas, the standout carne asada fajitas, and tasty *camarones diablo* (six broiled jumbo shrimp seasoned with spices). Anything mesquite grilled is sure to please. Servings are as large as the restaurant. Sunday brunch, also recommended, is served from 11am to 3pm. With so many people dining here, Lauriol Plaza is a good place to people-watch.

1835 18th St. NW. ℂ 202/387-0035. www.lauriolplaza.com. Reservations not accepted. Main courses $8–$17. AE, DC, DISC, MC, V. Sun 11am–11pm; Mon–Thurs 11:30am–11pm; Fri–Sat 11:30am–midnight. Metro: Dupont Circle.

Meskerem ETHIOPIAN   Washington has a number of Ethiopian restaurants, but this is probably the best. It's certainly the most attractive; the three-level high-ceilinged dining room (sunny by day, candlelit at night) has an oval skylight girded by a painted sunburst and walls hung with African art and musical instruments. On the mezzanine level, you sit at *messobs* (basket tables) on low, carved Ethiopian chairs or upholstered leather poufs. Ethiopian music enhances the ambience.

Diners share large platters of food, which they scoop up with a sourdough cre-pelike pancake called *injera* (no silverware here). Items listed as *watt* are hot and spicy; *alitchas* are milder and more delicately flavored. You might also share an entree—perhaps *yegeb kay watt* (succulent lamb in thick, hot *berbere* sauce)—along with a platter of five vegetarian dishes served with tomato and potato salads. Some combination platters comprise an array of beef, chicken, lamb, and vegetables. There's a full bar; the wine list includes Ethiopian wine and beer.

2434 18th St. NW (between Columbia and Belmont rds.). ℂ 202/462-4100. www.meskeremonline.com. Reservations recommended. Lunch and dinner main courses $8.95–$13. AE, DC, MC, V. Daily noon–midnight, with bar staying open until 3am Fri–Sat.

SUPER-CHEAP EATS

Mixtec (Value REGIONAL MEXICAN   This cheerful Adams-Morgan spot attracts a clientele of neighborhood folks, D.C. chefs, and Hispanics from all over, all of whom appreciate the delicious authenticity of the regional Mexican cuisine. The kitchen is open, the dining room colorfully decorated, and the Mexican music lively.

Two items are served here that you can't find at any of the many other Southwestern eateries in the capital: the authentic *menudo,* a stew of tripe and calf's feet (granted, not for everyone); and *tortas,* which are a kind of Mexican sub, layered with grilled pork, chiles, guacamole, and salsa. You will also find delicious small dishes called *antojitos* ("little whims"), in the $2.50 to $4.95 range, which include *queso fundido* (a bubbling hot dish of broiled Chihuahua cheese topped with shredded spicy chorizo sausage flavored with jalapeños and cilantro); and the *enrollados mexicanos,* large flour tortillas wrapped around a variety of fillings, including grilled chicken, beef, vegetables, and salmon. The freshly prepared guacamole is excellent. Choose from 30 kinds of tequila, tequila-mixed drinks, Mexican beers, and fresh fruit juices.

1792 Columbia Rd. (just off 18th St.). ℂ 202/332-1011. Main courses $3.95–$15. MC, V. Sun–Thurs 10am–10pm; Fri–Sat 10am–11pm.

Pasta Mia (Value ITALIAN   Right next door to Mixtec (see above) is another excellent and inexpensive choice that stays busy all night. You might have to wait for a table, too, especially on a Friday or Saturday night, since the restaurant doesn't take reservations. But you'll agree that it's worth it, after you dive into a plate heaped with one of the nearly 25 pasta dishes on the menu. Eight have meat sauces, three have seafood, and the remainder are vegetarian. I recommend the green fettuccine with creamy porcini-mushroom sauce. Bread is made in-house, and appetizers, like the Caesar salad or fresh mozzarella and tomatoes, are all flavorful. This place is as low-key as Washington gets, with a simple, brightly lit interior of red-checked covered tables packed together, and dishes served to a table as they are ready.

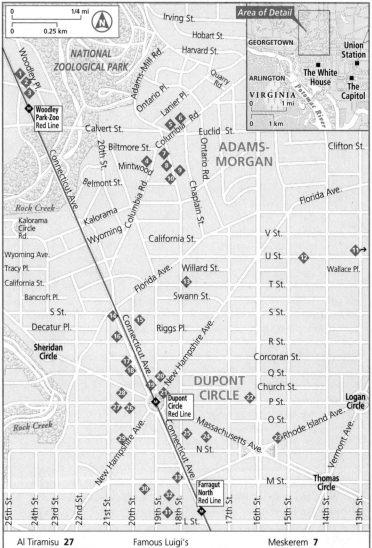

Area of Detail

GEORGETOWN

Union Station

ARLINGTON

The White House

VIRGINIA

The Capitol

0   1 mi

0   1 km

Potomac River

NATIONAL ZOOLOGICAL PARK

Irving St.

Hobart St.

Harvard St.

Adams-Mill Rd.

Ontario Pl.

Lanier Pl.

Quarry Rd.

Columbia Rd.

Euclid St.

Clifton St.

ADAMS-MORGAN

Woodley Pl.

Woodley Park-Zoo Red Line

Calvert St.

20th St.

Biltmore St.

Mintwood

Belmont St.

Connecticut Ave.

Rock Creek

Kalorama Circle Rd.

Kalorama

Wyoming Columbia Rd.

Ontario Rd.

Chaplain St.

Wyoming Ave.

Tracy Pl.

California St.

California St.

Bancroft Pl.

S St.

Decatur Pl.

Sheridan Circle

Florida Ave.

Willard St.

Swann St.

Florida Ave.

V St.

U St.

T St.

S St.

Wallace Pl.

Riggs Pl.

Connecticut Ave.

New Hampshire Ave.

R St.

Corcoran St.

Q St.

DUPONT CIRCLE

Church St.

P St.

O St.

Logan Circle

Dupont Circle Red Line

Rock Creek

New Hampshire Ave.

Massachusetts Ave.

Rhode Island Ave.

Vermont Ave.

N St.

Connecticut Ave.

Farragut North Red Line

M St.

Thomas Circle

25th St. 24th St. 23rd St. 22nd St. 21st St. 20th St. 19th St. 18th St. 17th St. 16th St. 15th St. 14th St. 13th St.

L St.

Al Tiramisu **27**	Famous Luigi's Pizzeria Restaurant **32**	Meskerem **7**
Ben's Chili Bowl **11**	Felix Restaurant and Lounge **10**	Mixtec **5**
Bistrot du Coin **14**		Oodles Noodles **31**
Bua **22**	15 Ria **23**	Pasta Mia **6**
Burrito Brothers **8**	Firefly **29**	Perry's **4**
Cashion's Eat Place **4**	Johnny's Half Shell **26**	Petits Plats **1**
The Childe Harold **17**	Kramerbooks & Afterwords Café **19**	Pizzeria Paradiso **28**
City Lights of China **15**		Raku **20**
Coppi's **12**	La Fourchette **9**	Sala Thai **27**
Daily Grill **33**	Lauriol Plaza **13**	Tabard Inn **24**
Dupont Grille **21**	Lebanese Taverna **2**	Teaism Dupont Circle **16**
Etrusco **18**	Luna Grill & Diner **25**	Tono Sushi **3**
		Vidalia **30**

137

Great Places to Picnic

One of the most sublime, and least expensive, pleasures to be had in Washington is to sit outdoors on a nice day enjoying a picnic lunch or supper. It's not hard to find a perfect setting when so much of the city is acres and acres of parkland. What is the National Mall, after all, but one long stretch of picnic lawn? Rock Creek Park, the C&O Canal, East Potomac Park, and private gardens offer some other options.

Pick up delicious picnic fare from the shop I recommend within the writeup or from one of the shops listed in chapter 8's "Gourmet Goodies to Go" section, then head for a park. Here are some spots that might appeal:

- **The Folger Shakespeare Library,** 201 E. Capitol St. SE (© **202/544-4600**). The Elizabethan Garden belonging to the library is small and private—holly-covered, wrought-iron fencing shields it from the street. The unmarked plantings are either mentioned in Shakespeare's plays or were grown during Elizabethan times. Purchase a delicious sandwich or salad at the nearby Le Bon Café (p. 118). You might combine your picnic with a garden tour, given April through October, every third Saturday at 10am and 11am. The garden is open during library hours, Monday through Saturday from 10am to 4pm.

- **Washington National Cathedral,** Massachusetts and Wisconsin avenues NW (© **202/537-6200**). The Bishop's Lawn cuts a wide swath of green on a slope beneath the towering Gothic cathedral. It's the perfect spot to hear the ringing of the cathedral bells, at about 12:30pm every Saturday, year-round; this is a carillon performance, in which 53 bells are rung in tuneful patterns. Sit here on Sunday after the 11am service, or on a Tuesday evening about 7:30pm and you will hear a peal bell performance, that is, the ringing of 10 different bells by 10 different people. (This, too, is a weekly event, year-round.) Adjoining the lawn is the medieval Bishop's Garden, an enclosure of garden "rooms," where every planting is marked. (You may picnic on the lawn, but not in the garden.) Another idea: take the 1-hour tour of the Bishop's Garden offered Wednesday at 10:30am April through October, and follow it up with a picnic on the lawn. The lawn and garden are open daily until dusk. For information about musical performances, call © **202/537-5757;** for info about garden tours, call © **202/244-0568.**

- **Victorian Garden,** Christian Heurich House Museum, 1307 New Hampshire Ave. NW. New owners purchased this estate in spring 2003, with the intention of keeping the house and garden open to visitors. The site had not yet reopened at the time of my research, and its phone

1790 Columbia Rd. NW. © **202/328-9114.** Reservations not accepted. Main courses $9–$10. MC, V. Mon–Sat 6:30–10pm.

WORTH A SPLURGE

Cashion's Eat Place ★★ *Finds* AMERICAN   Cashion's has all the pleasures of a neighborhood restaurant—easy, warm, comfortable—combined with cuisine that is out of this world. Owner/chef Ann Cashion continues to rack up culinary number, website, and hours of operation were not available. I recommend you stop by anyway, if you are in the Dupont Circle neighborhood, for the garden is such a pleasant spot. Like the Folger's, this garden is a small sanctuary. Smithsonian horticulturists designed the garden to include plants that might be found in a traditional Victorian England garden. You can sit on the grass or on one of the wooden or wrought-iron benches. Most of the garden is shaded.

- **Montrose Park,** on R Street between 30th and 31st streets NW, in upper Georgetown (© **202/282-1063**). Open daily until dusk, this wooded, 16-acre park is part of Rock Creek Park and offers a little of everything: open green lawn, with picnic tables and a few benches in the shade; two sets of first-come, first-served tennis courts; a pretty green pavilion with tables and benches; a modest-size playground; and walking/hiking trails, including a true Lover's Lane, down which trysting couples have wandered since 1900. On the other side of the lane is **Dumbarton Oaks,** whose formal gardens are worth viewing; you're not allowed to picnic there, though.
- **National Gallery of Art Sculpture Garden,** just across 7th Street from the West Wing of the National Gallery. Tourists and office workers like to come here on their lunch break, and all sorts of people find their way here Friday evenings in summer, when the garden hosts live jazz sets (see chapter 9's listing of free outdoor performances). The park takes up 2 city blocks and features open lawns; a central pool with a spouting fountain (the pool is converted into an ice rink in winter); 17 sculptures by renowned artists, like Roy Lichtenstein and Ellsworth Kelly (and Scott Burton, whose "Six-Part Seating" you're welcome to sit upon); and informally landscaped shrubs, trees, and plants. Buy your lunch from the cafe here and eat at one of the outside tables, or take your picnic fare over to the pool, where you can sit on its wide ledge, dip your toes in, and munch.
- **Wolf Trap Farm Park,** 1551 Trap Rd., Vienna, VA (© **703/255-1800** for general info, 202/255-1868 for box office). The National Park Service–administered Wolf Trap is not the only place where you can picnic to music, but it's the best. For the price of a lawn seat (usually $10 to $20) you can lie back in the sun or under the stars and take in a concert, pausing from time to time to delve into picnic fare.

   Note: Again, see chapter 9 for a listing of free indoor and outdoor entertainment within the District, and for more information about Wolf Trap and how to get there.

awards as easily as she pleases her patrons. Her menu changes daily, always featuring about eight entrees, split between seafood and meat: fritto misto of whole jumbo shrimp and black sea bass filet, served with onion rings and house-made tartar sauce, or fried sweetbreads on a bed of sautéed spinach, and so on. The side dishes that accompany each entree, such as lemon cannelloni bean purée or radish and sprout salad, are equally as appealing. Chocolate cinnamon mousse, lime tartalette, and other desserts are worth saving room for. Sunday brunch is popular, too; you can choose from breakfast fare (challah French toast, spinach and Gruyère omelets) or heartier items (grilled rainbow trout, croque monsieurs).

The charming dining room curves around a slightly raised bar. In warm weather, the glass-fronted Cashion's opens invitingly to the sidewalk, where you can also dine. Tables at the back offer a view of the small kitchen, where Cashion and her staff work away. In winter, ask for a table away from the front door, which lets in a blast of cold air with each new arrival.

1819 Columbia Rd. NW (between 18th St. and Mintwood Place). (C) **202/797-1819.** Reservations recommended. Brunch $8.95–$12; dinner main courses $17–$26. MC, V. Tues 5:30–10pm; Wed–Sat 5:30–11pm; Sun 11:30am–2:30pm and 5:30–10pm.

Felix Restaurant and Lounge ✿ (Moments AMERICAN   Felix is a supper club for the 21st century, featuring a different musical act every night, Ska to swing, as you enjoy your "Big City" martini and large portioned dinners. Consider as appetizers the fresh yellowfin tuna tartare with kumquats and tomatillos, or the veal carpaccio appetizer with olives, Roquefort cheese, and pickled mushrooms. Move on from there, to the tea-smoked pork tenderloin, and for dessert, the thin crust apple tart. Felix is famous for Friday night, kosher-style Sabbath dinners, serving everything from Matzoh ball soup to brisket of beef, but the restaurant cautions that its kitchen is not Kosher. Also see chapter 9 for a description of Felix's offspring, the Spy Lounge, which shares its entrance with Felix.

2406 18th St. NW. (C) **202/483-3549.** www.thefelix.com. Reservations recommended. Main courses $17–$27. AE, DC, DISC, MC, V. Nightly 5:30–11pm for dinner, bar stays open until 3am.

Perry's ✿ ASIAN FUSION   Celebrities seem to like this place—Keanu Reeves, Stevie Wonder, and President Bush's twin daughters are among those who've been spotted here—as do most Washingtonians in the 20- to 40-something age brackets. The biggest draw is Perry's rooftop deck, festively strung with yellow lights, open nightly from 5:30pm in the nicer months. The restaurant's whimsically hip interior has a 1920s feel, lots of wood, a fireplace, French windows framed by floor-to-ceiling red curtains, and an octopus-like chandelier suspended from a fire-engine-red plastic cushion. Seating includes low orange sofas at mahogany tables. Cuisine is Asian fusion, featuring entrees such as crisped red snapper, seared scallops, roast chicken, and sushi. Perry's makes a fine gingerbread for dessert.

Sunday brunch is another main attraction: Drag queens in over-the-top outfits (one slinks around the room in a black vinyl cat costume) appear every 15 minutes or so; they dance, flirt with male customers, camp it up, and lip synch to the music. The crowd is about half straight, half gay men and women, and everyone has a great time. The brunch buffet changes week to week but usually offers a spread of paella, French toast, smoked salmon, cold cuts, egg dishes, breakfast meats, grilled vegetables, cheeses, desserts, and more.

1811 Columbia Rd. NW (between Biltmore and Mintwood sts.). (C) **202/234-6218.** Main courses $14–$19; brunch $23. AE, DC, MC, V. Sun 11:30am–3pm and 5:30–11:30pm; Mon–Thurs 5:30–11:30pm; Fri–Sat 5:30pm–12:30am.

7 Dupont Circle

Bistrot du Coin ✿ FRENCH   When Michel Richard, acclaimed chef of Michel Richard Citronelle, is homesick, he visits this restaurant, because he thinks it feels like France. I think so, too. The wooden facade that draws your attention from the street, the way the whole glass front of the dining room opens right to the sidewalk, the zinc bar, the moody waiters—everything speaks of a Paris cafe, most of all the food.

I keep hearing that the mussels are the thing to order, either curried and creamed, or hiding in a thick gratin of leeks, but so far I have chosen other dishes and been pleased. The cassoulet is delicious, and not too hearty; the *tartine baltique* turned out to be an open-faced sandwich with smoked salmon, tamara onions, capers, and olive oil, and I slurped down every bite. The steak *frites* are just what you'd hope for, tasty and comforting. The menu presents a limited number of wines, but since these include a $10 glass of Veuve Cliquot champagne, I can't complain. Or select an aperitif from a list of 16, very reasonably priced. I chose the licorice-flavored Ricard, which is similar to pastis, and at $3.95, a delicious deal.

1738 Connecticut Ave. NW (near Florida Ave.). ℭ 202/234-6969. www.bistrotducoin.com. Main courses $13–$27. AE, DISC, MC, V. Sun 11am–11pm; Mon–Wed 11:30am–11pm; Thurs–Sat 11:30am–1am. Metro: Dupont Circle.

Bua THAI   Walk by on a Friday or Saturday night and you'll see the two-story restaurant packed, with tables full on the second floor outdoor balcony in summer. In spite of its two floors, Bua is not a large restaurant. The people who come here are mostly a neighborhood crowd, with office people filling the place weekdays for lunch. The food is inexpensive and the service gracious and honest; my server steered me away from the "heavenly wings" appetizer, pronouncing them "too crusty." Consider instead the satays, pad thai, and steamed seafood in banana leaves, all house specialties. The peanut sauce accompanying the satays is so good that Bua should sell containers of it for people to stock at home. The spring rolls are very delicate, not greasy.

1635 P St. NW. ℭ 202/265-0828. www.buathai.com. Reservations suggested. Lunch main courses $5.95–$7.75; dinner main courses $7.95–$13. AE, DC, DISC, MC, V. Mon–Fri 11:30am–2:30pm; Sat–Sun noon–4pm; Sun–Thurs 5–10:30pm; Fri–Sat 5–11pm. Metro: Dupont Circle, with a 10–15 min. walk.

The Childe Harold AMERICAN   In the old days, the Childe Harold used to feature live music. Performers would set up their equipment in the niche formed by the bay window of the Victorian town house, and play their hearts out. The past lives on in the menu, where sandwich favorites include the Bonnie Raitt (a BLT with curried chicken on rye), the Bruce Springsteen (crab cake on an English muffin), and the Emmylou Harris (avocado, bacon, and mayo on whole wheat), all named after just some of those who performed here. (The word is, that the Childe Harold plans to stage live music again—call to find out.) Besides the sandwiches, the hamburgers are noteworthy, and served with topping choices that range from blackened blue cheese to Brie with toasted almonds. Pastas, seafood, salads, and steak are also on the menu. It may be hard to consider anything more serious than the burgers and bar food, however, since a beery smell is ever present. If you're downstairs in the Pilgrimage Bar, you can add cigarette smoke to the mix. In warm weather, the outside patio opens up. If you're seated inside, upstairs, at the front of the Childe Harold, or outside on the patio, you're in a great position to people-watch.

1610 20th St. NW (between Q and R sts.). ℭ 202/483-6700. www.childeharold.com. Main courses mostly $6.95–$17; burgers, omelets, salads, and sandwiches $5.95–$9.95. AE, DC, DISC, MC, V. Upstairs Mon–Sat 11:30am–2pm and 5:30–11pm; brunch Sat 11:30am–3pm; Sun 10:30am–3pm. Downstairs Pilgrimage Bar open Sun–Thurs until midnight, Fri–Sat until 2am. Metro: Dupont Circle.

City Lights of China CHINESE   One of Washington's best Chinese restaurants outside of Chinatown, City Lights is a favorite of White House workaholics, whatever administration, who frequently order takeout from here. If you are staying at a nearby hotel, you might consider ordering food to go, as well; takeout prices are cheaper for some items. Some of the most popular dishes include crisp fried Cornish hen prepared in a cinnamon-soy marinade and served with a tasty dipping sauce, Chinese eggplant in garlic sauce, stir-fried spinach, crisp fried shredded beef, and Peking duck. The setting, a three-tiered dining room with much of the seating in comfortable leather booths and ban-quettes, is unpretentious. Neat white-linen tablecloths, cloth flower arrange-ments in lighted niches, and green neon track lighting complete the picture. There's a full bar.

1731 Connecticut Ave. NW (between R and S sts.). ℭ 202/265-6688. Reservations recommended. Lunch main courses $6.95–$24 (most are about $8.95); dinner main courses $9.95–$26 (most are about $13). AE, DC, DISC, MC, V. Mon–Fri 11:30am–11pm; Sat noon–11pm; Sun noon–10:30pm; dinner from 3pm daily. Metro: Dupont Circle.

Firefly ⚑ CONTEMPORARY AMERICAN   This is an intimate and popu-lar restaurant, which makes for a rollicking experience but also a crowded one— you can feel squeezed in here. A floor-to-ceiling "firefly tree" hung with lanterns heightens this feeling. The food is quite good. We enjoyed the potato gnocchi with smoke trout and sage brown butter and the grilled New York steak with housemade fries, watercress, and Smithfield ham. If fries don't come with your meal, it's worth ordering them as a side, as they're excellent and arrive hot and salty in a paper cone set in its own stand. (Sister restaurant Poste also serves fries "Belgian style.") At lunch, consider the grilled salmon BLT, or the Amish chicken Cobb salad. We had the caramelized apple tart for dessert, which was no good at all, and not even served warm. Firefly lies within the Hotel Madera, but has a separate entrance.

In the Hotel Madera, 1310 New Hampshire Ave. NW (between 20th and 21st sts.). ℭ 202/861-1310. www. firefly-dc.com. Reservations recommended. Brunch main courses $7.50–$14; lunch main courses $10–$17; dinner main courses $12–$23. AE, DC, DISC, MC, V. Mon–Fri 7–10am and 11:30am–2:30pm; Sat–Sun 10:30am–2:30pm; Sun–Thurs 5:30–10:30pm; Fri–Sat 5:30–11pm. Metro: Dupont Circle.

Johnny's Half Shell ⚑ (Finds SEAFOOD   Whenever a friend visits from out of town and I haven't gotten around to making a restaurant reservation, we usu-ally end up at Johnny's. It's easy, fun, and comfortable; it's open continuously from lunch through the afternoon to closing, and it takes no reservations, so you can usually walk right in and get something fresh from the sea (though weekend nights after 8:30pm, you'll probably have at least a 20-min. wait); and it feels like a hometown restaurant, a rare thing in a city whose residents tend to origi-nate from many other hometowns. Johnny's owners, Ann Cashion and John Fulchino, own another very popular restaurant, Cashion's Eat Place (p. 138) in Adams-Morgan. The restaurant is small, with a decor that features an aquarium behind the long bar, booths along one paneled wall, a tile floor, and a partly open kitchen. The professional yet friendly waiters seem to enjoy themselves.

Everything on the menu looks good, from the farm-raised chicken with old-fashioned Eastern Shore slippery dumplings, garden peas, and button mush-rooms, to the crab meat imperial with a salad of *haricots verts* (young green beans), tomatoes, and shallots. I recently opted for the delicious fried oyster po'boy sandwich, while my friend Sue went for the Maryland crab cakes with coleslaw and french fries; we both devoured every morsel. If the sautéed soft-shell crabs with Old Bay and basil beurre blanc and corn pudding are on the menu, get them. My daughter Cait likes the barbecued shrimp appetizer with Asiago cheese grits. Oysters, and Wellfleet clams on the half shell are always available, of course. The short wine list includes a few selections by the glass; there are four beers on tap. Desserts are simple but perfect, including homemade ice cream, a choice of hazelnut, almond, pecan, or chocolate tart, and chocolate angel food cake with caramel sauce.

2002 P St. NW. ℂ **202/296-2021.** Reservations not accepted. Lunch main courses $7.50–$12; dinner main courses $16–$22. AE, MC, V. Mon–Thurs 11:30am–10:30pm; Fri–Sat 11:30am–11pm (weekdays, between 3 and 5pm, a light fare menu of soups and salads is available); Sun 5–10pm. Metro: Dupont Circle.

Pizzeria Paradiso 𝒦 ITALIAN   Peter Pastan, master chef/owner of Obelisk (located right next door), owns this classy, often crowded, 16-table pizzeria. An oak-burning oven at one end of the charming room produces exceptionally doughy but light pizza crusts. As you wait, you can munch on mixed olives and gaze up at the ceiling painted to suggest blue sky peeking through ancient stone walls. Pizzas range from the plain Paradiso, which offers chunks of tomatoes covered in melted mozzarella, to the robust Siciliano, a blend of nine ingredients including eggplant and red onion. Or you can choose your own toppings from a list of 29. As popular as the pizzas are the *panini* (sandwiches) of homemade focaccia stuffed with marinated roasted lamb and vegetables and other fillings, and the salads, such as tuna and white bean. Good desserts, but a limited wine list. Pizzeria Paradiso has finally opened another location, at 3282 M St. NW (ℂ 202/337-1245), in Georgetown, right next door to Dean & Deluca. This location is larger, has a full bar, and a private party room.

2029 P St. NW. ℂ **202/223-1245.** Reservations not accepted. Pizzas $7.95–$17; sandwiches and salads $3.95–$6.95. DC, MC, V. Daily 11:30am–11pm. Metro: Dupont Circle.

Raku PAN ASIAN   Raku's glass-fronted restaurant occupies a prominent, excellent people-watching corner near Dupont Circle. Spring through fall, the scene gets even better when Raku's windowed walls open to its sidewalk cafe. Inside, you find artfully tied bamboo poles and Japanese temple beams, shoji screens, and TV monitors airing campy videos (anything from Godzilla to instructions for using chopsticks), as Asian pop music plays as background music. A curvilinear bar overlooks the kitchen, where chefs prepare the street food of China, Japan, Korea, and Thailand, presenting them as tapas or "big plates." Among the 24 tapas to recommend are the dumplings; chicken and veggie are tasty, but the best are the "pork juicy buns" (stuffed with roast pork, cabbage, soy, and ginger, served with black bean sauce). Also try the chicken yakitori, a meal comprised of skewered soy-sesame glazed chicken. "Big plates" include pad thai and a thrilling shrimp and coconut dish in which jumbo shrimp are sautéed with broccoli, peppers, crispy shallots, and carrots, and topped with a spicy coconut sauce. Raku also serves noodle dishes, salads (the Hunan chicken salad remains wildly popular), and sushi.

1900 Q St. NW. ℂ **202/265-7258.** Tapas $3.95–$8; main courses $6–$16. AE, MC, V. Sun–Thurs 11:30am–10pm; Fri–Sat 11:30am–11pm. Metro: Dupont Circle.

SUPER-CHEAP EATS

Kramerbooks & Afterwords Café AMERICAN   Bookstore/cafes may be ubiquitous now, but when Kramer's opened nearly 30 years ago, it was the only one, at least in Washington. It's the kind of place you go for cappuccino after the movies, for an intense discussion of your love life over a platter of fettuccine, or to linger over a good book and a cognac on a sunny afternoon. Sit indoors at tables crowded under a low beamed ceiling, at the bar (scene of monthly changing art exhibits), upstairs on a tiny balcony overlooking the bookstore, in a two-story glassed-in solarium, or at outdoor cafe tables.

The cafe opens early, serving traditional breakfast fare along with items ranging from quesadillas to Nova Scotia salmon served with caviar, sour cream, a bagel, and cream cheese. At weekend brunches (2am–3pm Sat–Sun), the price of an entree may cover the cost of a mimosa or other special drink. The long menu lists an eclectic mix of entrees: veggie chili, pasta with your choice of toppings, chicken and cheese quesadillas, and a fair number of fresh fish dishes. Numerous drink options include margaritas, ice cream/liqueur concoctions, microbrews, and premium wines by the glass. Indulge in a hot fudge sundae for dessert. Wednesday through Saturday nights there's live entertainment—mostly blues and jazz.

1517 Connecticut Ave. NW (between Q St. and Dupont Circle). ✆ 202/387-1462. Lunch main courses $8.75–$12; dinner main courses $10–$15; specials may cost a little more. AE, DISC, MC, V. Sun–Thurs 7:30am–1am; around the clock Fri 7:30am–Sun 1am. Metro: Dupont Circle.

Luna Grill & Diner *(Value)* AMERICAN   Close your eyes while you're eating and you'll think you're in an old-time diner—or at home, if someone in your family is a good cook. Luna's food is old-fashioned fare, but updated to be healthier and tastier. House-made bread comes with the meal, and it isn't spongy white bread, it's thick slices of delicious loaves whose flavor changes day to day: pimento, caper, basil, and the favorite, pesto. The turkey with stuffing and a choice of sides (try the thickly mashed potatoes) is a tasty deal for $8.95, and the gravy isn't greasy. Other things on the menu include lasagna, burgers, steak sandwiches, and big salads. Four or five wines by the glass are available for $4.25 to $5.50. (Luna has a full bar.) The restaurant draws mostly a younger, downtown crowd, maybe because of its location, just below Dupont Circle, on a stretch of Connecticut Avenue that includes clubs and bars. With its light wood tables, painted sunbursts, and gold Christmas balls dangling from the ceiling, the Luna doesn't look like a diner. Check out the pasta special, offered Sunday and Monday after 5pm; pastas are half the regular price of $6.95, and you can choose from a long list of toppings, which go for $1.50 to $2.50 each. Breakfast is served all day.

1301 Connecticut Ave. NW. ✆ 202/835-2280. Breakfast items $3–$8; main courses at lunch and dinner $6–$16; brunch $3–$10. AE, DC, DISC, MC, V. Mon–Thurs 8am–11pm; Fri 8am–midnight; Sat 8am–1am; Sun 8am–10pm; brunch Sat–Sun 10am–3pm. Metro: Dupont Circle or Farragut North.

Sala Thai THAI   At lunch, you'll see a lot of diners sitting alone and reading newspapers, happy to escape the office. At dinner, the restaurant is filled with groups and couples, plus the occasional family. Among the 53 items to recommend on the menu are no. 41, *nua kra ting tone,* which is spicy beef with onion, garlic, and parsley sauce ("not found at any other Thai restaurant in Washington," said my Thai waitress, sporting multicolored streaks in her hair), and, no. 26, *ka prow,* which is an even spicier dish of either beef, chicken, or pork sautéed with basil leaves and chile. The restaurant lies downstairs from the street; with no windows to watch what's happening on P Street, you're really here for the food, which is excellent and cheap. Even conventional pad thai doesn't disappoint. Pay attention if your waiter cautions you about the level of spiciness of a dish you order—for some dishes (like no. 38, stir-fried sliced pork in red curry sauce with peppers), you'll need an asbestos tongue.

2016 P St. NW. ✆ 202/872-1144. Reservations accepted for 5 or more. Lunch main courses $6.25–$9; dinner main courses $7.95–$20. AE, DC, DISC, MC, V. Mon–Thurs 11:30am–10:30pm; Fri 11:30am–11pm; Sat noon–11pm; Sun noon–10:30pm. Metro: Dupont Circle.

Teaism Dupont Circle *(Finds)* ASIAN FUSION   Occupying a turn-of-the-20th-century neoclassic building on a tree-lined street, Teaism has a lovely rustic interior such as you might find in the Chinese countryside. A display kitchen and tandoor oven dominate the sunny downstairs room, which offers counter seating along a wall of French windows, open in warm weather. Upstairs seating is on banquettes and small Asian stools at handcrafted mahogany tables.

The impressive tea list comprises close to 30 aromatic blends, most of them from India, China, and Japan. On the menu is light Asian fare served on stainless-steel plates or in lacquer lunch boxes (Japanese "bento boxes," which hold a delicious meal of, for example, teriyaki salmon, cucumber-ginger salad, a scoop of rice with seasoning, and fresh fruit—all $8). Dishes include Thai chicken curry with sticky rice, ostrich burger with Asian slaw, and a portobello and goat cheese sandwich. Baked goods, coconut rice pudding, and lime shortbread cookies are among desserts. At breakfast, you might try ginger scones or cilantro eggs and sausage with fresh tandoor-baked onion nan bread. Everything's available for takeout. Teapots, cups, and other gift items are for sale.

Note: Teaism has two other locations, both convenient for sightseeing. **Teaism Lafayette Square,** 800 Connecticut Ave. NW (© 202/835-2233), is across from the White House; it's open weekdays from 7:30am to 5:30pm and serves afternoon tea. **Teaism Penn Quarter** ✦, 400 8th St. NW (© 202/638-6010), which is near the MCI Center, the National Gallery, and nightspots, is the only branch that serves beer, wine, and cocktails. Teaism Penn Quarter is open daily, serving all three meals and afternoon tea, and brunch on Saturday and Sunday; its happy hour on Thursday and Friday, from 5:30 to 7:30pm, features free hors d'oeuvres (with purchased drink—try the mango or ginger margaritas) like curries and Asian noodle salads.

2009 R St. NW (between Connecticut and 21st sts.). © 202/667-3827. All menu items 90¢–$8. AE, MC, V. Mon–Thurs 8am–10pm; Fri 8am–11pm; Sat 9am–11pm; Sun 9am–10pm. Metro: Dupont Circle.

WORTH A SPLURGE

Al Tiramisu ✦✦ *(Finds* ITALIAN   I called last minute for a reservation and the staff was kind enough to squeeze in four of us (*squeeze* being the operative word, as the tables are a little snug in this narrow but intimate restaurant). But the charming servers have time to chat a little without keeping you waiting. It was refreshing to have our waiter, without any discussion, hand the wine list to me, rather than to one of the men at the table. Make sure you give the menu due consideration; this is one place where the mainstays are just as good (and certainly cheaper) than the daily specials. Al Tiramisu is known for its grilled fish and for its black and white truffles, a favorite item of certain Kennedy clan members. Also exceptional are the grilled squid, house-made spinach-ricotta ravioli with butter and sage sauce, and the osso buco. This is a place to come if you need cheering up. Ebullient chef/owner Luigi Diotaiuti makes his presence known sometimes—check out the restaurant's website for a taste of his personality. A little hokey, perhaps, but fun.

2014 P St. NW. © 202/467-4466. www.altiramisu.com. Reservations required. Lunch main courses $6–$17; dinner main courses $14–$20. AE, DC, MC, V. Mon–Fri noon–2:30pm; Mon–Sat 5:30–10:30pm; Sun 5–9:30pm. Metro: Dupont Circle.

Dupont Grille ✦ AMERICAN   Although the Dupont Grille is situated inside the Irish-owned Jurys Washington Hotel, the restaurant is thoroughly American, its chef, Cornell Coulon, hailing from New Orleans. The hotel faces Dupont Circle, but the restaurant, which has floor-to-ceiling glass panels that slide open at a slant, sits on 19th Street, which means you get the hustle and bustle of the neighborhood without the full-blown effect of traffic noise. This is a colorful dining spot, both design- and cuisine-wise. Banquettes are pumpkin-toned, and wall panels look like a Piet Mondrian painting—big squares of yellow, black, and white. We followed our waiter's suggestion and ordered a beef confit spring roll with sundried tomato, chutney, and basil dressing; the chopped salad with romaine, radicchio, blue cheese, and tomato topped with a garlicky dressing; and grilled Waluu (a moist and sweet fish found in the Pacific; it's also known as "Hawaiian butterfish"), served on a bed of sautéed snowpeas, daikon radish, preserved ginger, and rock shrimp, with a citrus/soy sauce. Quite delicious. A large bar lines the center back wall, and the restaurant opens to a sidewalk café in warm weather.

In the Jurys Washington Hotel, 1500 New Hampshire Ave. NW (entrance on 19th St. NW). ℂ **202/939-9596.** Reservations recommended. Breakfast main courses $8.95–$12; brunch $18; dinner main courses $17–$26. AE, DC, DISC, MC, V. Daily 7–11am; Sun brunch 11am–2:30pm; Sun–Thurs 5:30–10pm; Fri–Sat 5:30–11pm. Metro: Dupont Circle.

Etrusco ✹✹ ITALIAN   Etrusco is just the sort of place you'd hope to stumble upon as a stranger in town. It's pretty, with a sophisticated but relaxed atmosphere, and the food is excellent. Lately, diners have been complaining about indifferent service, though, and I hope that by the time you read this, the wait staff will have regained its former professionalism. From the slate terrace at street level with umbrella tables, you descend a short flight of steps to the exquisite dining room, which resembles a trattoria with ochre and burnt-sienna walls, arched skylight, and tile floor.

On the menu you'll find warm baby octopus salad, *ribollita* (minestrone thickened with bread and Parmesan cheese), pappardelle with shredded duck, crumb-coated grilled tuna, and the more traditional veal scaloppini and osso buco. It's all very, very good. End with "Grandfather's cake," a light chocolate pie.

1606 20th St. NW. ℂ **202/667-0047.** Reservations recommended. Main courses $14–$30. AE, DC, MC, V. Nightly 5:30–10:30pm. Metro: Dupont Circle.

Tabard Inn ✹ AMERICAN   The restaurant here is only a shade more conventional than the inn in which it resides (see chapter 5). From the cozy though tattered lounge, where you can enjoy a drink in front of a crackling fire, you enter a narrow room, where hanging plants dangle from skylights and a mural of a ponytailed waiter points the way to the kitchen. A small bar hugs one side of the passage, a series of small tables the other, and both lead to the main space. Or you can head up a set of stairs to another dining room and its adjoining courtyard. The restaurant staff, like the inn staff, is disarmingly solicitous.

The food is fresh and seasonal, making use of the inn's own homegrown and organically grown vegetables and herbs. The menu changes with the seasons, so sample dishes might include beef tenderloin with house made boudin blanc, pancetta wrapped tuna, or a seafood and green herb stew of spring vegetables, pistou, and crostini. Sunday brunch is an a la carte feast of both breakfast and supper choices, from vanilla brioche French toast, to roasted trout with roasted new potatoes. The Tabard is a favorite spot for Washingtonians.

1739 N St. NW. ℂ **202/833-2668.** www.tabardinn.com. Reservations recommended. Breakfast $2.50–$7.50; brunch $9–$14; lunch main courses $10–$16; dinner main courses $19–$27. AE, DC, MC, V. Daily 7–9:30am; Mon–Fri 11:30am–2:30pm; Sat 11am–2:30pm; Sun 10:30am–2:30pm and 6–9pm; Mon–Thurs 6–10pm; Fri–Sat 6–10:30pm. Metro: Dupont Circle.

8 Foggy Bottom/West End

Bertucci's ITALIAN   My friend Jane and 11 of her colleagues ate lunch here, ordering pizza, tea, and soda for all, and the bill came to $45, without tip. Pretty cheap, huh? Which is why you'll find a lot of George Washington University students eating here (Bertucci's is located within a little mall adjacent to the campus). What a lot of people don't realize is that you get a big salad bowl with pizza at lunch (11am–3pm, daily), and it's replenished for free. (This deal doesn't apply to carryout orders.) Pizzas are large, with a wide range of toppings offered, from standard tomato and cheese to shredded prosciutto, caramelized onions, and a lemon pepper cream sauce. Service is irregular. Bertucci's serves pastas and other main courses, but I can only recommend the pizzas, all of which, by the way, are cooked in a brick oven. Bertucci's is a national chain; another location in Washington is at 1218 Connecticut Ave. NW (© 202/463-7733), in the Dupont Circle neighborhood.

2000 Pennsylvania Ave. NW. © 202/296-2600. Reservations required for 8 or more. Pizzas and pastas from $7–$17 at lunch and dinner. AE, DISC, MC, V. Mon–Thurs 11am–10pm; Fri–Sat 11am–11pm; Sun noon–10pm. Metro: Foggy Bottom or Farragut West.

SUPER-CHEAP EATS

Cup'A Cup'A AMERICAN   George Washington University professors hang out here, along with Kennedy Center artists, patrons, and Watergate Condominium residents—Cup'A Cup'A is located in the Watergate complex, within view of the Kennedy Center. Keep it in mind if you're headed to the Center before or after a performance. This is an attractive restaurant and not just a place to have coffee, as its name might lead you to assume. In fact, the decor has a feel of Venice about it, thanks to Italian yellow walls hung with photos of that Italian city, and various cappuccino and coffee machines. The menu offers many delicious breakfast breads, like scones and muffins, side dishes of bacon and eggs, and, at lunch and dinner, huge sandwiches: roast beef, turkey, curried

---

(Value   Pretheater Dinners and Weekend Brunches = Great Deals

Some of Washington's finest restaurants offer some of the best deals in town, in the form of either the fixed price pretheater dinner or weekend brunch. At least one favorite, **Café Atlantico** 🦋🦋 (p. 128), serves both, and they are both winners. Café Atlantico's pretheater tasting menu, available from 5 to 6:30pm nightly, allows you three courses for $22; sample dishes are shrimp with tamarind oil and pineapple as a first course, lobster with a sauce of tomatoes, olives, onions, capers, and lime for the main course, and warm chocolate cake to finish. From Café Atlantico's Latino dim sum menu you may choose items a la carte or the all-you-can-eat feast for $25 (vegetarian) or $35 (regular) per person. The Latino dim sum is served Saturdays and Sundays 11:30am to 2:30pm, and features tapas-size portions of 25 different courses, ranging from tuna ceviche with coconut milk, to duck leg confit with passion fruit oil.

Take a look at **Bistro Français** (p. 150) to read about another pretheater dinner—its three-course $20 meal is served from 5 to 7pm and 10:30pm to 1am nightly, which makes the bistro a good spot for late night dining, too. Other restaurants in this chapter that offer brunches are **Georgia Brown's** (p. 129), whose $24 Sunday brunch includes jazz; **Old Glory Barbecue** 🦋 (p. 152), whose $12 ($6.95 for kids) all-you-can-eat meal is a steal; and the **Bombay Club** (p. 131), whose $19 Sunday brunch is an elegant but filling affair, with champagne, piano music, and a buffet of choices.

chicken, ham, and so on. Wines are available by the glass for $4.50. Beer is also served.

600 New Hampshire Ave. NW. *C* 202/466-3677. Sandwiches $4–$5.95 at lunch; $5–$7 at dinner. AE, DC, MC, V. Mon–Sat 6:30am–8pm; Sun 10am–6pm. Metro: Foggy Bottom.

WORTH A SPLURGE

Kaz Sushi Bistro JAPANESE   Amiable chef/owner Kazuhiro ("Kaz") Okochi opened his own place after having worked at Sushi-Ko (p. 156) for many years. This is said to be the best place for sushi in the Washington area, and aficionados vie for one of the six chairs at the bar to watch Kaz and his staff do their thing, preparing salmon roe, sea urchin, tuna, and many other fish for sushi. Besides sushi, Kaz is known for his napoleon of sea trout and wonton skins, his broiled scallops, and for his bento boxes, offering exquisite tastings of pan-seared salmon, spicy broiled mussels, and the like. Kaz is one of few chefs in the area trained to handle tora fugu, the blowfish, which can be poisonous if not cleaned properly. The blowfish, if available, is served in winter. This is also the place to come for premium sakes.

1915 I St. NW. *C* 202/530-5500. Reservations recommended. Sushi a la carte $3.25–$6.50; lunch main courses $9.25–$17; dinner main courses $14–$25. AE, DC, DISC, MC, V. Mon–Fri 11:30am–2pm; Mon–Sat 6–10pm. Metro: Farragut West.

Kinkead's ✦✦✦ AMERICAN/SEAFOOD   When a restaurant has been as roundly praised as Kinkead's, you start to think no place can be *that* good—but Kinkead's really is. An appetizer like grilled squid with creamy polenta and tomato fondue leaves you with a permanent longing for squid. The signature dish, pepita-crusted salmon with shrimp, crab, and chiles, provides a nice hot crunch before melting in your mouth. Vegetables you may normally disdain—sweet potatoes, for instance—taste delicious here.

Award-winning chef/owner Bob Kinkead is the star at this three-tier, 220-seat restaurant. He wears a headset and orchestrates his kitchen staff in full view of the upstairs dining room, where booths and tables neatly fill the nooks and alcoves of the town house. At street level is a scattering of tables overlooking the restaurant's lower level, the more casual bar and cafe, where a jazz group or pianist performs nearly every evening. ***Beware:*** If the waiter tries to seat you in the "atrium," you'll be stuck at a table mall-side just outside the doors of the restaurant—yuck.

Kinkead's menu (which changes daily for lunch and again for dinner) features primarily seafood, but always includes at least one beef and one poultry entree. The wine list comprises more than 300 selections, and you can trust expert sommelier Michael Flynn to lead you to one you'll enjoy. You can't go wrong with the desserts either, like the chocolate dacquoise with cappuccino sauce. If you're hungry but not ravenous in the late afternoon, stop in for some delicious light fare: fish and chips, lobster roll, soups, and salads.

2000 Pennsylvania Ave. NW. *C* 202/296-7700. www.kinkead.com. Reservations recommended. Lunch main courses $15–$22; dinner main courses $22–$29; light fare $11–$22. AE, DC, DISC, MC, V. Daily 11:30am–2:30pm (with light fare served daily 2:30–5:30pm); Sun–Thurs 5:30–10pm; Fri–Sat 5:30–10:30pm. Metro: Foggy Bottom.

Nectar ✦✦ AMERICAN   This tiny place, seating 42, opened in April 2003. Nectar has some intriguing features: Its short menu offers as many appetizers as entrees—six of each. The modest but unusual wine list offers every wine by the glass, half-bottle, or bottle, with prices per glass ranging from $7 to $100, and prices per bottle ranging from $29 to $450. The décor combines elegant: gilded mirrors and golden sponge-painted walls, with unpretentious: pipes are exposed, though painted. Three friends and I agreed that our meals were winners. For appetizers we chose a fresh and minty pea soup, salad greens topped with sesame dressing, and fresh asparagus; for entrees, we selected veal cheeks with butternut squash puree and Masala spices, pheasant on a bed of ramps, and scallops sautéed with *haricots verts,* chorizo, dried fruit, pistachio, and curry spices. Everything was cooked perfectly and flavored nicely. We found fault only with the service, which was a little slow. Also, when our plates had been placed in front of us, we had to wait politely as our server delivered his detailed description of each dish we had ordered. This was a little much, especially since we knew exactly what we had ordered and were impatient to start eating. He was an earnest young chap, though, and had spent summers in Maine, where we like to go too, so we forgave him.

In the George Washington University Inn, 824 New Hampshire Ave. NW (between H and I sts.). ℂ 202/298-8085. www.nectardc.com. Reservations recommended. Lunch main courses $12–$17; dinner main courses $17–$26. AE, DC, DISC, MC, V. Breakfast daily 7–10am; lunch Mon–Fri 11am–2:30pm; dinner Sun–Thurs 5–10pm and Fri–Sat 5–11pm. Metro: Foggy Bottom.

9 Georgetown

Aditi INDIAN   This charming two-level restaurant provides a serene setting in which to enjoy first-rate Indian cooking to the tune of Indian music. A must here is the platter of assorted appetizers, which features *bhajia* (a deep-fried vegetable fritter), deep-fried cheese-and-shrimp pakoras, and crispy vegetable samosas stuffed with spiced potatoes and peas. Favorite entrees include lamb biryani, which is basmati rice pilaf tossed with savory pieces of lamb, cilantro, raisins, and almonds; and the skewered jumbo tandoori prawns, chicken, lamb, or beef—all fresh and fork tender—barbecued in the tandoor. Sauces are on the mild side, so if you like your food fiery, inform your waiter. A *kachumber* salad, a medley of chopped cucumber, lettuce, green pepper, and tomatoes, topped with yogurt and spices, is a refreshing accompaniment to entrees. For dessert, try *kheer,* a cooling rice pudding garnished with chopped nuts. There's a full bar.

3299 M St. NW. ℂ 202/625-6825. Reservations recommended. Lunch main courses $7–$16; dinner main courses $9–$16. AE, DC, DISC, MC, V. Sun noon–2:30pm; Mon–Sat 11:30am–2:30pm; Sun–Thurs 5:30–10pm; Fri–Sat 5:30–10:30pm.

Bangkok Bistro THAI   The trend in Thai restaurants these days is toward hip decor with traditional Thai cuisine, and that's what you get at Bangkok Bistro. Table tops seem to change color, reflecting the sparkle from the light fixtures, and waiters' ties, I swear, catch the light and shine, too. Choose from a respectable pad thai to spicy crispy whole flounder with chili garlic. Biting into a two-star menu item, you may find, as my husband did, that "a tingling sensation lingers and spreads a hearty glow." Oddly enough, though, if you choose a spicier dish, you may be disappointed—the two-stars, when we were there, at least, seemed more potent than the triple-starred; four stars are the spiciest. Best advice: Tell the waiter if you really and truly like hot Thai food. Also recommended: kapow, either beef, chicken, or pork sautéed with garlic, chiles, and basil leaves; and "Sweet Surrender," coconut shrimp in mango sauce. Bangkok Bistro serves generous portions of mixed drinks and glasses of wine, for the price.

3251 Prospect St. NW. ℂ 202/337-2424. Reservations accepted. Lunch $6.95–$17 (average is $6.95); dinner $9.95–$17 (average is $9.95). AE, DC, DISC, MC, V. Mon–Thurs 11:30am–11pm; Fri 11:30am–midnight; Sat noon–midnight; Sun noon–11pm.

Bistro Français ★ *Value* FRENCH   In this authentically Parisian bistro—the late-night hangout of Washington's top chefs—wainscoted walls are hung with mahogany-framed mirrors and French period posters from the two world wars. Seating areas are defined by wrought-iron and brass railings, ceilings are ornate pressed copper, and etched- and stained-glass panels add to the cozy clutter. Candlelit tables, set with white linen and adorned with fresh flowers, strike an elegant note.

The Bistro is actually a two-part affair—half of it a casual cafe, the other half a more serious dining room. Depending on where you sit, you have different menus, though the offerings are similar. In either section, a good bet on weekdays from 5 to 7pm (also from 10:30pm–1am) is a prix-fixe meal for $20 that includes: a glass of house wine; soup du jour or homemade liver mousse or mussels Niçoise; an entree, chosen from a long list of specials (such as braised duck with raspberry sauce and Indian wild rice); and a selection from the pastry cart. A similar menu is offered Monday through Saturday from 11am to 4pm, for $15. A la carte listings include a selection of traditional French hors d'oeuvres (seafood terrine with horseradish sauce, escargots with vegetables and garlic butter, sherried chicken-liver pâté), and entrees (*poulet rôti* [roast chicken] with tarragon, *entrecôte au poivre* [steak with crushed peppercorns]). Desserts are also Parisian cafe standbys—chocolate mousse, crème brûlée, and such (the raspberry tarte is first-rate). Numerous daily specials supplement the menu, as does an extensive, mostly French, wine list. The Saturday and Sunday brunch menu includes all the champagne you can drink.

3124–28 M St. NW. ℰ 202/338-3830. Reservations recommended. Lunch main courses $7.95–$14; dinner main courses $14–$22; prix-fixe lunch $15; brunch $16; early-bird/late-night special $20. AE, DC, MC, V. Sun–Thurs 11am–3am; Fri–Sat 11am–4am; Sat–Sun brunch 11am–4pm.

Clyde's of Georgetown AMERICAN   Clyde's has been a favorite watering hole for an eclectic mix of Washingtonians since 1963. You'll see university students, Capitol Hill types, affluent professionals, Washington Redskins, romantic duos, and well-heeled ladies who lunch. A 1996 renovation transformed Clyde's from a saloon to a theme park, whose dining areas include a cherry-paneled front room with oil paintings of sport scenes, and an atrium with vintage model planes dangling from the glass ceiling and a 16th-century French limestone chimney piece in the large fireplace.

Clyde's is known for its burgers, chili, and crab-cake sandwiches. Appetizers are a safe bet, and Clyde's take on the classic Niçoise (chilled grilled salmon with greens, oven-roasted roma tomatoes, green beans, and grilled new potatoes in a tasty vinaigrette) is also recommended. Sunday brunch is a tradition, and some brunch items are available on Saturday, too. The menu is reassuringly familiar—steak and eggs, omelets, waffles—with variations thrown in for good measure. Among bar selections are about 10 draft beers. Wines are half-price on Sundays.

Note: You can park in the underground Georgetown Park garage for $1 per hour for the first 2 hours (a deal in Georgetown!). Just show your meal receipt and ask the mall concierge to validate your parking ticket.

3236 M St. NW. ℰ 202/333-9180. www.clydes.com. Reservations recommended. Lunch/brunch $7.95–$16; dinner main courses $11–$24 (most under $12); burgers and sandwiches (except for crab-cake sandwich) $10 or less. AE, DC, DISC, MC, V. Mon–Thurs 11:30am–midnight; Fri 11:30am–1am; Sat 10am–1am; Sun 9am–10:30pm (Sun brunch 9am–4pm).

Garrett's AMERICAN   The rooftop terrace at Garrett's is one of Washington's best-kept secrets. You reach it via a narrow stairway that bypasses a clattering

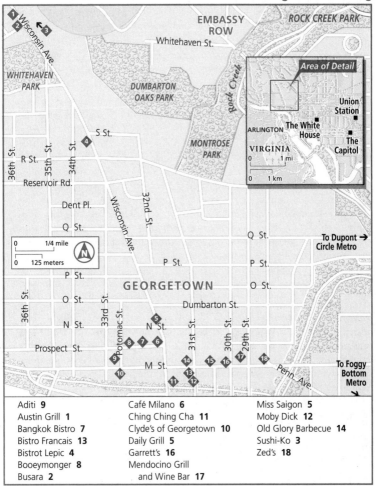

Aditi **9**
Austin Grill **1**
Bangkok Bistro **7**
Bistro Francais **13**
Bistrot Lepic **4**
Booeymonger **8**
Busara **2**

Café Milano **6**
Ching Ching Cha **11**
Clyde's of Georgetown **10**
Daily Grill **5**
Garrett's **16**
Mendocino Grill
  and Wine Bar **17**

Miss Saigon **5**
Moby Dick **12**
Old Glory Barbecue **14**
Sushi-Ko **3**
Zed's **18**

ground-floor bar. The second-story terrace—perfect for romantic dinners—has a sloped glass cathedral ceiling and glass walls framed in gleaming white that provide a solarium-like setting from which to view the streets and buildings of Georgetown while you dine. Candlelit tables are spaced far apart. Walls are hung with 19th-century railroad prints, and train artifacts (crossing signs, railroad lights) are much in evidence.

Consider an appetizer of piquantly sauced buffalo wings served with a blue cheese dip or nachos piled high with Monterey Jack, cheddar cheese, and spicy beef. Main dishes include burgers, salads, sandwiches (ranging from fresh oven-roasted turkey on multigrain bread to barbecued pork on a fresh roll, both with fries and coleslaw), pastas (perhaps fettuccine tossed with blackened chicken strips, mushrooms, and scallions, in a tangy Parmesan cream sauce), or a 12-ounce chargrilled New York strip steak served with a baked potato and vegetable. Save room for a big slab of Reese's ice cream peanut butter pie for dessert. There's a full bar.

An interesting footnote: Garrett's occupies a 200-year-old building that was originally the residence of Thomas Sim Lee, governor of Maryland and a forebear of Robert E. Lee.

3003 M St. NW. ✆ 202/333-1033. Reservations recommended. Sandwiches $4.75–$7.75; main courses mostly $6.95–$14. AE, DC, DISC, MC, V. Mon–Thurs 11:30am–2am; Fri 11:30am–3am; Sat noon–3am; Sun noon–2am.

Miss Saigon VIETNAMESE   This is a charming restaurant, with tables scattered amid a "forest" of tropical foliage, and twinkly lights strewn upon the fronds of the potted palms and ferns.

The food here is delicious and authentic, though the service can be a trifle slow when the restaurant is busy. To begin, there is the crispy calamari, or the shrimp and pork-stuffed garden rolls. House specialties include steamed flounder, caramel salmon, and "shaking beef" (cubes of tender Vietnamese steak, marinated in wine, garlic, butter, and soy sauce, then sautéed with onions and potatoes and served with rice and salad). There's a full bar. Desserts range from bananas *flambé au rhum* (fried bananas with rum sauce) to ice cream with Godiva liqueur. Not to be missed is drip-pot coffee, brewed table side and served iced over sweetened condensed milk.

3057 M St. NW. ✆ 202/333-5545. Reservations recommended, especially weekend nights. Lunch main courses $4.50–$8.95; dinner main courses $8.95–$23. AE, DC, MC, V. Mon–Fri 11:30am–10:30pm (lunch menu served until 3pm); Sat–Sun noon–11pm (dinner menu served all day).

Old Glory Barbecue *(Kids* BARBECUE   Raised wooden booths flank one side of the restaurant; an imposing, old-fashioned dark-wood bar with saddle-seat stools extends down the other. Recorded swing music during the day, more mainstream music into the night, plays in the background. Old Glory boasts the city's "largest selection of single-barrel and boutique bourbons" and a new rooftop deck with outdoor seating and views of Georgetown.

After 9pm or so, the two-story restaurant becomes packed with the hard-drinkin' young and restless. In early evening, though, Old Glory is prime for anyone—singles, families, or an older crowd—although it's almost always noisy. Come for the messy, tangy, delicious spare ribs; hickory-smoked chicken; tender, smoked beef brisket; or marinated, wood-fired shrimp. Six sauces are on the table, the spiciest being the vinegar-based East Carolina and Lexington. My Southern-raised husband favored the Savannah version, which reminded him of that city's famous Johnny Harris barbecue sauce. The complimentary corn muffins and biscuits; side dishes of collard greens, succotash, and potato salad; and desserts like apple crisp and coconut cherry cobbler all hit the spot.

3139 M St. NW. ✆ 202/337-3406. Reservations accepted for 6 or more Sun–Thurs, reservations not accepted Fri–Sat. Main courses $7.95–$22; Sun brunch buffet $12, $6.95 for children 11 and under. AE, DC, DISC, MC, V. Sun 11am–11:30pm (brunch from 11am–3pm); Mon–Thurs 11:30am–11:30pm; Fri–Sat 11:30am–midnight. Bar stays open later nightly.

Zed's ETHIOPIAN   Though Ethiopian cuisine has long been popular in Washington, few restaurants can match Zed's truly authentic, high-quality fare. Zed's is a charming little place with indigenous paintings, posters, and artifacts adorning pine-paneled walls. Tables are set with fresh flowers, and Ethiopian music enhances the ambience.

Diners eschew silverware in favor of using a sourdough crepelike pancake called *injera* to scoop up food. Highly recommended are the *doro watt* (chicken stewed in a tangy, hot red chile-pepper sauce), the *infillay* (strips of tender chicken breast flavored with seasoned butter and honey wine served with a delicious chopped spinach and rice side dish), flavorful lamb dishes, and the deep-fried whole fish. Vegetables have never been tastier. Consider ordering more of the garlicky chopped collard greens, red lentil purée in spicy red-pepper sauce, or a chilled purée of roasted yellow split peas mixed with onions, peppers, and garlic. There's a full bar, and, should you have the inclination, there are Italian pastries for dessert.

1201 28th St. NW (at M St.). ℭ 202/333-4710. Reservations accepted for 6 or more. Main courses $9–$15. AE, DC, DISC, MC, V. Sun–Thurs 11am–10pm; Fri–Sat 11am–11pm.

SUPER-CHEAP EATS

Booeymonger DELI   This is the original Booeymonger's (there's another, in suburban Maryland). The deli is situated on a side street, at the corner; a few tables outside allow you to dine with a view of some typical old Georgetown town houses. Inside are two brick-walled rooms, usually filled with students, construction workers, and people from the neighborhood. One look at the menu is enough to tell you the Booeymonger's been around for a while: it offers quiche, for one thing, and sandwiches with names like the "Patty Hearst" (turkey, bacon, and melted provolone cheese with Russian dressing on French bread), and the "Tuna Turner" (tuna with lettuce, tomato, house dressing, and veggies on a kaiser roll). You can order the basics, too; this is about as cheap as it gets in Georgetown.

3265 Prospect St. NW. ℭ 202/333-4810. Breakfast items 60¢–$4.50; sandwiches $2.75–$5.95. MC, V. Mon–Fri 7:30am–midnight; Sat–Sun 8am–midnight.

Ching Ching Cha *(Finds* CHINESE   Located just below M Street, this skylit Chinese tearoom offers a pleasant respite from the crowds. You can sit on pillows at low tables or on chairs set at rosewood tables. Choices are simple: individual items like a tea-and-spice boiled egg, puff pastry stuffed with lotus-seed paste, or five-spice peanuts; or the tea meal, which consists of miso soup, three marinated cold vegetables, rice, a salad, and tastings of soy-ginger chicken, salmon with mustard-miso sauce, or steamed teriyaki-sauced tofu. Tea choices include several different green, black, medicinal, and oolong teas, plus a Fujian white tea and a ginseng brew. A typical dish might be the $11 "tea meal," which includes curried chicken with vegetables, soup, and salad (tofu and salmon tea meals are also available).

1063 Wisconsin Ave. NW. ℭ 202/333-8288. Reservations not accepted. All items $4–$20. AE, DISC, MC, V. Tues–Sat 11:30am–9pm; Sun 11:30am–7pm.

Moby Dick, House of Kabob ✪ MIDDLE EASTERN   Moby Dick has about six places in the D.C. area, one of which happens to be located just down the street from where I live, a fact for which I will be forever grateful. Moby Dick is my backup for dinner, on days that have been too long. All Moby Dicks offer the same mouthwatering dishes. Our favorites are the gyro sandwiches and chicken souvlaki. The beef on the gyro is exquisitely seasoned, as is the chicken, and both come with a tangy yogurt cucumber sauce. The huge pita bread is made right behind the counter in the traditional clay oven. The hummus is the best I've had anywhere, and my children enjoy the rice, which they say tastes different (meaning "better") than mine. My girls, ages 11 and 16, usually split a gyro, which at $4.50, proves to be a real deal. The only unremarkable dishes are the salads. Moby Dick has a dining room (no bar), or you can order to go.

1070 31st St. NW (just below M St.). ℭ 202/333-4400. Sandwiches/platters/traditional dishes $4.15–$12. Daily 11am–10pm, with hours extended to 4am Sat and Sun mornings.

WORTH A SPLURGE

Bistrot Lepic & Wine Bar 🐪🐪 FRENCH   Tiny Bistrot Lepic is the real thing—a charming French restaurant that seems plucked right off a Parisian side street. The atmosphere is bustling and cheery, and you hear a lot of French spoken—not just by the waiters, but also by customers. The Bistrot is a neighborhood place, and you'll often see diners waving hellos across the room to each other, or even leaving their table to visit with those at another. In its nine years, the restaurant has made some changes to accommodate its popularity, most recently turning the upstairs into a wine bar and lounge; this means that if you arrive early for your reservation, you now have a place to wait (in the past, one had to hover hungry-eyed at the door). Or you can come just to hang out, sip a glass of wine, and munch on delicious little somethings from the wine bar menu, where the most expensive item is the $12 terrine of homemade foie gras. No need to make a reservation at the wine bar unless you plan to order dinner from the regular menu.

This is traditional French cooking, updated. The seasonal menu offers such entrees as grilled rainbow trout with carrot sauce, beef medallions with polenta and shiitake mushroom sauce, and sautéed sea scallops with ginger broccoli mousse. We opted for specials: rare tuna served on fennel with citrus vinaigrette, and grouper with a mildly spicy lobster sauce upon a bed of spinach.

The modest French wine list offers a fairly good range. The house red wine, Le Pic Saint-Loup, is a nice complement to most menu choices and is $23 a bottle.

1736 Wisconsin Ave. NW (near S St.). ℂ 202/333-0111. www.bistrotlepic.net. Reservations recommended. Lunch main courses $13–$17; dinner main courses $14–$23. AE, DC, DISC, MC, V. Tues–Sun 11:30am–2:30pm; Tues–Thurs 5:30–10pm; Fri-Sat 5:30–10:30pm; wine bar Tues–Thurs and Sun 5:30–11:30pm; Fri–Sat 5:30 pm–12:30am.

Café Milano 🐪 ITALIAN   The beautiful people factor rises exponentially here as the night wears on. Café Milano has long been a magnet for Washington's famous and attractive, and their visitors. In fact, the restaurant plays up its reputation, staging occasional "fashion brunches," where models strut their stuff while you dine. But this restaurant/nightclub/bar also serves very good food. Salads are big, pasta servings are small, and fish and meat entrees are just the right size. We had the endive, radicchio, and arugula salad topped with thin sheets of Parmesan cheese; a *panzanella* salad of tomatoes, potatoes, red onion, celery, and cucumber basking in basil and olive oil; *cappellacci* (round ravioli) pockets of spinach and ricotta in cream sauce; sautéed sea bass on a bed of vegetables with lemon chive sauce; and the Santa Babila pizza, which has tomatoes, fresh mozzarella, oregano, and basil on a light pizza crust. All were delicious. At Café Milano, it's the nonsmokers who are relegated to the back room, while the smoking section takes over the main part of the restaurant and bar, which opens through the glass front to the sidewalk cafe. A bevy of good-humored waiters takes care of you. For best value, try the four-course, $35 fixed price menu, which changes nightly.

3251 Prospect St. NW (between Wisconsin Ave. and Potomac St.). ℂ 202/333-6183. www.cafemilano.net. Reservations recommended. Lunch main courses $9.50–$19; dinner main courses $13–$30; fixed price dinner $35. Sun–Wed 11:30am–11pm (bar menu served until midnight); Thurs–Sat 11:30am–midnight (bar menu served until 1am).

Mendocino Grille and Wine Bar 🐪AMERICAN   As its name suggests, you should come here to enjoy West Coast wine, along with contemporary American cuisine and a California-casual ambience. All of the 125-or-so bottles on the wine list are California vintages, and waiters are knowledgeable about the specifics of each, so don't hesitate to ask questions. California-casual doesn't mean cheap, though: Bottles range from $20 to $500, although most fall in the $50 to $60 range. The restaurant offers 22 wines by the glass, in different sizes, the better for tastings, and most of these run from $7 to $9 each.

New owner (in 2003) Eli Hengst wants to keep Mendocino's already delicious cuisine, but hopes eventually to be using 40% or more organic ingredients in the kitchen. Highlights on the menu include an Amish farmed free-range chicken served with scallion mashed potatoes and grilled vegetables, a New York strip of Kobe beef, and mustard spiced yellowfin tuna presented on orzo with English peas and artichokes.

Rough-textured slate walls alternate with painted patches of Big Sur sky to suggest a West Coast winery in California's wine-growing region. The wall sconces resemble rectangles of sea glass and the dangling light fixtures look like turned-over wineglasses. It's a very pleasant place, where Georgetown neighbors tend to congregate. Thursday through Saturday, the restaurant serves small dishes and desserts from about 10pm until 1am.

2917 M St. NW. ✆ 202/333-2912. Reservations recommended. Lunch main courses $6.75–$19; dinner main courses $17–$29; prix fixe: lunch $20, dinner $33. AE, DC, DISC, MC, V. Mon–Sat 11:30am–3pm; Sun–Thurs 5:30–10pm; Fri–Sat 5:30–11pm; Thurs–Sat 10pm–1am for small dishes.

10 Glover Park

Buses (the no. 30 series) travel to Glover Park, which is just north of Georgetown. Even better, hop on one of the blue Georgtown Metro Connection shuttle buses (see chapter 4 for more information on the buses), which travel up Wisconsin Avenue as far as 35th Street, putting you just south of the following restaurants. Or, you can take a taxi.

Austin Grill (Kids SOUTHERN/SOUTHWESTERN   Rob Wilder opened his grill in 1988 to replicate the easygoing lifestyle, Tex-Mex cuisine, and music he loved when he lived in Austin. The good food and festive atmosphere make this a great place for the kids, a date, or a group of friends. Austin Grill is loud; as the night progresses, conversation eventually drowns out the sound of the recorded music (everything from Ry Cooder to Natalie Merchant).

Fresh ingredients are used to create outstanding crab-meat quesadillas, "Lake Travis" nachos (tostadas slathered with red onion, refried beans, and cheese), a daily fish special (like rockfish fajitas), Key lime pie, and excellent versions of standard fare (chicken enchiladas, guacamole, pico de gallo, and so on). The margaritas are awesome.

Austin Grill's upstairs overlooks the abbreviated bar area below. An upbeat decor includes walls washed in shades of teal and clay and adorned with whimsical coyotes, cowboys, Indians, and cacti. Arrive by 6pm weekends if you don't want to wait; weekdays are less crowded.

This is the original Austin Grill; another District Austin Grill is located near the MCI Center at 750 E St. NW (✆ 202/393-3776). Suburban locations include one in Old Town Alexandria (see chapter 10).

2404 Wisconsin Ave. NW. ✆ 202/337-8080. www.austingrill.com. Reservations not accepted. Main courses $8–$17. AE, DC, DISC, MC, V. Mon 11:30am–10:30pm; Tues–Thurs 11:30am–11pm; Fri 11:30am–midnight; Sat 11am–midnight; Sun 11am–10:30pm.

Busara THAI   Like many Thai restaurants, Busara gives you big portions for a pretty good price. The pad thai is excellent—less sweet than most—the satays are well marinated, and an appetizer called "shrimp bikini" serves up not-at-all-greasy deep-fried shrimp in a thin spring-roll covering.

Busara's dining room is large, with a picture window overlooking Wisconsin Avenue, modern art on the neon-blue walls, and dimly set track lighting angled this way and that. Service is solicitous, but not pushy. If the dining room is full, you can eat at the bar (at dinner only), which is in a separate, rather inviting room. In warm weather, Busara also serves diners in its Oriental garden.

2340 Wisconsin Ave. NW. © 202/337-2340. Reservations recommended. Lunch main courses $7–$9; dinner main courses $10–$17. AE, DISC, MC, V. Daily 11:30am–3pm; Sun–Thurs 5–10:30pm; Fri–Sat 5–11:30pm.

Sushi-Ko ✦ JAPANESE Sushi-Ko was Washington's first sushi bar when it opened 28 years ago and it remains popular. The sushi chefs are fun to watch—try to sit at the sushi bar. You can expect superb sushi and sashimi standards, but the best items are daily specials, like a sea trout napoleon (diced sea trout layered between rice crackers), the delicately fried soft shell crab (in season, spring and summer), and the "small dishes," like the grilled baby octopus with mango, or asparagus with smoked salmon and mustard dashi sauce. The tempuras and teriyakis are also excellent. And there's a long list of sakes, as well as burgundy wines and Japanese beer.

2309 Wisconsin Ave. NW. © 202/333-4187. www.sushiko.us. Reservations recommended. Main courses $11–$21. AE, MC, V. Tues–Fri noon–2:30pm; Mon–Thurs 6–10:30pm; Fri 6–11pm; Sat 5:30–11pm; Sun 5:30–10pm.

11 Woodley Park

Lebanese Taverna MIDDLE EASTERN This family-owned restaurant gives you a taste of Lebanese culture—its cuisine, decor, and music. It's very popular on weekends, so expect to stand in line (reservations are accepted for seating before 6:30pm only). Diners, once seated in the courtyardlike dining room, where music plays and prayer rugs hang on the walls, hate to leave. The wood-burning oven in the back bakes the pita breads and several appetizers. Order a *demi mezze,* with pita for dipping, and you get 10 sampling dishes, including hummus, tabbouleh, baba ghanoush, and pastry-wrapped spinach pies (*fatayer bi sabanikh*), enough for dinner for two or hors d'oeuvres for four, and a pretty good deal at $45 for the platter. The wealth of meatless dishes will delight vegetarians, while rotisserie items, especially the chicken and the char-grilled kebabs of chicken and shrimp, will please all others.

There are other Lebanese Tavernas in the area but this is the only one in the District.

2641 Connecticut Ave. NW. © 202/265-8681. www.lebanesetaverna.com. Reservations accepted before 6:30pm. Lunch main courses $7.75–$15; dinner main courses $11–$19. AE, DC, DISC, MC, V. Mon–Fri 11:30am–2:30pm; Sat 11:30am–3pm; Mon–Thurs 5:30–10:30pm; Fri–Sat 5:30–11pm; Sun 5–10pm. Metro: Woodley Park–Zoo.

Tono Sushi JAPANESE You can sit outside at sidewalk tables, inside upstairs or down, at the sushi bar, or at two low tables. Likewise, the menu offers endless choices. There's sushi, of course, interpreted in brave new ways, from sushi of oysters to three kinds of salmon over rice. Specials list things like monkfish liver pâté. For the best bargain, try a meal-in-a-bowl soup, like the tempura soba, which combines buckwheat noodles, shrimp, fishcake, and broth. For traditionalists, there are plenty of tempura, teriyaki, yakitori, and sukiyaki dishes.

2605 Connecticut Ave. NW. © 202/332-7300. Reservations suggested. Lunch $6.95–$19; dinner $7.95–$19; sushi $1.50–$4 per piece. AE, MC, V. Daily 11:30am–2:30pm and 5–10pm. Metro: Woodley Park–Zoo.

WORTH A SPLURGE

Petits Plats ☞ FRENCH   Petits Plats is another French bistro, and a very pretty one, ensconced in a town house that's situated directly across from the Woodley Park Metro entrance and the Marriott Wardman Park Hotel. You can sit at the sidewalk cafe, on the porch above, or in the front room, back room, or upstairs rooms of the town house. Watching the passersby on busy Connecticut Avenue is a major amusement. Bistro fare includes shrimp bisque with crab meat; five different mussels dishes, like the mussels in a mustard, cream, and white wine sauce (each comes with french fries); Provençal-styled shrimp on an artichoke-bottom dish; Belgian endive salad with apples, walnuts, and Roquefort; and roasted rack of lamb with potatoes au gratin. The reasonably priced Petits Plats becomes even more so Tuesday through Friday at lunch, when a two-course set menu is available for $14; daily at early dinner, 5:30 to 7pm, when a three-course set menu is available for $19; and at Saturday and Sunday brunch, when $16 gets you a choice of entree (from eggs Benedict to steak *frites*), a house salad, and all the champagne you like. Since it opened in spring 2000, Petits Plats has gained a loyal following.

2653 Connecticut Ave. NW. ℂ **202/518-0018.** www.petits-plats.com. Reservations recommended. Lunch main courses $11–$16; dinner main courses $15–$22. AE, MC, V. Tues–Fri 11:30am–2:30pm; Sat–Sun 11:30am–4pm; Tues–Thurs and Sun 5:30–10pm; Fri–Sat 5:30–11pm. Metro: Woodley Park–Zoo.

7

Exploring Washington, D.C.

Throughout other chapters of this book, I've made the claim that Washington, D.C., can be paradise for the traveler on a budget. If you haven't been convinced yet, this chapter and the sightseeing it guides you to, ought to do it. Of the nearly 50 major attractions described herein, only six sites charge admission, and three of the six call it a "donation," which means you probably won't be turned away if you arrive with empty pockets. This chapter also recommends a number of less famous sites (see box on "Museums of Special Interest"), which are either free to visit or ask a minimal admission. The most expensive attractions? The International Spy Museum, whose entrance fee has already increased twice since its 2002 opening to the current $13 per adult, $11 per child charge; and organized city tours, like Tourmobile, which charges $20 per adult and $10 per child for its most popular route.

The point is, you can tour the capital inside and out, without spending a dime. Your bigger problem is time. My advice is to consider the whole picture and then decide what it is that really interests you. Don't assume that you need to follow the crowd. The National Air and Space Museum continues to be the most visited attraction in Washington, and it is, indeed, marvelous (and almost always swarming with visitors). But if its exhibits don't appeal, don't go. There's plenty else to do.

Here's what I mean. While you are in the neighborhood of the "big name" sights, you may want to pop in to a lesser known attraction for a different kind of experience. For example, the Capitol, the Supreme Court, and the Library of Congress all dovetail nicely at the intersection of First Street and East Capitol Street. But if you crave a fix of something unrelated to government, walk 1 block past the Library of Congress on East Capitol to the Folger Shakespeare Library, where you can admire Tudor architecture and exhibits from the collection of Renaissance books, paintings, and musical instruments. Take a break and stroll south to Pennsylvania Avenue for some takeout food and return here to picnic in the Elizabethan garden. And at night, if the Folger Theatre is staging a production, you owe it to yourself to attend, for these performances are priceless (see chapter 9 for more information along those lines). I'm getting carried away, perhaps, but that's what I want you to do: get carried away by your experiences. Go at your own pace, see what you want to see, allow for the unexpected, and if you don't get to everything, come back for another visit.

A lot is new in the capital, from museum openings to enhanced security procedures, so be sure to read both the "Head's Up" and the "Openings & Closings" boxes that follow.

As you prepare for sightseeing around the capital, keep aware of what's going on in the world, and build in some extra time for security procedures, which are in place at most attractions. You'll notice barriers erected around the Capitol grounds and monuments, but don't let the sight of them, nor the tighter security precautions,

Head's Up

The terrorist attacks of September 11, 2001, our country's invasion of Iraq in 2003, and other world events have necessitated the implementation of stricter security procedures around the capital. In addition, the U.S. Department of Homeland Security sometimes issues color code warnings, which may affect the operation of attractions you'd like to see. Generally, you should know that a "Code Red," is the only warning that would close museums and most other attractions. The next level down, "Code Orange," may prompt some sites to close, but not usually. For instance, when a Code Orange was issued during the time our country was at war with Iraq, the Capitol canceled its public tours of the building; once the war ended, the Code Orange was lifted, and the Capitol resumed its public tours. A few weeks later, Homeland Security issued another Code Orange alert, in response to a possible threat from Al Qaeda—this time, the Capitol stayed open for tours. Meanwhile, the Bureau of Engraving and Printing decided to remain closed throughout the duration of all Code Orange warnings.

deter you. At many museums, like the Smithsonian's Air and Space, Natural History, and American History museums, you now must walk past metal detectors, which means that, during the busy spring and summer seasons, especially, you may be standing in line outside, as you wait for your turn to pass through security. Other museums have staff hand-search handbags, briefcases, and backpacks. At government buildings, like the Capitol, security procedures run the gamut, including the use of X-ray machines, metal detectors, and hand searches. Make things easy on yourself and everyone else by carrying as little as possible, and certainly no sharp objects. Museums no longer offer the use of lockers.

SUGGESTED ITINERARIES

If You Have 1 Day

Make the Mall your destination, visiting whichever museums appeal to you the most. Then take a breather: If you have young kids, take them for a ride on the carousel across from the Smithsonian's Arts & Industries Building. With or without kids, stroll across the Mall to the National Gallery Sculpture Garden, where you

can get a bite to eat in the cafe or relax by the reflecting pool. Rest up, dine in Dupont Circle, stroll Connecticut Avenue, then take a cab to visit the Lincoln Memorial at night.

If You Have 2 Days

On your first day, take a narrated tour of the city (see the list of tours at the end of this chapter) for an overview of the city's attractions, stopping at the Jefferson, FDR, Lincoln, and Vietnam War Veterans memorials, and at the Washington Monument. Use the tour to determine which Mall museums you'll want to visit. After taking in the Washington Monument, walk up 15th Street to F Street, turn right, and walk to Red Sage at 14th and F for some Southwestern fare in the restaurant's open-all-day Border Café (which doesn't take reservations). Following lunch, visit your top-pick museums on the Mall.

Start your second day by visiting the Capitol, followed by a tour of the Supreme Court. For lunch, choose from one of the great dining room deals available in the Supreme Court, the Capitol, or the Library of Congress. Then spend the afternoon visiting the Library of Congress, the

Washington, D.C., Attractions

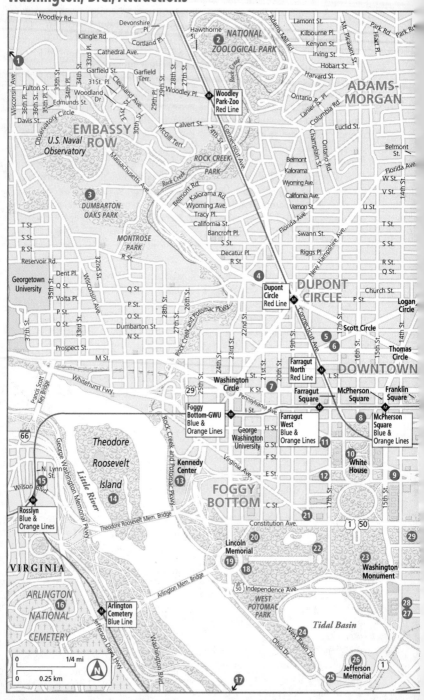

NATIONAL ZOOLOGICAL PARK

ADAMS-MORGAN

Woodley Park-Zoo Red Line

EMBASSY ROW

U.S. Naval Observatory

ROCK CREEK PARK

DUMBARTON OAKS PARK

MONTROSE PARK

Georgetown University

DUPONT CIRCLE

Dupont Circle Red Line

Scott Circle

DOWNTOWN

Logan Circle

Thomas Circle

Farragut North Red Line

Washington Circle

Farragut Square

McPherson Square

Franklin Square

Foggy Bottom-GWU Blue & Orange Lines

George Washington University

Farragut West Blue & Orange Lines

McPherson Square Blue & Orange Lines

Theodore Roosevelt Island

Kennedy Center

White House

FOGGY BOTTOM

Rosslyn Blue & Orange Lines

VIRGINIA

ARLINGTON NATIONAL CEMETERY

Arlington Cemetery Blue Line

Lincoln Memorial

Constitution Ave.

Washington Monument

WEST POTOMAC PARK

Independence Ave.

Tidal Basin

Jefferson Memorial

0   1/4 mi
0   0.25 km

Openings & Closings

Much is happening in D.C. in 2004, a lot of it to do with construction and renovation. But first, what's new: In December 2003, the National Air and Space Museum's auxiliary gallery opened in Virginia, near Washington-Dulles International Airport; the **Steven F. Udvar-Hazy Center** is free and open to the public, displaying 200 aircraft and 135 spacecraft. In fall 2004, the Smithsonian's much heralded **National Museum of the American Indian** opens on the National Mall, its three permanent exhibit halls displaying up to 2,000 objects from the museum's 800,000-piece collection. The museum also has a theater and an outdoor performance space. On May 29, 2004, the dedication of the **National World War II Memorial** takes place, on the National Mall.

Throughout 2004, the Smithsonian's American Art Museum and National Portrait Gallery remain closed for renovation, as does the FBI Building and the annex of the Phillips Collection (the main building at the Phillips stays open). The Kennedy Center of the Performing Arts is going on with all shows, though the place looks like construction-central, as it will for the coming decade while its grand expansion, including a pedestrian plaza, is in production. The new Newseum is still under construction. For security reasons, not renovations, the White House and the Pentagon are both closed to walkup tours, but each allows some tours by certain student, youth, veterans, or military groups who have arranged visits through a senator or congressperson.

Folger Shakespeare Library, and, if you have time, Union Station and the National Postal Museum. Have dinner in Georgetown and browse the shops.

If You Have 3 Days

Spend your first 2 days as described above.

On the morning of your third day, tour the National Archives, followed by the National Gallery of Art. Enjoy lunch in nearby Chinatown or MCI Center neighborhood, such as at Matchbox or Jaleo (see chapter 6 for addresses and other suggestions), and then visit the National Museum of Women in the Arts. Have a pretheater dinner at one of the many restaurants that offer these good deals (Café Atlantico and the Bombay Club near the White House are two fine choices, and they're described along with others in chapter 6). Then head to the Kennedy Center for a performance.

If You Have 4 Days or More

Spend your first 3 days as suggested above.

On the fourth day, visit the U.S. Holocaust Memorial Museum (not recommended for children under 12); this will require most of your day. Have dinner in Adams-Morgan, followed by club-hopping up and down 18th Street. (Or take in a salsa lesson at Habana Village, on Columbia Road in Adams Morgan; see chapter 9 for other suggestions for places to boogie.)

If you have a fifth day, consider a day trip to Alexandria, Virginia. Or board a boat for Mount Vernon and spend most of the morning touring the estate (see chapter 10 for details), with the afternoon set aside for seeing sights you've missed. Have dinner in downtown Washington at one

THE THREE HOUSES OF GOVERNMENT

Call Ahead

If there were only one piece of advice I could give to a visitor, it would be to call ahead to the places you plan to tour, to make sure they're open. I don't mean in advance of your trip (although that can't hurt)—I mean on each day of touring, before you set out. Many of Washington's government buildings, museums, memorials, and monuments are open to the general public nearly all the time—except when they are not.

Because buildings like the Capitol, the Supreme Court, and the White House are "offices" as well as tourist destinations, the business of the day always poses the potential for closing one of those sites, or at least sections, to sightseers. (The White House is probably most vulnerable to this situation.) This caveat is even more important in the wake of the terrorist attack on the Pentagon; touring procedures change and then change again in response to the perceived need for security measures. (See box, "Head's Up," above.)

In addition to the security issue, there's the matter of maintenance. The steady stream of visitors to Washington's attractions necessitates ongoing caretaking and, sometimes, new construction, which may require closing an entire landmark, or part of it, to the public, or put in place new hours of operation or procedures for visiting. (Construction of the Capitol's Visitor Center is one such example; see information within the Capitol's description, later in this chapter.)

Finally, Washington's famous museums, grand halls, and public gardens double as settings for press conferences, galas, special exhibits, festivals, and other special events, so you might arrive at, say, the National Air and Space Museum on a Sunday afternoon, as I did not long ago, only to find some of its galleries off limits because caterers were setting up for an event.

Want to avoid frustration and disappointment? Call ahead.

of the 7th Street–district restaurants, then see Shakespeare performed at the Shakespeare Theatre, or head to the Blue Bar at the Henley Park Hotel to sip a nightcap as you listen to live jazz.

1 The Three Houses of Government

Three of the most visited sights in Washington have always been the buildings housing the executive, legislative, and judicial branches of the U.S. government. All three, the White House, the Capitol, and the Supreme Court, are stunning and offer fascinating lessons in American history and government. The terrorist attacks of September 11, 2001, have resulted in restricted public access, but it is still possible to tour all three buildings. Here is some information that will help you as you go.

The Capitol ★★★   The Capitol is as majestic up close at it is from afar. For 135 years it sheltered not only both houses of Congress, but also the Supreme Court and, for 97 years, the Library of Congress as well. When you tour the Capitol, you'll learn about America's history as you admire the place in which it unfolded.

Classical architecture, interior embellishments, and hundreds of paintings, sculptures, and other artworks are integral elements of the Capitol.

On the massive bronze doors leading to the **Rotunda** are portrayals of events in the life of Columbus. The Rotunda—a huge 96-foot-wide circular hall capped by a 180-foot-high dome—is the hub of the Capitol. The dome was completed, at Lincoln's direction, while the Civil War was being fought. Nine presidents have lain in state here; when Kennedy's casket was displayed, the line of mourners stretched 40 blocks. On the circular walls are eight immense oil paintings of events in American history, such as the presentation of the Declaration of Independence and the surrender of Cornwallis at Yorktown. In the dome is an allegorical fresco masterpiece by Constantino Brumidi, *Apotheosis of Washington,* a symbolic portrayal of George Washington surrounded by Roman gods and goddesses watching over the progress of the nation. Brumidi was known as the "Michelangelo of the Capitol" for the many works he created throughout the building. (Take another look at the dome and find the woman directly below Washington; the triumphant *Armed Freedom* figure is said to be modeled after Lola Germon, a beautiful young actress with whom the 60-year-old Brumidi had a child.) Beneath the dome is a trompe-l'oeil frieze depicting events in American history, from the arrival of Columbus through the Wright brothers' flight at Kitty Hawk.

Also in the Rotunda is the sculpture of suffragists Elizabeth Cady Stanton, Susan B. Anthony, and Lucretia Mott. For a long time, the ponderous monument had been relegated to the Crypt, one level directly below the Rotunda. Women's groups successfully lobbied for its more prominent position in the Rotunda.

The **National Statuary Hall** was originally the chamber of the House of Representatives. In 1864, it became Statuary Hall, and the states were invited to send two statues each of native sons and daughters to the hall. There are 97 statues in all, since three states, Nevada, New Mexico, and North Dakota, have sent only one. As the room filled up, statues spilled over into the Hall of Columns, corridors, and any space that might accommodate the bronze and marble artifacts. Many of the statues honor individuals who played important roles in American history, such as Henry Clay, Ethan Allen, Daniel Webster, and six women, including Jeannette Rankin, the first woman to serve in Congress.

You will not see them on your tour, but the **south and north wings** of the Capitol hold the House and Senate chambers, respectively. The House of Representatives chamber is the largest legislative chamber in the world, and the setting for the president's annual State of the Union addresses. (See information further along about watching Senate and House activity when the bodies are in session.) The Capitol also houses the **Old Supreme Court Chamber,** which has been restored to its mid-19th-century appearance. The Old Supreme Court Chamber is where Chief Justice John Marshall established the foundations of American constitutional law. Allow at least an hour for touring here, longer if you plan to attend a session of Congress. Remember to allow time for waiting in line, too.

Very Important Note: In mid-2002, construction started on a comprehensive, underground Capitol Visitor Center, with completion scheduled for 2005. Since the Capitol Visitor Center is being created directly beneath the plaza where people traditionally line up for tours on the east side of the Capitol, touring procedures have changed. The best thing to do is to call ahead (© **202/225-6827**) to find out the new procedures in place for the time you are visiting, and whether the construction work will temporarily close parts of the building you wish to visit.

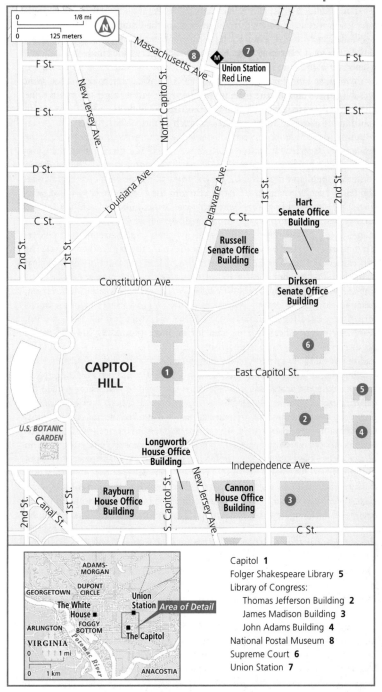

0 1/8 mi

0 125 meters

Massachusetts Ave.

8 Ⓜ 7

Union Station Red Line

F St.

F St.

New Jersey Ave.

North Capitol St.

E St.

E St.

D St.

Louisiana Ave.

Delaware Ave.

C St.

1st St.

2nd St.

Hart Senate Office Building

C St.

Russell Senate Office Building

2nd St.

1st St.

Dirksen Senate Office Building

Constitution Ave.

6

CAPITOL HILL

1

East Capitol St.

5

2

4

U.S. BOTANIC GARDEN

Longworth House Office Building

New Jersey Ave.

Independence Ave.

Cannon House Office Building

S. Capitol St.

3

2nd St.

Canal St.

1st St.

Rayburn House Office Building

C St.

ADAMS-MORGAN

DUPONT CIRCLE

GEORGETOWN

Union Station

Area of Detail

The White House ■

ARLINGTON

FOGGY BOTTOM

Potomac River

VIRGINIA

0 1 mi

■ **The Capitol**

0 1 km

ANACOSTIA

Capitol **1**
Folger Shakespeare Library **5**
Library of Congress:
   Thomas Jefferson Building **2**
   James Madison Building **3**
   John Adams Building **4**
National Postal Museum **8**
Supreme Court **6**
Union Station **7**

At this time, I can tell you that self-guided tours and "VIP" tours (tours reserved in advance by individuals through their congressional offices) have been suspended, for the foreseeable future. The only way now to tour the Capitol Building is in groups of 40. A Capitol Guide Service guide conducts each tour, which is free and lasts about 30 minutes.

You have two options: If you are part of an organized bunch, say a school class on a field trip, you may arrange a tour in advance, putting together groups of no more than 40 each, by contacting your congressional office at least one month ahead, and following the procedures that office outlines for you. If you are on your own, or with family or friends, you will want to get to the Capitol early, by 7:30am, to stand in line for one of a limited number of timed tickets the Capitol distributes daily, starting at 9am. Head to the ticket kiosk at the southwest corner of the Capitol grounds, near the intersection of First Street and Independence Avenue SW, across First Street from the U.S. Botanic Gardens. It's a first-come, first-served system, with only one ticket given to each person, and each person, including children of any age, must have a ticket. The good news is that once you receive your ticket, you are free to go somewhere nearby to get a bite to eat, or to sightsee, while you wait for your turn to tour the Capitol. The bad news is that all of you, even 1-year-old baby Louie, have to rise early and get to the Capitol by about 7:30am and then stand in line for another hour or more to be sure of touring the Capitol that day. Still, I think this is an improvement over the old touring procedure, which required all of you to stay in the queue until you entered the Capitol—if you left the line, you lost your place. Again, I emphasize that you must call the recorded information line (✆ **202/225-6827**) on the morning of your planned visit to confirm exactly where you should go and what you should do to obtain your ticket.

Now, if you wish to visit either or both the House and Senate galleries, you follow a different procedure. These galleries are open to visitors only when the galleries are **in session** ✮✮✮, but you must have a pass to visit each gallery. (Families, take note that children under 6 are not allowed in the Senate gallery.) Once obtained, the passes are good through the remainder of the Congressional session. To obtain visitor passes in advance, contact your representative for a House gallery pass, or your senator for a Senate gallery pass; District of Columbia and Puerto Rico residents should contact their delegate to Congress. If you don't receive visitor passes in the mail (not every senator or representative sends them), they're obtainable at your senator's office on the Constitution Avenue side of the building or your representative's or delegate's office on the Independence Avenue side. (Visitors who are not citizens can obtain a gallery pass by presenting a passport at the Senate or House appointments desk, located on the first floor of the Capitol.) Call the Capitol switchboard at ✆ **202/224-3121** to contact the office of your senator or congressperson. Your congressional office will issue you a pass and direct you to the House or Senate Gallery line outside the Capitol, for entry into the Capitol.

You'll know the House and/or the Senate is in session if you see flags flying over their respective wings of the Capitol (House: south side, Senate: north side), or you can check the weekday "Today in Congress" column in the *Washington Post* for details on times of the House and Senate sessions and committee hearings. This column also tells you which sessions are open to the public, allowing you to pick one that interests you.

At the east end of the Mall, entrance on E. Capitol St. and 1st St. NW. ✆ **202/225-6827**. www.aoc.gov, www.house.gov, www.senate.gov. Free admission. Year-round 9am–4:30pm Mon–Sat, with first tour starting at 9:30am and last tour starting at 3:30pm. Closed for tours Sun and Jan 1, Thanksgiving, and Dec 25. Parking at Union Station or on neighborhood streets. Metro: Union Station or Capitol South.

The Supreme Court of the United States ⭒⭒   The highest tribunal in the nation, the Supreme Court is charged with deciding whether actions of Congress, the president, the states, and lower courts are in accord with the Constitution, and with applying the Constitution's enduring principles to novel situations and a changing country. The Supreme Court's chief justice and eight associate justices have the power of judicial review—that is, authority to invalidate legislation or executive action that conflicts with the Constitution. Out of the 7,000 or so cases submitted to it each year, the Supreme Court hears only about 100 cases, many of which deal with issues vital to the nation. The Court's rulings are final, reversible only by another Supreme Court decision, or in some cases, an Act of Congress or a constitutional amendment.

Until 1935, the Supreme Court met in the Capitol. Architect Cass Gilbert designed the stately Corinthian marble palace that houses the Court today. The building was considered rather grandiose by early residents: One justice remarked that he and his colleagues ought to enter such pompous precincts on elephants.

If you're in town when the Court is in session, try to **see a case being argued** ⭒⭒⭒ (call ☏ **202/479-3211** for details). The Court meets Monday through Wednesday from 10am to noon, and, on occasion, from 1 to 2pm, starting the first Monday in October through late April, alternating in approximately 2-week intervals between "sittings" to hear cases and deliver opinions and "recesses" for consideration of Court business and writing opinions. From mid-May to late June, you can attend brief sessions (about 15 min.) at 10am on Monday, when the justices release orders and opinions. You can find out what cases are on the docket by checking the *Washington Post*'s "Supreme Court Calendar." Arrive at least an hour early—even earlier for highly publicized cases—to line up for seats, about 150 of which are allotted to the general public.

There are many rituals here. At 10am, the entrance of the justices is announced by the marshal, and all present rise and remain standing while the justices are seated following the chant: "The Honorable, the Chief Justice and Associate Justices of the Supreme Court of the United States. Oyez! Oyez! Oyez! All persons having business before the Honorable, the Supreme Court of the United States, are admonished to draw near and give their attention, for the Court is now sitting. God save the United States and this Honorable Court!" Unseen by the gallery is the "conference handshake"; following a 19th-century tradition symbolizing a "harmony of aims if not views," each justice shakes hands with each of the other eight when they assemble to go to the bench. The Court has a record before it of prior proceedings and relevant briefs, so each side is allowed only a 30-minute argument.

Call the Supreme Court information line to find out days and times that court arguments will take place. You may view these on a first-come, first-served basis, choosing between the 3-minute line, which ushers visitors in and out of the court every 3 minutes, starting at 10am in the morning and at 1pm in the afternoon; or the "regular" line, which admits visitors who wish to stay for the entire argument, starting at 9:30am and 12:30pm (you should try to arrive about 90 min. ahead of time to snag a spot).

The Supreme Court is cloaked in mystery, purposefully. You can't take cameras or recording devices into the courtroom, and you're not allowed to take notes, either. The justices seldom give speeches and never give press conferences.

When the Court is not in session, you can tour the building and attend a **free lecture** in the courtroom about Court procedure and the building's architecture. Lectures are given every hour on the half-hour from 9:30am to 3:30pm. After the talk, explore the Great Hall and go down a flight of steps to see the **24-minute film** on the workings of the Court. On the same floor is an exhibit highlighting the "History of High Courts Around the World," on display indefinitely. If you tour the building on your own, you should allow about an hour. You might also consider contacting your senator or congressperson—at least 2 months in advance—to arrange for a 40-minute guided tour of the building led by a Supreme Court staff member, who will take you places you won't be able to go on your own.

There's also a gift shop and a cafeteria that's open to the public and serves good food.

One 1st St. NE (between E. Capitol St. and Maryland Ave. NE). ✆ 202/479-3000. www.supremecourtus.gov. Free admission. Mon–Fri 9am–4:30pm. Closed all federal holidays. Metro: Capitol South or Union Station.

The White House 🐿🐿★ It's amazing when you think about it: This house has served as a residence, office, reception site, and world embassy for every U.S. president since John Adams. The White House is the only private residence of a head of state that has opened its doors to the public for tours, free of charge. It was Thomas Jefferson who started this practice, which is stopped only during wartime; the administration considers that we are currently fighting a war on terrorism, and, therefore, the White House, at this writing, remains closed for public tours. The White House is open for tours by certain groups, however: school and youth groups (students in grades 1–12), and organized military and veterans groups. **If you are hoping to arrange a White House tour for your student or military/veterans group, you must submit a request to your senator or congressperson's office.** For those who have arranged such tours, and in the hope that general public tours have resumed by the time you read this, I provide the following information. To find out the latest White House tour information, call ✆ **202/456-7041.**

An Act of Congress in 1790 established the city, now known as Washington, District of Columbia, as the seat of the federal government. George Washington and city planner Pierre L'Enfant chose the site for the White House (or "President's House," as it was called before whitewashing brought the name "White House" into use) and staged a contest to find a builder. Although Washington picked the winner—Irishman James Hoban—he was the only president never to live in the White House. The structure took 8 years to build, starting in 1792, when its cornerstone was laid, and its facade is made of the same stone as that used to construct the Capitol. In 1814, during the War of 1812, the British set fire to the White House, gutting the interior; the exterior managed to endure only because a rainstorm extinguished the fire. What you see today is Hoban's basic creation: a building modeled after an Irish country house (in fact, Hoban had in mind the house of the duke of Leinster in Dublin).

Alterations over the years have incorporated the South Portico in 1824, the North Portico in 1829, and electricity in 1891, during Benjamin Harrison's presidency. In 1902, repairs and refurnishings of the White House cost nearly $500,000. No other great change took place until Harry Truman's presidency, when the interior was completely renovated, after the leg of Margaret Truman's piano cut through the dining room ceiling. The Trumans lived at Blair House across the street for nearly 4 years while the White House interior was shored up with steel girders and concrete. It's as solid as Gibraltar now.

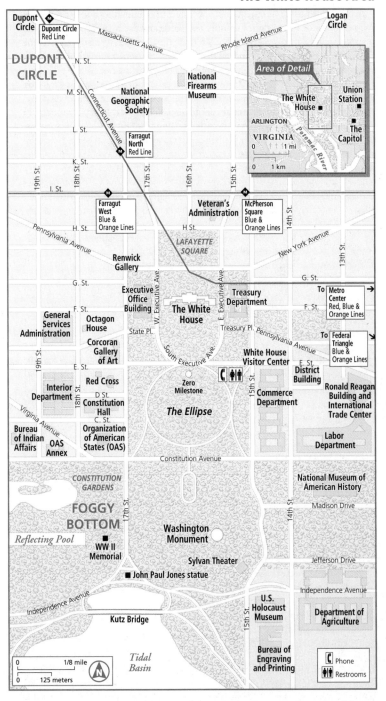

The White House Area

Logan Circle

Dupont Circle — Dupont Circle Red Line

Massachusetts Avenue

Rhode Island Avenue

DUPONT CIRCLE

N. St.

Connecticut Avenue

M. St.

National Geographic Society

National Firearms Museum

L. St.

Farragut North Red Line

K. St.

I. St.

Area of Detail

The White House ■

Union Station ■

ARLINGTON

VIRGINIA

The Capitol ■

Potomac River

0 — 1 mi

0 — 1 km

19th St. · 18th St. · 17th St. · 16th St. · 15th St.

Farragut West Blue & Orange Lines

Veteran's Administration

McPherson Square Blue & Orange Lines

14th St.

Pennsylvania Avenue

H. St.

H St.

LAFAYETTE SQUARE

New York Avenue

13th St.

Renwick Gallery

G. St.

G. St.

Executive Office Building

W. Executive Ave.

The White House

E. Executive Ave.

Treasury Department

To Metro Center Red, Blue & Orange Lines →

General Services Administration

Octagon House

F. St.

State Pl.

Treasury Pl.

Pennsylvania Avenue

F. St.

To Federal Triangle Blue & Orange Lines →

Corcoran Gallery of Art

E. St.

White House Visitor Center

E. St.

District Building

19th St.

Interior Department

18th St.

Red Cross

D St.

Constitution Hall

C. St.

South Executive Ave.

Zero Milestone

C ▮▮

15th St.

Commerce Department

Ronald Reagan Building and International Trade Center

Virginia Avenue

The Ellipse

Bureau of Indian Affairs

OAS Annex

Organization of American States (OAS)

Labor Department

Constitution Avenue

CONSTITUTION GARDENS

17th St.

National Museum of American History

Madison Drive

FOGGY BOTTOM

Reflecting Pool

■ WW II Memorial

Washington Monument

14th St.

Sylvan Theater

Jefferson Drive

■ John Paul Jones statue

Independence Avenue

Independence Avenue

U.S. Holocaust Museum

15th St.

Department of Agriculture

Kutz Bridge

Tidal Basin

0 — 1/8 mile

0 — 125 meters

Bureau of Engraving and Printing

C Phone

▮▮ Restrooms

In 1961, Jacqueline Kennedy formed a Fine Arts Committee to help restore the famous rooms to their original grandeur, ensuring treatment of the White House as a museum of American history and decorative arts. "It just seemed to me such a shame when we came here to find hardly anything of the past in the house, hardly anything before 1902," Mrs. Kennedy observed. Presidents and their families through the years have put their own stamp on the White House, the most recent example being President Bush's addition of the T-ball field to the South Lawn.

Highlights of the tour include the **Gold-and-White East Room,** the scene of presidential receptions, weddings (Lynda Bird Johnson, for one), and other dazzling events. This is where the president entertains visiting heads of state and the place where seven of the eight presidents who died in office (all but Garfield) laid in state. It was also where Nixon resigned. The room's early-18th-century style was adopted during the Theodore Roosevelt renovation of 1902; it has parquet Fontainebleau oak floors and white-painted wood walls with fluted pilasters and classical relief inserts. Note the famous Gilbert Stuart portrait of George Washington that Dolley Madison saved from the British torch during the War of 1812. The portrait is the only object to have remained continuously in the White House since 1800 (except during times of reconstruction).

You'll visit the **Green Room,** which was Thomas Jefferson's dining room but today is used as a sitting room. Mrs. Kennedy chose the green watered-silk-fabric wall covering. In the **Oval Blue Room,** decorated in the French Empire style chosen by James Monroe in 1817, presidents and first ladies have officially received guests since the Jefferson administration. It was, however, Van Buren's decor that began the "blue room" tradition. The walls, on which hang portraits of five presidents (including Rembrandt Peale's portrait of Thomas Jefferson and G. P. A. Healy's of Tyler), are covered in reproductions of early-19th-century French and American wallpaper. Grover Cleveland, the only president to wed in the White House, was married in the Blue Room. This room was also where the Reagans greeted the 52 Americans liberated after being held hostage in Iran for 444 days, and every year it's the setting for the White House Christmas tree.

The **Red Room,** whose satin-covered walls and Empire furnishings are red, is used as a reception room, usually for afternoon teas. Several portraits of past presidents and a Gilbert Stuart portrait of Dolley Madison, hang here. Dolley Madison used the Red Room for her famous Wednesday-night receptions.

From the Red Room, you enter the **State Dining Room.** Modeled after late-18th-century neoclassical English houses, this room is a superb setting for state dinners and luncheons. Below G. P. A. Healy's portrait of Lincoln is an inscription written by John Adams on his second night in the White House (FDR had it carved into the mantel): "I Pray Heaven to Bestow The Best of Blessings on THIS HOUSE and on All that shall here-after Inhabit it. May none but Honest and Wise Men ever rule under this Roof."

White House tours take place mornings only, Tuesday through Saturday. There are no public restrooms or telephones in the White House, and picture-taking and videotaping are prohibited.

Note: Even if you have successfully reserved a White House tour for your group, you should still call ℭ **202/456-7041** before setting out in the morning; in case the White House is closed on short notice because of unforeseen events. If this should happen to you, you should make a point of walking by the White House anyway, since its exterior is still pretty awesome. Stroll past it on Pennsylvania Avenue, down 15th Street past the Treasury Building, and along the backside and South Lawn, on E Street.

1600 Pennsylvania Ave. NW (visitor entrance gate at E St. and E. Executive Ave.). ✆ **202/456-7041** or 202/208-1631. www.whitehouse.gov. Free admission. Tours only for school and veterans groups, which have arranged the tour through their congressional offices. Metro: McPherson Square.

The White House Visitor Center ⭐   Even—especially—if you are not able to tour the White House, you should stop here. The Visitor Center opened in 1995 to provide extensive interpretive data about the White House (as well as other Washington tourist attractions) and to serve as a ticket-distribution center (though that function is suspended indefinitely). It is run under the auspices of the National Park Service and the staff is particularly well informed. Try to catch the 30-minute video about the White House, *Within These Walls,* which provides interior views of the presidential precincts (it runs continuously throughout the day). Before you leave the Visitor Center, pick up a copy of the National Park Service's brochure on the White House, which tells you a little about what you'll see in the eight or so rooms you tour and a bit about the history of the White House. The White House Historic Association runs a small shop here.

The association operates an informative website, **www.whitehousehistory.org**, although much of it seems designed to make you order something.

Before you leave the Visitor Center, take a look at the exhibits, which include:

Architectural History of the White House, including the grounds and extensive renovations to its structure and interior that have taken place since its cornerstone was laid in 1792.

Symbol and Image, showing how the White House has been portrayed by photographers, artists, journalists, political cartoonists, and others.

First Families, with displays about the people who have lived here (such as prankster Tad Lincoln, who once stood in a window above his father and waved a Confederate flag at a military review).

The Working White House, focusing on the vast staff of servants, chefs, gardeners, Secret Service people, and others who maintain this institution.

Ceremony and Celebration, depicting notable White House events, from a Wright Brothers' aviation demonstration in 1911 to a ballet performance by Baryshnikov during the Carter administration.

White House Interiors, Past and Present, including photographs of the ever-changing Oval Office as decorated by administrations from Taft through Clinton.

1450 Pennsylvania Ave. NW (in the Dept. of Commerce Building, between 14th and 15th sts.). ✆ **202/208-1631** for recorded information. Free admission. Daily 7:30am–4pm. Closed Jan 1, Thanksgiving, and Dec 25. Metro: Federal Triangle.

2 The Major Memorials

The capital's major memorials honor esteemed presidents, war veterans, and founding fathers. In the offing is a memorial to Dr. Martin Luther King Jr. But this year, on May 29, 2004, the American Battle Monuments Commission dedicates the National Mall's newest memorial, the **National World War II Memorial.** Located at the east end of the Reflecting Pool between the Lincoln Memorial and the Washington Monument, the World War II Memorial is the first national memorial dedicated to all who served during World War II, and honors all military veterans of the war, citizens on the home front, and the nation at large. For more information about the memorial and the dedication ceremony, go to the website, www.wwiimemorial.com, or call ✆ 800/639-4WW2.

All of these memorials are located in picturesque **West Potomac Park** (see p. 216 for full details on the park and its famous **cherry blossoms**), which lies at the western end of the National Mall, where it borders the Potomac River and encircles the Tidal Basin. Unfortunately, none of the memorials lie directly on a Metro line, so you can expect a bit of a walk from the specified station.

The easiest thing to do, if you're up to it, is to walk from one monument or memorial to the next. You'll want to dress for the weather: light clothing, shades, and sunscreen in summer; a hat, gloves, and warm jacket in winter—these monuments are set in wide open spaces, providing no or little protection from the elements. But when the weather is lovely, so is the experience of sauntering around West Potomac Park.

Or, you can go by **Tourmobile** (p. 221), which continually picks up and discharges passengers at each of these sites throughout the day. The National Park Service manages all of these properties and maintains information about each of them, including upcoming events, at **www.nps.gov** (click on the "Visit Your Parks" function to find the one you want).

Some believe the best time to visit the memorials is at night, when they're illuminated in all their imposing white-stone glory and all the crowds are gone. Try it—all of the memorials are safe to visit after dark, with park rangers on hand until 11:45pm year-round, except for the Washington Monument, which closes at 5pm now. You may view the exteriors any time.

Washington Monument ★★★ *Kids*   The idea of a tribute to George Washington first arose 16 years before his death, at the Continental Congress of 1783. But the new nation had more pressing problems and funds were not readily available. It wasn't until the early 1830s, with the 100th anniversary of Washington's birth approaching, that any action was taken.

Then there were several fiascoes. A mausoleum was provided for Washington's remains under the Capitol Rotunda, but a grand-nephew, citing Washington's will, refused to allow the body to be moved from Mount Vernon. In 1830, Horatio Greenough was commissioned to create a memorial statue for the Rotunda. He came up with a bare-chested Washington, draped in classical Greek garb; a shocked public claimed he looked as if he were "entering or leaving a bath," and so the statue was relegated to the Smithsonian. Finally, in 1833, prominent citizens organized the Washington National Monument Society. Treasury Building architect Robert Mills's design (originally with a circular colonnaded Greek temple base, which was later discarded for lack of funds) was accepted.

The cornerstone was laid on July 4, 1848, and for the next 37 years, watching the monument grow, or not grow, was a local pastime. Declining contributions and the Civil War brought construction to a halt at an awkward 150 feet (you can still see a change in the color of the stone about halfway up). The unsightly stump remained until 1876, when President Grant approved federal monies to complete the project. Dedicated in 1885, it was opened to the public in 1888.

A major 2-year restoration completed in 2000 repaired the monument's exterior masonry and mortar, refurbished its elevator, installed a new climate-control system, scrubbed the 897 interior steps, and polished the 193 carved commemorative stones.

Visiting the Washington Monument: The Washington Monument is the world's tallest freestanding work of masonry. It stands at the very center of Washington, D.C., landmarks, and the 360-degree views from the top are spectacular. Due east are the Capitol and Smithsonian buildings; due north is the White

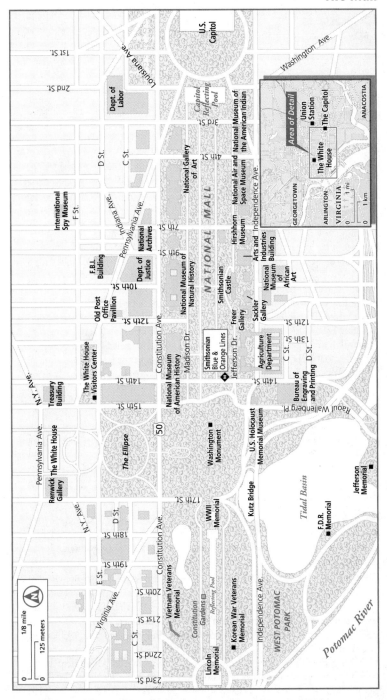

The Mall

U.S. Capitol

1st St.

2nd St.

Louisiana Ave.

Dept. of Labor

Washington Ave.

Capitol Reflecting Pool

3rd St.

D St.

C St.

National Gallery of Art

4th St.

International Spy Museum

F St.

Pennsylvania Ave.

Indiana Ave.

National Archives

7th St.

NATIONAL MALL

National Museum of the American Indian

Independence Ave.

National Air and Space Museum

Hirshhorn Museum

Arts and Industries Building

9th St.

F.B.I. Building

Dept. of Justice

Smithsonian Castle

National Museum of African Art

Old Post Office Pavillion

10th St.

National Museum of Natural History

Freer Gallery

Sackler Gallery

12th St.

The White House Visitors Center

Constitution Ave.

Madison Dr.

Smithsonian Blue & Orange Lines

Jefferson Dr.

Agriculture Department

13th St.

C St.

D St.

14th St.

Treasury Building

N.Y. Ave.

14th St.

National Museum of American History

15th St.

Bureau of Engraving and Printing

Raoul Wallenberg Pl.

Pennsylvania Ave.

The White House

Renwick Gallery

50

The Ellipse

Washington Monument

U.S. Holocaust Memorial Museum

N.Y. Ave.

D St.

17th St.

Kutz Bridge

Tidal Basin

Jefferson Memorial

18th St.

19th St.

E St.

Constitution Ave.

WWII Memorial

F.D.R. Memorial

Virginia Ave.

20th St.

Vietnam Veterans Memorial

Constitution Gardens

Reflecting Pool

Korean War Veterans Memorial

Independence Ave.

WEST POTOMAC PARK

Potomac River

21st St.

C St.

22nd St.

Lincoln Memorial

23rd St.

N

0 — 1/8 mile

0 — 125 meters

Area of Detail

Union Station

The Capitol

ANACOSTIA

GEORGETOWN

The White House

VIRGINIA

ARLINGTON

0 — 1 mi

0 — 1 km

Impressions

May the spirit which animated the great founder of this city descend to future generations.

—John Adams

House; due west is the Lincoln Memorial (with Arlington National Cemetery beyond); and due south is the Jefferson Memorial, overlooking the Tidal Basin and the Potomac River. It's like being at the center of a compass, and it provides a marvelous orientation to the city.

Climbing the 897 steps is not allowed, but the large elevator whisks visitors to the top in just 70 seconds. If you're dying to see more of the interior, take a **"Walk Down" tour,** which is given everyday at 10am and 2:30pm. For details, call before you go or ask a ranger on duty. On this tour you'll learn more about the building of the monument and get to see the 193 carved stones inserted into the interior walls. The stones are gifts from foreign countries, all 50 states, organizations, and individuals. The most expensive stone was given by the state of Alaska in 1982—it's pure jade and worth millions. There are stones from Siam (now Thailand), the Cherokee Nation, and the Sons of Temperance. Allow half an hour here, plus time spent waiting in line.

Light snacks are sold at a snack bar on the grounds, where you'll also find a few picnic tables. There's limited but free 2-hour **parking** at the 16th Street Oval.

Ticket Information: Although admission to the Washington Monument is free, you'll still have to get a ticket. The ticket booth is located at the bottom of the hill from the monument, on 15th Street NW between Independence and Constitution avenues. It's open daily from 8am to 4:30pm. Tickets are usually gone by 9:30am, so plan to get there by 7:30 or 8am, especially in peak season, if you really want to ascend to the top of the monument. The tickets grant admission at half-hour intervals between the stated hours, on the same day you visit. If you want to save yourself the trouble and get them in advance, call the National Park Reservation Service (✆ **800/967-2283**) or go online at http://reservations.nps.gov; you'll pay $1.50 per ticket plus a 50¢ service charge per transaction.

Directly south of the White House (at 15th St. and Constitution Ave. NW). ✆ 202/426-6841. Free admission. Daily 9am–5pm. Last elevators depart 15 min. before closing (arrive earlier). Closed Dec 25, open until noon July 4. Metro: Smithsonian, then a 10-min. walk.

Lincoln Memorial ★★★ *Kids*   This beautiful and moving testament to the nation's greatest president attracts millions of visitors annually. Like its fellow presidential memorials, this one was a long time in the making. Although it was planned as early as 1867—2 years after Lincoln's death—it was not until 1912 that Henry Bacon's design was completed, and the memorial itself was dedicated in 1922.

The neoclassical templelike structure, similar in architectural design to the Parthenon in Greece, has 36 fluted Doric columns representing the states of the Union at the time of Lincoln's death, plus two at the entrance. On the attic parapet are 48 festoons symbolizing the number of states in 1922, when the monument was erected. Hawaii and Alaska are noted in an inscription on the terrace. Due east is the Reflecting Pool, lined with American elms and stretching 2,000 feet toward the Washington Monument and the Capitol beyond.

The memorial chamber has limestone walls inscribed with the Gettysburg Address and Lincoln's Second Inaugural Address. Two 60-foot-high murals by

Jules Guerin on the north and south walls depict, allegorically, Lincoln's principles and achievements. On the south wall, an Angel of Truth freeing a slave is flanked by groups of figures representing Justice and Immortality. The north-wall mural depicts the unity of North and South and is flanked by groups of figures symbolizing Fraternity and Charity. Most powerful, however, is Daniel Chester French's 19-foot-high seated statue of Lincoln, which disappears from your sightline as you get close to the base of the memorial, then emerges slowly into view as you ascend the stairs.

Lincoln's legacy has made his memorial the site of numerous demonstrations by those seeking justice. Most notable was a peaceful demonstration of 200,000 people on August 28, 1963, at which the Rev. Dr. Martin Luther King Jr. proclaimed, "I have a dream." Look for the words "I have a dream. Martin Luther King, Jr., The March on Washington for Jobs and Freedom, August 28, 1963" inscribed and centered on the granite step, 18 steps down from the chamber. The inscription, which the National Park Service added in July 2003, marks the precise spot where King stood to deliver his famous speech.

An information booth, a small museum, and a bookstore are on the premises. Rangers present 20- to 30-minute programs as time permits throughout the day. Limited free **parking** is available along Constitution Avenue and south along Ohio Drive. Twenty to thirty minutes is sufficient time for viewing this memorial.

Directly west of the Mall in Potomac Park (at 23rd St. NW, between Constitution and Independence aves.). © 202/426-6842. Free admission. Daily 8am–11:45pm. Closed Dec 25. Metro: Foggy Bottom, then a 30-min. walk.

Korean War Veterans Memorial ⭐

This privately funded memorial, founded in 1995, honors those who served in Korea, a 3-year conflict (1950–53) that produced almost as many casualties as Vietnam. It consists of a circular "Pool of Remembrance" in a grove of trees and a triangular "Field of Service," highlighted by lifelike statues of 19 infantrymen, who appear to be trudging across fields. In addition, a 164-foot-long black-granite wall depicts the array of combat and support troops that served in Korea (nurses, chaplains, airmen, gunners, mechanics, cooks, and others); a raised granite curb lists the 22 nations that contributed to the U.N.'s effort there; and a commemorative area honors KIAs, MIAs, and POWs. Plan to spend 15 minutes for viewing. Limited parking is available along Ohio Drive.

Tip: If you don't mind a walk, try to snag a **parking** spot along West Basin Drive near the FDR Memorial; the Korean War and the Vietnam War Veterans memorials, as well as the Lincoln Memorial, are then all within reach.

Just across from the Lincoln Memorial (east of French Dr., between 21st and 23rd sts. NW). © 202/426-6841. Free admission. Rangers on duty daily 8am–11:45pm except Dec 25. Ranger-led interpretive programs are given throughout the day. Metro: Foggy Bottom.

Vietnam Veterans Memorial ⭐⭐

The Vietnam Veterans Memorial is possibly the most poignant sight in Washington: two long, black-granite walls in the shape of a V, each inscribed with the names of the men and women who gave their lives, or remain missing, in the longest war in American history. Even if no one close to you died in Vietnam, it's wrenching to watch visitors grimly studying the directories to find out where their loved ones are listed, or rubbing pencil on paper held against a name etched into the wall. The walls list close to 60,000 people, many of whom died very young.

Because of the raging conflict over U.S. involvement in the war, Vietnam veterans had received almost no recognition of their service before the memorial was conceived by Vietnam veteran Jan Scruggs. The nonprofit Vietnam Veterans Memorial Fund raised $7 million and secured a 2-acre site in tranquil Constitution Gardens to erect a memorial that would make no political statement about the war and would harmonize with neighboring memorials. By separating the issue of the wartime service of individuals from the issue of U.S. policy in Vietnam, the VVMF hoped to begin a process of national reconciliation.

Yale senior Maya Lin's design was chosen in a national competition open to all citizens over 18 years of age. The two walls are angled at 125° to point to the Washington Monument and the Lincoln Memorial. The wall's mirrorlike surface reflects surrounding trees, lawns, and monuments. The names are inscribed in chronological order, documenting an epoch in American history as a series of individual sacrifices from the date of the first casualty in 1959. The park service continues to add names over the years, of those Vietnam veterans who die eventually of injuries sustained during the war.

The wall was erected in 1982. In 1984, a life-size sculpture of three Vietnam soldiers by Frederick Hart was installed at the entrance plaza. Near the statue, a flag flies from a 60-foot staff. Another sculpture, the *Vietnam Veterans Women's Memorial*, which depicts three servicewomen tending a wounded soldier, was installed on Veterans Day 1993. You should allow about 20 minutes here.

The park rangers at the Vietnam Veterans Memorial are very knowledgeable and are usually milling about—be sure to seek them out if you have any questions. Limited **parking** is available along Constitution Avenue.

Just across from the Lincoln Memorial (east of Henry Bacon Dr. between 21st and 22nd sts. NW). ☏ 202/426-6841. Free admission. Rangers on duty daily 8am–11:45pm except Dec 25. Ranger-led programs are given throughout the day. Metro: Foggy Bottom.

Franklin Delano Roosevelt Memorial ✹✹✹

The FDR Memorial has proven to be one of the most popular of the presidential memorials since it opened on May 2, 1997. Its popularity has to do as much with its design as the man it honors. This is a 7½-acre outdoor memorial that lies beneath a wide-open sky. It stretches out, rather than rising up, across the stone-paved floor. Granite walls define the four "galleries," each representing a different term in FDR's presidency from 1933 to 1945. Architect Lawrence Halprin's design includes waterfalls, sculptures (by Leonard Baskin, John Benson, Neil Estern, Robert Graham, Thomas Hardy, and George Segal), and Roosevelt's own words carved into the stone.

One drawback of the FDR Memorial is the noise. Planes on their way to or from nearby Reagan National Airport zoom overhead, and the many displays of cascading water can sound thunderous. When the memorial first opened, adults and children alike arrived in bathing suits and splashed around on warm days (the memorial is unsheltered and unshaded). Park rangers don't allow that anymore, but they do allow you to dip your feet in the various pools. A favorite time to visit is at night, when dramatic lighting reveals the waterfalls and statues against the dark parkland.

Conceived in 1946, the FDR Memorial had been in the works for 50 years. Part of the delay in its construction can be attributed to the president himself. FDR had told his friend Supreme Court Justice Felix Frankfurter, "If they are to put up any memorial to me, I should like it to be placed in the center of that green plot in front of the Archives Building. I should like it to consist of a block about the size [of this desk]." In fact, such a plaque sits in front of the National Archives Building. Friends and relatives struggled to honor Roosevelt's request to leave it at that, but Congress and national sentiment overrode them.

As with other presidential memorials, this one opened to some controversy. Advocates for people with disabilities were incensed that the memorial sculptures did not show the president in a wheelchair, which he used from the age of 39 after he contracted polio. President Clinton asked Congress to allocate funding for an additional statue portraying a wheelchair-bound FDR. You will now see a small statue of FDR in a wheelchair, placed at the very front of the memorial, to the right. Step inside the gift shop to view a replica of Roosevelt's wheelchair, as well as one of the rare photographs of the president sitting in a wheelchair. The memorial is probably the most accessible tourist attraction in the city; as at most of the National Park Service locations, wheelchairs are available for free use on-site.

If you don't see a posting of tour times, look for a ranger and request a tour; the rangers are happy to oblige. Thirty minutes is sufficient time to allot here.

In West Potomac Park, about midway between the Lincoln and Jefferson memorials, on the west shore of the Tidal Basin. ℭ 202/426-6841. Free admission. Ranger staff on duty daily 8am–11:45pm. Closed Dec 25. Free parking along W. Basin and Ohio drs. Metro: Smithsonian, with a 30-min. walk; or take the Tourmobile.

George Mason Memorial ⊛   This memorial honors George Mason, author of the Virginia Declaration of Rights, which had much to do with the establishment of our national Bill of Rights. Dedicated on April 9, 2002, the memorial consists of a bronze statue of Mason, set back in a landscaped grove of trees and flower beds (lots and lots of pansies), arranged in concentric circles around a pool and fountain. Mason appears in 18th-century garb, from buckled shoes to tricorn hat, seated on a marble bench, but leaning backward on one arm and gazing off in the general direction of the Washington Monument. Two stone slabs are inscribed with some of Mason's words, like these, referring to Mason's rejection of slavery, "that slow Poison, which is daily contaminating the Minds & Morals of our People." Wooden benches placed within the circles of flowers present a pleasant opportunity to learn about Mason, and take a break, before moving on.

In West Potomac Park, on Ohio Drive at the Tidal Basin, between the Jefferson and FDR memorials. ℭ 202/426-6841. Free admission. Always open, though rangers generally are not posted here. To find out more about George Mason from a park ranger, visit the Jefferson Memorial, a 5-min. walk around the Tidal Basin, where park rangers are on duty 8am–11:45pm. Closed Dec 25. Free parking along W. Basin and Ohio Drives. Metro: Smithsonian, with a 2- to 3-min. walk, or take the Tourmobile.

Jefferson Memorial ⊛⊛   President John F. Kennedy, at a 1962 dinner honoring 29 Nobel Prize winners, told his guests that they were "the most extraordinary collection of talent, of human knowledge, that has ever been gathered together at the White House, with the possible exception of when Thomas Jefferson dined alone." Jefferson penned the Declaration of Independence and served as George Washington's secretary of state, John Adams's vice president, and America's third president. He spoke out against slavery, although, like many of his countrymen, he kept slaves himself. In addition, he established the University of Virginia and pursued wide-ranging interests, including architecture, astronomy, anthropology, music, and farming.

The site for the Jefferson Memorial was of extraordinary importance. The Capitol, the White House, and the Mall were already located in accordance with architect Pierre L'Enfant's master plan for the city, but there was no spot for such a project that would maintain L'Enfant's symmetry. So the memorial was built on land reclaimed from the Potomac River, now known as the Tidal Basin. Franklin Delano Roosevelt, who laid the cornerstone in 1939, had all the trees between the Jefferson Memorial and the White House cut down so that he could see the memorial every morning.

> **Tips Parking Near the Mall**
>
> First of all: Don't drive. Use the Metro.
>
> But if you're hell-bent on driving on a weekday, set out early to nab one of the Independence or Constitution avenues spots that become legal at 9:30am, when rush hour ends. Arrive about 9:15am and just sit in your car until 9:30am (to avoid getting a ticket), then hop out and stoke the meter. So many people do this that if you arrive at 9:30am or later, you'll find most of the street parking spots gone.

The memorial is a columned rotunda in the style of the Pantheon in Rome, whose classical architecture Jefferson himself introduced to this country (he designed his home, Monticello, and the earliest University of Virginia buildings in Charlottesville). On the Tidal Basin side, the sculptural group above the entrance depicts Jefferson with Benjamin Franklin, John Adams, Roger Sherman, and Robert Livingston, all of whom worked on drafting the Declaration of Independence. The domed interior of the memorial contains the 19-foot bronze statue of Jefferson standing on a 6-foot pedestal of black Minnesota granite. The sculpture is the work of Rudolph Evans, who was chosen from more than 100 artists in a nationwide competition. Jefferson is depicted wearing a fur-collared coat given to him by his close friend, the Polish general Tadeusz Kosciuszko.

Rangers present 20- to 30-minute programs throughout the day as time permits. Twenty to thirty minutes is sufficient time to spend here.

Spring through fall, a refreshment kiosk at the Tourmobile stop offers snacks. A gift shop, a small museum, and a bookstore are located on the bottom floor of the memorial. There's free 1-hour **parking.**

South of the Washington Monument on Ohio Dr. SW (at the south shore of the Tidal Basin). ☎ **202/ 426-6841.** Free admission. Daily 8am–11:45pm. Closed Dec 25. Metro: Smithsonian, with a 20- to 30-min. walk; or take the Tourmobile.

3 The Smithsonian Museums

Wealthy English scientist James Smithson (1765–1829), the illegitimate son of the duke of Northumberland, never explained why he willed his vast fortune to the United States, a country he had never visited. Speculation is that he felt a new nation, lacking established cultural institutions, most needed his bequest. Smithson died in Genoa, Italy, in 1829. Congress accepted his gift in 1836; 2 years later, half a million dollars' worth of gold sovereigns (a considerable sum in the 19th century) arrived at the U.S. Mint in Philadelphia. For the next 8 years, Congress debated the best possible use for these funds. Finally, in 1846, James Polk signed an act into law establishing the Smithsonian Institution and authorizing a board to receive "all objects of art and of foreign and curious research, and all objects of natural history, plants, and geological and mineralogical specimens . . . for research and museum purposes."

Since then, private donations have swelled Smithson's original legacy many times over. Although the Smithsonian acquires approximately 70% of its yearly budget from congressional allocations, the institution depends quite heavily on these monies from private donors. Lately, the Smithsonian's pursuit of contributions has been criticized by people both within (some longtime Smithsonian curators and directors have resigned) and without the organization, who fear that donors are given too much say in curatorial matters, that important research is underfunded, and that the institution itself is being crassly commercialized as its new wings and exhibits open bearing the names of the companies and individuals who have paid for them. Stay tuned.

The Smithsonian's collection of nearly 141 million objects spans the entire world and all of its history, its peoples and animals (past and present), and our attempts to probe into the future. The sprawling institution comprises 14 museums (the opening of the National Museum of the American Indian this year brings that number to 15, with 10 of them on the Mall; see "The Mall," on p. 173), as well as the National Zoological Park in Washington, D.C. (there are two additional museums in New York City). Still, the Smithsonian's collection is so vast that its museums display only about 1% or 2% of the collection's holdings at any given time. Its holdings, in every area of human interest, range from a 3.5-billion-year-old fossil to part of a 1902 Horn and Hardart Automat. Thousands of scientific expeditions sponsored by the Smithsonian have pushed into remote frontiers in the deserts, mountains, polar regions, and jungles.

To find out information about any of the Smithsonian museums, you call the same number: © **202/357-2700** or TTY 202/357-1729. The information specialists who answer are very professional and always helpful. The Smithsonian museums also share the same website, **www.si.edu**, which will help get you to their individual home pages.

Smithsonian Information Center (the "Castle")   Make this your first stop. Built in 1855, this Norman-style red-sandstone building, popularly known as the "Castle," is the oldest building on the Mall, yet it holds the impressively high-tech and comprehensive Smithsonian Information Center.

The main information area here is the Great Hall, where a 24-minute video overview of the institution runs throughout the day in two theaters. There are two large schematic models of the Mall (as well as a third in Braille), and two large electronic maps of Washington allow visitors to locate nearly 100 popular attractions and Metro and Tourmobile stops. Interactive videos, some at children's heights, offer extensive information about the Smithsonian and other capital attractions and transportation (the menus seem infinite).

The entire facility is accessible to persons with disabilities and information is available in a number of foreign languages. Daily Smithsonian events appear on monitors; in addition, the information desk's volunteer staff can answer questions and help you plan a Smithsonian sightseeing itinerary. Most of the museums are within easy walking distance of the facility.

While you're here, notice the charming vestibule, which has been restored to its turn-of-the-20th-century appearance. It was originally designed to display exhibits at a child's eye level. The gold-trimmed ceiling is decorated to represent a grape arbor with brightly plumed birds and blue sky peeking through the trellis.

1000 Jefferson Dr. SW. © **202/357-2700** or TTY 202/357-1729. Daily 9am–5:30pm, info desk 9am–4pm. Closed Dec 25. Metro: Smithsonian.

Tips Information, Please

If you want to know what's happening at any of the Smithsonian museums, just get on the phone. **Dial-a-Museum** (© **202/357-2020**, or 202/633-9126 for Spanish), a recorded information line, lists daily activities and special events. For other information, call © 202/357-2700.

Anacostia Museum and Center for African-American History and Culture   This museum is inconveniently located, but that's because it was initially created in 1967 as a neighborhood museum (which makes it unique among the Smithsonian branches). It's devoted to the African-American experience, focusing on Washington, D.C., and the Upper South. The permanent collection includes about 7,000 items, ranging from videotapes of African-American church services to art, sheet music, historic documents, textiles, glassware, and anthropological objects. In addition, the Anacostia produces a number of shows each year and offers a comprehensive schedule of free educational programs and activities in conjunction with exhibit themes. Allow about an hour here.

1901 Fort Place SE (off Martin Luther King Jr. Ave.). © 202/287-3306. www.si.edu/anacostia. Free admission. Daily 10am–5pm. Closed Dec 25. Metro: Anacostia, head to the exit marked "Local," turn left after exiting, then take a W2 or W3 bus directly to the museum.

Arthur M. Sackler Gallery ✦   Asian art is the focus of this museum and the neighboring Freer (together, they form the National Museum of Asian Art in the United States). The Sackler opened in 1987, thanks to a gift from Arthur M. Sackler of 1,000 priceless works. Since then, the museum has received 11th- to 19th-century Persian and Indian paintings, manuscripts, calligraphies, miniatures, and bookbindings from the collection of Henri Vever. In spring 2003, art collector Robert O. Muller bequeathed the museum his entire collection of 4,000 Japanese prints and archival materials.

The Sackler's permanent collection displays Khmer ceramics; ancient Chinese jades, bronzes, paintings, and lacquerware; 20th-century Japanese ceramics and works on paper; ancient Near Eastern works in silver, gold, bronze, and clay; and stone and bronze sculptures from South and Southeast Asia. With the addition of Muller's bequest, the Sackler now has a sumptuous graphic arts inventory, covering a century of work by Japanese master printmakers. Supplementing the permanent collection are traveling exhibitions from major cultural institutions in Asia, Europe, and the United States. In the past, these have included such wide-ranging areas as 15th-century Persian art and culture, photographs of Asia, and art highlighting personal devotion in India. A visit here is an education in Asian decorative arts, but also in antiquities.

To learn more, arrive in time for a highlights tour, offered daily, except Wednesday, at 12:15pm. Also enlightening, and more fun, are the public programs that both the Sackler and the Freer Gallery frequently stage, such as performances of contemporary Asian music, tea ceremony demonstrations, and Iranian film screenings. All are free, but you might need tickets; for details, call the main information number or check out the website. Allow at least an hour to tour the Sackler.

The Sackler is part of a museum complex that also houses the National Museum of African Art. And it shares its staff and research facilities with the adjacent Freer Gallery, to which it is connected via an underground exhibition space.

1050 Independence Ave. SW. © 202/633-4880. www.asia.si.edu. Free admission. Daily 10am–5:30pm; in summer, museum often stays open Thurs until 8pm, but call to confirm. Closed Dec 25. Metro: Smithsonian.

Arts & Industries Building *Kids*   Completed in 1881 as the first U.S. National Museum, this redbrick and sandstone structure was the scene of President Garfield's Inaugural Ball. (It looks quite similar to the Castle, so don't be confused; from the Mall, the Arts & Industries Building is the one on the left.) From 1976 through the mid-1990s, it housed exhibits from the 1876 U.S. International Exposition in Philadelphia—a celebration of America's centennial that featured the latest advances in technology. Some of these Victorian tools, products, art, and other objects are on permanent display. The building displays rotating exhibits, such as one offered in 2003: "Changing the Face of Power: Women in the U.S. Senate," which displayed 35 black-and-white photographs of women senators.

Singers, dancers, puppeteers, and mimes perform in the **Discovery Theater** (open all year except Aug, with performances weekdays and on selected Sat). Call ✆ **202/357-1500** for show times and ticket information; admission of about $5 is charged.

Don't miss the charming Victorian-motif shop on the first floor. Weather permitting, a 19th-century **carousel** operates across the street, on the Mall.

Note: The Arts and Industries Building is a prime place for early birds. The museum holds a Seattle's Best Coffee booth, which opens at 8:30am, selling coffee, muffins, sandwiches, and the like. You can sit inside the rotunda (the rest of the museum is off limits until 10am), sipping coffee and planning your day.

900 Jefferson Dr. SW (on the south side of the Mall). ✆ **202/357-2700.** www.si.edu/ai. Free admission. Daily 10am–5:30pm. Closed Dec 25. Metro: Smithsonian.

Freer Gallery of Art ★ Charles Lang Freer, a collector of Asian and American art from the 19th and early 20th centuries, gave the nation 9,000 of these works for his namesake gallery's opening in 1923. Freer's original interest was American art, but his good friend James McNeill Whistler encouraged him to collect Asian works as well. Eventually the latter became predominant. Freer's gift included funds to construct a museum and an endowment to add to the Asian collection only, which now numbers more than 28,000 objects. It includes Chinese and Japanese sculpture, lacquer, metalwork, and ceramics; early Christian illuminated manuscripts; Iranian manuscripts, metalwork, and miniatures; ancient Near Eastern metalware; and South Asian sculpture and paintings.

The Freer is mostly about Asian art, but it also displays some of the more than 1,200 American works (the world's largest collection) by **Whistler.** Most remarkable and always on view is the famous **Peacock Room.** Originally a dining room designed for the London mansion of F. R. Leyland, the Peacock Room displayed a Whistler painting called *The Princess from the Land of Porcelain.* But after his painting was installed, Whistler was dissatisfied with the room as a setting for his work. When Leyland was away from home, Whistler painted over the very expensive leather interior and embellished it with paintings of golden peacock feathers. Not surprisingly, a rift ensued between Whistler and Leyland. After Leyland's death, Freer purchased the room, painting and all, and had it shipped to his home in Detroit. It is now permanently installed here. Other American painters represented in the collections are Thomas Wilmer Dewing, Dwight William Tryon, Abbott Henderson Thayer, John Singer Sargent, and Childe Hassam. All in all, you could spend a happy 1 to 2 hours here.

Housed in a grand granite-and-marble building that evokes the Italian Renaissance, the pristine Freer has lovely skylit galleries. The main exhibit floor centers on an open-roof garden court. An underground exhibit space connects the Freer to the neighboring Sackler Gallery, and both museums share the **Meyer Auditorium,**

Freeze Frame

About 90% of the American works in the Freer are in their original frames, many of them designed by architect Stanford White or painter James McNeill Whistler.

which is used for free chamber-music concerts, dance performances, Asian feature films, and other programs. Inquire about these, as well as children's activities and free tours given daily, at the information desk.

On the south side of the Mall (at 1050 Independence Ave. SW). ℭ **202/633-4880.** www.asia.si.edu. Free admission. Daily 10am–5:30pm; in summer, gallery often stays open Thurs until 8pm, but call to confirm. Closed Dec 25. Metro: Smithsonian.

Hirshhorn Museum & Sculpture Garden 🐾

This museum of modern and contemporary art is named after Latvian-born Joseph H. Hirshhorn, who, in 1966, donated his vast art collection—more than 4,000 drawings and paintings and some 2,000 pieces of sculpture—to the United States "as a small repayment for what this nation has done for me and others like me who arrived here as immigrants." At his death in 1981, Hirshhorn bequeathed an additional 5,500 artworks to the museum, and numerous other donors have greatly expanded his legacy.

Constructed 14 feet above ground on sculptured supports, the doughnut-shaped concrete-and-granite building shelters a verdant plaza courtyard where sculpture is displayed. The light and airy interior follows a simple circular route that makes it easy to see every exhibit without getting lost in a honeycomb of galleries. Natural light from floor-to-ceiling windows makes the inner galleries the perfect venue for viewing sculpture—second only, perhaps, to the beautiful tree-shaded sunken **Sculpture Garden** 🐾 across the street (don't miss it). Paintings and drawings are installed in the outer galleries, along with intermittent sculpture groupings.

A rotating show of about 600 pieces is on view at all times. The collection features just about every well-known 20th-century artist and touches on most of the major trends in Western art since the late 19th century, with particular emphasis on our contemporary period. Among the best-known pieces are Rodin's *The Burghers of Calais* (in the Sculpture Garden), Hopper's *First Row Orchestra,* de Kooning's *Two Women in the Country,* and Warhol's *Marilyn Monroe's Lips.*

Pick up a free calendar when you enter to find out about free films, lectures, concerts, and temporary exhibits. An outdoor cafe is open during the summer. Free tours of the collection and the Sculpture Garden are given daily; call about them.

On the south side of the Mall (at Independence Ave. and 7th St. SW). ℭ **202/633-4674.** www.si.edu/ hirshhorn. Free admission. Museum daily 10am–5:30pm; in summer museum often stays open Thurs until 8pm, but call to confirm. Sculpture Garden daily 7:30am–dusk. Closed Dec 25. Metro: L'Enfant Plaza (Smithsonian Museums/Maryland Ave. exit) or Smithsonian.

National Air and Space Museum 🐾🐾 *Kids*

This museum chronicles the story of the mastery of flight, from Kitty Hawk to outer space. It holds the largest collection of historic aircraft and spacecraft in the world—so many, in fact, that the museum is able to display only about 20% of its artifacts at any one time. To supplement its space, the National Air and Space Museum has just opened an extension gallery, the Steven F. Udvar-Hazy Center, at Washington-Dulles International Airport, to display many more. The center, which debuted in December 2003, will also serve as the Air and Space Museum's primary restoration facility. Shuttle buses run regularly between the two sites, but allow lots of time for the excursion, since the Udvar-Hazy Center is at least 45 minutes away. The 2003 timing was intentional, since 2003 marked the 100th anniversary of Orville and Wilbur Wright's 12-second flight in 1903. The National Air and Space Museum commemorated the event at this location by staging a special exhibit, "The Wright Brothers and the Invention of the Aerial Age," which continues into 2005. (See box, "Museum Exhibits Scheduled for 2004.")

At any rate, you should plan to spend a couple of hours here. During the tourist season and on holidays, arrive before 10am to make a beeline for the film ticket line when the doors open. The not-to-be-missed **IMAX films** ✒ shown here are immensely popular, and tickets to most shows sell out quickly. You can purchase tickets up to 2 weeks in advance, but they are available only at the Lockheed Martin IMAX Theater box office on the first floor. Two or more films play each day, most with aeronautical or space-exploration themes; *To Fly* and *Space Station 3D* are two that should continue into 2004. Tickets cost $7.50 for adults, $6 for ages 2 to 12 and 55 or older; they're free for children under 2. You can also see IMAX films most evenings after the museum's closing; call for details (© **202/357-1686**).

You'll also need tickets to attend a show at the **Albert Einstein Planetarium** ✒, which creates "an astronomical adventure" as projectors display blended space imagery upon a 70-foot diameter dome, making you feel as if you're traveling in three dimensions through the cosmos. The planetarium's main feature, called "Infinity Express, A 20-Minute Tour of the Universe," gives you the sensation that you are zooming through the solar system, as it explores such questions as "how big is the universe?" and "where does it end?" Tickets are $7.50 for adults, $6 for ages 2 to 12 and 55 or older; you can buy an IMAX film and planetarium combo ticket for $12 per adult, $10 per child.

How Things Fly, a gallery that opened in 1996 to celebrate the museum's 20th anniversary, includes wind and smoke tunnels, a boardable Cessna 150 airplane, and dozens of interactive exhibits that demonstrate principles of flight, aerodynamics, and propulsion. All the aircraft, by the way, are originals.

Kids love the walk-through **Skylab orbital workshop** on the first floor. Other galleries here highlight the solar system, U.S. manned space flights, sea-air operations, and aviation during both world wars. An important exhibit is **Beyond the Limits: Flight Enters the Computer Age,** illustrating the primary applications of computer technology to aerospace. **Explore the Universe** presents the major discoveries that have shaped the current scientific view of the universe; it illustrates how the universe is taking shape, and probes the mysteries that remain. In 2002, the museum added a set of six, two-seat **Flight Simulators** to its first floor galleries (the Udvar-Hazy Center has several more), allowing visitors to climb aboard and use a joystick to pilot an aircraft. For 3 minutes you truly feel as if you are in the cockpit and airborne, maneuvering your craft up, down, and upside-down on a wild adventure, thanks to virtual reality images and high-tech sounds. You must pay $6.50 to enjoy the ride and measure at least 48 inches to go it alone; children under 48 inches must measure at least 42 inches and be accompanied by an adult.

The museum's cafeteria, The Wright Place, offers food from three popular American chains: McDonald's, Boston Chicken, and Donato's Pizza. Best of all, the cafeteria serves up a great view of the Capitol.

On the south side of the Mall (at 7th and Independence Ave. SW), with entrances on Jefferson Dr. or Independence Ave. © **202/357-2700,** or 202/357-1686 for IMAX ticket information. www.nasm.edu. Free admission (fee for some features). Daily 10am–5:30pm. The museum often opens at 9am in summer, but call to confirm. Free 1½-hr. highlight tours daily at 10:15am and 1pm. Closed Dec 25. Metro: L'Enfant Plaza (Smithsonian Museums/Maryland Ave. exit) or Smithsonian.

National Museum of African Art ✒

Founded in 1964, and part of the Smithsonian since 1979, the National Museum of African Art moved to the Mall in 1987 to share a subterranean space with the Sackler Gallery (see above) and the Ripley Center. Its aboveground domed pavilions reflect the arch motif of the neighboring Freer.

Museum Exhibits Scheduled for 2004

The following listing, though hardly comprehensive, is enough to give you an idea about upcoming or current exhibits at major Washington museums. Because schedules sometimes change, it's always a good idea to call ahead. See individual entries in this chapter for phone numbers and addresses.

Anacostia Museum and Center for African-American History and Culture "In Their Own Words: African-American Slave Narratives" (Sep 14, 2003–Mar 7, 2004) presents a slave's perspective, drawing on the narratives of slaves, letters to and from their descendants, and folktales handed down through generations.

Arts and Industries Building "The Beatles! Backstage and Behind the Scenes" (Dec 1, 2003–Mar 31, 2004) showcases 70 black and white *Life* magazine and CBS photographs taken during the 1964 Beatles tour to the U.S., including their performance on the Ed Sullivan Show.

Corcoran Gallery of Art "W. Eugene Smith" (Jan 31–Apr 12, 2004) is the first museum show in Washington, D.C., of Smith's photographs. The retrospective encompasses approximately 60 photographs drawn from the collection of the photographer's son, Kevin Smith.

Folger Shakespeare Library "Voices for Tolerance in an Age of Persecution" (June to mid Oct 2004) draws on the library's collection of 16th- and 17th-century books, manuscripts, and art to highlight voices who argued for tolerance in early modern Europe.

Hirshhorn Museum and Sculpture Garden "Douglas Gordon" (Feb 12– May 9, 2004). This is a survey of works by the Scottish artist best known

The museum collects and exhibits ancient and contemporary art from the entire African continent, but its permanent collection of more than 7,000 objects (shown in rotating exhibits) highlights the traditional arts of the vast sub-Saharan region. Most of the collection dates from the 19th and 20th centuries. Also among the museum's holdings are the *Eliot Elisofon Photographic Archives,* comprising 300,000 photographic prints and transparencies and 120,000 feet of film on African arts and culture. Permanent exhibits include *The Ancient West African City of Benin, a.d. 1300–1897* (cast-metal heads, figures, and architectural plaques that depict kings and attendants); *The Ancient Nubian City of Kerma, 2500–1500 b.c.* (ceramics, jewelry, and ivory animals); *The Art of the Personal Object* (everyday items such as chairs, headrests, snuffboxes, bowls, and baskets); and *Images of Power and Identity (masks, sculptures, and other visual arts from Africa, south of the Sahara).*

Inquire at the desk about special exhibits, workshops (including excellent children's programs), storytelling, lectures, docent-led tours, films, and demonstrations. A comprehensive events schedule provides a unique opportunity to learn about the diverse cultures and visual traditions of Africa. Plan on spending a minimum of 30 minutes here.

950 Independence Ave. SW. ✆ 202/357-4600. www.si.edu/nmafa. Free admission. Daily 10am–5:30pm. Closed Dec 25. Metro: Smithsonian.

for his video installations using classic Hollywood films, like *Psycho* and *Taxi Driver*, as his subjects.

National Gallery of Art   "Courtly Art of the Ancient Maya" (Apr 4–Jul 25, 2004) and "The Drawings Of Jim Dine" (Mar 21–Aug 29, 2004) are two exhibits overlapping at the gallery.

National Air and Space Museum   "The Wright Brothers and the Invention of the Aerial Age" (Oct 11, 2003–TBD), celebrates the 100th anniversary of powered flight. The Wright brothers' 1903 Wright Flyer is displayed at street level, and the exhibit includes 250 photographs and 150 artifacts related to the lives of the brothers.

National Museum of Natural History   "Baseball as America" (Apr 3–Aug 15, 2004) displays the treasures of the Baseball Hall of Fame, the first time these objects have been shown outside their home in Cooperstown, NY.

National Postal Museum   "The Art of the Stamp" (Jul 31, 2003–Feb 16, 2004) exhibits original artwork by more than 70 artists and designers, representing 40 years of illustration history.

Phillips Collection   "The Paintings of Joan Mitchell" (Summer 2004, dates TBD). This retrospective features works by the renowned Abstract Expressionist American painter, who was born in 1925 and died in 1992. This exhibit is the final stop of a tour organized by the Whitney Museum of American Art.

Renwick Gallery   "Jewels and Gems" (Sept. 26, 2003–Feb 9, 2004) shows 100 jewelry pieces, often called "wearable sculpture," that span the last 100 years or so, from the Arts and Crafts Movement to the present.

National Museum of American History ★★★ *Kids*   Well, you could spend days in here (okay, just plan on a few hours). This museum and its neighbor, the National Museum of Natural History, are the behemoths of the Smithsonian, each filled to the gills with artifacts. American History deals with "everyday life in the American past" and the external forces that have helped to shape our national character. Its massive contents range from General Washington's Revolutionary War tent to Archie Bunker's chair. It's all very interesting, but since you do have a life to lead, consider this approach to touring.

Start at the top, that is, the third floor, where **The American Presidency** exhibit explores the power and meaning of the presidency by studying those who have held the position. (There's a gift shop just for this exhibit on this floor.) Also on this floor, don't miss the first American flag to be called Old Glory (1824).

If you are interested in ship models, uniforms, weapons, and other military artifacts; the experiences of GIs in World War II (and the postwar world); the wartime internment of Japanese Americans; money, medals, textiles, printing and graphic arts, or ceramics, check out third-floor exhibits on those subjects. Otherwise, head downstairs to the second floor.

Here, don't miss the intriguing opportunity to see the huge **original Star-Spangled Banner** ★★★, whose 30-by-34-foot expanse has just been painstakingly conserved by expert textile conservators. This is the very flag that inspired Francis

Scott Key to write the poem that became the U.S. national anthem in 1814. Though its 3-year conservation was completed in 2002, the flag remains on view and outstretched, flat, behind glass, in its specially designed conservation lab.

One of the most popular exhibits on the second floor is **First Ladies: Political Role and Public Image,** which displays the first ladies' gowns (look for that of our current first lady, Laura Welch Bush, in the American Presidency exhibit), and tells you a bit about each of these women. Infinitely more interesting, I think, is the neighboring exhibit, **From Parlor to Politics: Women and Reform in America, 1890–1925,** which chronicles the changing roles of women as they've moved from domestic to political and professional pursuits. Following that, find the exhibit called **Within These Walls . . . ,** which interprets the rich history of America by tracing the lives of the people who lived in this 200-year-old house, transplanted from Ipswich, MA. If this personal approach to history appeals to you, continue on to **Field to Factory,** which tells the story of African-American migration from the South between 1915 and 1940.

Finally, you're ready to hit the first floor, where some exhibits explore the development of farm machinery, power machinery, timekeeping, phonographs, and typewriters. A temporary exhibit that opened in August 2002 may still be here when you visit and is worth touring: **Bon Appetit: Julia Child's Kitchen at the Smithsonian,** which is a presentation of the famous chef's actual kitchen from her home in Cambridge, Massachusetts. When she moved to California in late 2001, Child donated her kitchen and all that it contained (1,200 items in all) to the museum. Most of these are on display, vegetable peeler to kitchen sink. A new permanent exhibit that opened in November 2003 on this level is **America on the Move,** which details the story of transportation in America since 1876.

Longtime exhibits continue: **Material World** displays artifacts from the 1700s to the 1980s, everything from a spinning wheel to a jukebox. You can have your mail stamped "Smithsonian Station" at a post office that had been located in Headsville, West Virginia, from 1861 to 1971, when it was brought, lock, stock, and barrel, to the museum. Best of all is the **Palm Court Ice Cream Parlor,** where you can stop and have an ice cream; the Palm Court includes the interior of Georgetown's Stohlman's Confectionery Shop as it appeared around 1900, and part of an actual 1902 Horn and Hardart Automat.

The museum holds many other major exhibits. Inquire at the information desk about highlight tours, films, lectures, concerts, and hands-on activities for children and adults. The museum has four gift shops, and its main one is vast—it's the second-largest of the Smithsonian shops (the largest is the one at the National Air and Space Museum).

On the north side of the Mall (between 12th and 14th sts. NW), with entrances on Constitution Ave. and Madison Dr. (©) **202/357-2700.** www.americanhistory.si.edu. Free admission. Daily 10am–5:30pm. Closed Dec 25. Metro: Smithsonian or Federal Triangle.

National Museum of Natural History ⭐⭐ (Kids) Before you step inside the museum, stop outside first, on the 9th Street side of the building, to visit the new **butterfly garden.** Four habitats—wetland, meadow, wood's edge, and urban garden—are on view, designed to beckon butterflies and visitors alike. The garden is at its best in warm weather, but it's open year-round.

Now go inside. Children refer to this Smithsonian showcase as "the dinosaur museum," since there's a dinosaur hall, or sometimes "the elephant museum," since a huge African bush elephant is the first amazing thing you see if you enter the museum from the Mall. Whatever you call it, the National Museum of Natural

History is the largest of its kind in the world, and one of the most visited museums in Washington. It contains more than 124 million artifacts and specimens, everything from Ice Age mammoths to the legendary Hope Diamond. The same warning applies here as at the National Museum of American History: You're going to suffer artifact overload, so take a reasoned approach to sightseeing.

If you have children in your crew, you might want to make your first stop the first-floor **Discovery Room,** which is filled with creative hands-on exhibits "for children of all ages." Call ahead or inquire at the information desk about hours. Also popular among little kids is the second floor's **O. Orkin Insect Zoo** ✹, where they enjoy looking at tarantulas, centipedes, and the like, and crawling through a model of an African termite mound. The Natural History, like its sister Smithsonian museums, is struggling to overhaul and modernize its exhibits, some of which are quite dated in appearance, if not in the facts presented. So a renovation of the gems and minerals hall has made the **Janet Annenberg Hooker Hall of Geology, Gems, and Minerals** ✹✹ worth a stop. You can learn all you want about earth science, from volcanology to the importance of mining in our daily lives. Interactive computers, animated graphics, and a multimedia presentation of the "big picture" story of the earth are some of the things that have moved the exhibit and the museum a bit further into the 21st century.

Scheduled to open on the first floor (the Rotunda floor) in November 2003 is the **Kenneth E. Behring Hall of Mammals,** where visitors can operate interactive dioramas that explain how mammals evolved and adapted to changes in habitat and climate over the course of millions of years. At least 274 models of mammals and a dozen fossils are on display. This exhibit represents the first time the mammal hall has been updated since 1963. Also, don't miss **African Voices Hall,** which presents the people, cultures, and lives of Africa, through photos, videos, and more than 400 objects.

Other Rotunda-level displays include the **fossil collection,** which traces evolution back billions of years and includes a 3.5-billion-year-old stromatolite (blue-green algae clump) fossil—one of the earliest signs of life on Earth—and a 70-million-year-old dinosaur egg. **Life in the Ancient Seas** features a 100-foot-long mural depicting primitive whales, a life-size walk-around diorama of a 230-million-year-old coral reef, and more than 2,000 fossils that chronicle the evolution of marine life. The **Dinosaur Hall** displays giant skeletons of creatures that dominated the earth for 140 million years before their extinction about 65 million years ago. Suspended from the ceiling over Dinosaur Hall are replicas of ancient birds, including a life-size model of the pterosaur, which had a 40-foot wingspan. Also residing above this hall is the jaw of an ancient shark, the *Carcharodon megalodon,* which lived in the oceans 5 million years ago. A monstrous 40-foot-long predator, with teeth 5 to 6 inches long, it could have consumed a Volkswagen Bug in one gulp. In an effort to update this exhibit, the museum in 2001 mounted a digital triceratops (that is, a computerized rendering of that dinosaur); you can manipulate the image to learn more about it.

Don't miss the **Discovery Center,** funded by the Discovery Channel, featuring the Johnson **IMAX theater** with a six-story-high screen for 2-D and 3-D movies (*Jane Goodall's Wild Chimpanzees* and *Ghosts of the Abyss,* which explored the wreck of the *Titanic,* were among the films shown in 2003), a six-story Atrium Cafe with a food court, and expanded museum shops. In spring 2002, the museum opened the small **Fossil Café,** located within the dinosaur exhibit on the first floor. In this 50-seat cafe, the tables' clear plastic tops are actually fossil cases that present fossilized plants and insects for your inspection as you munch away on smoked turkey sandwiches, goat cheese quiche, and the like.

The theater box office is on the first floor of the museum; purchase tickets as early as possible, or at least 30 minutes before the screening. The box office is open daily from 9:45am through the last show. Films are shown continuously throughout the day. Ticket prices are $7.50 for adults and $6 for children (2–12) and seniors 55 or older. On Friday nights from 6 to 10pm, the theater stages live (no cover) jazz nights, starring excellent local musicians.

On the north side of the Mall (at 10th St. and Constitution Ave. NW), with entrances on Madison Dr. and Constitution Ave. ℂ 202/357-2700, or 202/633-4629 for information about IMAX films. www.mnh.si.edu. Free admission to museum; IMAX tickets $7.50 adults, $6 children ages 2–12 and seniors age 55 or older. Daily 10am–5:30pm. In summer the museum often stays open until 8pm, but call to confirm. Closed Dec 25. Free highlight tours Mon–Thurs 10:30am and 1:30pm, Fri 10:30am. Metro: Smithsonian or Federal Triangle.

National Postal Museum ⟡   This museum is, somewhat surprisingly, a hit, a pleasant hour spent for the whole family. Bring your address book and you can send postcards to the folks back home through an interactive exhibit that issues a cool postcard and stamps it. That's just one feature that makes this museum visitor-friendly. Many of its exhibits involve easy-to-understand activities, like postal-themed video games.

The museum documents America's postal history from 1673 (about 170 years before the advent of stamps, envelopes, and mailboxes) to the present. (Did you know that a dog sled was used to carry mail in Alaska until 1963, when it was replaced by an airplane?) In the central gallery, titled **Moving the Mail,** three planes that carried mail in the early decades of the 20th century are suspended from a 90-foot atrium ceiling. Here, too, are a railway mail car, an 1851 mail/passenger coach, a Ford Model-A mail truck, and a replica of an airmail beacon tower. In **Binding the Nation,** historic correspondence illustrates how mail kept families together in the developing nation. Several exhibits deal with the famed Pony Express, a service that lasted less than 2 years but was romanticized to legendary proportions by Buffalo Bill and others. In the Civil War section you'll learn about Henry "Box" Brown, a slave who had himself "mailed" from Richmond to a Pennsylvania abolitionist in 1856.

The Art of Cards and Letters gallery displays rotating exhibits of personal (sometimes wrenching, always interesting) correspondence taken from different periods in history, as well as greeting cards and postcards. And an 800-square-foot gallery, called **Artistic License: The Duck Stamp Story,** focuses on federal duck stamps (first issued in 1934 to license waterfowl hunters), with displays on the hobby of duck hunting and the ecology of American water birds. In addition, the museum houses a vast research library for philatelic researchers and scholars, a stamp store, and a museum shop. Inquire about free walk-in tours at the information desk.

Opened in 1993, this most recent addition to the Smithsonian complex occupies the lower level of the palatial beaux arts quarters of the City Post Office Building, which was designed by architect Daniel Burnham and is situated next to Union Station.

2 Massachusetts Ave. NE (at 1st St.). ℂ 202/357-2991. www.si.edu/postal. Free admission. Daily 10am–5:30pm. Closed Dec 25. Metro: Union Station.

National Zoological Park ⟡⟡ (Kids)   The **giant pandas** are the zoo's biggest draw, but don't stop with Mei Xiang and Tian Tian.

Established in 1889, the National Zoo is home to some 500 species, many of them rare and/or endangered. A leader in the care, breeding, and exhibition of animals, it occupies 163 beautifully landscaped and wooded acres and is one of the country's most delightful zoos. You'll see cheetahs, zebras, camels, elephants, tapirs, antelopes, brown pelicans, kangaroos, hippos, rhinos, giraffes, apes, and, of course, lions, tigers, and bears (oh my). In spring 2004, the zoo opens a new permanent exhibit entitled "Kids' Farm," which will be exactly as it sounds, a family-friendly farm, complete with dairy cow and barns.

Consider calling ahead (allow at least 4 weeks and call during weekday business hours) for a **free 90-minute highlights tour** (© 202/673-4671), though it's not recommended for kids under age 4. Tours take place only on weekends. The tour guide will tell you how to look at the animals; where, why, and when to look; and will fill your visit with lots of surprises.

Pointers: Enter the zoo at the Connecticut Avenue entrance; you'll be right by the Education Building, where you can pick up a map and find out about feeding times and any special activities. Note that from this main entrance, you're headed downhill; the return uphill walk can prove trying if you have young children and/or it's a hot day. But the zoo rents strollers, and snack bars and ice-cream kiosks are scattered throughout the park.

The zoo animals live in large, open enclosures—simulations of their natural habitats—along two easy-to-follow numbered paths: **Olmsted Walk** and the **Valley Trail.** You can't get lost and it's hard to miss a thing. Be sure to catch **Amazonia,** where you can hang out for an hour peering up into the trees and still not spy the sloth (do yourself a favor and ask the attendant where it is).

Zoo facilities include stroller-rental stations, a number of gift shops, a bookstore, and several paid-parking lots. The lots fill up quickly, especially on weekends, so arrive early or take the Metro.

Adjacent to Rock Creek Park, main entrance in the 3000 block of Connecticut Ave. NW. © 202/673-4800 (recording), or 202/673-4717. www.si.edu/natzoo. Free admission. Daily Apr–Oct (weather permitting): grounds 6am–8pm, animal buildings 10am–6pm. Daily Oct–Apr: grounds 6am–6pm, animal buildings 10am–4:30pm. Closed Dec 25. Metro: Woodley Park–Zoo or Cleveland Park.

Renwick Gallery of the Smithsonian American Art Museum 🎢 *Finds*

A department of the Smithsonian American Art Museum (though located nowhere near it), the Renwick is a showcase for American creativity in crafts, housed in a historic mid-1800s landmark building of the French Second Empire style. The original home of the Corcoran Gallery, it was saved from demolition by First Lady Jacqueline Kennedy in 1963, when she recommended that it be renovated as part of the Lafayette Square restoration. In 1965, it became part of the Smithsonian and was renamed for its architect, James W. Renwick, who also designed the Smithsonian Castle.

Although the setting—especially the magnificent Victorian Grand Salon with its wainscoted plum walls and 38-foot skylight ceiling—evokes another era, the museum's contents are mostly contemporary. On view on the first floor are temporary exhibits of American crafts and decorative arts. On the second floor, the museum's rich and diverse displays boast changing crafts exhibits and contemporary works from the museum's permanent collection, such as Larry Fuente's *Game Fish,* or Wendell Castle's *Ghost Clock.* The **Grand Salon** on the second floor, styled in 19th-century opulence, is newly refurbished and currently displays 170 paintings and sculptures from the American Art Museum, which is closed for renovation. The great thing about this room, besides its fine art and grand design, is its cushiony, velvety banquettes, perfect resting stops for the weary sightseer. Tour the gallery for about an hour, rest for a minute, then go on to your next destination.

The Renwick offers a comprehensive schedule of crafts demonstrations, lectures, and films. Inquire at the information desk. And check out the museum shop near the entrance for books on crafts, design, and decorative arts, as well as craft items, many of them for children. *Note:* It is the main branch of the Smithsonian American Art Museum that is closed for renovation, not this offshoot.

750 9th St. NW (at Pennsylvania Ave. and 17th St. NW). (C) **202/357-2700.** http://americanart.si.edu. Free admission. Daily 10am–5:30pm. Closed Dec 25. Metro: Farragut West or Farragut North.

4 Elsewhere on the Mall

National Archives After being closed for renovation since July 5, 2001, the Rotunda of the National Archives reopened on September 18, 2003. Once again, our country's most important original documents, the Declaration of Independence, the Constitution of the United States, and the Bill of Rights (collectively known as the Charters of Freedom) are on display. New cases allow for better viewing, especially for children and those in wheelchairs, and, for the first time, you will be able to view all four pages of the Constitution in one visit. Also added are 14 new document cases tracing the story of the creation of the Charters and the ongoing influence of these fundamental documents on the nation and the world. Two larger-than-life murals painted by Barry Faulkner have also been restored. One, entitled *The Declaration of Independence,* shows Thomas Jefferson presenting a draft of the Declaration to John Hancock, the presiding officer of the Continental Congress; the other, entitled *The Constitution,* shows James Madison submitting the Constitution to George Washington and the Constitutional Convention.

The renovation of the Rotunda is phase I of a comprehensive project called "The National Archives Experience." Phase II is due for completion September 2004, when the National Archives debuts new exhibition spaces in its public vaults. Exhibits here will feature interactive technology and displays of documents and artifacts to explain our country's development in the use of records, from Indian treaties to presidential websites. The new exhibit area will include a theater that, during the day, continually runs dramatic films illustrating the relationship between records and democracy in the lives of real people, and at night, serves as a premier documentary film venue for the city. A special exhibition gallery will showcase exhibits of timely topics that will then travel to other museums.

This federal institution is charged with sifting through the accumulated papers of a nation's official life—billions of pieces a year—and determining what to save and what to destroy. The Archives' vast accumulation of census figures, military records, naturalization papers, immigrant passenger lists, federal documents, passport applications, ship manifests, maps, charts, photographs, and motion picture film (and that's not the half of it) spans 2 centuries. Anyone is welcome to use the National Archives center for genealogical research—this is where Alex Haley began his work on *Roots.*

And it's all available for the perusal of anyone age 16 or over (call for details). If you're interested, visit the building, entering on Pennsylvania Avenue, and head to the fourth floor, where a staff member can advise you about the time and effort that will be involved, and, if you decide to pursue it, exactly how to proceed.

The National Archives building itself is worth an admiring glance. The neoclassical structure, designed by John Russell Pope (also the architect of the National Gallery of Art and the Jefferson Memorial) in the 1930s, is an impressive example of the beaux arts style. Seventy-two columns create a Corinthian colonnade on each of the four facades. Great bronze doors mark the Constitution Avenue entrance and four large sculptures representing the Future, the Past, Heritage, and Guardianship sit on pedestals near the entrances. Huge pediments crown both the Pennsylvania Avenue and Connecticut Avenue entrances to the building.

700 Pennsylvania Ave. NW (between 7th and 9th sts.; enter on Pennsylvania Ave.). ℂ **866/272-6272** or ℂ 202/501-5000 for general information, or ℂ 202/501-5400 for research information. www.nara.gov. Free admission. Call for visiting and research hours. Closed Dec 25. Metro: Archives–Navy Memorial.

National Gallery of Art ✰✰✰   Most people don't realize it, but the National Gallery of Art is not part of the Smithsonian complex. Housing one of the world's foremost collections of Western painting, sculpture, and graphic arts, spanning from the Middle Ages through the 20th century, the National Gallery has a dual personality. The original West Building, designed by John Russell Pope (architect of the Jefferson Memorial and the National Archives), is a neoclassic marble masterpiece with a domed rotunda over a colonnaded fountain and high-ceilinged corridors leading to delightful garden courts. It was a gift to the nation from Andrew W. Mellon, who also contributed the nucleus of the collection, including 21 masterpieces from the Hermitage, two Raphaels among them. The ultramodern East Building, designed by I. M. Pei and opened in 1978, is composed of two adjoining triangles with glass walls and lofty tetrahedron skylights. The pink Tennessee marble from which both buildings were constructed was taken from the same quarry; it forms an architectural link between the two structures.

The West Building: On the main floor of the West Building, about 1,000 paintings are always on display. To the left (as you enter off the Mall) is the **Art Information Room,** housing the **Micro Gallery,** where those so inclined can design their own tours of the permanent collection and enhance their knowledge of art via user-friendly computers.

To the right and left of the rotunda are sculpture galleries. On view are more than 800 works from the museum's permanent collection, mostly European sculptures from the Middle Ages to the early 20th century. Among the masterpieces here are Honoré Daumier's entire series of bronze sculptures, including all 36 of his caricatured portrait busts of French government officials.

The National Gallery is in the midst of a renovation, closing sections of the gallery as it goes. In 2003, the West Building's Dutch, Northern Renaissance, Italian, French, Spanish, 17th- through early 19th-century galleries were closed and may still be in 2004—call ℂ **202/842-6179** for information.

The **National Gallery Sculpture Garden** ✰, just across 7th Street from the West Wing, opened to the public in May 1999. The park takes up 2 city blocks and features open lawns; a central pool with a spouting fountain (the pool turns into an ice rink in winter); an exquisite glassed-in pavilion housing a cafe; 17 sculptures by renowned artists like Roy Lichtenstein and Ellsworth Kelly (and Scott Burton, whose *Six-Part Seating* you're welcome to sit upon) and, the latest installment, a Paris Metro sign; and informally landscaped shrubs, trees, and plants. It continues to be a hit, especially in warm weather, when people sit on

---

Tips **Avoiding the Crowds at the National Gallery of Art**

The best time to visit the National Gallery is Monday morning; the worst is Sunday afternoon.

the wide rim of the pool and dangle their feet in the water while they eat their lunch. Friday evenings in summer, the gallery stages live jazz performances here.

The East Building: Hard to miss outside the building is Frank Stella's giant sculpture, newly installed at the corner of 3rd Street and Pennsylvania Avenue. Called "Prince of Homburg," the aluminum and fiberglass creation is more than 30 feet high, weighs 10 tons, and moves with the wind.

Inside this wing is a showcase for the museum's collection of 20th-century art, including works by Picasso, Miró, Matisse, Pollock, and Rothko; this is also the home of the art history research center. Always on display are the massive aluminum Calder mobile dangling under a seven-story skylight and an exhibit called **Small French Paintings,** which I love.

Altogether, you should allow a leisurely 2 hours to see everything here.

Pick up a floor plan and calendar of events at an information desk to find out about National Gallery exhibits, films, tours, lectures, and concerts. Highly recommended are the free highlight tours (call for exact times) and audio tours. The gift shop is a favorite. The gallery offers several good dining options, among them the concourse-level Cascade Café, which has seven food stations; the Garden Café, on the ground floor of the West Building, which sometimes tailors its menu to complement a particular exhibit; and the sculpture garden's Pavilion Café.

4th St. and Constitution Ave. NW, on the north side of the Mall (between 3rd and 7th sts. NW). Enter the gallery from the National Mall or through its 6th St. entrances; the 7th and 4th street entrances are closed until further notice, for security reasons. ⓒ 202/737-4215. www.nga.gov. Free admission. Mon–Sat 10am–5pm; Sun 11am–6pm. Closed Jan 1 and Dec 25. Metro: Archives, Judiciary Square, or Smithsonian.

United States Holocaust Memorial Museum ⭐⭐
This museum remains a top draw, as it has been since it opened in 1993. If you arrive without a reserved ticket specifying an admission time, you'll have to join the line of folks seeking to get one of the 1,575 day-of-sale tickets the museum makes available each day (see the note titled "Holocaust Museum Touring Tips," below). The museum opens its doors at 10am and the tickets are usually gone by 10:30am. Get in line early in the morning (around 8am).

The noise and bustle of so many visitors can be disconcerting, and it's certainly at odds with the experience that follows. But things settle down as you begin your tour. When you enter, you will be issued an identity card of an actual victim of the Holocaust. By 1945, 66% of those whose lives are documented on these cards were dead.

The tour begins on the fourth floor, where exhibits portray the events of 1933 to 1939, the years of the Nazi rise to power. On the third floor (documenting 1940–44), exhibits illustrate the narrowing choices of people caught up in the Nazi machine. You board a Polish freight car of the type used to transport Jews

---

ⓘ Tips Holocaust Museum Touring Tips

Because so many people want to visit the museum (it has hosted as many as 10,000 visitors in a single day), tickets specifying a visit time (in 15-min. intervals) are required. Reserve as many as 10 tickets in advance via Tickets.com (ⓒ 800/400-9373; www.tickets.com) for a small service charge. If you order well in advance, you can have tickets mailed to you at home. If you didn't plan ahead, you can also get same-day tickets at the museum beginning at 10am daily (lines form earlier, usually around 8am). Note that same-day tickets are limited, and one person may obtain a maximum of four.

from the Warsaw ghetto to Treblinka and hear recordings of survivors telling what life in the camps was like. This part of the museum documents the details of the Nazis' "Final Solution" for the Jews.

The second floor recounts a more heartening story: It depicts how non-Jews throughout Europe, by exercising individual action and responsibility, saved Jews at great personal risk. Denmark—led by a king who swore that if any of his subjects wore a yellow star, so would he—managed to hide and save 90% of its Jews. Exhibits follow on the liberation of the camps, life in Displaced Persons camps, emigration to Israel and America, and the Nuremberg trials. A highlight at the end of the permanent exhibition is a 30-minute film called *Testimony,* in which Holocaust survivors tell their personal stories. The tour concludes in the hexagonal Hall of Remembrance, where you can meditate on what you've experienced and light a candle for the victims. The museum notes that most people take 2 to 3 hours on their first visit; many people take longer.

In addition to its permanent and temporary exhibitions, the museum has a Resource Center for educators, which provides materials and services to Holocaust educators and students; an interactive computer learning center; and a registry of Holocaust survivors, a library, and archives, which researchers may use to retrieve historic documents, photographs, oral histories, films, and videos.

The museum recommends not bringing children under 11; for older children, it's advisable to prepare them for what they'll see. There's a cafeteria and museum shop on the premises.

You can see some parts of the museum without tickets. These include two special areas on the first floor and concourse: **Daniel's Story: Remember the Children** and the **Wall of Remembrance** (Children's Tile Wall), which commemorates the 1.5 million children killed in the Holocaust, and the **Wexner Learning Center.**

100 Raoul Wallenberg Place SW (formerly 15th St. SW; near Independence Ave., just off the Mall). © 202/ 488-0400. www.ushmm.org. Free admission. Daily 10am–5:30pm, staying open until 8pm Tues and Thurs mid-Apr to mid-June. Closed Yom Kippur and Dec 25. Metro: Smithsonian.

5 Other Government Agencies

Bureau of Engraving & Printing *Kids*   This is where they will literally show you the money. A staff of 2,600 works around the clock churning it out at the rate of about $700 million a day. Everyone's eyes pop as they walk past rooms overflowing with new greenbacks. But although the money draws everyone in, it's not the whole story. The bureau prints many other products, including 25 billion postage stamps a year, presidential portraits, and White House invitations.

Note: The Bureau of Engraving and Printing responds to Department of Homeland Security "Code Orange" warnings by halting its public tours. So just be sure to call ahead to confirm that tours are still on a normal schedule when you're here.

Let's assume that you're planning a trip during "normal times." Many people line up each day to get a peek at all the moola, so arriving early, especially during the peak tourist season, is essential.

Consider securing VIP tickets from your senator or congressperson; VIP tours are offered Monday through Friday at 8:15 and 8:45am, with additional 4, 4:15, 4:30 and 5pm tours added in summer, and last about 45 minutes. Write at least 3 months in advance for tickets.

Tickets for general public tours are required every day, and every person taking the tour must have a ticket. To obtain a ticket, go to the ticket booth on

Raoul Wallenberg Place and show a valid photo ID. You will receive a ticket specifying a tour time for that same day, and be directed to the 14th Street entrance of the bureau. Booth hours are from 8am to 2pm all year long, and reopening in summer from 3:30 to 7pm.

The 40-minute guided tour begins with a short introductory film. Then you'll see, through large windows, the processes that go into the making of paper money: the inking, stacking of bills, cutting, and examination for defects. Most printing here is done from engraved steel plates in a process known as *intaglio,* the hardest to counterfeit, because the slightest alteration will cause a noticeable change in the portrait in use. Additional exhibits include bills no longer in use, counterfeit money, and a $100,000 bill designed for official transactions (since 1969, the largest denomination printed for the general public is $100).

After you finish the tour, allow time to explore the **Visitor Center,** open from 8:30am to 3:30pm (until 8pm in summer), where exhibits include informative videos, money-related electronic games, and a display of $1 million. Here, too, you can buy gifts ranging from bags of shredded money—no, you can't tape it back together—to copies of documents such as the Gettysburg Address.

14th and C sts. SW. ⓒ **800/874-3188** or 202/874-2330. www.moneyfactory.com. Free admission. Mon–Fri 9am–2pm (last tour begins at 1:40pm); in summer, (June–Aug) extended hours 3:30–7pm (the building and ticket booth close to the public between 2 and 3:30pm). Closed Dec 25–Jan 1 and federal holidays. Metro: Smithsonian (Independence Ave. exit).

Federal Bureau of Investigation   Closed for public tours during renovation, which continues until 2005.

Library of Congress ⭐   The question most frequently asked by visitors to the Library of Congress is: Where are the books? The answer is: on the 532 miles of shelves located throughout the library's three buildings: the **Thomas Jefferson, James Madison Memorial,** and **John Adams** buildings. Established in 1800, "for the purchase of such books as may be necessary for the use of Congress," the library today serves the nation, with holdings for the visually impaired (for whom books are recorded on cassette and/or translated into Braille), research scholars, and college students—and tourists. Its first collection of books was destroyed in 1814 when the British burned the Capitol (where the library was then housed) during the War of 1812. Thomas Jefferson then sold the institution his personal library of 6,487 books as a replacement, and this became the foundation of what would grow to become the world's largest library.

Today, the collection contains a mind-boggling 121 million items. Its buildings house more than 18 million catalogued books, 54 million manuscripts, 12 million prints and photographs, 2.5 million audio holdings (discs, tapes, talking books, and so on), more than 700,000 movies and videotapes, musical instruments from the 1700s, and the letters and papers of everyone from George Washington to Groucho Marx. The library offers a year-round program of free concerts, lectures, and poetry readings, and houses the Copyright Office.

Just as impressive as the scope of the library's holdings is its architecture. Most magnificent is the ornate Italian Renaissance–style **Thomas Jefferson Building,** which was erected between 1888 and 1897 to hold the burgeoning collection and establish America as a cultured nation with magnificent institutions equal to anything in Europe. Fifty-two painters and sculptors worked for 8 years on its interior. There are floor mosaics of Italian marble, allegorical paintings on the overhead vaults, more than 100 murals, and numerous ornamental cornucopias, ribbons, vines, and garlands within. The building's exterior has 42 granite sculptures and yards of bas-reliefs. Especially impressive are the exquisite marble **Great Hall** and the **Main Reading Room,** the latter under a 160-foot dome. Originally intended to hold the fruits of at least 150 years of collecting, the Jefferson Building was, in fact, filled up in a mere 13 years. It is now supplemented by the James Madison Memorial Building and the John Adams Building.

On permanent display in the Jefferson Building's Great Hall are several exhibits: The **American Treasures of the Library of Congress** rotates a selection of more than 200 of the rarest and most interesting items from the library's collection—like Thomas Jefferson's rough draft of the Declaration of Independence with notations by Benjamin Franklin and John Adams in the margins, and the contents of Lincoln's pockets when he was assassinated. Across the Great Hall from the American Treasures exhibit is one that showcases the **World Treasures of the Library of Congress.** Its multimedia display of books, maps, videos, and illustrations invites visitors to examine artifacts from the library's vast international collections. Tucked away in a corner of the Jefferson Building is another permanent exhibit, the **Bob Hope Gallery of American Entertainment,** which presents on a rotating basis, film clips, memorabilia, and manuscript pages from a collection that the comedian donated to the library in 2000.

If you are waiting for your tour to start (see schedule below), take in the 12-minute orientation film in the Jefferson's visitors' theater or browse in its gift shop. Pick up a calendar of events when you visit. Concerts take place in the Jefferson Building's elegant **Coolidge Auditorium.** The concerts are free but require tickets, which you can obtain through Ticketmaster (© **800/551-7328** or 202/432-7328).

The **Madison Building,** across Independence Avenue from the Jefferson Building, at 10 Independence Ave. SE, offers interesting exhibits and features classic, rare, and unusual films in its **Mary Pickford Theater.** Find out more about the library's free film series by accessing the LOC website (www.loc.gov), clicking on "News and Events," then scrolling down to find the postings for the free concert series and the free film series. The Madison Building also houses a cafeteria and the more formal Montpelier Room restaurant, both of which are open for lunch weekdays.

Anyone over high school age may use the library's collections, but first you must obtain a user card with your photo on it. Go to Reader Registration in Room LM 140 (street level of the Madison Bldg.) and present a driver's license or passport. Then head to the Information Desk in either the Jefferson or Madison buildings to find out about the research resources available to you and how to use them. Most likely, you will be directed to the Main Reading Room. All books must be used on-site.

1st St. SE (between Independence Ave. and E. Capitol St.). © **202/707-8000.** www.loc.gov. Free admission. Madison Bldg. Mon–Fri 8:30am–9:30pm; Sat 8:30am–6pm. Jefferson Bldg. Mon–Sat 10am–5pm. Closed federal holidays. Stop at the information desk inside the Jefferson Building's west entrance on 1st St. to obtain same-day free tickets to tour the Library. Tours of the Great Hall: Mon–Fri 10:30 and 11:30am, and 1:30, 2:30, and 3:30pm; Sat 10:30 and 11:30am, and 1:30 and 2:30pm. Metro: Capitol South.

6 More Museums

Art Museum of the Americas   Within this Spanish–Colonial style building are works of contemporary Latin and Caribbean artists. A bicentennial gift to the United States from the Organization of American States (OAS) member countries, the museum has a rotating permanent collection; anywhere between 80 and 200 works are on display at any given time. Most major Latin American artists are represented. Be sure to see the art exhibit on the first floor and stroll through the formal Aztec Garden out back. The garden leads to the OAS head-quarters building, at 17th Street and Constitution Avenue NW, which houses an art gallery displaying paintings by Latin artists. This gallery is open weekdays only, but welcomes the public free of charge.

201 18th St. NW (at Virginia Ave.). ✆ **202/458-6016.** www.oas.org. Free admission. Tues–Sun 10am–5pm. Closed federal holidays and Good Friday. Metro: Farragut West, then walk south about 6 blocks.

B'nai B'rith Klutznick National Jewish Museum This interesting museum documents 20 centuries of Jewish history. Much of the collection consists of cere-monial and folk-art objects. Among permanent exhibits are a worldwide collection of ancient and modern Torahs, menorahs, prayer shawls, Passover plates, religious books, kiddush cups, marriage contracts, candlesticks, and coins. American Jewish history is documented in correspondence between presidents and Jewish groups, including a letter from George Washington to a Hebrew congregation in Newport, R.I. ("The Government of the United States . . . gives to bigotry no sanction and to persecution no assistance . . . ") In addition, the museum displays works by con-temporary artists. And a Sports Hall of Fame honors American Jewish athletes and sports personalities such as "Red" Auerbach, Hank Greenberg, Mel Allen, and Sandy Koufax. There's a small sculpture garden on the premises.

2020 K St. NW. ✆ **202/857-6583.** www.bbinet.org, then click on "Klutznick." The museum is free and open to the public Mon–Thurs, noon–3pm, by advance reservation only: Call the number listed, or better yet, e-mail the museum at museum@bnaibrith.org. Metro: Farragut North or Farragut West.

City Museum ⭐ Long overdue, this museum presents the story of "the people, events, and communities" of Washington, D.C. A main feature is the 25-minute multimedia show, in which historical figures and contemporary characters come to life, going backwards and forwards in time, as they reveal the main events and personalities that formed this city. "Washington Stories," as the show is called, runs every 30 minutes and focuses on the early days of D.C. It's a little goofy—the character of Pierre L'Enfant wants to be called "Peter"—and seems designed for viewers with short attention spans, since the presentation of information jumps from bit to bit. But it's successful in conveying certain ideas, for instance, that Washington has always been a city of diversity. An exhibit on the first floor enti-tled "Washington Perspectives" covers the history of the city through displays of old ticket stubs, photographs, advertisements, and other artifacts, with printed explanations and sometimes recorded voices. The room is divided into 4 chrono-logical sections, and as you move through each time period, you pick up details, whether it's about the bustle of market life in the 18th century, or segregation in the 1950s. At some point, you'll notice people bent over in the middle of the room, peering at the floor: they're looking at the lit-up map beneath their feet, pieced together from aerial photographs taken in 1999. Your fellow museum-goers are trying to locate specific places on the map. Upstairs are two more exhibits. "Sandlots to Stadiums" basically traces the history of sports and recreation in the city. To me, the much more interesting exhibit is "Mapping the City, It's in the Details," which displays old maps, receipts, and drawings; headphones on stands in front of many of the artifacts provide audio recordings of historians giving con-text to and information about what you are seeing.

The City Museum resides in the restored and gorgeous Carnegie Library building and its interior is all grand white marble, Palladian windows, and grace-ful double staircases. I visited the museum soon after it opened in May 2003, when it wasn't complete. By the time you read this, it should also offer a café, library, shop, galleries on the communities of Chinatown and Mount Vernon Square, an archaeology lab, and an education center. (I hope, too, that a museum brochure will have been produced and that the air conditioning system will have grown quieter.) The early 20th century Beaux Arts designed structure serves as fine counterpoint to the brand new, ultramodern and huge D.C. Convention Center, directly across the street.

801 K St. NW (at Mount Vernon Square, between 7th and 9th sts.). © 202/383-1800. www.citymuseumdc.org. Admission: exhibits $3 adults, $2 students and seniors; multimedia show $6 adults, $5 students and seniors; combination ticket: $8 adults, $6 students and seniors. Tues–Sun 10am–5pm; 3rd Thurs every month until 9pm. Closed Mon and major holidays. Metro: Mount Vernon Square/Convention Center or Gallery Place/Chinatown.

The Corcoran Gallery of Art ★★   This elegant art museum, a stone's throw from the White House, is a favorite party site in the city, hosting everything from inaugural balls to wedding receptions.

The first art museum in Washington, the Corcoran Gallery was housed from 1869 to 1896 in the redbrick and brownstone building that is now the Renwick. The collection outgrew its quarters and was transferred in 1897 to its present beaux arts building, designed by Ernest Flagg.

The collection, shown in rotating exhibits, focuses chiefly on American art. A prominent Washington banker, William Wilson Corcoran was among the first wealthy American collectors to realize the importance of encouraging and supporting this country's artists. Enhanced by further gifts and bequests, the collection comprehensively spans American art from 18th-century portraiture to 20th-century moderns like Nevelson, Warhol, and Rothko. Nineteenth-century works include Bierstadt's and Remington's imagery of the American West; Hudson River School artists; expatriates like Whistler, Sargent, and Mary Cassatt; and two giants of the late 19th century, Homer and Eakins.

The Corcoran is not exclusively an American art museum. On the first floor is the collection from the estate of Senator William Andrews Clark, an eclectic grouping of Dutch and Flemish masters; European painters; French Impressionists; Barbizon landscapes; Delft porcelains; a Louis XVI *salon dore* transported in toto from Paris; and more. Clark's will stated that his diverse collection, which any curator would undoubtedly want to disperse among various museum departments, must be shown as a unit. He left money for a wing to house it and the new building opened in 1928. Don't miss the small walnut-paneled room known as "Clark Landing," which showcases 19th-century French Impressionist and American art; a room of exquisite Corot landscapes; another of medieval Renaissance tapestries; and numerous Daumier lithographs donated by Dr. Armand Hammer. Allow an hour for touring the collection.

Pick up a schedule of events—temporary exhibits, gallery talks, concerts, art auctions, and more. Families should inquire about the Corcoran's series of Saturday Family Days and Sunday Traditions. (Family Days are especially fun and always feature great live music.) Both programs are free, but you need to reserve a slot for the Sunday events. There is some street parking.

(**Fun Fact**   **The Height of Her Powers**

Displayed on the second floor of the Corcoran is the white-marble female nude, *The Greek Slave,* by Hiram Powers, considered so daring in its day that it was shown on alternate days to men and women.

The charming Café des Artistes is open for lunch Wednesday through Saturday from 11am to 2pm, for dinner on Thursday from 4 to 8pm, and for Sunday brunch from 10:30am to 2pm (reservations accepted for parties of 6 or more), which costs $24 per adult, $11 per child (12 and under), and includes live gospel music singers; call ☏ 202/639-1786 for more information. The Corcoran has a nice gift shop.

500 17th St. NW (between E St. and New York Ave.). ☏ **202/639-1700.** www.corcoran.org. $5 adults, $3 seniors, $1 students 13–18, $8 families, free for children under 12; free admission all day Mon, and Thurs after 5pm. Open Wed–Mon 10am–5pm, with extended hours Thurs until 9pm. Free walk-in tours daily (except Tues) at noon, as well as at 7:30pm Thurs and at 2:30pm Sat and Sun. Closed Jan 1 and Dec 25. Metro: Farragut West or Farragut North.

Dumbarton Oaks *Finds* Many people associate Dumbarton Oaks, a 19th-century Georgetown mansion named for a Scottish castle, with the 1944 international conference that led to the formation of the United Nations. Today the 16-acre estate is a research center for studies in Byzantine and pre-Columbian art and history, as well as landscape architecture. Its yards, which wind gently down to Rock Creek Ravine, are magical, modeled after European gardens. The pre-Columbian museum, designed by Philip Johnson, is a small gem, and the Byzantine collection is a rich one.

This unusual collection originated with Robert Woods Bliss and his wife, Mildred. In 1940, they turned over their estate, their extensive Byzantine collection, a library of works on Byzantine civilization, and 16 acres (including 10 acres of exquisite formal gardens) to Mr. Bliss's alma mater, Harvard, and provided endowment funds for continuing research in Byzantine studies. In the early 1960s, they also donated their pre-Columbian collection and financed the building of a wing to house it, as well as a second wing for Mrs. Bliss's collection of rare books on landscape gardening. The Byzantine collection includes illuminated manuscripts, a 13th-century icon of St. Peter, mosaics, ivory carvings, a 4th-century sarcophagus, jewelry, and more. The pre-Columbian works feature Olmec jade and serpentine figures, Mayan relief panels, and sculptures of Aztec gods and goddesses.

The historic music room, furnished in European antiques, was the setting for the 1944 Dumbarton Oaks Conversations about the United Nations. It has a painted 16th-century French-style ceiling and an immense 16th-century stone fireplace. Among its notable artworks is El Greco's *The Visitation.*

Pick up a self-guiding brochure to tour the staggeringly beautiful **formal gardens,** which include an Orangery, a Rose Garden, wisteria-covered arbors, groves of cherry trees, and magnolias. Unless you're a fan of Byzantine or pre-Columbian art, you're likely to spend more time in the garden, as much as an hour when everything is in bloom. Exit at R Street, turn left, cross an honest-to-goodness Lovers' Lane, and proceed next door to Montrose Park, where you can picnic. There is parking on the street.

1703 32nd St. NW (entrance to the collections on 32nd St., between R and S sts.; garden entrance at 31st and R sts.). ☏ 202/339-6401. www.doaks.org. Collections: suggested donation $1 year-round. Garden Mar 15–Oct $5 adults, $3 children under 12 and senior citizens; Nov–Mar 15 free admission. Garden Mar 15–Oct daily 2–6pm; Nov–Mar 2–5pm, weather permitting. Collections year-round Tues–Sun 2–5pm. Gardens and collections are closed national holidays and Dec 24.

Folger Shakespeare Library *Finds* "Shakespeare taught us that the little world of the heart is vaster, deeper, and richer than the spaces of astronomy," wrote Ralph Waldo Emerson in 1864. A decade later, Amherst student Henry Clay Folger was profoundly affected by a lecture Emerson gave similarly extolling the bard. Folger purchased an inexpensive set of Shakespeare's plays and went on to amass the world's largest (by far) collection of the bard's works, today housed in the Folger Shakespeare Library. By 1930, when Folger and his wife, Emily, laid the cornerstone of a building to house the collection, it comprised 93,000 books, 50,000 prints and engravings, and thousands of manuscripts. The Folgers gave it all as a gift to the American people.

The building itself has a marble facade decorated with nine bas-relief scenes from Shakespeare's plays; it is a striking example of Art Deco classicism. A statue of Puck stands in the west garden. An **Elizabethan garden** on the east side of the building is planted with flowers and herbs of the period. Inquire about guided tours scheduled on certain Saturdays from April to October. The garden is also a quiet place to have a picnic.

The facility, which houses some 250,000 books, 100,000 of which are rare, is an important research center not only for Shakespearean scholars, but also for those studying any aspect of the English and continental Renaissance. A multimedia computer exhibition called *The Shakespeare Gallery* offers users a close-up look at some of the Folger's treasures, as well as Shakespeare's life and works. And the oak-paneled **Great Hall,** reminiscent of a Tudor long gallery, is a popular attraction for the general public. On display are rotating exhibits from the permanent collection: books, paintings, playbills, Renaissance musical instruments, and more. Plan on spending at least 30 minutes here.

At the end of the Great Hall is a theater designed to suggest an Elizabethan inn-yard where plays, concerts, readings, and Shakespeare-related events take place (see chapter 9 for details).

201 E. Capitol St. SE. ✆ 202/544-7077. www.folger.edu. Free admission. Mon–Sat 10am–4pm. Free walk-in tours daily at 11am, with an extra tour added Sat at 1pm. Closed federal holidays. Metro: Capitol South or Union Station.

Ford's Theatre & Lincoln Museum *Kids* On April 14, 1865, President Abraham Lincoln was in the audience at Ford's Theatre, one of the most popular playhouses in Washington. Everyone was laughing at a funny line from Tom Taylor's celebrated comedy, *Our American Cousin,* when John Wilkes Booth crept into the president's box, shot the president, and leapt to the stage, shouting *"Sic semper tyrannis!"* ("Thus ever to tyrants!") With his left leg broken from the vault, Booth mounted his horse in the alley and galloped off. Doctors carried Lincoln across the street to the house of William Petersen, where the president died the next morning.

The theater was closed after Lincoln's assassination and used as an office by the War Department. In 1893, 22 clerks were killed when three floors of the building collapsed. It remained in disuse until the 1960s, when it was remodeled and restored to its appearance on the night of the tragedy. Except when rehearsals or matinees are in progress (call before you go), visitors can see the theater and trace Booth's movements on that fateful night. Free 15-minute talks on the history of the theater and the story of the assassination are given throughout the day. Be sure to visit the Lincoln Museum in the basement, where exhibits—including the Derringer pistol used by Booth and a diary in which he outlines his rationalization for the deed—focus on events surrounding Lincoln's assassination and the trial of the conspirators. Thirty minutes is plenty of time to spend here.

The theater stages productions most of the year (see chapter 9 for information).

517 10th St. NW (between E and F sts.). ✆ 202/426-6925. www.nps.gov/foth. Free admission. Daily 9am–5pm. Closed Dec 25. Metro: Metro Center.

Museums of Special Interest

In addition to the many superb museums described within this chapter, there are many wonderful lesser-known ones around the city, usually focusing on very specific interests. They don't appeal to everyone, but if you're a buff of some kind, you might find one of them fascinating. Don't try to drop in without calling, because most of these museums are not open daily and some require appointments.

Anderson House, 2118 Massachusetts Ave. NW (© 202/785-2040): A century-old, 50-room mansion of amazing design and impressive art and furnishings. The mansion is headquarters for the Society of the Cincinnati, which was founded in 1783 by Continental officers (including George Washington) who had served in the American Revolution. Metro: Dupont Circle.

Art Museum of the Americas, 201 18th St. NW, within the Organization of American States (© 202/458-6016): Permanent collection of 20th-century Latin American art. Metro: Farragut West, then walk south about 6 blocks.

Capital Children's Museum, 800 3rd St. NE (© 202/675-4120): Hands-on educational complex. Metro: Union Station.

Daughters of the American Revolution (DAR) Museum, 1776 D St. NW (© 202/879-3241): Early American furnishings and decorative arts. Metro: Farragut West, then walk south about 5 blocks.

Decatur House (★, 748 Jackson Place (© 202/842-0920): Historic house museum with permanent collection of Federalist and Victorian furnishings. Metro: Farragut West or McPherson Square.

Dumbarton House, 2715 Q St. NW (© 202/337-2288): Another historic house museum, with a permanent collection of 18th- and 19th-century English and American furniture and decorative arts. Metro: Dupont Circle, with a 20-minute walk along Q Street.

Frederick Douglass National Historic Site, 1411 W St. SE (© 202/426-5961): Last residence of the famous African-American 19th-century abolitionist. Metro: Anacostia, then catch bus no. B2, which stops right in front of the house.

Hillwood Museum and Gardens, 4155 Linnean Ave. NW (© 202/686-8500): Newly renovated estate of Marjorie Merriweather Post, who collected art and artifacts of 18th-century France and Imperial Russia. Formal gardens, grand rooms, high tea. Metro: Van Ness or Cleveland Park.

Interior Department Museum, 1849 C St. NW (© 202/208-4743): Permanent exhibits relating to American historical events and locales, including murals by prominent Native American artists, newly on view on the ninth floor. Metro: Farragut West, then walk about 6 blocks south.

Kreeger Museum, 2401 Foxhall Rd. NW (© 877/337-3050 or 202/227-3050): This museum in a residential neighborhood is a treasure trove of art from the 1850s to 1970s, including Impressionist paintings and the works of many American artists. No Metro; take a cab.

Mary McLeod Bethune Council House National Historic Site, 1318 Vermont Ave. NW (© 202/673-2402): Last residence of African-American activist/educator Bethune, who was a leading champion of black and women's rights during FDR's administration. Metro: McPherson Square.

National Building Museum, 401 F St. NW (✆ **202/272-2448**): Housed within a historic building of mammoth proportions is this fine museum devoted to architecture, building, and historic preservation. Metro: Judiciary Square.

Octagon 🕭, 1799 New York Ave. NW (✆ **202/638-3105**): Another historic house museum, it also features exhibits on architecture (its neighbor is the American Institute of Architects headquarters). Metro: Farragut West.

Old Stone House, 3051 M St. NW (✆ **202/426-6851**): 1765 structure said to be the oldest in D.C. still standing on its original foundations. Colonial appearance, English garden. Metro: Foggy Bottom, with a 15-minute walk.

Pope John Paul II Cultural Center, 3900 Harewood Rd. NE (✆ **202/635-5400**): A large multimedia facility that uses interactive presentations to engage visitors of all denominations in exploring issues of religion, world culture, and spirituality in the new millennium. Metro: Brookland–Catholic University; the center runs a free shuttle every 30 minutes on the half-hour between the Metro stop and the center.

Sewall-Belmont House, 144 Constitution Ave. NE (✆ **202/546-3989**): A must for those interested in women's history, the historic house displays memorabilia of the women's suffrage movement, which got its start here. Metro: Union Station.

Textile Museum, 2320 S St. NW (✆ **202/667-0441**): Historic and contemporary handmade textile arts, housed in historic John Russell Pope mansion. Metro: Dupont Circle, Q Street exit, then walk a couple of blocks up Massachusetts Avenue until you see S Street.

Tudor Place, 1644 31st St. NW (✆ **202/965-0400**): An 1816 mansion with gardens, home to Martha Washington's descendants until 1984. Metro: Dupont Circle, with a 25-minute walk along Q Street.

United States Navy Memorial and Naval Heritage Center, 701 Pennsylvania Ave. NW (✆ **202/737-2300**): Outside plaza honors men and women of the U.S. Navy; museum features interactive video kiosks used to learn about Navy ships, aircraft, and history. Metro: Archives–Navy Memorial.

Woodrow Wilson House, 2340 S St. NW (✆ **202/387-4062**): The intriguing former home of this president, preserved the way it was when he lived here in the 1920s. Docents guide visitors on hour-long tours, pointing out objects, such as the French Gobelin tapestry given to Wilson by the French ambassador, and the marble mosaic gift from Pope Benedict; telling stories about our 28th president (he liked to whistle the tune "Oh You Beautiful Doll" to his beloved wife, Edith). Metro: Dupont Circle, then walk a couple of blocks up Massachusetts Avenue until you reach S Street.

The House Where Lincoln Died (the Petersen House) *Kids* After he was mortally wounded at Ford's Theatre, the doctors attending Lincoln had him carried out into the street, where boarder Henry Safford, standing in the open doorway of his rooming house, gestured for them to bring the president inside. So Lincoln died in the home of William Petersen, a German-born tailor. Now furnished with period pieces, the dark, narrow town house looks much as it did on that fateful April night. It takes about 5 minutes to troop through the building. You'll see the front parlor where an anguished Mary Todd Lincoln spent the night with her son, Robert. In the back parlor, Secretary of War Edwin M. Stanton held a cabinet meeting and questioned witnesses. From this room, Stanton announced at 7:22am on April 15, 1865, "Now he belongs to the ages." Lincoln died, lying diagonally because he was so tall, on a bed the size of the one you see here. (The Chicago Historical Society owns the actual bed and other items from the room.) In 1896, the government bought the house for $30,000 and it is now maintained by the National Park Service.

516 10th St. NW. *©* 202/426-6924. Free admission. Daily 9am–5pm. Closed Dec 25. Metro: Metro Center.

International Spy Museum *Kids* Months after we visited the Spy Museum, my 11-year-old and I still like to test each other's powers of observation. We'll be standing in a store or other public place and look around for signs of "hostile surveillance, security systems, and unexpected risk or unlucky breaks." We're putting into practice some tips we picked up at the museum, in a section called "Tricks of the Trade," where interactive monitors teach you what to look for, when it comes to suspicious activity. This tradecraft area is the first you come to in the museum, after you've seen the 5-minute briefing film, and it's easy to spend a lot of time here. In addition to the surveillance games, the section displays trick equipment (e.g., a shoe transmitter used by Soviets as a listening device, and a single-shot pistol disguised as a lipstick tube) and continuously runs film in which spies talk about bugging devices and locks and picks. You can watch a video that shows individuals being made up for disguise, from start to finish, and you can crawl on your belly through duct work in the ceiling overhead. (The conversations you hear are taped, not floating up from the room of tourists below.)

Try to pace yourself, though, because there's still so much to see, and you can easily reach your personal limit before you get through the 68,000-square-foot museum. The next section covers the history of spying ("the second oldest profession") and tells about famous spymasters over time, from Moses; to Sun Tzu, the Chinese general, who wrote *The Art of War* in 400 B.C.; to George Washington, whose Revolutionary War letter of 1777 setting up a network of spies in New York, is on view. You learn about the use of codes and codebreaking in spying, with one room of the museum devoted to the Enigma cipher machine used by the Germans (whose "unbreakable" codes the Allied cryptanalysts succeeded in deciphering) in World War II. An actual Enigma machine is displayed, and interactive monitors allow you to simulate the experience of using an Enigma machine, while learning more about its invention and inventor.

Much more follows: artifacts from all over (this is the largest collection of international espionage artifacts ever put on public display); a re-created tunnel beneath the divided city of Berlin during the Cold War; the intelligence-gathering stories of those behind enemy lines and of those involved in planning D-Day in World War II; an exhibit on escape and evasion techniques in wartime; the tales of spies of recent times, told by the CIA and FBI agents involved in identifying them; and a mockup of an intelligence agency's 21st century operations center. You exit the museum directly to its gift shop, which leads to the Spy City Café.

While you may look with suspicion on everyone around you when you leave the museum, you can trust that what you've just learned at the museum is authoritative: the Spy Museum's executive director was with the CIA for 36 years and his advisory board includes two former CIA directors, two former CIA disguise chiefs, and a retired KGB general.

The International Spy Museum has been immensely popular ever since its mid-2002 opening, which translates into long lines for admission. Consider ordering advance tickets for next-day or future date tours through Ticketmaster (*C* **202/432-SEAT**), which you can pick up at the Will Call desk inside the museum. You can also purchase advance tickets, including those for tours later in the day, at the box office.

800 F St. NW (at 8th St. NW). *C* **866/779-6873** or 202/393-7798. www.spymuseum.org. Admission $13 adults, $10 children ages 5–18. Apr–Oct daily 10am–7pm; Nov–Mar daily 10am–5pm; museum closes 1 hr. after last admission. Closed Thanksgiving, Dec 25, and Jan 1. Metro: Gallery Place/Chinatown or National Archive/Navy Memorial.

National Geographic Society's Explorers Hall   Explorers Hall rotates exhibits related to exploration, adventure, and earth sciences, using interactive programs and artifacts. A recent exhibit included *Sir Edmund Hillary: Everest and Beyond,* celebrating the 50th anniversary of Hillary's ascent of Mount Everest. Most exhibits consume about an hour of touring time. If you are a fan of National Public Radio's Diane Rehm talk show, you may want to join the audience for the Friday morning live broadcast of the show produced in this building, in the Grosvenor Auditorium. Rehm's 10am to noon, Friday show always uses the first hour to host a panel of journalists discussing and analyzing the top news stories; and the second hour to feature conversations with a scientist, author, or newsmaker. Call *C* **202/857-7700** or e-mail drshow@ngs.org, by 4:30pm of the preceding day to reserve a seat in the audience. Admission is free, but you must have a reservation and bring a photo ID. When you make your reservation, you will be asked to indicate the date of the show you'd like to attend, the name of everyone in your party, your daytime phone number, and whether you intend to stay for the first, second, or entire 2 hours.

17th and M sts. NW. *C* 202/857-7588. www.nationalgeographic.com. Free admission. Mon–Sat and holidays 9am–5pm; Sun 10am–5pm. Closed Dec 25. Metro: Farragut North (Connecticut Ave. and L St. exit).

National Museum of Women in the Arts   Seventeen years after it opened, this stunning collection remains the foremost museum in the world dedicated to celebrating "the contribution of women to the history of art." Founders Wilhelmina and Wallace Holladay, who donated the core of the permanent collection—more than 250 works by women from the 16th through the 20th century—became interested in women's art in the 1960s. After discovering that no women were included in H. W. Janson's *History of Art,* a standard text (which, by the way, did not address this oversight until 1986!), the Holladays began collecting art by women, and the concept of a women's art museum soon evolved.

Since its opening, the collection has grown to more than 2,700 works by more than 800 artists, including Rosa Bonheur, Frida Kahlo, Helen Frankenthaler, Barbara Hepworth, Georgia O'Keeffe, Camille Claudel, Lila Cabot Perry, Mary Cassatt, Elaine de Kooning, Käthe Kollwitz, and many other lesser-known artists from earlier centuries. You will discover here, for instance, that the famed Peale family of 19th-century portrait painters included a very talented sister,

Sarah Miriam Peale. The collection is complemented by an ongoing series of changing exhibits. You should allow an hour here.

The museum is housed in a magnificent Renaissance Revival landmark building designed in 1907 as a Masonic temple by noted architect Waddy Wood. Its sweeping marble staircase and splendid interior make it a popular choice for wedding receptions.

1250 New York Ave. NW (at 13th St.). ✆ **800/222-7220** or 202/783-5000. www.nmwa.org. $8 adults, $6 students over 18 with ID and seniors over 60; free for youth 18 and under. Mon–Sat 10am–5pm; Sun noon–5pm. Closed Jan 1, Thanksgiving, and Dec 25. Metro: Metro Center (13th St. exit).

Phillips Collection ★★ Conceived as "a museum of modern art and its sources," this intimate establishment, occupying an elegant 1890s Georgian Revival mansion and a more youthful wing, houses the exquisite collection of Duncan and Marjorie Phillips, avid collectors and proselytizers of modernism. Carpeted rooms with leaded- and stained-glass windows, oak paneling, plush chairs and sofas, and fireplaces establish a comfortable, homelike setting. Today the collection includes more than 2,500 works. Among the highlights: superb Daumier, Dove, and Bonnard paintings; some splendid small Vuillards; five van Goghs; Renoir's *Luncheon of the Boating Party;* seven Cézannes; and six works by Georgia O'Keeffe. Ingres, Delacroix, Manet, El Greco, Goya, Corot, Constable, Courbet, Giorgione, and Chardin are among the "sources" or forerunners of modernism represented. Modern notables include Rothko, Hopper, Kandinsky, Matisse, Klee, Degas, Rouault, Picasso, and many others. It's a collection you'll enjoy viewing for an hour or so. Don't be put off by the sight of construction; the Phillips is in the midst of an expansion, but the main building will remain open throughout.

A full schedule of events includes temporary shows with loans from other museums and private collections, gallery talks, lectures, and free concerts in the ornate music room. (Concerts take place Sept–May on Sun at 5pm; arrive early. Although the concert is free, admission to the museum on weekends costs $8.) On Thursday, the museum stays open until 8:30pm for **Artful Evenings** with music, gallery talks, and a cash bar; admission is $5.

On the lower level, a charming little restaurant serves light fare, right next to the gift shop, which holds clever collectibles tied to the art of the museum.

1600 21st St. NW (at Q St.). ✆ **202/387-2151**. www.phillipscollection.org. Admission Sat–Sun $8 adults, $6 students and seniors, free for children 18 and under; contribution accepted Tues–Fri. Special exhibits may require an additional fee. Tues–Sat 10am–5pm year-round (Thurs until 8:30pm); Sun noon–5pm. Free tours Wed and Sat 2pm. Closed Jan 1, July 4, Thanksgiving, and Dec 25. Metro: Dupont Circle (Q St. exit).

7 Other Attractions

Cathedral of Saint Matthew the Apostle Completed in 1895 after 2 years of construction, this majestic cathedral honors the patron saint of civil servants and is the seat of the Archbishop of Washington. It was here that Pope John Paul II celebrated Mass on Oct. 6, 1979, during the Washington portion of his visit to the United States, and it was here that President John F. Kennedy's funeral Mass was said on Nov. 25, 1963. Every fall, the cathedral celebrates a "Red Mass," attended by those in the legal profession, including Supreme Court justices and members of Congress and government agencies, the White House Cabinet, the diplomatic corps, and, sometimes, the President, to pray for guidance from the Holy Spirit in conducting their legal business.

Step inside to admire the Romanesque style, mosaic-covered walls, gilded Corinthian capitals, and overall design intended to replicate the form of the cross. Its dome rises 190 feet; the church seats 1,254 people, with the use of its chapels.

1725 Rhode Island Ave. NW, off Connecticut Ave. NW. © 202/347-3215. www.stmatthewscathedral.org. Free admission. Sun–Fri 7am–6pm, Sat 8am–6pm. Weekday Masses 7am, 8am, 12:10pm, 5:30pm; Saturday Masses 8am, 12:10pm, 5:30pm; Sunday Masses 7am, 8:30am, 10am (Latin), 11:30am (interpreted for the deaf), 1pm (in Spanish), 5:30pm. Metro: Farragut North or Dupont Circle.

John F. Kennedy Center for the Performing Arts ✿   Opened in 1971, the Kennedy Center is both the national performing arts center and a memorial to John F. Kennedy. Set on 17 acres overlooking the Potomac, the striking facility, designed by noted architect Edward Durell Stone, encompasses an opera house, a concert hall, two stage theaters, a theater lab, and a film theater. The best way to see the Kennedy Center is to take a free 50-minute guided tour (which takes you through some restricted areas). You can beat the crowds by writing in advance to a senator or congressperson for passes for a free VIP tour, given year-round Monday through Friday at 9:30am and 4:30pm, and at 9:30am only on Saturday. Call © 202/467-4600 for details.

The tour begins in the **Hall of Nations,** which displays the flags of all nations diplomatically recognized by the United States. Throughout the center you'll see gifts from more than 40 nations, including all the marble used in the building (3,700 tons), which Italy donated. First stop is the **Grand Foyer,** scene of many free concerts and programs and the reception area for all three theaters on the main level; the 18 crystal chandeliers are a gift from Sweden. You'll also visit the **Israeli Lounge** (where 40 painted and gilded panels depict scenes from the Old Testament); the **Concert Hall,** home of the National Symphony Orchestra; the **Opera House** (which may be closed for renovations during your visit); the **African Room** (decorated with beautiful tapestries from African nations); the **Eisenhower Theater;** the **Hall of States,** where flags of the 50 states and four territories are hung in the order they joined the Union; the **Performing Arts Library;** and the **Terrace Theater,** a bicentennial gift from Japan. If there's a rehearsal going on, the tour skips the visits to the theaters.

If you'd like to attend performances during your visit, check out the website or call the toll-free number above and request the current issue of *Kennedy Center News Magazine,* a free publication that describes all Kennedy Center happenings and prices. See chapter 9 for specifics on theater, concert, and film offerings.

Add another 15 minutes after the tour to walk around the building's terrace for a panoramic view of Washington.

The Kennedy Center, like a lot of other places around town, is undergoing a grand renovation. Try not to let it bother you. Eventually, the center will add two new buildings to the 8-acre plaza in front of the center, and better connect the center to the rest of the city. Right now, it's a mess, even though the center's performances, and tours, continue uninterrupted.

The construction affects the parking situation, which is limited. Until construction is completed, you should avoid driving here. If you do, you can expect to pre-pay a flat rate of $12 when you enter the garage after 1pm weekdays and all day on weekends, and $8 when you enter and leave the garage between 10am and 7pm weekdays.

2700 F St. NW (at New Hampshire Ave. NW and Rock Creek Pkwy.). © 800/444-1324, or 202/467-4600 for information or tickets. www.kennedy-center.org. Free admission. Daily 10am–midnight. Free guided tours Mon–Fri 10am–5pm; Sat–Sun 10am–1pm. Metro: Foggy Bottom (there's a free shuttle service between the station and the center, running every 15 min. from 9:45am–midnight weekdays, 10am–midnight Sat, and noon–midnight Sun). Bus: no. 80 from Metro Center.

Saint John's Church, Lafayette Square Union Station   Every president of the United States since James Madison has worshiped at the Episcopal church across Lafayette Square from the White House, hence its nickname, "Church of the Presidents." The church even has a pew traditionally designated for the president: pew 54. The Madisons were charter members of the congregation. Other parishioner presidents have included James Monroe, Andrew Jackson, Martin Van Buren, William Henry Harrison, John Tyler, Zachary Taylor, Franklin Pierce, and Chester A. Arthur. The morning after John F. Kennedy's assassination, Lyndon Johnson came here for quiet prayer. And President Ford attended services almost every Sunday when he was in town, as did President Bush.

A Greek Revival building with a dome and colonnaded-portico entrance, St. John's was designed by Benjamin Latrobe, the architect famous for his work on the Capitol and the White House. In 1883 another famous architect, James Renwick, was commissioned to add a Palladian window over the altar (*The Last Supper,* designed by the curator of stained-glass windows at Chartres). Other notable stained-glass windows added in the 1880s include one presented by Chester A. Arthur in memory of his wife, who was a St. John's choir member. The window faces the White House (so that Arthur could see it from his office). The *Adoration of the Magi* window commemorates Presidents Madison, Monroe, and Van Buren. On the opposite side of the church, the *Sower's Window* is a memorial to William H. Seward, Lincoln's secretary of state. And the beautiful *Madonna of the Chair* window in the south transept of the balcony is modeled after a painting by Raphael.

The Parish House next door served as the residence of British Minister Lord Ashburton during U.S.-British negotiations in 1842 to settle the Canadian boundary dispute. Here Secretary of State Daniel Webster and Lord Ashburton smoothed over the difficulties of negotiation with sumptuous meals, balls, parties, and receptions.

A guided tour of the church is offered the first Sunday of every month after the last morning service, or you can call to schedule a tour.

Across from Lafayette Sq., 16th and H sts. NW. ✆ 202/347-8766. www.stjohns-dc.org. Free admission. Daily 9am–3pm; services Mon–Fri 12:10pm; Sun 8, 9, and 11am, and 1pm (in Spanish). Summer Sun services are at 8 and 10:30am. Metro: McPherson Sq. (Vermont Ave. exit).

Union Station ⚐   In Washington, D.C., even the very train station where you arrive is an attraction. Union Station, built between 1903 and 1907 in the great age of rail travel, was painstakingly restored in the 1980s at a cost of $160 million. The station was designed by noted architect Daniel H. Burnham, who modeled it after the Baths of Diocletian and Arch of Constantine in Rome.

When it opened in 1907, this was the largest train station in the world. The Ionic colonnades outside were fashioned from white granite. The facade contains 100 eagles. In the front of the building, a replica of the Liberty Bell and a monumental statue of Columbus hold sway. Six carved fixtures over the entranceway represent Fire, Electricity, Freedom, Imagination, Agriculture, and Mechanics. You enter the station through graceful 50-foot Constantine arches and walk across an expanse of white-marble flooring. The **Main Hall** is a massive rectangular room with a 96-foot barrel-vaulted ceiling and a balcony adorned with 36 Augustus Saint-Gaudens sculptures of Roman legionnaires. Off the Main Hall is the **East Hall,** shimmering with scagliola marble walls and columns, a gorgeous hand-stenciled skylight ceiling, and stunning murals of classical scenes inspired by ancient Pompeiian art. Today it's the station's nicest shopping venue.

In its heyday, this "temple of transport" witnessed many important events. President Wilson welcomed General Pershing here in 1918 on his return from France. South Pole explorer Rear Admiral Richard Byrd was also feted at Union Station on his homecoming. And Franklin D. Roosevelt's funeral train, bearing his casket, was met here in 1945 by thousands of mourners.

But after the 1960s, with the decline of rail travel, the station fell on hard times. Rain caused parts of the roof to cave in, and the entire building—with floors buckling, rats running about, and mushrooms sprouting in damp rooms—was sealed in 1981. That same year, Congress enacted legislation to preserve and restore this national treasure.

Today, Union Station is once again a vibrant entity patronized by locals and visitors alike. Every square inch of the facility has been cleaned, repaired, and/or replaced according to the original design. About 120 retail and food shops on three levels offer a wide array of merchandise. And you'll be happy to find that most of the offerings in the Food Court are not fast-food joints but an eclectic mix of restaurants. The skylit **Main Concourse,** which extends the entire length of the station, is the primary shopping area as well as a ticketing and baggage facility. A nine-screen **cinema complex** lies on the lower level, across from the Food Court. The remarkable restoration, which involved hundreds of European and American artisans using historical research, bygone craft techniques, and modern technology, is meticulous in every detail. You could spend half a day here shopping, or about 20 minutes touring.

Stop by the visitor kiosk in the Main Hall. See chapter 8 for information about **shops.**

50 Massachusetts Ave. NE. ⒸⓉ 202/371-9441. www.unionstationdc.com. Free admission. Daily 24 hr. Shops Mon–Sat 10am–9pm; Sun 10am–6pm. Parking: $1 for 2 hr. with store or restaurant's stamped validation; for 2–3 hr., you pay $6 with validated ticket. Without validation, parking rates start at $5 for the 1st hr., and go up from there. Metro: Union Station.

Washington National Cathedral ⚑   Pierre L'Enfant's 1791 plan for the capital city included "a great church for national purposes," but possibly because of early America's fear of mingling church and state, more than a century elapsed before the foundation for Washington National Cathedral was laid. Its actual name is the Cathedral Church of St. Peter and St. Paul. The church is Episcopal, but it has no local congregation and seeks to serve the entire nation as a house of prayer for all people. It has been the setting for every kind of religious observance, from Jewish to Serbian Orthodox.

A church of this magnitude—it's the sixth largest cathedral in the world, and the second largest in the United States—took a long time to build. Its principal (but not original) architect, Philip Hubert Frohman, worked on the project from 1921 until his death in 1972. The foundation stone was laid in 1907 using the mallet with which George Washington set the Capitol cornerstone. Construction was interrupted by both world wars and by periods of financial difficulty. The cathedral was completed with the placement of the final stone atop a pinnacle on the west front towers on September 29, 1990, 83 years (to the day) after it was begun.

English Gothic in style (with several distinctly 20th-century innovations, such as a stained-glass window commemorating the flight of *Apollo 11* and containing a piece of moon rock), the cathedral is built in the shape of a cross, complete with flying buttresses and 110 gargoyles. It is, along with the Capitol and the Washington Monument, one of the dominant structures on the Washington skyline. Its 57-acre landscaped grounds have two lovely gardens (the lawn is ideal for picnicking), four schools, a greenhouse, and two gift shops.

Over the years the cathedral has seen much history. Services to celebrate the end of world wars I and II were held here. It was the scene of President Wilson's funeral (he and his wife are buried here), as well as President Eisenhower's. Helen Keller and her companion, Anne Sullivan, were buried in the cathedral at her request. And during the Iranian crisis, a round-the-clock prayer vigil was held in the Holy Spirit Chapel throughout the hostages' captivity. When they were released, the hostages came to a service here.

The best way to explore the cathedral is to take a 30- to 45-minute **guided tour;** they leave continually from the west end of the nave. You can also walk through on your own, using a self-guiding brochure available in several languages. Call about group and special-interest tours, both of which require reservations and fees (© **202/537-5700**). Allow additional time to tour the grounds or "close" and to visit the **Observation Gallery** ☆, where 70 windows provide panoramic views. Tuesday and Wednesday afternoon tours are followed by a high tea in the Observation Gallery for $18 per person; reservations required. Call © **202/537-8993.**

The cathedral hosts numerous events: organ recitals; choir performances; an annual flower mart; calligraphy workshops; jazz, folk, and classical concerts; and the playing of the 53-bell carillon. Check the cathedral's website for schedules.

P.S. for fans of *The West Wing:* That really was the nave of the Washington National Cathedral, up and down whose center aisle President Jed Bartlet paced as he railed at God during the final episode of the 2001 season.

Massachusetts and Wisconsin aves. NW (entrance on Wisconsin Ave.). © 202/537-6200. www.cathedral. org/cathedral. Donation $3 adults, $2 seniors, $1 children. Cathedral daily 10am–4:30pm; May 1 to Labor Day, the nave level stays open Mon–Fri until 9pm. Gardens daily until dusk. Regular tours Mon–Sat 10–11:30am and 12:45–3:30pm; Sun 12:45–2:30pm. No tours on Palm Sunday, Easter, Thanksgiving, Dec 25, or during services. Worship services vary throughout the year, but you can count on a weekday Evensong service at 4:30pm, a weekday noon service, and an 11am service every Sun; call for other service times. Metro: Tenleytown, with a 20-min. walk. Bus: Any N bus up Massachusetts Ave. from Dupont Circle or any 30-series bus along Wisconsin Ave. This is a stop on the Old Town Trolley Tour.

WALKING TOUR	**HISTORIC HOMES NEAR THE WHITE HOUSE**

Start:	748 Jackson Place NW (corner of H Street NW on Lafayette Square; Farragut West Metro Station).
Finish:	2017 I St. NW (near Foggy Bottom Metro Station).
Time:	Approximately 3 hours.
Best Times:	If you want to see all of the historic houses, you should start mid-morning, Tuesday through Sunday.

Worst Times: In late afternoon, or Monday, when the houses are closed or getting ready to close. This walking tour centers on a main thoroughfare, Pennsylvania Avenue, best-known as the street on which the President lives. You'll walk by the White House on this tour, but won't go in—tours of the White House are currently available to school and veterans groups only, and must be arranged in advance through the office of your congressperson or senator. Each of the houses on this tour lies in proximity to the White House, so it makes sense that their individual histories intertwine with particular presidencies. As you make your way to these historic homes, you'll be mingling with the many office workers, college students, and administrators who keep this part of town bustling during the day.

Walking Tour: Historic Homes Near the White House

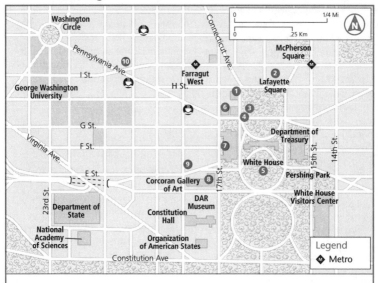

1 Decatur House
2 St. John's Episcopal Church
3 Lafayette Square
4 Pennsylvania Avenue
5 The White House
6 Renwick Gallery
7 Old Executive Office Building
8 Corcoran Gallery
9 Octagon
10 Arts Club of Washington

STARTING OUT
Weekdays, stop in for breakfast at **Bread Line**, 1751 Pennsylvania Ave. NW (℗ **202/822-8900**). Just a block from the White House, and close to Stop 1, Bread Line sells individual danishes, muffins, croissants, cookies, and other baked goods, all created from scratch on-site, as well as gourmet sandwiches made with fresh-baked breads. (Owner Mark Furstenburg is generally credited with revolutionizing bread-baking in Washington.) You can sit inside or out, or carry out.

From Bread Line, you turn left from Pennsylvania Avenue onto 17th Street and right on H Street to reach Stop 1. If you're heading directly to Stop 1 from the Farragut West Metro station, 17th Street exit, turn left on 17th Street and walk down 17th Street to H Street, which you cross. Turn left and proceed to the entrance at 1610 H Street.

❶ Decatur House

Noted architect Benjamin Latrobe (the Capitol, the White House) designed this Federal-style brick town house at 748 Jackson Place NW, on Lafayette Square (℗ **202/842-0920;** www.decaturhouse.org), in 1817 for Commodore Stephen Decatur, famous War of 1812 naval hero.

Decatur and his wife Susan established themselves as gracious hosts in the 14 short months they lived here. Two days after hosting a ball for President James Monroe's daughter, Marie, in March 1820, Decatur was killed in a "gentleman's duel" by his former mentor, James Barron, who blamed Decatur for his 5-year suspension from the Navy following a court-martial in which Decatur had played an active role. Susan moved to Georgetown.

Other distinguished occupants have been Henry Clay (while secretary of state), Martin Van Buren, and George M. Dallas (vice president from 1845–49). In 1872, Californians Edward Fitzgerald Beale and his wife, Mary, bought Decatur House, repairing and remodeling the interior in accordance with Victorian tastes. The Beales left Decatur House to their son, Truxton, whose widow bequeathed it to the National Trust for Historic Preservation in 1956. The Trust continues to maintain and operate Decatur House, and has converted the house into a museum and bookstore.

Tours given every hour (lasting from 30–45 min.) inform you about the house's history, architecture, and interior design. It's a good idea to call ahead to confirm that the house is not closed for a special group tour, which sometimes take place.

Decatur House is open for guided tours only, Tuesday, Wednesday, Friday, and Saturday 10am to 5pm, Thursday 10am to 8pm, and Sunday noon to 4pm. Donations are appreciated. Closed Thanksgiving, Christmas, and New Year's.

Your tour puts you back on H Street, where you want to continue on H Street, past Lafayette Square, past the Hay-Adams Hotel to:

❷ St. John's Church

Every president of the United States since James Madison has worshiped at this Episcopal church across Lafayette Square from the White House, at 16th and H streets NW (ℂ **202/347-8766**), which explains why St. John's is often called the "church of the presidents." If you tour the church, look for pew 54, which is the one traditionally reserved for the current president and first family. See the listing for St. John's on p. 206 for more information. The church offers a guided tour the first Sunday of every month after the last morning's service.

Next door to the church is the Parish House, which served as the residence of Lord Alexander Ashburton, British minister to America in the mid–19th century. It was here that Ashburton and U.S. secretary of state Daniel Webster helped to settle the U.S.-British dispute over Canadian boundaries.

Retrace your steps along H Street to stop at:

❸ Lafayette Square

Until recently, this small public park was a favorite gathering spot for protestors and homeless people. Security concerns sometimes keep the square off limits to the public; this policy seems to change from day to day. Let's assume you're here on a good day.

Originally an open-air market and military encampment, the square takes its name from the day in 1824 when Lafayette visited Washington and crowds swarmed the park for a sight of him. But it's General Andrew Jackson whose statue centers the park—his was America's first equestrian statue when erected in 1853. Sculptor Clark Mills somehow trained a horse to maintain a reared-up pose so that Mills could study how the horse balanced its weight.

Elsewhere in the square are memorials to those from other countries who helped the colonists fight in the War for Independence, the Marquis de Lafayette, Steuben (the Prussian drillmaster of Valley Forge), and Kosciuszko (Polish soldier and statesman) among them.

Walk through the square to reach:

❹ Pennsylvania Avenue

This 2-block section has been closed to traffic since 1995 in an effort to thwart terrorists and crazies from getting near the president. The closing of the street has been controversial, but one good result (aside from ensuring the safety of the president, that is) is that the street has turned into a pleasant promenade area, especially in warm weather, a place where office workers and tourists can stroll at their leisure without fear of traffic.

Hovering over Pennsylvania Avenue is:

❺ The White House

Although the White House no longer is open to the general public, you're free to view its exterior. (If you want to learn some history, you need to stop by the **White House Visitor Center** at 1450 Pennsylvania Ave. NW (© **202/ 208-1631**); see writeup earlier in this chapter).

Take a few minutes to walk around the outside of the White House to study the architecture. Its design is that of Irishman James Hoban, who entered his architectural draft in a contest held by George Washington, beating out 52 other entries, including one submitted by Thomas Jefferson. Though Washington picked the winner, he was the only president never to live in the White House, or president's palace, as it was called before whitewashing brought the name "white house" into use.

The White House took 8 years to build, starting in 1792, when its cornerstone was laid, and its facade is made of the same stone as that used to construct the Capitol. In 1814, during the War of 1812, the British set fire to the White House, gutting the interior; the only reason the exterior endured is because a rainstorm extinguished the fire. What you see today is Hoban's basic creation: a building modeled after an Irish country house; in fact, Hoban had in mind the house of the Duke of Leinster, in Dublin.

From the front entrance to the White House, facing the White House, turn right down Pennsylvania Avenue to where it meets 17th Street NW. There you'll find the:

❻ Renwick Gallery of the Smithsonian American Art Museum

This building, designed by James Renwick, was the first Corcoran Gallery, created in 1859 to house William Wilson Corcoran's grand art collection. The Civil War interrupted that plan, just as the building was nearing completion. The federal government usurped the use of the structure, while Corcoran, a Confederate sympathizer, left for Europe. Upon his return in 1869, Corcoran reclaimed his building; he finally opened his gallery in 1870. Before the end of the century, however, Corcoran's collection had outgrown this space and a second Corcoran Gallery was built (see below) to house Corcoran's art. The Renwick building was used this time as a U.S. Court of Claims, before falling into disrepair. In 1963, First Lady Jacqueline Kennedy recommended the structure be saved as part of the Lafayette Square restoration.

The building became part of the Smithsonian in 1965 and today the museum (© **202/357-2700;** http:// americanart.si.edu) operates as an annex of the Smithsonian American Art Museum. Step inside for a look at the newly refurbished Victorian Grand Salon on the second floor, which currently displays 170 paintings and sculptures from the American Art Museum (closed until 2006 for renovation), and to browse through the galleries, which display American crafts.

Turn left on 17th Street, where you walk right by the:

❼ Old Executive Office Building

This structure at 17th Street NW and Pennsylvania Avenue is not to be confused with the New Executive Office Building, located behind the Renwick Gallery. Known as the "OEB" by insiders who work in or with the Executive Office of the President, this huge, ornately styled building originally was called the State, War, and Navy Building. It was constructed between 1872 and 1888; on completion, it was the largest office building in the world. During the Iran-Contra scandal of the Reagan presidency, the OEB became famous as the site of document shredding by Colonel Oliver North and his secretary, Fawn Hall. The OEB is closed for tours, as I write this, but call © **202/395-5895** in case the policy changed after presstime.

Cross 17th Street, walk a couple of blocks to New York Avenue, and turn right. Across New York Avenue is:

⑧ The Corcoran Gallery of Art

This beaux arts building at 500 17th St. NW (☎ **202/639-1700;** www. corcoran.org), designed by Ernest Flagg, houses a grand collection, shown in rotating exhibits, of mostly American art. On view are works by Nevelson, Rothko, Bierstadt, Remington, Whistler, Sargent, Cassatt, and their peers (see the full listing on p. 197 for more information). The interior is magnificent and, thanks to the Café des Artistes, in the great hall on the first floor of the museum, you have the opportunity to sit and admire the view.

> **TAKE A BREAK**
> Take a seat at the **Café des Artistes** (☎ **202/639-1786**) and enjoy one of the cafe's superior sandwiches or salads, as you gaze at the museum's wide marble staircase, fluted columns, and skylight ceiling. You might try the roast beef on pumpernickel, salmon on brioche, smoked turkey with stuffing and bacon on sourdough, or a Caesar salad. Sandwiches and salads range from about $8.95 to $12; hot entrees are available and cost a bit more. The charming cafe also offers wine, beer, and a host of other beverages. It's open for lunch Wednesday through Saturday 11am to 2pm; for dinner 4 to 8pm Thursday; and for Sunday brunch 10:30am to 2pm (reservations are not accepted for the buffet brunch, which costs $24 per adult, $11 per child 12 and under, and includes live gospel music singers).

Back outside, follow New York Avenue to 18th Street and you have found:

⑨ The Octagon

One of the oldest houses in Washington, The Octagon, 1799 New York Ave. NW (☎ **202/638-3221;** www. theoctagon.org), is also one of the most interesting. The 1801 building served as a temporary president's home for James and Dolley Madison after the British burned the White House in 1814. President Madison sat at the circular table in the upstairs circular room and signed the Treaty of Ghent, ending the War of 1812. The Octagon, which has only six sides, was designed by Dr. William Thornton, first architect of the U.S. Capitol (and Tudor Place, see below), and completed in 1801. Built for the wealthy Tayloe family, it is an exquisite example of Federal-period architecture, with unusual features: round rooms, an oval-shaped staircase that curves gracefully up three floors, hidden doors, and triangular chambers.

Tours are guided and last about an hour, during which you learn more about the house and about the Tayloes, their slaves, and life in the 1800s. The museum hosts changing exhibits, usually on an architectural theme, in two upstairs rooms, and has a permanent exhibit in the English basement, where you learn about the "downstairs" side of life in the 1800s—these were the servants' quarters and work rooms. The American Architectural Foundation administers The Octagon, which is open Tuesday through Sunday, 10am to 4pm. Admission is $5 for adults, $3 for children and seniors.

From The Octagon, head up 18th Street to Pennsylvania Avenue and turn left. Cross Pennsylvania Avenue at 20th Street, proceed 1 block to I Street, and turn left again. In the middle of the block is the:

⑩ Arts Club of Washington

You'll have to ring the buzzer for entry to this structure at 2017 I St. NW (☎ **202/331-7282;** www.artsclubof washington.com), and then you'll find you're on your own to wander. Chances are, too, that a luncheon or some other soiree will be in full swing in the first floor rooms. The Arts Club, founded in 1916 to promote the arts in greater Washington, occupies this town house duplex and allows members and others to rent its facilities for special events.

The site is historic because this is where James Monroe lived for the first 6 months of his presidency, while the White House was being rebuilt after being torched by the British in the War of 1812. Monroe's inaugural ball was held here. The rear wing of the structure dates from 1802, the front portion from 1805.

It's a little bit funky now, as you'll see if you explore a bit: Flights of stairs take you into little alcoves and hidden wings. Art by local artists hangs on the walls throughout the adjoining buildings.

The Arts Club is free and open to the public Tuesday through Friday 10am to 5pm, Saturday 10am to 2pm. Call in advance if you'd like a guided tour of the club.

8 Just Across the Potomac: Arlington

The land that today comprises Arlington County was originally carved out of Virginia as part of the nation's new capital district. In 1847, the land was returned to the state of Virginia, although it was known as Alexandria County until 1920, when the name was changed to avoid confusion with the city of Alexandria.

The county was named to honor Arlington House, built by George Washington Parke Custis, a descendant of Martha Washington whose daughter married Robert E. Lee. The Lees lived in Arlington House on and off until the onset of the Civil War in 1861. After the first Battle of Bull Run, at Manassas, several Union soldiers were buried here; the beginnings of Arlington National Cemetery date from that time. The Arlington Memorial Bridge leads directly from the Lincoln Memorial to the Robert E. Lee Memorial at Arlington House, symbolically joining these two figures into one Union after the Civil War.

Arlington has long been a residential community, with most people commuting into Washington to work and play. In recent years, however, the suburb has come into its own, booming with business, restaurants, and nightlife, giving residents reasons to stay put and tourists more of an inducement to visit (see the box, "Arlington Row," in chapter 9). Here are a couple of sites worth seeing:

Arlington National Cemetery *ᴋᴋ*   Upon arrival, head over to the **Visitor Center,** where you can view exhibits, pick up a detailed map, use the restrooms (there are no others until you get to Arlington House), and purchase a **Tourmobile ticket** ($6 per adult, $3 for children 3–11), which allows you to stop at all major sites in the cemetery and then reboard whenever you like. Service is continuous and the narrated commentary is informative; this is the only guided tour of the cemetery offered. If you've got plenty of stamina, consider doing part or all of the tour on foot. Remember as you go that this is a memorial frequented not just by tourists but also by those attending burial services or visiting the graves of beloved relatives and friends who are buried here.

This shrine occupies approximately 612 acres on the high hills overlooking the capital from the west side of the Memorial Bridge. It honors many national heroes and more than 260,000 war dead, veterans, and dependents. Many graves of the famous at Arlington bear nothing more than simple markers. Five-star Gen. John J. Pershing's is one of those. Secretary of State John Foster Dulles is buried here. So are President William Howard Taft and Supreme Court Justice Thurgood Marshall. Cemetery highlights include:

The Tomb of the Unknowns, containing the unidentified remains of service members from both world wars, the Korean War, and, until 1997, the Vietnam War. In 1997, the remains of the unknown soldier from Vietnam were identified as those of Air Force 1st Lt. Michael Blassie, whose A-37 was shot down in

South Vietnam in 1962. Blassie's family, who had reason to believe that the body was their son's, had beseeched the Pentagon to exhume the soldier's remains and conduct DNA testing to determine if what the family suspected was true. Upon confirmation, the Blassies buried Michael in his hometown of St. Louis. The crypt honoring the dead but unidentified Vietnam War soldiers remains empty for the time being. The entire tomb is an unembellished, massive white-marble block, moving in its simplicity. A 24-hour honor guard watches over the tomb, with the changing of the guard taking place every half-hour April to September, every hour on the hour October to March, and every hour at night.

Within a 20-minute walk, all uphill, from the Visitor Center is **Arlington House** (© 703/235-1530). From 1831 to 1861, this was the legal residence of Robert E. Lee, where he and his family lived off and on until the Civil War. Lee married the great-granddaughter of Martha Washington, Mary Anna Randolph Custis, who inherited the estate. It was here that Lee resigned his commission in the U.S. Army when his native Virginia seceded from the Union. During the Civil War, the estate was taken over by Union forces and troops were buried here. A year before the defeat of the Confederate forces at Gettysburg, the U.S. government bought the estate. A fine melding of the styles of the Greek Revival and the grand plantation houses of the early 1800s, the house has been administered by the National Park Service since 1933.

You tour the house on your own; park rangers are on-site to answer your questions. About 30% of the furnishings are original. Slave quarters and a small museum adjoin. Admission is free. It's open daily from 9:30am to 4:30pm (closed Jan 1 and Dec 25).

Pierre Charles L'Enfant's grave was placed near Arlington House at a spot that is believed to offer the best view of Washington, the city he designed.

Below Arlington House, an 8-minute walk from the Visitor Center, is the **Gravesite of John Fitzgerald Kennedy.** John Carl Warnecke designed a low crescent wall embracing a marble terrace, inscribed with the 35th president's most famous utterance: "And so my fellow Americans, ask not what your country can do for you, ask what you can do for your country." Jacqueline Kennedy Onassis rests next to her husband, and Robert Kennedy is buried close by. The Kennedy graves attract streams of visitors. Arrive close to 8am to contemplate the site quietly; otherwise, it's mobbed. Looking north, there's a spectacular view of Washington.

In 1997, the **Women in Military Service for America Memorial** (© 800/222-2294 or 703/533-1155; www.womensmemorial.org) was added to Arlington Cemetery to honor the more than 1.8 million women who have served in the armed forces from the American Revolution to the present. The impressive new memorial lies just beyond the gated entrance to the cemetery, a 3-minute walk from the Visitor Center. As you approach the memorial, you see a large, circular reflecting pool, perfectly placed within the curve of the granite wall rising behind it. Arched passages within the 226-foot-long wall lead to an upper terrace and dramatic views of Arlington National Cemetery and the monuments of Washington; an arc of large glass panels (which form the roof of the memorial hall) contains etched quotations from servicewomen (and a couple from men). Behind the wall and completely underground is the **Education Center,** housing a **Hall of Honor,** a gallery of exhibits tracing the history of women in the military, a theater, and a computer register of servicewomen, which visitors may access for information about individual military women, past and present. Hours are 8am to 5pm (until 7pm Apr–Sept). Stop at the reception desk for a brochure that details a self-guided tour through the memorial. The memorial is open every day but Christmas.

Plan to spend half a day at Arlington Cemetery and the Women in Military Service Memorial.

Just across the Memorial Bridge from the base of the Lincoln Memorial. © **703/607-8052.** www.arlington cemetery.org. Free admission. Apr–Sept daily 8am–7pm; Oct–Mar daily 8am–5pm. Metro: Arlington National Cemetery. If you come by car, parking is $1.25 an hr. for the 1st 3 hr., $2 an hr. thereafter. The cemetery is also accessible via Tourmobile.

Newseum & Freedom Park 🦆 *Kids*   The Newseum opened in 1997 as the world's first museum dedicated exclusively to news, it's been such a hit that it's already outgrown its location. This location is closed, and a new, larger, and higher-profile headquarters is under construction at 6th Street and Pennsylvania Avenue NW, just off the Mall, though it won't open until 2006. You can visit Freedom Park and the Freedom Forum Journalists Memorial, however.

Adjoining the museum, **Freedom Park,** which opened in the summer of 1996 and sits atop a never-used elevated highway, celebrates the spirit of freedom and the struggle to preserve it. Here, too, are many intriguing exhibits: segments of the Berlin Wall (the largest display of the wall outside of Germany), stones from the Warsaw Ghetto, a bronze casting of a South African ballot box, a headless statue of Lenin (one of many that were pushed over and beheaded when the Soviet Union collapsed in 1991), and a bronze casting of Martin Luther King Jr.'s Birmingham jail-cell door. The glass and steel Freedom Forum Journalists Memorial (honoring more than 900 journalists killed while on assignment) rises above the Potomac, offering views of the Washington Monument, the Lincoln and Jefferson memorials, and the National Cathedral.

1101 Wilson Blvd. (at N. Kent St.). © **888-NEWSEUM** or 703/284-3544. www.newseum.org. Freedom Park daily dawn–dusk. Limited parking is available in the building. Metro: Rosslyn.

The Pentagon   Damaged in the shocking September 11, 2001, terrorist attack in which a hijacked commercial jet crashed into the building, killing 125 people working at the Pentagon, and 64 more people aboard the plane, the Pentagon building has been restored, but at this writing, it remains closed for general public tours, although school and military groups may be able to arrange for tours (call the information number listed below).

The Pentagon is the headquarters of the American military establishment. This immense five-sided structure was built during the early years of World War II. It's one of the world's largest office buildings, housing approximately 23,000 employees. For their convenience, it contains a complete indoor shopping mall, including two banks, a post office, an Amtrak ticket office, a beauty salon, a dry cleaner, and more. It's a self-contained world. There are many mind-boggling statistics to underscore the vastness of the Pentagon—for example, the building contains enough phone cable to circle the globe three times.

Off I-395. © **703/697-1776.** www.defenselink.mil/pubs/pentagon. Free admission. Call to find out whether tours are being offered. Metro: Pentagon.

9 Parks & Gardens

Washington is extensively endowed with vast natural areas, all centrally located within the District. Included in all this greenery are thousands of parkland acres, two rivers, the mouth of a 185-mile-long tree-lined canal-side trail, an untamed wilderness area, and a few thousand cherry trees. And there's much more just a stone's throw away.

GARDENS

Enid A. Haupt Garden   Named for its donor, a noted supporter of horticul-
tural projects, this stunning garden presents elaborate flower beds and borders,
plant-filled turn-of-the-20th-century urns, 1870s cast-iron furnishings, and lush
baskets hung from reproduction 19th-century lampposts. Although on ground
level, the garden is actually a 4-acre rooftop garden above the subterranean Sackler and African Art museums. An **"Island Garden"** near the Sackler Gallery,
entered via a 9-foot moon gate, has benches backed by English boxwoods under
the shade of weeping cherry trees.

A **"Fountain Garden"** outside the African Art Museum provides granite seating
walls shaded by hawthorn trees. Three small terraces, shaded by black sour-gum
trees, are located near the Arts & Industries Building. And five majestic linden trees
shade a seating area around the Downing Urn, a memorial to American landscapist
Andrew Jackson Downing. Elaborate cast-iron carriage gates made according to a
19th-century design by James Renwick, flanked by four red sandstone pillars, have
been installed at the Independence Avenue entrance to the garden.

10th St. and Independence Ave. SW. ℭ 202/357-2700. Free admission. Late May–Aug daily 7am–8pm; Sept
to mid-May daily 7am–5:45pm. Closed Dec 25. Metro: Smithsonian.

United States Botanic Garden ⭐   The Botanic Garden reopened in late
2001 after a major, 5-year renovation. In its new incarnation, the grand conservatory devotes half of its space to exhibits that focus on the importance of plants
to people, and half to exhibits that focus on ecology and the evolutionary biol-
ogy of plants. A 93-foot-high Palm House encloses a jungle of palms, ferns, and
vines, the Orchid Room holds 12,000 varieties of orchids, and the new National
Garden outside the conservatory includes a First Ladies Water Garden, a formal
rose garden, and a lawn terrace. You'll also find a Meditation Garden and gardens created especially with children in mind.

Also visit the garden annex across the street, **Bartholdi Park.** The park is
about the size of a city block, with a stunning cast-iron classical fountain created
by Frédéric Auguste Bartholdi, designer of the Statue of Liberty. Charming
flower gardens bloom amid tall ornamental grasses, benches are sheltered by
vine-covered bowers, and a touch and fragrance garden contains such herbs as
pineapple-scented sage.

245 1st St. ℭ 202/225-8333. www.usbg.gov. Free admission. Daily 10am–5pm. Metro: Federal Center SW.

PARKS
POTOMAC PARK

West and East Potomac parks, their 720 riverside acres divided by the Tidal Basin,
are most famous for their spring display of **cherry blossoms** and all the hoopla
that goes with it. So much attention is lavished on Washington's cherry blossoms
that the National Park Service devotes a home page to the subject: **www.
nps.gov/nacc/cherry**. You can access this site to find out forecasts for the blooms
and assorted other details. You can also call the National Park Service (ℭ **202/
485-9880**) for information. In all, there are more than 3,700 cherry trees planted
along the Tidal Basin in West Potomac Park, East Potomac Park, the Washington
Monument grounds, and in other pockets of the city.

To get to the Tidal Basin by car (*not* recommended in cherry-blossom season),
you want to get on Independence Avenue and follow the signs posted near the
Lincoln Memorial that show you where to turn to find parking and the FDR
Memorial. If you're walking, you'll want to cross Independence Avenue where it

intersects with West Basin Drive (there's a stoplight and crosswalk), and follow the path to the Tidal Basin. There is no convenient Metro stop near here.

West Potomac Park encompasses Constitution Gardens; the Vietnam, Korean, Lincoln, Jefferson, and FDR memorials; a small island where ducks live; and the Reflecting Pool (see "The Major Memorials," earlier in this chapter for full listings of the memorials). It has 1,628 trees bordering the Tidal Basin, some of them Akebonos with delicate pink blossoms, but most Yoshinos with white, cloudlike flower clusters. The blossoming of the cherry trees is the focal point of a 2-week-long celebration, including the lighting of the 300-year-old Japanese Stone Lantern near Kutz Bridge, presented to the city by the governor of Tokyo in 1954. (This year's Cherry Blossom Festival is scheduled to run Mar 27–Apr 11, 2004.) The trees bloom for a little less than 2 weeks beginning sometime between March 20 and April 17; April 5 is the average date. Planning your trip around the blooming of the cherry blossoms is an iffy proposition, and I wouldn't advise it. All it takes is one good rain and those cherry blossoms are gone. The cherry blossoms are not illuminated at night.

East Potomac Park has 1,681 cherry trees in 11 varieties. The park also has picnic grounds, tennis courts, three golf courses, a large swimming pool, and biking and hiking paths by the water.

Created in 1890, **Rock Creek Park** (www.nps.gov/rocr) was purchased by Congress for its "pleasant valleys and ravines, primeval forests and open fields, its running waters, its rocks clothed with rich ferns and mosses, its repose and tranquillity, its light and shade, its ever-varying shrubbery, its beautiful and extensive views." A 1,750-acre valley within the District of Columbia, extending 12 miles from the Potomac River to the Maryland border, it's one of the biggest and finest city parks in the nation. Parts of it are still wild; it's not unusual to see a deer scurrying through the woods in more remote sections.

The park's offerings include the Old Stone House, Carter Barron Amphitheater (see chapter 9), playgrounds, an extensive system of beautiful hiking and biking trails, sports facilities, remains of Civil War fortifications, and acres and acres of wooded parklands. See also p. 198 for a description of the formal gardens at **Dumbarton Oaks,** which border Rock Creek Park in upper Georgetown.

For full information on the wide range of park programs and activities, visit the **Rock Creek Nature Center and Planetarium,** 5200 Glover Rd. NW (© **202/ 895-6070**), Wednesday through Sunday from 9am to 5pm; or Park Headquarters, 3545 Williamsburg Lane NW (© **202/895-6015**), Monday through Friday from 7:45am to 4:15pm. To get to the Nature Center by public transportation, take the Metro to Friendship Heights and transfer to bus no. Y2, Y3, or Y4 to Military Road and Oregon Avenue/Glover Road. Call © **202/895-6070** to request a brochure that provides details on picnic locations.

The Nature Center and Planetarium itself is the scene of numerous activities, including weekend planetarium shows for kids (minimum age 4) and adults; nature films; crafts demonstrations; live animal demonstrations; guided nature walks; plus a daily mix of lectures, films, and other events. A calendar is available on request. Self-guided nature trails begin here. All activities are free, but for planetarium shows you need to pick up tickets a half-hour in advance. There are also nature exhibits on the premises. The Nature Center is closed on federal holidays.

Not far from the Nature Center is **Fort DeRussey,** one of 68 fortifications erected to defend the city of Washington during the Civil War. From the intersection of Military Road and Oregon Avenue, you walk a short trail through the woods to reach the fort, whose remains include high earth mounds with openings where guns were mounted, surrounded by a deep ditch/moat.

At Tilden Street and Beach Drive, you can see a water-powered 19th-century gristmill, which normally is grinding corn and wheat into flour (© **202/426-6908**). It's called **Peirce Mill** (a man named Isaac Peirce built it), but it's currently closed for repairs. Peirce's old carriage house is now the **Rock Creek Gallery** (© **202/244-2482**), where works of local artists are shown; it's open Thursday through Sunday from noon to 6pm (closed federal holidays and 1 month in summer, either July or Aug).

Poetry readings and workshops are held during the summer at **Miller's Cabin,** the one-time residence of High Sierra poet Joaquin Miller, Beach Drive north of Military Road. Call © **202/895-6070** for information.

There's convenient free **parking** throughout the park.

THEODORE ROOSEVELT ISLAND PARK ⭐⭐

A serene 91-acre wilderness preserve, Theodore Roosevelt Island is a memorial to the nation's 26th president, in recognition of his contributions to conservation. During his administration, Roosevelt, an outdoor enthusiast and expert field naturalist, set aside a total of 234 million acres of public lands for forests, national parks, wildlife and bird refuges, and monuments.

Native American tribes were here first, inhabiting the island for centuries, until the arrival of English explorers in the 1600s. Over the years, the island passed through many owners before becoming what it is today—an island preserve of swamp, marsh, and upland forest that's a haven for rabbits, chipmunks, great owls, fox, muskrat, turtles, and groundhogs. It's a complex ecosystem in which cattails, arrow arum, and pickerelweed grow in the marshes, and willow, ash, and maple trees root on the mud flats. You can observe these flora and fauna in their natural environs on 2½ miles of foot trails.

In the northern center of the island, overlooking an oval terrace encircled by a water-filled moat, stands a 17-foot bronze statue of Roosevelt. From the terrace rise four 21-foot granite tablets inscribed with tenets of his conservation philosophy.

To drive to the island, take the George Washington Memorial Parkway exit north from the Theodore Roosevelt Bridge. The parking area is accessible only from the northbound lane; park there and cross the pedestrian bridge that connects the lot to the island. You can also rent a canoe at Thompson's Boat Center (p. 223) and paddle over, or take the pedestrian bridge at Rosslyn Circle, 2 blocks from the Rosslyn Metro station. You can picnic on the grounds near the memorial; if you do, allow about an hour or two here.

In the Potomac River, between Washington and Rosslyn, VA. See access information above. © **703/289-2500**. www.nps.gov/gwmp. Free admission. Daily dawn–dusk. Metro: Rosslyn, then walk 2 blocks to Rosslyn Circle and cross the pedestrian bridge to the island.

ACTIVITIES ON THE C&O CANAL

One of the great joys of living in Washington is the **C&O Canal** (**www.nps.gov/choh**) and its unspoiled 184½-mile towpath. You leave urban cares and stresses behind while hiking, strolling, jogging, cycling, or boating in this lush, natural setting of ancient oaks and red maples, giant sycamores, willows, and wildflowers. But the canal wasn't always just a leisure spot for city people. It was built in the 1800s, when water routes were considered vital to transportation. Even before it was completed, the canal was being rendered obsolete by the B&O Railroad, which was constructed at about the same time and along the same route. Today, its role as an oasis from unrelenting urbanity is even more important.

A good source of information about the canal is the National Park Service office at **Great Falls Tavern Visitor Center,** 11710 MacArthur Blvd., Potomac, MD (*②* **301/769-3714**). At this 1831 tavern, you can see museum exhibits and a film about the canal; there's also a bookstore on the premises. The park charges an entrance fee, $5 per car, $3 per walker or cyclist.

In Georgetown, the **Georgetown Information Center,** 1057 Thomas Jefferson St. NW (*②* **202/653-5190**), can also provide maps and information.

Hiking any section of the flat dirt towpath or its more rugged side paths is a pleasure (and it's free). There are picnic tables, some with barbecue grills, about every 5 miles on the way to Cumberland, beginning at **Fletcher's Boat House** (*②* **202/244-0461**), which is about 3¼ miles out of Georgetown and is a good place to rent bikes or boats or to purchase bait, tackle, and a fishing license. Enter the towpath in Georgetown below M Street via Thomas Jefferson Street. If you hike 14 miles, you'll reach **Great Falls,** a point where the Potomac becomes a stunning waterfall plunging 76 feet. Or drive to Great Falls Park on the Virginia side of the Potomac.

Much less strenuous than hiking is a **mule-drawn 19th-century canal boat trip** led by Park Service rangers in period dress. They regale passengers with canal legend and lore and sing period songs. These boats depart from mid-April to early November; departure times and tickets are available at the Georgetown Information Center (see above). Both the Georgetown and Great Falls barge rides last about 1 hour and 10 minutes and cost $8 for adults, $6 for seniors over 61, and $5 for children ages 3 to 14.

Call any of the above information numbers for details on riding, rock climbing, fishing, bird-watching, concerts, ranger-guided tours, ice skating, camping, and other canal activities.

10 Especially for Kids

Who knows what kids might enjoy in Washington better than other kids? So I asked my children, Caitlin (16) and Lucy (11), who offer these suggestions:

Caitlin: "I recommend going to see a play at the Folger Theatre [at the Folger Shakespeare Library], which is really cute. The theater is set up as it would have been in the 1500s, and you feel like you're in those times. Both plays that I saw here, *She Stoops to Conquer,* and *Twelfth Night,* were hilarious and the acting was really good."

Lucy: "I like to go to the Planetarium [Einstein Planetarium, in the National Air and Space Museum], because I like looking up and seeing the stars and constellations, and a voice tells you what you are seeing, in case you can't tell. My friend Annie says that the simulators [flight simulator machines at the museum] are fun, but she said that they can be a little scary, but I still want to try those, the next time we go."

For more ideas, consult the Friday "Weekend" section of the *Washington Post,* which lists numerous activities (mostly free) for kids: special museum events, children's theater, storytelling programs, puppet shows, video-game competitions, and so forth. Call the Kennedy Center, the Lisner, and the National Theatre to find out about children's shows; see chapter 9 for details. Also read the write-up of Discovery Theater, within the Smithsonian's Arts & Industries Building, earlier in this chapter.

I've checked out hotels built with families in mind in chapter 5's "Family-Friendly Hotels"; that hotel pool may rescue your sanity for an hour or two. The "Organized Tours" and "Outdoor Activities" sections below may also be your saving grace when you've either run out of steam or need a jump-start to your day.

FAVORITE CHILDREN'S ATTRACTIONS

Check for special children's events at museum information desks when you enter. As noted within the listings for individual museums, some children's programs are also great fun for adults. I recommend the programs at the **Corcoran Gallery of Art,** the **Folger Shakespeare Library,** the **Phillips,** and the **Sackler Gallery** in particular. (The gift shops in most of these museums have wonderful toys and children's books.) Call ahead to find out which programs are running. Here's a rundown of the biggest kid-pleasers in town (for details, see the full entries earlier in this chapter):

- **Ford's Theatre & Lincoln Museum and The House Where Lincoln Died** (p. 199): Booth's gun and diary, the clothes Lincoln was wearing the night he was assassinated, and other such grisly artifacts. Kids adore the whole business.
- **International Spy Museum** (p. 202): Both kids and adults enjoy pretending to be spies, testing their powers of observation, and trying to figure out how the Enigma machine works.
- **Lincoln Memorial** (p. 174): Kids know a lot about Lincoln and enjoy visiting his memorial. A special treat is visiting after dark (the same goes for the Washington Monument and Jefferson Memorial).
- **National Air and Space Museum** (p. 182): Spectacular IMAX films (don't miss), planetarium shows, missiles, rockets, a walk-through orbital workshop, and flight simulators.
- **National Museum of Natural History** (p. 186): A Discovery Room just for youngsters, the butterfly garden, an insect zoo, shrunken heads, and dinosaurs, and the IMAX theater showing 2-D and 3-D films.
- **National Zoological Park** (p. 188): Pandas! Kids always love a zoo, and this is an especially good one.
- **Washington Monument** (p. 172): Easy to get them up there, hard to get them down. If only they could use the steps, they'd be in heaven.

11 Organized Tours

ON FOOT

Tour de Force (📞 **703/525-2948;** www.atourdeforce.com) is historian and raconteur Jeanne Fogel's 19-year-old company. She offers a variety of walking and bus tours around the city, revealing little-known anecdotes and facts about neighborhoods, historic figures, and the most visited sites. Fogel's tours are custom designed for groups, not individuals. Call for rates.

TourDC, Walking Tours of Georgetown, Dupont Circle & Embassy Row (📞 **301/588-8999;** www.tourdc.com) conducts 90-minute ($12) walking tours of Georgetown, telling about the neighborhood's history up to the present and taking you past the homes of notable residents.

Guided Walking Tours of Washington 🔍 (📞 **301/294-9514;** www.dcsightseeing.com) offers 2-hour walks through the streets of Georgetown, Adams-Morgan, and other locations, guided by author/historian Anthony S. Pitch. Inquire about private tours. Rates are $10 per person, $6 for seniors and students.

BY BUS

TOURMOBILE   Best-known and least expensive, **Tourmobile Sightseeing** (© **888/868-7707** or 202/554-5100; www.tourmobile.com) is a good choice if you're looking for an easy-on/easy-off tour of major sites. The comfortable red, white, and blue sightseeing trams travel to as many as 24 attractions (the company changes its schedule and number of stops, depending on whether sites are open for public tours), including Arlington National Cemetery. Tourmobile is the only narrated sightseeing shuttle tour authorized by the National Park Service. The company offers a number of different tours, but the most popular is the **American Heritage Tour,** which stops at 21 sites on or near the National Mall and at three sites in Arlington Cemetery. (Again, the number of stops may be fewer than 21, if regularly scheduled stops, like the White House, are not open for public tours due to increased security.) Normally, stops include the memorials and Washington Monument, Union Station, the National Gallery, most of the Smithsonian museums (National Air and Space, National Museum of American History, National Museum of Natural History, and the Arts & Industries Building/Hirshhorn Museum), the Capitol, and several other locations. In Arlington Cemetery, the bus stops at the Kennedy grave sites, the Tomb of the Unknowns, and Arlington House.

You simply hop on a Tourmobile at any of the locations, paying the driver when you first board the bus (you can also purchase a ticket at the booth at the Washington Monument or inside the Arlington National Cemetery Visitor Center, or, for a small surcharge, order your ticket in advance from Ticketmaster at © **800/551-SEAT**). Along the route, you may get off at any stop to visit monuments or buildings. When you finish exploring each area, just show your ticket and climb aboard the next Tourmobile that comes along. The buses travel in a loop, serving each stop about every 15 to 30 minutes. One fare allows you to use the buses for a full day. The charge for the American Heritage Tour is $20 for anyone 12 and older, $10 for children 3 to 11. For Arlington Cemetery only, those 12 and older pay $6, children $3. Children under 3 ride free. Buses follow figure-eight circuits from the Capitol to Arlington Cemetery and back. Well-trained narrators give commentaries about sights along the route and answer questions.

Though heated in winter, these trams are not air-conditioned in summer, and though the windows stay open, they can get hot and uncomfortable. Readers also report that Tourmobiles, being the largest trams, take a long time to load and unload passengers, which can be frustrating to those anxious to see the sights.

Tourmobiles operate 9:30am–4:30pm, daily year-round, except Christmas. (In busy tourist season, Tourmobile sometimes extends its hours.)

Call Tourmobile or access the website for further information and rates for other tours.

OLD TOWN TROLLEY   Old Town Trolley tours (© **202/832-9800;** www.oldtowntrolley.com) offer fixed-price, on-off service as you travel in a loop around the city. You can purchase your ticket at the booth at Union Station, or board without a ticket and purchase it en route. (One exception is the Lincoln Memorial stop. The National Park Service does not allow any tour bus service other than Tourmobile to solicit business on its lands, which means you must have a prepaid ticket to board an Old Town Trolley at the Lincoln Memorial.) Buses operate daily from 9am to 5:30pm year-round. The cost is $27 for adults, $13 for children 4 to 12, free for children under 4. The full tour, which is narrated, takes 2 hours (if you never get off), and trolleys come by every 30 minutes or so. Old Town Trolley tours cost more but stop at certain hotels, like the Capital Hilton and the JW Marriott, and travel to neighborhoods, like Georgetown, and attractions away from the Mall, like the National Geographic Society.

MARTZ GRAYLINE L'IL RED TROLLEY TOURS Martz Grayline Tours (© 202/289-1995; www.graylinedc.com) operates these red trolleys in the same fashion as Tourmobile and Old Town Trolleys, providing on-and-off service for a fixed price ($28 for adults, $14 for children ages 11 and under) as the trolley travels around the city, stopping at more than 25 sites. Trolley stops overlap with those of the other companies, and include stops at hard-to-reach destinations, like Adams-Morgan.

BY BOAT

Since Washington is a river city, why not see it by boat? Potomac cruises allow sweeping vistas of the monuments and memorials, Georgetown, the Kennedy Center, and other Washington sights. Read the information below carefully, since not all boat cruises offer guided tours.

Some of the following boats leave from the Washington waterfront and some from Old Town Alexandria:

Spirit of Washington Cruises, Pier 4 at Sixth and Water streets SW (© 866/211-3811 or 202/554-8000; www.spiritcruises.com; Metro: Waterfront), offers a variety of trips daily, including evening dinner, lunch, and brunch, and moonlight dance cruises, as well as a half-day excursion to Mount Vernon and back. Lunch and dinner cruises include a 40-minute high-energy musical revue. Prices range from $39 for a lunch excursion to $121 for a first class dinner cruise. Call to make reservations.

The *Spirit of Washington* is a luxury climate-controlled harbor cruise ship with carpeted decks and huge panoramic windows designed for sightseeing. There are three well-stocked bars on board. Mount Vernon cruises are aboard an equally luxurious sister ship, the *Potomac Spirit.*

Potomac Party Cruises (© 703/683-6076; www.dandydinnerboat.com) operates *The Dandy* and *Nina's Dandy,* both climate-controlled, all-weather, glassed-in floating restaurants that run year-round. Lunch, evening dinner/dance, and special charter cruises are available daily. You board both vessels in Old Town Alexandria, at the Prince Street pier, between Duke and King streets. Trips range from $33 for a 2½-hour weekday lunch cruise to $81 for a 3-hour Saturday dinner cruise.

Odyssey III (© 888/741-0281; www.odysseycruises.com) was designed specifically to glide under the bridges that cross the Potomac. The boat looks like a glass bullet, with its snub-nosed port and its streamlined 240-foot-long glass body. The wraparound see-through walls and ceiling allow for great views. Like *The Dandy,* the *Odyssey* operates all year. You board the *Odyssey* at the Gangplank Marina, on Washington's waterfront, at Sixth and Water streets SW (Metro: Waterfront). Cruises available include lunch, Sunday brunch, and dinner excursions, with live entertainment provided during each cruise. It costs $47 for a 2-hour weekday lunch cruise and $115 for a 3-hour Saturday dinner cruise.

The **Potomac Riverboat Company** ♿ (© 703/548-9000; www.potomacriverboatco.com) offers three narrated tours April through October aboard the *Matthew Hayes,* on a 90-minute tour past Washington monuments and memorials; the *Admiral Tilp,* on a 40-minute tour of Old Town Alexandria's waterfront; and the *Miss Christin,* which cruises to Mount Vernon, where you hop off and reboard after you've toured the estate. You board the boats at the pier behind the Torpedo

Factory in Old Town Alexandria, at the foot of King Street; or, for the Washington monuments and memorials tour, Georgetown's Washington Harbour. *Matthew Hayes* tickets are $16 for adults, $8 for children ages 2 to 12; *Admiral Tilp* tickets are $8 for adults, $5 for children ages 2 to 12; and *Miss Christin* tickets are $27 for adults, $15 for children ages 6 to 10, and include admission to Mount Vernon. A concession stand selling light refreshments and beverages is open during the cruises.

The **Capitol River Cruise's** *Nightingale I* and *Nightingale II* (© **800/405-5511** or 301/460-7447; www.capitolrivercruises.com) are historic 65-foot steel riverboats that can accommodate up to 90 people. The *Nightingale's* narrated jaunts depart Georgetown's Washington Harbour every hour on the hour, from noon to 9pm, April through October. The 50-minute narrated tour travels past the monuments and memorials as you head to National Airport and back. A snack bar on board sells light refreshments, beer, wine, and sodas; you're welcome to bring your own picnic aboard. The price is $10 per adult, $5 per child ages 3 to 12. To get here, take the Metro to Foggy Bottom and then take the Georgetown Metro Connection Shuttle or walk into Georgetown, following Pennsylvania Avenue, which becomes M Street. Turn left on 31st Street NW, which dead-ends at the Washington Harbour complex.

A BOAT ON WHEELS Old Town Trolley also operates the **DC Ducks** (© **202/832-9800;** www.dcducks.com), which feature unique land and water tours of Washington aboard the *DUKW,* an amphibious army vehicle (boat with wheels) from World War II that accommodates 30 passengers. Ninety-minute guided tours aboard the open-air canopied craft include a land portion taking in major sights—the Capitol, Lincoln Memorial, Washington Monument, White House, and Smithsonian museums—and a 30-minute Potomac cruise. Tickets can be purchased inside Union Station at the information desk; you board the vehicle just outside the main entrance to Union Station. There are departures daily during tour season (Mar–Oct); hours vary, but departures usually follow an 11am and 1 and 3pm schedule. Tickets cost $26 for adults, $13 for children 5 to 12, free for children under 5.

BY BIKE

Bike the Sites, Inc. ✹ (© 202/842-2453; www.bikethesites.com) offers a more active way to see Washington. The company has designed several different biking tours of the city, including the popular Capital Sites Ride, which takes 3 hours, covers 55 sites along an 8-mile stretch, and costs $40 per adult, $30 per child 12 and under. Bike the Sites provides you with a 21-speed Trek Hybrid bicycle fitted to your size, bike helmet, handlebar bag, water bottle, light snack, and two guides to lead the ride. Guides impart historical and anecdotal information as you go. The company will customize bike rides to suit your tour specifications.

12 Outdoor Activities

The Washington area offers plenty of opportunities for outdoor activities. See "Parks & Gardens," earlier in this chapter for complete coverage of the city's loveliest green spaces.

Joggers can enjoy a run on the Mall or along the path in Rock Creek Park.

Rent a bike at **Fletcher's Boat House,** Reservoir and Canal roads (© **202/244-0461;** www.fletchersboathouse.com), or **Thompson's Boat Center,** 2900 Virginia Ave. at Rock Creek Parkway NW (© **202/333-4861** or 202/333-9543; www.thompsonboatcenter.com; Metro: Foggy Bottom, with a 10-min. walk); both Fletcher's and Thompson's rent bikes from about late March to

November. At **Big Wheel Bikes,** 1034 33rd St. NW, right near the C&O Canal just below M Street (© **202/337-0254**), you can rent a bike year-round, Tuesday through Sunday. If you need suggested routes or want company, check out Friday's *Washington Post* "Weekend" section listing cycling trips. Rock Creek Park has an **11-mile paved bike route** ✈ from the Lincoln Memorial through the park into Maryland. Or you can follow the bike path from the Lincoln Memorial and go over the Memorial Bridge to pedal to Old Town Alexandria and to Mount Vernon (see chapter 10 for details). On weekends and holidays, a large part of Rock Creek Parkway is closed to vehicular traffic. The C&O Canal and the Potomac parks, described earlier in "Parks & Gardens," also have extended bike paths. A new 7-mile path, the **Capital Crescent Trail,** takes you from Georgetown to the suburb of Bethesda, Maryland, following a former railroad track that parallels the Potomac River for part of the way and passes by old trestle bridges and pleasant residential neighborhoods.

Thompson's Boat Center and Fletcher's Boat House (see above for both addresses and phone numbers) also rent boats (of course), following the same schedule as their bike rental season, basically March to November. Thompson's has canoes, kayaks, and rowing shells (recreational and racing), and is open for boat and bike rentals daily from 6am to 8pm. Fletcher's is right on the C&O Canal, about 3¼ wonderfully scenic miles from Georgetown. The same family has owned it since 1850! In addition to renting bikes and canoes, Fletcher's also sells fishing licenses, bait, and tackle. Fletcher's is accessible by car (west on M St. to Canal Rd.) and has plenty of free parking.

From late March to mid-September, you can rent **paddleboats** ✈ on the north end of the Tidal Basin off Independence Avenue (© **202/479-2426**). Four-seaters rent for $16 an hour; two-seaters are $8 an hour. You can rent boats daily from 10am to about an hour before sunset.

Hikers will be happy to know about Washington's numerous **hiking paths.** The C&O Canal offers 184½ miles; Theodore Roosevelt Island has more than 88 wilderness acres to explore, including a 2½-mile nature trail (short but rugged); and Rock Creek Park boasts 20 miles of hiking trails (maps are available at the Visitor Information Center or Park Headquarters; see above for information about the parks).

If you're coming to Washington in winter, you can go **ice skating** on the C&O Canal (call © **301/299-3613** for information on ice conditions), as long as you bring your own skates. For a really fun experience, head to the **National Gallery Sculpture Garden Ice Rink** ✈, on the Mall at 7th Street and Constitution Avenue NW (© **202/289-3360**), where you can rent skates, twirl in view of the sculptures, and enjoy hot chocolate and a sandwich in the Pavilion Café, right next to the rink. Another outdoor rink where you can rent skates is **Pershing Park,** at 14th Street and Pennsylvania Avenue NW (© **202/737-6938**).

If you're here in summer and your hotel doesn't have a pool, you might consider one of the neighborhood pools run by the District's Department of Parks and Recreation. These include a large outdoor pool at 25th and N streets NW (© **202/727-3285**); and the Georgetown outdoor pool at 34th Street and Volta Place NW (© **202/282-2366**). Keep in mind that these are likely to be crowded.

Tennis lovers will have a hard time finding public courts in Washington. **East Potomac Park** has nine tennis courts, including five indoors (© **202/554-5962**). Fees vary with court surface and time of play; call for details. **Montrose Park** (p. 139), right next to Dumbarton Oaks in Georgetown has several courts available for free on a first-come, first-served basis; but they're often in use.

Shopping

The Washington shopping scene is expanding, I'm happy to say. Better yet, much of the expansion is taking place where it is most needed: in the heart of downtown, around the MCI Center, convenient to residents and tourists, alike. By the time you read this, new retail options should include H&M (for Hennes & Mauritz), a trendy Swedish fashion store, at 11th and F streets NW; and Gallery Place, a multi-purpose complex of at least 10 retailers, plus offices, condominiums, and a 14-screen movie theater, located adjacent to the MCI Center, on 7th Street NW.

Bargain hunters will have to look further afield (though easily accessible by Metro), but again, your choices have improved in the past year or so. The tony neighborhood of Chevy Chase, MD, home to Neiman-Marcus, Saks Fifth Avenue, and Tiffany's, saw the debut in July 2003 of a Stein Mart, the Florida-based retail store known for selling high-end clothes at low prices. Stein Mart is located on the upper level of the Chevy Chase Pavilion, which also has an Ann Taylor Loft store (an Ann Taylor spinoff selling less expensive clothes for younger women); right next door is a two-level "off-price" Loehmann's store that opened in 2003; across the street are discount clothiers T.J. Maxx and Filene's Basement. Suddenly one of the richest parts of town is also the best place to get a deal. Read this chapter for information about these affordable shopping options (see, in particular, the section on "Discount Shopping") and suggestions for other places to shop, or at least, to browse.

1 The Shopping Scene

Washington-area stores are usually open daily from 10am to 5 or 6pm Monday through Saturday, with one late night (usually Thurs) when hours extend to 9pm. Sunday hours are usually from noon to 5 or 6pm. Exceptions are the malls, which are open late nightly, and antiques stores and art galleries, which tend to keep their own hours. Play it safe and call ahead if there's a store you really want to get to.

Sales tax on merchandise is 5.75% in the District, 5% in Maryland, and 4.5% in Virginia.

Most gift, arts, and crafts stores, including those at the Smithsonian museums, will handle shipping for you; clothes stores generally do not.

If you're a true bargain hunter, scope out the *Washington Post* website (**www.washingtonpost.com**) in advance of your trip to see which stores are having sales. Once you get to the *Post*'s home page, hit "Entertainment" at the top of your screen, click on "Shopping," and then click on "Sales and Bargains," a column that's updated weekly.

2 Great Shopping Areas

Union Station　The only legitimate shopping area on Capitol Hill, Union Station has more than 100 specialty shops, selling jewelry, apparel, and gifts, and more than 45 eateries.

Downtown　The area bounded east and west by 7th and 14th streets NW, and north and south by New York and Pennsylvania avenues NW, is in a frenzy of development. In addition to the new H&M and Gallery Place stores, mentioned in the introduction, shops here include the chi-chi Chanel Boutique, located within the Willard Inter-Continental hotel's courtyard, and the four-level Shops at National Place, with Casual Corner and Filene's Basement being among your options. Look for the huge Borders bookstore at 14th and F streets NW, in the grand old Garfinckel's Building. The adaptable and reliable Hecht's, at 12th and G streets, continues as the sole department store downtown. Metro: Metro Center.

Adams-Morgan　Centered on 18th Street and Columbia Road NW, Adams-Morgan is a neighborhood of ethnic eateries and nightclubs interspersed with the odd secondhand bookshop and eclectic collectibles stores. It's a fun area for walking and shopping. Parking is possible during the day but impossible at night. Closest Metro: You have two choices: Woodley Park–Adams Morgan, then walk south on Connecticut Avenue NW until you reach Calvert Street, cross Connecticut Avenue and follow Calvert Street across the bridge until you reach the junction of Columbia Road NW and 18th Street NW. On Saturday, you can catch the no. 98 Adams Morgan–U Street Link shuttle bus, which departs every 15 minutes from the Woodley Park station and takes you to Adams-Morgan. With a Metrorail transfer from the Woodley Park Metro station, the cost is 40¢; with no transfer, you pay $1.20. Second choice: Dupont Circle; exit at Q Street NW and walk up Connecticut Avenue NW to Columbia Road NW.

Connecticut Avenue/Dupont Circle　Running from the mini–Wall Street that is K Street north to S Street, Connecticut Avenue NW is a main thoroughfare, where you'll find traditional clothing at Brooks Brothers, Talbots, and Burberry's; casual duds at The Gap; discount items at Filene's Basement; and haute couture at Rizik's. Closer to Dupont Circle are coffee bars and neighborhood restaurants, as well as art galleries; funky boutiques; gift, stationery, book, and record shops; and stores with a gay and lesbian slant. Metro: Farragut North at one end, Dupont Circle at the other.

Georgetown　Georgetown is the city's main shopping area. In the heart of the neighborhood, stores line Wisconsin Avenue and M Street NW, and they also fan out along side streets from the central intersection. You'll find both chain and one-of-a-kind shops, chic as well as thrift. Sidewalks and streets are almost always crowded, and parking can be tough. Weekends, especially, bring out all kinds of yahoos, who are mainly here to drink. Visit Georgetown on a weekday morning, if you can. Weeknights are another good time to visit, for dinner and strolling afterward. Metro: Foggy Bottom, then catch the bright blue Georgetown Metro Connection bus, which runs every 10 minutes, takes only a few minutes to reach Georgetown, and costs 35¢ with a Metrorail transfer, or $1 without a transfer. Metrobuses (the no. 30-series: 30, 32, 34, 36) travel through Georgetown from different parts of the city. Otherwise, consider taking a taxi. If you drive, you'll find parking lots expensive and tickets even more so, so be careful where you plant your car.

Upper Wisconsin Avenue Northwest   In a residential section of town known as Friendship Heights on the D.C. side and Chevy Chase on the Maryland side (7 miles north of Georgetown, going straight up Wisconsin Ave.) is a quarter-mile shopping district that extends from Saks Fifth Avenue at one end to Sur La Table at the other. In between lie Lord & Taylor, Neiman Marcus, and Hecht Company department stores; a bevy of top shops, such as Tiffany's and Versace; two malls, the Mazza Gallerie and the Chevy Chase Pavilion; and several stand-alone staples, such as Banana Republic. As mentioned in the introduction, a number of discount stores are located here: Stein Mart, Filene's Basement, T.J. Maxx, and Loehmann's. The street is too wide and traffic always too snarled to make this a fun place to stroll, although teenagers do love to loiter here. Drive here if you want; the Hecht's store parking lot offers 2 hours of free parking with validation. Or Metro it; the strip is right on the Red Line, with the "Friendship Heights" exits leading directly into each of the malls and into Hecht's.

Old Town Alexandria   Old Town, a Virginia neighborhood beyond National Airport, is becoming increasingly like Georgetown, warts (heavy traffic, crowded sidewalks, difficult parking) and all. Old Town extends from the Potomac River in the east to the King Street Metro station in the west, and from about First Street in the north to Green Street in the south, but the best shopping is in the center, where King and Washington streets intersect. Weekdays are a lot tamer than weekends. It's always a nice place to visit, though; the drive alone is worth the trip. See chapter 10 for full coverage of Alexandria. Metro: King Street, then hop on a blue and gold DASH bus and pay $1 to reach the heart of Old Town.

3 Shopping A to Z
ANTIQUES
A few miles north of the city is not too far to go for the good deal or true bonanza you're likely to discover on **Antique Row.** Some 40 antiques and collectible shops line Howard Avenue in Kensington, Maryland, offering every sort of item in a wide variety of styles, periods, and prices. If you don't drive or catch a cab, you'll have to take the Metro and two buses. From Dupont Circle, board an L2 bus and get a transfer from the driver. Ask him to tell you when you reach the transfer point for the L8 bus. When you reach that juncture, board the L8 bus and ask to be let off at Connecticut and Knowles avenues. Howard Avenue is 1 block north of Knowles.

Brass Knob Architectural Antiques   When early homes and office buildings are demolished in the name of progress, these savvy salvage merchants spirit away saleable treasures, from chandeliers to wrought-iron fencing. 2311 18th St. NW. ⓒ 202/332-3370. www.thebrassknob.com. Metro: Woodley Park or Dupont Circle. There's a second location across the street called the **Brass Knob's Back Doors Warehouse,** 2329 Champlain St. NW (ⓒ 202/265-0587).

cherry   This is an antiques store, all right, but as its name suggests, a little offbeat. Expect affordable eclectic furnishings and decorative arts, and lots of mirrors and sconces. 1526 Wisconsin Ave. NW. ⓒ 202/342-3600. Metro: Foggy Bottom, then walk or take the Georgetown Metro Connection shuttle.

Cherub Antiques Gallery   The Cherub Antiques Gallery specializes in Art Nouveau and Art Deco, art glass (signed Tiffany, Steuben, Lalique, and Gallé), Liberty arts and crafts, and Louis Icart etchings. 2918 M St. NW. ⓒ 202/337-2224. Metro: Foggy Bottom, then take the Georgetown Metro connection.

Gore-Dean   Though its offerings include some American pieces, the store specializes in 18th- and 19th-century European furnishings, decorative accessories, paintings, prints, and porcelains. Recently added are a lampshade shop, garden shop, and framing studio. 1525 Wisconsin Ave. NW. ✆ **202/625-1776.** www.gore-dean.com. Metro: Foggy Bottom, then take the Georgetown Metro Connection.

Marston-Luce   Stop in here at least to admire, if not buy, a beautiful 18th or 19th century French furnishing or two. 1651 Wisconsin Ave. NW. ✆ **202/333-6800.** Metro: Foggy Bottom, then take the Georgetown Metro Connection.

Millennium   This is antiques shopping for the TV generation, where anything made between the 1930s and the 1970s is considered collectible. The shop works with nearly a score or so of dealers; stock changes weekly. Funky wares run from Bakelite to Heywood-Wakefield blond-wood beauties to used drinking glasses. 1528 U St. NW. ✆ **202/483-1218.** Metro: U St.–Cardozo.

Old Print Gallery   This gallery carries original American and European prints from the 17th through the 19th century, including political cartoons, maps, and historical documents. It's one of the largest antique print and map shops in the United States. 1220 31st St. NW. ✆ **202/965-1818.** www.oldprintgallery.com. Metro: Foggy Bottom, then take the Georgetown Metro Connection.

Susquehanna Antiques   This Georgetown store specializes in American, English, and European furniture, paintings, and garden items of the late 18th and early 19th centuries. 3216 O St. NW. ✆ **202/333-1511.** www.susquehannaantiques.com. Metro: Foggy Bottom, then take the Georgetown Metro Connection.

ART GALLERIES

Art galleries abound in Washington, but especially proliferate in Dupont Circle and Georgetown, and along Seventh Street downtown.

For a complete listing of local galleries, get your hands on a copy of **"Galleries,"** a monthly guide to major galleries and their shows; the guide is available free at many hotel concierge desks and at many galleries.

DUPONT CIRCLE

For all galleries listed below, the closest Metro stop is Dupont Circle.

Affrica   Authentic and traditional African masks, figures, and artifacts. The gallery's clients include major museums and private collectors from around the world. 2010 ½ R St. NW. ✆ **202/745-7272.** www.affrica.com.

Anton Gallery   Expect to find contemporary American paintings, as well as sculpture, functional ceramics, and prints. Anton represents national and international artists. 2108 R St. NW. ✆ **202/328-0828.** www.antongallery.com.

Kathleen Ewing Gallery   This gallery features vintage and contemporary photography. 1609 Connecticut Ave. NW. ✆ **202/328-0955.** www.kathleenewinggallery.com.

The Mansion on O Street   Not an art gallery in the usual sense, H. H. Leonards' Mansion consists of three Victorian town houses joined together and decorated throughout with more than 5,000 antiques and artworks, in styles ranging from Art Deco to avant-garde. H's place is also her home, a special-events spot, and a luxurious B&B to boot. 2020 O St. NW. ✆ **202/496-2000.** www.omansion.com. Open by appointment only.

GEORGETOWN

For all the galleries listed below, the closest stop is Foggy Bottom, with a transfer to the Georgetown Metro Connection bus to get you the rest of the way.

Addison/Ripley Fine Art   This gallery represents both nationally and region-ally recognized artists, from the 19th century to the present; works include paint-ings, sculpture, photography, and fine arts. 1670 Wisconsin Ave. NW. ✆ **202/338-5180.** www.addisonripleyfineart.com.

Govinda Gallery   This place, a block from the campus of Georgetown Uni-versity, generates a lot of media coverage, since it often shows artwork created by famous names and features photographs of celebrities. My husband and I wan-dered in last winter and we had the gallery to ourselves as we enjoyed the pho-tographs of a young Bob Dylan, taken by the renowned Barry Feinstein. 1227 34th St. NW. ✆ **202/333-1180.** www.govindagallery.com.

Guarisco Gallery, Ltd.   Its display of 19th- and early-20th-century paintings, watercolors, and sculptures by the likes of Camille Pissarro, T. Robinson, and H. Lebasque make this gallery as much a museum as a shop. 2828 Pennsylvania Ave. NW (in the courtyard of the Four Seasons Hotel). ✆ **202/333-8533.** www.guariscogallery.com.

Spectrum Gallery   A cooperative venture since 1966, in which 30 professional Washington-area artists, including painters, potters, sculptors, photographers, col-lagists, and printmakers, share in shaping gallery policy, maintenance, and opera-tion. The art is reasonably priced. 1132 29th St. NW (just below M St.). ✆ **202/333-0954.** www.spectrumgallery.org.

SEVENTH STREET ARTS CORRIDOR
A couple of these galleries predate the renaissance taking place in this downtown neighborhood. To get here, take the Metro to either the Archives/Navy Memo-rial (Blue–Orange Line) or Gallery Place/Chinatown/MCI Center (Red–Yellow Line) stations.

406 Art Galleries   Several first-rate art galleries, some of them interlopers from Dupont Circle, occupy this historic building, with its 16-foot-high ceilings and spacious rooms. Look for the **David Adamson Gallery** (✆ **202/628-0257;** www. adamsoneditions.com), which showcases digital printmaking and photography and the works of contemporary artists, like locals Kevin MacDonald and Renee Stout, and national artists KiKi Smith and William Wegman. The **Touchstone Gallery** (✆ **202/347-2787;** www.touchstonegallery.com), on the second floor, is a self-run co-op of 35 to 40 artists who take turns exhibiting their work; and the third floor **Eklektikos Gallery of Art** (✆ **202/783-8444;** www.eklektikos. com) represents regional, national, and international artists. 406 7th St. NW, between D and E sts.

Zenith Gallery   Across the street from the 406 Group, Zenith shows diverse works by contemporary artists, most American, about half of whom are local. You can get a good deal here, paying anywhere from $50 to $50,000 for a piece. Among the things you'll find are annual humor shows, neon exhibits, realism, abstract expressionism, and landscapes. 413 7th St. NW. ✆ **202/783-2963.** www.zenith gallery.com.

BOOKS
Washingtonians are readers, so bookstores constantly pop up throughout the city. An increasingly competitive market means that chain bookstores do a brisk business, even though D.C. can claim more general-interest independent book-stores than any other city. Here are my favorite bookstores in general, used, and special-interest categories. *Note:* Websites for chain bookstores are for the chain itself, not individual stores.

GENERAL

Barnes & Noble   This wonderful three-story shop has sizable software, travel book, and children's title sections. A cafe on the second level sometimes hosts concerts. 3040 M St. NW. 📞 **202/965-9880.** www.barnesandnoble.com. Metro: Foggy Bottom, then take the Georgetown Metro Connection shuttle. Other area locations include 555 12th St. NW (📞 202/347-0176) and 4801 Bethesda Ave., in Bethesda, Maryland (📞 301/986-1761).

B. Dalton   This is an all-purpose bookstore, heavy on the bestsellers and carrying magazines, too. Union Station. 📞 **202/289-1724.** www.barnesandnoble.com. Metro: Union Station. There's another location in Chevy Chase Pavilion (📞 202/686-6542). See entries under "Malls" for more information about this location.

Borders   With its overwhelming array of books, records, videos, and magazines, this outpost of the expanding chain has taken over the town. Many hardcover bestsellers are 30% off. The store often hosts performances by local musicians. 1800 L St. NW. 📞 **202/466-4999.** www.borders.com. Metro: Farragut North. Other Borders stores in the District include 5333 Wisconsin Ave. NW (📞 202/686-8270), in upper northwest D.C.; and 600 14th St. NW (📞 202/737-1385).

Bridge Street Books   A small, serious shop specializing in politics, poetry, literature, history, philosophy, and publications you won't find elsewhere. Bestsellers and discounted books are not its specialty. 2814 Pennsylvania Ave. NW (next to the Four Seasons Hotel). 📞 **202/965-5200.** Metro: Foggy Bottom, then take the Georgetown Metro Connection shuttle.

Chapters, A Literary Bookstore   Chapters is strong in new and backlisted fiction (no discounts, though), and is always hosting author readings. Tea is always available, and on Friday afternoons they break out the sherry and cookies. 455 11th St. NW (inside building at 1001 Pennsylvania Ave.). 📞 **202/347-5495.** www.chapters literary.com. Metro: Archives-Navy Memorial or Federal Triangle.

Kramerbooks & Afterwords Café *(Finds)*   The first bookstore/cafe in Washington, maybe in this country, this place has launched countless romances. It's jammed and often noisy, stages live music Wednesday through Saturday evenings, and is open all night weekends. Paperback fiction takes up most of its inventory, but the store carries a little of everything. No discounts. 1517 Connecticut Ave. NW. 📞 **202/387-1400.** www.kramers.com. Metro: Dupont Circle.

Olsson's Books and Records.   This 30-year-old independent, quality bookstore chain has about 60,000 to 70,000 books on its shelves. Members of its helpful staff know what they're talking about and will order books they don't have in stock. Some discounts are given on books, tapes, and CDs, and their regular prices are pretty good, too.

Besides this location, there are two other Olsson's bookstores in the District: at 418 7th St. NW (📞 202/638-7610), and at 1307 19th St. NW (📞 202/785-1133). In the suburbs are five other Olsson's: in Bethesda, Maryland, at 7647 Old Georgetown Rd. (📞 301/652-3336); in Old Town Alexandria, Virginia, at 106 S. Union St. (📞 703/684-0077); in Arlington, Virginia, at 2111 Wilson Blvd. (📞 703/525-4227) and at 1735 N. Lynn St. (📞 703/812-2103); and at National Airport (📞 703/417-1087). The stores on 7th Street, in Alexandria, and on Wilson Boulevard in Arlington each have a creditable cafe, known for its loungy atmosphere, made-in-house selections, and artistic crowd. 12th and F sts. NW (📞 **202/347-3686**). www.olssons.com. Metro: Metro Center.

Politics and Prose Bookstore   Located a few miles north of downtown in a residential area, this much cherished two-story shop may be worth going out of your way for. It has vast offerings in literary fiction and nonfiction alike and an excellent children's department. The store has expanded again and again over the years to accommodate its clientele's love of books, its most recent enlargement in 2002-2003 adding more space and books overall, but especially to the travel and children's sections. The shop hosts author readings nearly every night of the year. A warm, knowledgeable staff will help you find what you need. Downstairs is a cozy coffeehouse. Staff-recommended books are 20% off. 5015 Connecticut Ave. NW. ℂ 202/364-1919. www.politics-prose.com. Metro: Van Ness–UDC, and walk, or transfer to an "L" bus to take you the ¾ mile from there.

Trover Shop   The only general-interest bookstore on Capitol Hill, Trover specializes in its political selections and its magazines. The store discounts 30% on the *Washington Post* hardcover fiction and nonfiction bestsellers. 221 Pennsylvania Ave. SE. ℂ 202/547-BOOK. www.trover.com. Metro: Capitol South.

OLD & USED BOOKS

Second Story Books   If it's old, out of print, custom bound, or a small-press publication, this is where to find it. The store also specializes in used CDs and vinyl, and has an interesting collection of antique French and American advertising posters. 2000 P St. NW. ℂ 202/659-8884. www.secondstorybooks.com. Metro: Dupont Circle. Also at 4836 Bethesda Ave., in Bethesda, MD (ℂ 301/656-0170).

SPECIAL-INTEREST BOOKS

ADC Map and Travel Center   Here you'll find street maps and atlases for the East Coast, from Philadelphia to Atlanta, as well as an extensive collection of maps and guidebooks for the entire world. Globes and atlases are also for sale. 1636 I St. NW. ℂ 800/544-2659 or 202/628-2608. www.adcmap.com. Metro: Farragut West or Farragut North.

American Institute of Architects Bookstore   This store is geared toward architects, selling mostly theory and history books, although it does carry some coffee-table architectural photograph books and some gifts. 1735 New York Ave. NW. ℂ 202/626-7475. Metro: Farragut West.

Back Stage Books and Costumes   Back Stage is headquarters for Washington's theatrical community, which buys its books, scripts, trades, and sheet music here. It's also a favorite costume-rental shop. 545 8th St. SE. ℂ 202/544-5744. Metro: Eastern Market.

Franz Bader Bookstore   This store stocks books on art, art history, architecture, and photography, as well as exhibition catalogs. 1911 I St. NW. ℂ 202/337-5440. Metro: Farragut West or Farragut North.

Lambda Rising   It was a big deal when this gay and lesbian bookstore opened with a plate-glass window revealing its interior to passersby. Now it's an unofficial headquarters for the gay/lesbian/bi community, carrying every gay, lesbian, bisexual, and transgender book in print, as well as videos, music, and gifts. 1625 Connecticut Ave. NW. ℂ 202/462-6969. Metro: Dupont Circle.

National Museum of American History Giftshop   In this museum gift shop, you'll find a wonderful selection of books on American history and culture, including some for children. Constitution Ave. between 12th and 14th sts. NW. ℂ 202/357-1784. www.smithsonianstore.com. Metro: Federal Triangle or Smithsonian.

Reiter's Bookstore   This independent bookstore in the middle of the George Washington University campus is one of the leading scientific, technical, medical, and professional bookshops in the area. It's a great place to stumble in to, even if you're not scientifically inclined, because it also has a fine children's science section, some amusing mathematical and scientific toys, and humorous T-shirts ("Hey You, Get Out of the Gene Pool!"). 2021 K St. NW. © 202/223-3327. www.reiters.com. Metro: Foggy Bottom.

CAMERAS & FILM DEVELOPING

Photography is a big business in this image-conscious tourist town. A wide range of services and supplies, from inexpensive point-and-shoot cameras to deluxe German and Japanese equipment, is available at competitive prices. Some shops offer repair services and have multilingual staff.

National Geographic Society I just found out that the film lab here is open to the public. Drop off your film and you can pick up expert quality slides four hours later. 1145 17th St. NW. © 202/857-7582. www.nationalgeographic.com. Metro: Farragut North.

Penn Camera Exchange Across the street from the FBI Building, Penn Camera does a brisk trade with professionals and concerned amateurs. The store offers big discounts on major brand-name equipment, such as Olympus and Canon. Penn has been owned and operated by the Zweig family since 1953; its staff is quite knowledgeable, and its inventory wide-ranging. Their specialty is quality equipment and processing—not cheap, but worth it. 840 E St. NW. © 202/347-5777. www.penncamera.com. Metro: Gallery Place or Metro Center. Also at 1015 18th St. NW (© 202/785-7366).

Ritz Camera Centers Ritz sells camera equipment for the average photographer and offers 1-hour film processing. Call for other locations; there are many throughout the area. 1740 Pennsylvania Ave. NW. © 202/466-3470. www.ritzpix.com. Metro: Farragut West.

CRAFTS

A mano Owner Adam Mahr frequently forages in Europe and returns with the unique handmade, imported French and Italian ceramics, linens, and other decorative accessories that you'll covet here. 1677 Wisconsin Ave. NW. © 202/298-7200. www.amanoinc.com. Metro: Foggy Bottom, then take the Georgetown Metro Connection shuttle.

American Studio Plus This store features exquisite contemporary handcrafted American ceramics and jewelry, plus international objets d'art. 2906 M St. NW. © 202/965-3273. Metro: Foggy Bottom, then take the Georgetown Metro Connection shuttle.

Appalachian Spring Country comes to Georgetown. This store sells pottery, jewelry, newly made pieced and appliqué quilts, stuffed dolls and animals, candles, rag rugs, handblown glassware, an incredible collection of kaleidoscopes, glorious weavings, and wooden kitchenware. Everything is made by hand in the United States. 1415 Wisconsin Ave. NW, at P St. © 202/337-5780. Metro: Foggy Bottom, then take the Georgetown Metro Connection shuttle. There's another branch in Union Station (© 202/682-0505).

Indian Craft Shop *Finds* The Indian Craft Shop has represented authentic Native American artisans since 1938, selling their hand-woven rugs and hand-crafted baskets, jewelry, figurines, paintings, pottery, and other items. You need a photo ID to enter the building. Use the C Street entrance, which is the only one open to the public. Open weekdays and the third Saturday of each month. Department of the Interior, 1849 C St. NW, Room 1023. © 202/208-4056. www.indiancraftshop.com. Metro: Farragut West or Foggy Bottom.

The Phoenix   Around since 1955, the Phoenix still sells those embroidered Mexican peasant blouses popular in hippie days; high-end Mexican folk and fine art; handcrafted sterling silver jewelry from Mexico and all over the world; clothing in natural fibers from Mexican and American designers like Eileen Fisher and Flax; collectors' quality masks; and decorative doodads in tin, brass, copper, and wood. 1514 Wisconsin Ave. NW. ✆ 202/338-4404. Metro: Foggy Bottom, then take the Georgetown Metro Connection shuttle.

Torpedo Factory Art Center   Once a munitions factory, this three-story building built in 1918 now houses more than 84 working studios and the works of about 165 artists, who tend to their crafts before your very eyes, pausing to explain their techniques or to sell their pieces. Artworks include paintings, sculpture, ceramics, glasswork, and textiles. 105 N. Union St. ✆ 703/838-4565. www.torpedofactory.org. Metro: King St., then take the DASH bus (AT2, AT5, or AT7) eastbound to the waterfront.

DEPARTMENT STORE

Hecht's   This old reliable has outlasted other D.C. department stores, updating its merchandise to keep up with the times, as it marks prices down to beat the competition. You can buy just about anything here, brand name fashions, household appliances, makeup, shoes, linens, electronics, luggage. The one thing it does not carry, I discovered the other day, is children's shoes. 1201 G St. NW. ✆ 202/628-6661. www.hechts.com. Metro: Metro Center. Also at 5400 Wisconsin Ave. NW (✆ 301/654-7600; Metro: Friendship Heights).

DISCOUNT SHOPPING

Discount shops in Washington are few and far between. Stores like Wal-Mart and Target are all in the far 'burbs. Still, I've got some suggestions for you. First, check out the Washington Post website, www.washingtonpost.com, click on "Entertainment," then click on "Shopping," then click on "Sales and Bargains," to see whether any stores are having sales while you're here. Second, head to Hecht's department store (see its separate listing under "Department Store"), located downtown, or to Hecht's Chevy Chase, MD, location, where you'll find a number of other bargain stores on the same block (see others listed below); Hecht's is not a discount store but regularly holds sales and marks down prices on its upscale merchandise. For a recommended secondhand bookstore, read about Second Story Books under "Old and Used Books." Finally, review the following list of D.C.'s best bargain stores and the two succeeding sections directing you to thrift, secondhand, and consignment stores, and farmer's and flea markets.

Filene's Basement *(Value*   This Boston-based store may have gone bankrupt at home but continues to be a hit in Washington, selling designer and famous-name clothes and accessories, and now home furnishings. 1133 Connecticut Ave. NW, downtown. ✆ 202/872-8430. www.filenesbasement.com. Metro: Farragut North. Also at 529 14th St. NW, in the Shops at National Place complex (✆ 202/638-4110), and in the Mazza Gallerie in upper northwest Washington, 5300 Wisconsin Ave. NW (✆ 202/966-0208).

Loehmann's   This two-level store on upper Wisconsin Avenue, next to the Chevy Chase Pavilion and across from Filene's Basement in the Mazza Gallerie, sells brand name clothes at discount prices ("the biggest deal in designer clothes"), claiming to price their merchandise at 30% to 65% less than what other department stores charge. 5333 Wisconsin Ave. NW ✆ 202/362-4733. www.loehmanns.com. Metro: Friendship Heights.

Potomac Mills Mall *Value*   When you're stuck in the traffic that always clogs this section of I-95, you may wonder if a trip to Potomac Mills is worth it. Believe it or not, this place attracts more visitors than any other site in the Washington area; it's one of the largest indoor outlet malls around, with more than 220 shops such as Saks Fifth Avenue, Nordstrom Rack, L.L. Bean, and Polo Ralph Lauren. A huge IKEA store, which used to anchor the mall, has seceded, moving to its separate location across the street from Potomac Mills. 30 miles south on I-95. Accessible by car, or by shuttle bus leaving from designated places throughout the area, including Dupont Circle and Metro Center. Call ✆ **800/VA-MILLS** or 703/643-1770 for information about Potomac Mills; call ✆ 703/551-1050 for information about the shuttle-bus service. www.potomacmills.com.

Stein Mart   The Florida-based retailer opened this, its only D.C. store, in the Chevy Chase Pavilion in July 2003, taking over the upper level of the mall to purvey its department store brands at reduced prices. Along with apparel, the store sells shoes, jewelry, and bedding. 5335 Wisconsin Ave. NW. ✆ **202/363-7075.** www.steinmart.com. Metro: Friendship Heights.

T.J.Maxx   Half of this discount store is devoted to women's clothes, the other half is a mix of men's and children's clothes, shoes, and housewares. You can expect to find prices at 20% to 60% off department store prices. A no frills sort of place. 4350 Jenifer St. NW. ✆ **202/237-7616.** www.tjmaxx.com. Metro: Friendship Heights.

THRIFT/CONSIGNMENT/SECONDHAND SHOPS
Christ Child Opportunity Shop *Value*   Proceeds from merchandise sales go to children's charities. Among the first-floor items—all donations—are the usual thrift-shop jumble of jewelry, clothes, shoes, hats, and odds and ends. Upstairs, higher-quality merchandise is left on consignment; it's more expensive, but if you know antiques, you might find bargains in jewelry, silver, china, quilts, and other items. Closed in August. 1427 Wisconsin Ave. NW (at P St.). ✆ **202/333-6635.** Metro: Foggy Bottom, then take the Georgetown Metro Connection shuttle.

Secondhand Rose *Value*   This upscale second-floor consignment shop specializes in designer merchandise. Creations by Chanel, Armani, Donna Karan, Calvin Klein, Yves Saint-Laurent, Ungaro, Ralph Lauren, and others are sold at about a third of the original price. A stunning Scaasi black-velvet and yellow-satin ball gown might go for $400 (from $1,200 new); Yves Saint-Laurent pumps in perfect condition can be had for as little as $45. Everything is in style, in season, and in excellent condition. Secondhand Rose is also a great place to shop for gorgeous furs, designer shoes and bags, and costume jewelry. 1516 Wisconsin Ave. NW, between P St. and Volta Place. ✆ **202/337-3378.** Metro: Foggy Bottom, then take the Georgetown Metro Connection shuttle.

Secondi Inc.   On the second floor of a building right above Starbucks is this high-style consignment shop that sells women's clothing and accessories, including designer suits, evening wear, and more casual items, with nothing more than 2 years old—everything from Kate Spade to Chanel. 1702 Connecticut Ave. NW. (between R St. and Florida Ave.). ✆ **202/667-1122.** Metro: Dupont Circle.

FARMERS' & FLEA MARKETS
Alexandria Farmers' Market   The oldest continuously operating farmers' market in the country (since 1752), this market offers the usual assortment of locally grown fruits and vegetables, along with delectable baked goods, cut flowers, and plants. Open year-round, Saturday mornings from 5 to 10am. 301 King

St., at Market Square in front of the city hall, in Alexandria. © 703/838-4770. Metro: King St., then take the DASH bus (AT2, AT5, or AT7) eastbound to Market Square.

Dupont Circle FreshFarm Market *(Kids)*   Fresh flowers, produce, eggs, and cheeses are for sale here. The market also features kids' activities and guest appearances by chefs and owners of some of Washington's best restaurants: Bis, Vidalia, Restaurant Nora, Tosca, and 1789. Held Sundays from 9am to 1pm, April through December. On 20th St. NW, between Q St. and Massachusetts Ave., and in the adjacent Riggs Bank parking lot. © 202/362-8889. Metro: Dupont Circle, Q St. exit.

Eastern Market *(Value)*   This is the one everyone knows about, even if they've never been here. In continuous operation since 1873, this Capitol Hill institution holds an inside bazaar Tuesday through Sunday, where greengrocers, butchers, bakers, farmers, artists, craftspeople, florists, and other merchants sell their wares. Saturday morning is the best time to go. On Saturday and Sunday, outside stalls become a flea market. Tuesday through Saturday 7am to 6pm, Sunday 9am to 4pm. 225 7th St. SE, between North Carolina Ave. and C St. SE. © 202/546-7612 or 202/543-7293. Metro: Eastern Market.

Georgetown Flea Market *(Finds)*   Grab a coffee at Starbucks across the lane and get ready to barter. The Georgetown Flea Market is frequented by all types of Washingtonians looking for a good deal—they often get it—on antiques, painted furniture, vintage clothing, and decorative garden urns. Nearly 100 vendors sell their wares here. Open year-round on Sunday from 9am to 5pm.

The school recently converted part of its parking lot into an athletic field, sending another 50 of its original 100 vendors to set up at a new location: Georgetown Flea Market at U Street, 1345 U St. NW, which is open every Saturday and Sunday from 9am to 5pm. In the Hardy Middle School parking lot bordering Wisconsin Ave., between S and T sts. NW. Metro: Foggy Bottom, then take the Georgetown Metro Connection shuttle.

Montgomery County Farm Woman's Cooperative Market   Vendors set up inside every Saturday year-round from 7am to about 3:30pm to sell preserves, homegrown veggies, cut flowers, slabs of bacon and sausages, and mouthwatering pies, cookies, and breads; there's an abbreviated version on Wednesday. Outside, on Saturday, Sunday and Wednesday, you'll find flea-market vendors selling rugs, tablecloths, furniture, sunglasses—everything. 7155 Wisconsin Ave., in Bethesda. © 301/652-2291. Metro: Bethesda.

FASHION
See also "Discount Shopping," above, and "Shoes," later in this section.

CHILDREN'S CLOTHING
One-of-a-kind children's stores don't do well in downtown Washington. But if your youngster has spilled grape juice all over his favorite outfit and you need a suitable replacement, you can always head to **Hecht's** (p. 233) or to the nearest **Gap Kids:** in Georgetown at 1267 Wisconsin Ave. NW. (© 202/333-2411) or at 2000 Pennsylvania Ave. NW (© 202/429-6862). Also check out these two stores:

April Cornell *(Kids)*   Too precious for words, this store is almost entirely for girls (and their moms), selling lots of pretty, flowing, flowery dresses, plus linens and nightgowns. Some shirts for little boys. 3278 M St. NW. © 202/625-7887. www.aprilcornell.com. Metro: Foggy Bottom, then take the Georgetown Metro Connection shuttle.

Kid's Closet *Kids*   Its storefront display of cute kids' clothes stands out among the bank and restaurant facades in this downtown block; inside are clothes and accessories mostly with brand names like OshKosh and Little Me. 1226 Connecticut Ave. NW. ℂ 202/429-9247. Metro: Dupont Circle.

MEN'S CLOTHING

Local outlets of **Banana Republic** are at Wisconsin and M streets in Georgetown (ℂ **202/333-2554**) and F and 13th streets NW (ℂ 202/638-2724). **Eddie Bauer** has a store at 3040 M St. NW (ℂ **202/342-2121**) in Georgetown.

Beau Monde   This boutique sells mostly Italian-made clothes, in all the latest styles, including suits, sports coats, ties, slacks, shirts, and accessories. International Square, 1814 K St. NW. ℂ 202/466-7070. Metro: Farragut West.

Brooks Brothers   Brooks sells traditional men's clothes, as well as the fine line of Peal's English shoes. This store made the news as the place where Monica Lewinsky bought a tie for President Clinton. It also sells an extensive line of women's clothes. 1201 Connecticut Ave. NW. ℂ 202/659-4650. www.brooksbrothers.com. Metro: Dupont Circle or Farragut North. Other locations are at Potomac Mills (p. 234), at National Airport (ℂ 703/417-1071), and at 5504 Wisconsin Ave., in Chevy Chase, MD (ℂ 301/654-8202).

Burberry's   Here you'll find those plaid-lined trench coats, of course, along with well-tailored but conservative English clothing for men and women. Hot items include cashmere sweaters and camel's hair duffel coats for men. 1155 Connecticut Ave. NW. ℂ 202/463-3000. Metro: Farragut North.

Thomas Pink   For those who like beautifully made, bright-colored shirts, this new branch of the London-based high-end establishment should please. The store also sells ties, boxer shorts, women's shirts, cufflinks, and other accessories. 1127 Connecticut Ave. NW (inside the Mayflower Hotel). ℂ 202/223-5390. www.thomaspink.com. Metro: Farragut North.

Urban Outfitters   For the latest in casual attire, from fatigue pants to tube tops. The shop has a floor of women's clothes, a floor of men's clothes, as well as housewares, inflatable chairs, books, cards, and candles. 3111 M St. NW. ℂ 202/342-1012. www.urbn.com. Metro: Foggy Bottom, then take the Georgetown Metro Connection shuttle.

WOMEN'S CLOTHING

Washington women have many more clothing stores to choose from than men. Stores selling classic designs dominate, including **Ann Taylor,** at Union Station (ℂ **202/371-8010**), 1140 Connecticut Ave. NW (ℂ 202/659-0120), 600 13th St. NW (ℂ 202/737-0325), and Georgetown Park, 3222 M St. NW (ℂ 202/338-5290); and **Talbots,** at 1122 Connecticut Ave. NW (ℂ **202/887-6973**) and Georgetown Park, 3222 M St. NW (ℂ 202/338-3510). Beneath their modest apparel, however, Washington women like to wear racy **Victoria's Secret** lingerie—you'll find stores in Union Station (ℂ **202/682-0686**) and Georgetown Park (ℂ 202/965-5457), as well as at Connecticut and L streets NW (ℂ 202/293-7530).

See "Men's Clothing," immediately above, for locations of Banana Republic, Eddie Bauer, Brooks Brothers, and Urban Outfitters, all of which also sell women's clothes.

Hip boutiques and upscale shops proliferate as well:

all about jane   The independent-minded will enjoy pawing through the animal print, plaid, tweed, and colorful fashions that are making this newcomer a success in Adams-Morgan. 2438½ 18th St. NW. ☎ 202/797-9710. www.allaboutjane.net. Metro: Woodley Park, then a 20-min. walk.

Betsey Johnson   New York's flamboyant flower-child designer personally decorated the bubble-gum pink walls in her Georgetown shop. Her sexy, offbeat play-dress-up styles are great party and club clothes for the young and the still-skinny young at heart. This is the only Betsey Johnson store in D.C. 1319 Wisconsin Ave. NW. ☎ 202/338-4090. www.betseyjohnson.com. Metro: Foggy Bottom, then take the Georgetown Metro Connection shuttle.

Betsy Fisher   A walk past the store is all it takes to know that this shop is a tad different. Its windows and racks show off whimsically feminine fashions by new American designers. 1224 Connecticut Ave. NW. ☎ 202/785-1975. www.betsyfisher.com. Metro: Dupont Circle.

Chanel Boutique   A modest selection of Chanel's signature designs, accessories, and jewelry, at immodest prices. 1455 Pennsylvania Ave. NW, in the courtyard of the Willard Inter-Continental Hotel. ☎ 202/638-5055. Metro: Metro Center.

Commander Salamander   Loud music, young crowd, and funky clothes. Commander Salamander has a little bit of everything, including designer items (Dolce & Gabbana for instance), some of which are quite affordable. Too cool. 1420 Wisconsin Ave. NW. ☎ 202/337-2265. Metro: Foggy Bottom, then a 25-min. walk.

French Connection   This outpost of the London-based chain features clothes that are hip but not outrageous. 1229 Wisconsin Ave. NW. ☎ 202/965-4690. www.french connection.com. Metro: Foggy Bottom, then take the Georgetown Metro Connection shuttle.

Nana's   Owner Jackie Flanagan left the world of advertising and publishing to open this store last year, naming it after her fashion-wise grandmother. The shop sells new and vintage styles of work and play clothes, the idea being to mix old and new for a fresh look. Handbags, gifts, and bath products are also on sale. 1534 U St. NW. (between 15th and 16th sts.) ☎ 202/667-6955. www.nanadc.com. Metro: U St.–Cardozo.

Pirjo   Come here for the funky, baggy, and pretty creations of European designers like Marimekko, Rundholz, and Lillith. Styles range from casual to dressy. Pirjo sells elegant jewelry to boot. 1044 Wisconsin Ave. NW, in Georgetown. ☎ 202/337-1390. www.pirjos.com. Metro: Foggy Bottom, then take the Georgetown Metro Connection shuttle.

Rizik Brothers   In business since 1908, this downtown high-fashion store sells designs by Caroline Herrera, Oscar de la Renta, Geoffrey Beene, and other European and American designers. 1100 Connecticut Ave. NW. ☎ 202/223-4050. www.riziks. com. Metro: Farragut North.

Saks-Jandel   This store displays elegant day and evening wear by major European and American designers—Giorgio Armani, Louis Féraud, Christian Dior, Valentino, Isaac Mizrahi (this was the site of the designer's promo for his movie, *Unzipped*), John Galliano, and many others. Saks-Jandel has an international clientele. 5510 Wisconsin Ave., Chevy Chase, MD. ☎ 301/652-2250. Metro: Friendship Heights. Also at the Watergate, 2522 Virginia Ave. NW (☎ 202/337-4200).

GIFTS/SOUVENIRS

See also "Crafts," earlier in this section, and "Museum Shopping," below.

Chocolate Moose *Finds*   My husband endears himself to me and our daughters when he brings home gifts at Valentine's Day and other occasions from this shop: chunky, transparent, red heart-shaped earrings, wacky cards, paperweight snow globes with figurines inside, candies, eccentric clothing, and other funny, lovely, and useful presents. 1800 M St. NW. ✆ 202/463-0992. Metro: Farragut North.

Made in America   Union Station is full of gift shops, actually, but stop here if you want to pick up a baseball cap with a "DEA," "CIA," or "Police SWAT" insignia on its bill; White House guest towels; and other impress-the-folks-back-home items. Union Station. ✆ 202/842-0540. www.americastore.com. Metro: Union Station. Or save your shopping for the airport; Made in America has 1 location at National (✆ 703/417-1782) and 3 at Dulles (Terminal B: ✆ 703/572-2543; Terminal C: ✆ 703/572-6058; Terminal D: ✆ 703/572-6070).

GOURMET GOODIES TO GO

Demanding jobs and hectic schedules leave Washingtonians less and less time to prepare their own meals. Or so they say. At any rate, a number of fine-food shops and bakeries are happy to come to the rescue. Even the busiest bureaucrat can find the time to pop into one of these gourmet shops for a movable feast.

See also "Farmer's & Flea Markets," above.

Bread Line *Finds*   Owner Mark Furstenberg is credited with revolutionizing bread baking in Washington. He started the Marvelous Market chain (see below), though he has since bowed out. At Bread Line, he concentrates on selling freshly baked loaves of wheat bread, flatbreads, baguettes, and more; sandwiches like the roast pork bun or the muffaletta; tasty soups; and desserts such as bread puddings, pear tarts, and delicious cookies. Seating is available, but most people buy carryout. Open weekdays only, 7:30am to 3:30pm. 1751 Pennsylvania Ave. NW. ✆ 202/822-8900. Metro: Farragut West or Farragut North.

Dean & Deluca   This famed New York store has set down roots in Washington, in a historic Georgetown building that was once an open-air market. Though it is now closed in, this huge space still feels airy, with its high ceiling and windows on all sides. You'll pay top prices, but the quality is impressive—charcuterie, fresh fish, produce, cheeses, prepared sandwiches and cold pasta salads, hot-ticket desserts, like crème brûlée and tiramisu, and California wines. Also on sale are housewares; on site is an espresso bar/cafe. 3276 M St. NW. ✆ 202/342-2500. www.deandeluca.com. Metro: Foggy Bottom. There's 1 other cafe location, at 1299 Pennsylvania Ave. NW (✆ 202/628-8155).

Firehook Bakery   Known for its sourdough baguettes, apple-walnut bread, fresh fruit tarts, and, at its Farragut Square store, 912 17th St. NW (✆ 202/429-2253), for sandwiches like smoked chicken on sesame semolina bread. 1909 Q St. NW. ✆ 202/588-9296. www.firehook.com. Metro: Dupont Circle. Also at 3241 M St. NW (✆ 202/625-6247), 3411 Connecticut Ave. NW (✆ 202/362-2253), 215 Pennsylvania Ave. SE (✆ 202/544-7003), 431 11th St. NW (✆ 202/638-1637), 441 4th St. NW (✆ 202/347-1760), and at 2 locations in Alexandria, Virginia.

Lawson's Gourmet   Sitting at Lawson's cluster of outside tables and chairs, you'll see all of Washington pass by, from sharply dressed lawyers to bohemian artistes and panhandlers. You can buy elaborate sandwiches made to order and very nice desserts, wines, breads, and salads. 1350 Connecticut Ave. NW. ✆ 202/775-0400. Metro: Dupont Circle. Also at 1350 I St. (✆ 202/789-1440), 1776 I St. (✆ 202/296-3200), and Metro Center, 601 13th St. NW (✆ 202/393-5500).

Marvelous Market   First there were the breads: sourdough, baguettes, olive, rosemary, croissants, scones. Now, there are things to spread on the bread, including smoked salmon mousse and tapenade; pastries to die for, from gingerbread to flourless chocolate cake; and prepared foods, such as soups, empañadas, and pasta salads. The breakfast spread on Sunday mornings is sinful, and individual items, like the croissants, are tastier and less expensive here than at other bakeries. The location is grand, with 18th-century chandeliers, an antique cedar bar, and a small number of tables. 1511 Connecticut Ave. NW. ℭ **202/332-3690**. www.marvelous market.com. Metro: Dupont Circle. Also at 3217 P St. NW (ℭ 202/333-2591) and 5035 Connecticut Ave. NW (ℭ 202/686-4040).

JEWELRY

Beadazzled   The friendly staff helps you assemble your own affordable jewelry from an eye-boggling array of beads and artifacts. The store also sells textiles, woodcarvings, and other crafts from around the world. 1507 Connecticut Ave. NW. ℭ **202/265-BEAD**. www.beadazzled.net. Metro: Dupont Circle.

Chas Schwartz & Son   In business since 1888, Chas Schwartz specializes in diamonds and sapphires, rubies and emeralds, and is one of the few distributors of Hidalgo jewelry (enameled rings and bracelets). The professional staff also repairs watches and jewelry. 1400 F St. NW, or enter through the Willard Hotel, at 1401 Pennsylvania Ave. NW. ℭ **202/737-4757**. Metro: Metro Center. There's another branch at the Mazza Gallerie (ℭ 202/363-5432); Metro: Friendship Heights.

Keith Lipert Gallery   This decorative arts gallery sells Venetian glassware, high-end costume jewelry by designers such as Oscar de la Renta, and cute little old things, like art deco styled handbags. 2922 M St. NW. ℭ **202/965-9736**. Metro: Foggy Bottom, then take the Georgetown Metro Connection.

Tiffany & Co.   Tiffany is known for exquisite diamonds and other jewelry that can cost hundreds of thousands of dollars. But you may not know that the store carries less expensive items as well, like $35 candlesticks. Tiffany will engrave, too. Other items include tabletop gifts and fancy glitz: china, crystal, flatware, and a bridal registry service. 5500 Wisconsin Ave., Chevy Chase, MD. ℭ **301/657-8777**. www.tiffany.com. Metro: Friendship Heights.

Tiny Jewel Box   The first place Washingtonians go for estate and antique jewelry, but the six-story store next to the Mayflower Hotel sells the pieces of many designers, from Links of London to Christian Tse, as well as crystal and other house gifts. 1147 Connecticut Ave. NW. ℭ **202/393-2747**. www.tinyjewelbox.com. Metro: Farragut North.

MALLS

Also see the listing for **Potomac Mills** on p. 234.

Chevy Chase Pavilion   This is a manageably sized mall with about 25 stores and restaurants, anchored by an Embassy Suites Hotel. The inside is unusually pretty, with three levels winding around a skylit atrium. Stores include a two-level Pottery Barn, Stein Mart, Hold Everything, Talbots, Georgette Klinger, and J.Crew. The Cheesecake Factory, Starbucks, and a food court are among the dining options. 5335 Wisconsin Ave. NW. ℭ **202/686-5335**. Metro: Friendship Heights.

Fashion Center at Pentagon City   Nordstrom and Macy's are the biggest attractions in this elegant five-story shoppers' paradise. There's also the Ritz-Carlton Hotel where Ken Starr nabbed Monica Lewinsky, multiplex theaters, and a sprawling food court. Williams-Sonoma, Crate & Barrel, and Kenneth Cole are among the more than 170 shops. 1100 S. Hayes St., Arlington, VA. ℭ **703/415-2400**. www.shopsimon.com. Metro: Pentagon City.

Mazza Gallerie   Neiman Marcus anchors this modest-sized though upscale mall, which holds a nine-screen movie theater, a large Williams-Sonoma, a Saks Fifth Avenue Men's Store, Filene's Basement, Ann Taylor, Harriet Kassman, and about 18 other stores. 5300 Wisconsin Ave. NW. ✆ **202/966-6114**. www.mazzagallerie.net. Metro: Friendship Heights.

Pavilion at the Old Post Office   Not so much a mall as a tourist trap with souvenir shops and a food court. But TICKETplace has a booth here, selling half-price, day-of-show tickets to performances at area theaters and concert halls (see p. 244 for more information), and you can ride the elevator 315 feet up to the top of the building's clock tower, for a fab view of the city—for free (call ✆ 202/606-8691 for more information from the National Park Service, who operates this service). 1100 Pennsylvania Ave. NW. ✆ **202/289-4224**. www.oldpostofficedc.com. Metro: Federal Triangle.

Ronald Reagan Washington National Airport   Allow extra time before your flight and you can do all of your souvenir shopping here. The 100 stores include Brooks Brothers and Brookstone, and gift shop outlets of the Smithsonian, the National Zoo, and the National Geographic Society. Arlington, VA. ✆ **703/417-8600**. www.mwaa.com/National.

Shops at Georgetown Park   This is a deluxe mall, where you'll see the beautiful people shopping for beautiful things. Ann Taylor, Abercrombie & Fitch, J. Crew, and Polo/Ralph Lauren are just a few of the trendy stores. Sharper Image and Crabtree & Evelyn are here, too.

   The Old Town Trolley stops here (see chapter 7) and you can buy trolley tickets from two vendor stalls in the Food Court: PretzelMaker and A Little Bit of Buffalo. There are several restaurants, including Clyde's of Georgetown (see p. 150 for details), gourmet emporium/cafe Dean & Deluca, and the parklike Canal Walk Café Food Court. 3222 M St. NW. ✆ **202/298-5577**. www.shopsatgeorge townpark.com. Metro: Foggy Bottom, then take the Georgetown Metro Connection shuttle.

Shops at National Place   National Place has more than 75 shops and eateries, including Casual Corner, Filene's Basement discount department store, and an international food court. 1331 Pennsylvania Ave. NW. (enter through the J. W. Marriott Hotel or at F St., between 13th and 14th sts.). ✆ **202/662-1250**. Metro: Metro Center.

Tysons Corner Center and Tysons Corner II, The Galleria   Facing each other across Chain Bridge Road, these two gigantic malls could lead to shopper's overload. Tysons Corner Center, the first and less expensive, has Nordstrom, Bloomingdale's, and L.L. Bean, and specialty stores, such as Abercrombie & Fitch and Crabtree & Evelyn. The Galleria has Macy's, Saks Fifth Avenue, and more than 100 upscale boutiques. Tysons Corner Center, 1961 Chain Bridge Rd., McLean, VA. ✆ **703/893-9400**. www.shoptysons.com. Tysons Corner II, The Galleria, 2001 International Dr., McLean, VA. ✆ **703/827-7700**. www.shoptysonsgalleria.com. Metro: West Falls Church; take shuttle.

Union Station   One of the most popular tourist stops in Washington, Union Station boasts magnificent architecture and more than 120 shops, including Ann Taylor, Pendleton's, and Appalachian Spring (p. 232). Among the places to eat are America, B. Smith, and an impressive food court. There's also a nine-screen movie-theater complex. 50 Massachusetts Ave. NE. ✆ **202/289-1908**. www.union stationdc.com. Metro: Union Station.

White Flint Mall   Another Bloomingdale's, another long trip in the car or on the Metro; but once you're there, you can shop, take in a movie, and dine cheaply or well. Notable stores include Lord & Taylor, a huge Borders, Laura Ashley, and Coach. 11301 Rockville Pike, Kensington, MD. ✆ 301/468-5777. www.shop whiteflint.com. Metro: White Flint, then take the free White Flint shuttle, which runs every 15 min.

MISCELLANEOUS

Al's Magic Shop *(Kids)*   The drinks in our house always come with flies frozen inside the ice cubes (okay, so the flies are plastic), thanks to my daughter's last visit to this first-rate novelty store. Longtime owner and local character Al Cohen sold his store in 2002 to Cindy and Steve Brown, who have kept Al's name and spirit going here. 1012 Vermont Ave. NW. ✆ 202/789-2800. Metro: McPherson Square.

Fahrneys Pens, Inc.   People come from all over to purchase the finest fountain pens, or to have them engraved or repaired. In business since 1929, Fahrneys is an institution, selling Montblanc, Cross, Waterman, the best in the business. 1317 F St. NW (between 13th and 14th sts.). ✆ 800/624-7367 or 202/628-9525. www.fahrneyspens.com. Metro: Metro Center.

Ginza, "Things Japanese"   Everything Japanese, from incense and kimonos to futons to Zen rock gardens. 1721 Connecticut Ave. NW. ✆ 202/331-7991. www.ginza online.com. Metro: Dupont Circle.

Hats in the Belfry   In business for 26 years now, this hat store features designer hats, floppy hats, straw hats, Panama hats, all sorts of hats, for men and women, some for children, and some handbags. Go ahead, try some on. 1237 Wisconsin Ave. NW. ✆ 202/342-2006. www.hatsinthebelfry.com. Metro: Foggy Bottom, with a 25-min. walk.

Home Rule *(Value)*   Unique housewares; bath, kitchen, and office supplies; and gifts cram this tiny new store. You'll see everything from French milled soap to martini glasses. 1807 14th St. NW (at S St.). ✆ 202/797-5544. www.homerule.com. Metro: U St.–Cardozo.

MUSIC

See also the listing for **Olsson's Books and Records** on p. 230.

Borders   Besides being a great bookstore, Borders offers the best prices in town for CDs and tapes, and a wide range of music. At 18th and L sts. NW. ✆ 202/466-4999. Metro: Farragut North. (See other locations under "Books," earlier in this chapter.)

DCCD   This store sells new and used CDs, new records, and new and used video games. Known best as Washington's independent rock record store, DCCD features in-store performances by local and national bands. 2423 18th St. NW. ✆ 202/588-1810. Metro: Woodley Park, then a 20-min. walk.

DJ Hut   Everything for lovers of hip-hop, reggae, R&B, and go-go. 2010 P St. NW, 2nd floor. ✆ 202/659-2010. Metro: Dupont Circle.

Melody Record Shop   CDs, cassettes, and tapes, including new releases, are discounted here, plus the shop always has a table of unused but not newly released CDs that sell for about $10 each. Melody offers a wide variety of rock, classical, jazz, pop, show, and folk music, as well as a vast number of international selections. This is also a good place to shop for discounted portable electronic equipment, blank tapes, and cassettes. Its knowledgeable staff is a plus. 1623 Connecticut Ave. NW. ✆ 202/232-4002. www.melodyrecords.com. Metro: Dupont Circle, Q St. exit.

Tower Records   When you need a record at midnight on Christmas Eve, you go to Tower. This large, funky store, across the street from George Washington

Museum Shopping

Just what kinds of gifts can you find in museums, anyway? A couple of Christmases ago, I decided to find out. Shunning the malls, I turned to Washington museums and landmarks for all of my holiday shopping, and brought home a bounty of unique presents that (I'm pretty sure) everyone liked. Here's a little of what I gleaned:

The **National Museum of American History store** has an outstanding collection of books, CDs, and tapes (CDs from the Ken Burns PBS special on Jazz for one of my sisters, a CD of old baseball tunes for my then-6-year-old nephew), but also a lot of junky trinkets. Look to the **Library of Congress** for beautiful stationery and unusual books (I chose a book on Bach for my aunt, a leather-bound journal for my brother-in-law), but don't buy the jewelry, which is overpriced and unattractive. The **Textile Museum shop** sells exquisite and one-of-a-kind clothes and accessories (I snagged a silk purse from Japan for one sister and a Turkish tote bag for another), but you can expect to pay a bundle. Overall, the **National Building Museum** offers the best inventory for its surprising, useful, and cleverly designed housewares and interesting games. Here I bought heavy bookends embossed with a Celtic design for my mom and a museum board game for my niece; I still regret not grabbing the Koziol plastic caterpillar CD rack.

Other things to note: The largest museum shop is at the **National Air and Space Museum** (three floors!); and the shop at the **Smithsonian's Arts and Industries Building** carries a selection of the most popular items from all of the other Smithsonian shops.

You can check out some of the stores' merchandise online ahead of time: Point your browser to **www.smithsonianstore.com** (for the Smithsonian shops), **www.nbm.org/shop** then click on "Shop." (for the National Building Museum), and **www.loc.gov**, and click on "Shop" (for the Library of Congress). The Textile Museum website, **www.textile museum.org**, lists only its book titles. For the Web addresses of other museums, see their individual listings in chapter 7.

University, has a wide choice of records, cassettes, and CDs in every category— but the prices are high. 2000 Pennsylvania Ave. NW. ✆ 202/331-2400. www.tower.com. Metro: Foggy Bottom.

POLITICAL MEMORABILIA

Capitol Coin and Stamp Co. Inc.   A museum of political memorabilia—pins, posters, banners—and all of it is for sale. This is also a fine resource for the endangered species of coin or stamp collectors. 1100 17th St. NW, Suite 503. ✆ 202/296-0400. Metro: Farragut North.

SHOES

For men's dress shoes, try **Brooks Brothers** (p. 236). There are local outlets of **Foot Locker** at Union Station (✆ 202/289-8364), 3221 M St. NW (✆ 202/333-7640), and 1934 14th St. NW (✆ 202/319-8934). **Nine West** sells women's shoes from locations at Union Station (✆ 202/216-9490), 1008 Connecticut

Ave. NW (𝄞 202/452-9163), and 1227 Wisconsin Ave. NW (𝄞 202/337-7256).

Comfort One Shoes   Despite its unhip name, this store sells a great selection of popular styles for both men and women, including Doc Martens, Birkenstocks, and Ecco. You can always find something that actually feels comfortable. 1636 Connecticut Ave. NW. 𝄞 **202/328-3141.** www.comfortoneshoes.com. Metro: Dupont Circle. Also at 1607 Connecticut Ave. NW (𝄞 202/667-5300), 3222 M St. NW (𝄞 202/333-3399), and other locations.

Steve Madden   The music's so loud, you may not be able to hear a word the salesperson says. This is the city's only Steve Madden location, the women's shoe store that's really popular among the college-age crowd for its chunky platforms, sandals, and thongs. 3109 M St. NW. 𝄞 **202/342-6195.** Metro: Foggy Bottom, then take the Georgetown Metro Connection shuttle.

TOYS

The gift shops at museums and tourist attractions are really your best bets for children's gifts. One other suggestion:

Flights of Fancy *(Kids)*   Picture books, Playmobil toys, board games, and assorted other toys and amusements cram this small store. Union Station. 𝄞 **202/371-9800.** Metro: Union Station.

WINE & SPIRITS

Calvert Woodley Liquors   This is a large store with a friendly staff, nice selections, and good cheeses (about 300 to choose from) and other foods to go along with your drinks. 4339 Connecticut Ave. NW. 𝄞 **202/966-4400.** Metro: Van Ness–UDC.

Central Liquor *(Value)*   This is like a clearinghouse for liquor: Its great volume allows the store to offer the best prices in town on wines and liquor. The store carries more than 250 single-malt scotches. 917 F St. NW. 𝄞 **800/835-7928** or 202/737-2800. Metro: Gallery Place.

MacArthur Liquor   With a knowledgeable and enthusiastic staff, and an extensive and reasonably priced selection of excellent wines, both imported and domestic, this shop is always busy. 4877 MacArthur Blvd. NW. 𝄞 **202/338-1433.** www.bassins.com. Bus: D4 from Dupont Circle.

9

Washington, D.C., After Dark

The capital presents an astonishing array of free, top-notch entertainment. You may come to town to see Congress in action, to view art and exhibits at the Smithsonian and other museums, and to stroll through the city's beautiful parks. But you may come away just as excited about the live Latin jazz combo you heard—for free—at the National Museum of Natural History, or the exhilarating outdoor music festival you attended (well, for $3), featuring Blues Traveler and other class acts performing on a stage on Pennsylvania Avenue, with the Capitol in the background.

Many of those very same sightseeing landmarks for which D.C. is famous also host free and open-to-the-public entertainments. Check out the first section of this chapter, "Free & Almost-Free Entertainment," for a list of indoor and outdoor performances slated throughout the year, at venues that range from the Kennedy Center for the Performing Arts to the U.S. Capitol. No doubt, you'll see something appealing scheduled for the same days you plan to be here.

Most of Washington's nightlife and entertainment options are not free, of course. Again, don't despair: this chapter talks about how to purchase half-price tickets, and how to cash in on your status as a: student/senior/member of the military, or some other classification that might grant you entry or a reduced price at the door. If it's just a good bar you're after, I point you to a few places that offer complimentary food at happy hour. Read over the listings that follow to see which forms of entertainment most interest you. For up-to-date schedules of events, from live music and theater, to children's programs and flower shows, check the Friday "Weekend" section of the *Washington Post,* or go online, and browse the *Post*'s nightlife information at **www.washingtonpost.com**. The *City Paper,* available free at restaurants, bookstores, and other places around town, is another good source.

TICKETS

TICKETplace, Washington's only discount day-of-show ticket outlet, has one location: in the Old Post Office Pavilion, 1100 Pennsylvania Ave. NW (Metro: Federal Triangle). Call 🕿 **202/TICKETS** (842-5387), for information. You can purchase tickets there, or online at www.ticketplace.org. To purchase tickets at the Pavilion, go to the building's South Plaza entrance, on 12th Street NW, where you pass through metal detectors. On the day of performance only (except Sun and Mon; see below), you can buy half-price tickets (with cash, select debit and credit cards, or traveler's checks) to performances with tickets still available at most major Washington-area theaters and concert halls, as well as for performances of the opera, ballet, and other events. TICKETplace is open Tuesday through Saturday from 11am to 6pm; half-price tickets for Sunday and Monday shows are sold on Saturday. Though tickets are half-price, you have to pay a per-ticket service charge of 10% of the full face value of the ticket.

Tickets are available online Tuesday through Friday, between noon and 4pm. Again, the tickets sold are for same-day performances, at half-price, plus the per-ticket service charge, which for online sales, is 15% of the full face value of the ticket. You must pay by credit card, using MasterCard or Visa, then pick up the tickets at the "Will Call" booth of the theater you're attending; bring your credit card and a photo ID. TICKETplace is a service of the Cultural Alliance of Washington, in partnership with the Kennedy Center, the *Washington Post,* and Ticketmaster.

You can buy full-price tickets for most performances in town through **Ticketmaster** (© 202/432-SEAT; www.ticketmaster.com), if you're willing to pay a hefty service charge. Purchase tickets to Washington theatrical, musical, and other events before you leave home by going online or by calling © **800/551-SEAT.** Or you can wait until you get here and visit one of Ticketmaster's 18 locations throughout the city, including the TICKETplace outlet in the Old Post Office Pavilion (see above); Hecht's Department Store, 12th and G streets NW (Metro: Metro Center); George Washington University's Marvin Center, across from Lisner Auditorium, at 21st Street and H Street NW (Metro: Foggy Bottom); the DC Visitor Center in the Ronald Reagan Building, at 1300 Pennsylvania Ave. NW (Metro: Federal Triangle); and the MCI Center (Metro: Gallery Place). When you pay by credit card at TICKETplace and Ticketmaster, you have to show an ID to prove you are the credit card holder.

Another similar ticket outlet is **Tickets.com** (formerly Protix). You can order tickets by calling © **800/955-5566** or 703/218-6500, or by accessing its website at www.tickets.com.

1 Free & Almost-Free Entertainment

On any given day year-round, a concert or other live performance is taking place, at no charge, in an art gallery, museum, historic house, park, or other setting. And don't think you'll be listening to amateurs—for the most part, performances are by seasoned professionals, whose names may not be known to you, but who are recognized in their fields nonetheless.

Many people are aware of Washington's extensive outdoor concert offerings in summer, but few Washingtonians even know what a feast of free indoor entertainment is also available winter, spring, and fall.

Here's a list of those places around the city that feature free or almost-free shows. In most cases, you just show up; when you need tickets, reservations, or to arrive early to snag a seat, I've noted it. If a venue sounds particularly appealing, call for more information, since reservation policies and schedules do change. Also, check the Friday "Weekend" section of the *Washington Post,* which lists details of upcoming concerts, repertory films, and general performances, free or otherwise.

INDOOR ENTERTAINMENT
- **Arts Club of Washington,** 2017 I St. NW (© 202/331-7282). Housed in an early 19th-century brick town house that was home to James Monroe during the first 6 months of his presidency (when the British had torched the White House during the War of 1812), the Arts Club hosts free concerts—mostly classical and chamber music—most Fridays at noon, in every month but August and September.
- **Corcoran Gallery of Art,** 500 17th St. NW (© 202/639-1700). Free jazz concerts are held at 12:30pm most Wednesdays year-round in the Frances

Washington, D.C., After Dark

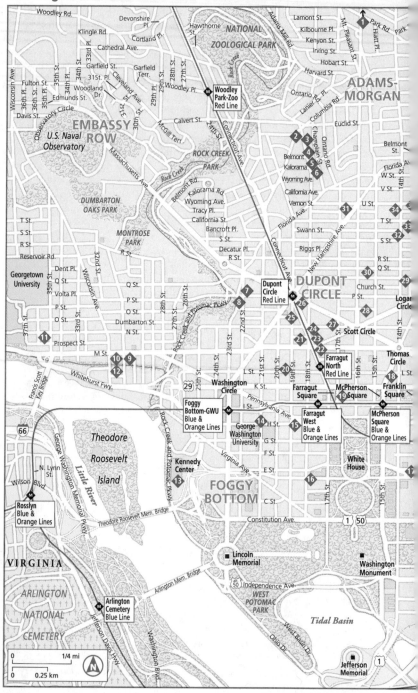

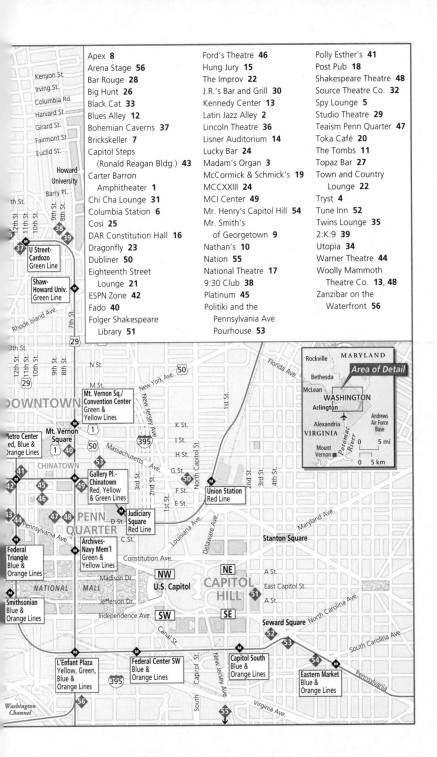

Apex **8**
Arena Stage **56**
Bar Rouge **28**
Big Hunt **26**
Black Cat **33**
Blues Alley **12**
Bohemian Caverns **37**
Bricskeller **7**
Capitol Steps
  (Ronald Reagan Bldg.) **43**
Carter Barron
  Amphitheater **1**
Chi Cha Lounge **31**
Columbia Station **6**
Cosi **25**
DAR Constitution Hall **16**
Dragonfly **23**
Dubliner **50**
Eighteenth Street
  Lounge **21**
ESPN Zone **42**
Fado **40**
Folger Shakespeare
  Library **51**

Ford's Theatre **46**
Hung Jury **15**
The Improv **22**
J.R.'s Bar and Grill **30**
Kennedy Center **13**
Latin Jazz Alley **2**
Lincoln Theatre **36**
Lisner Auditorium **14**
Lucky Bar **24**
Madam's Organ **3**
McCormick & Schmick's **19**
MCCXXIII **24**
MCI Center **49**
Mr. Henry's Capitol Hill **54**
Mr. Smith's
  of Georgetown **9**
Nathan's **10**
Nation **55**
National Theatre **17**
9:30 Club **38**
Platinum **45**
Politiki and the
  Pennsylvania Ave.
  Pourhouse **53**

Polly Esther's **41**
Post Pub **18**
Shakespeare Theatre **48**
Source Theatre Co. **32**
Spy Lounge **5**
Studio Theatre **29**
Teaism Penn Quarter **47**
Toka Café **20**
The Tombs **11**
Topaz Bar **27**
Town and Country
  Lounge **22**
Tryst **4**
Tune Inn **52**
Twins Lounge **35**
2:K:9 **39**
Utopia **34**
Warner Theatre **44**
Woolly Mammoth
  Theatre Co. **13, 48**
Zanzibar on the
  Waterfront **56**

and Armand Hammer auditorium. Call for a schedule of evening lectures and performances, for which the Corcoran charges admission. The Corcoran's **Café des Artistes** (ℂ **202/639-1786**) hosts a jazz gospel brunch every Sunday. It's $24 a person; no reservations taken for fewer than six people.

- **Georgetown Park Mall,** 3222 M St. NW (ℂ **202/342-8190**). From May through September, every Saturday from 1 to 3pm, the mall hosts "Concerts on the Canal," a series of free pop, jazz, and light classical concerts, held behind the mall, outside along the canal.

- **Kennedy Center for the Performing Arts,** New Hampshire Avenue and F Street NW (ℂ **800/444-1324** or 202/467-4600). In addition to its open houses (see the "Calendar of Events" listings in chapter 2), the Kennedy Center offers a nightly series of free concerts by soloists, choruses, bands, and ensembles, at 6pm on the **Millennium Stage** in its Grand Foyer. No tickets or reservations are required—just show up.

- **Library of Congress,** 1st Street SE and Independence Avenue (ℂ **202/707-5677**). Fall through spring, the library offers a series of classical, jazz, and other concerts in its Coolidge Auditorium, and films in its Mary Pickford Theater. Most events are free but require tickets. See the listing for the Library of Congress on p. 194 in chapter 7 for further information, or log onto www.loc.gov, and click on "News & Events." The Library of Congress also hosts free summer and fall concerts on its Neptune Plaza, in front of the Jefferson Building, at 10 1st St. SE; concerts are at noon, on occasional Wednesdays; check the website for details.

- **National Building Museum,** 401 F St. NW (ℂ **202/272-2448;** www.nbm.org). This series offers only three concerts per year, so check the website calendar for exact dates. If you're in town, bring your lunch and enjoy free pop or light classical ensemble music at 1:15pm in the Great Hall.

- **National Gallery of Art,** West Garden Court of the West Building, at 6th Street and Constitution Avenue NW (ℂ **202/842-6941**). One of the longest-running free weekly series—2004 marks its 63rd season—the National Gallery's Sunday concerts, offered October through June at 7pm, are certainly one of the most popular free offerings in town. Noted artists like jazz pianist Marian McPartland often perform, and the music sometimes ties in with a particular exhibit. Tickets and reservations are not needed, though you might wish they were, when you see the number of people queuing for first-come, first-served spots in the 500-seat garden court. Get there by 6pm.

- The National Gallery also presents **short films** with art-related subjects year-round, most Wednesday, Thursday, and Friday afternoons. On Saturday afternoons and Sunday evenings, classic and avant-garde feature films are shown. Admission is free; films are screened in the 461-seat auditorium in the East Building, at 4th Street and Constitution Avenue NW (ℂ **202/842-6799;** www.nga.gov). Call for exact times, and arrive 15 to 20 minutes ahead, to ensure a seat. Finally, in summer, the gallery hosts jazz sets in its sculpture garden; see listing below, under "Outdoor Performances."

- **National Museum of Natural History,** 10th and Constitution avenues NW (ℂ **202/633-7400;** www.mnh.si.edu/imax). This winning concert series features live jazz by groups like Marshall Keys, Sid Jacobs, and the Rick Whitehead Trio, every Friday night, 6 to 10pm, in the Atrium Café. A winner.

- **National Theatre,** 1321 Pennsylvania Ave. NW (ℂ **202/783-3372;** www.nationaltheatre.org). On Monday evenings in fall and spring, the National

Theatre presents free entertainment by local groups and performers at 6 and 7:30pm. Also ongoing throughout the school year is "Saturday Morning at the National," which features children's entertainment at 9:30 and 11am most Saturday mornings. The theater's summer cinema series highlights a theme or the movies of a particular director or actor ("Show Business" was the theme the summer of 2003); movies are shown Monday evenings in summer. For each of these free events, plan to arrive 30 minutes ahead to make sure you get a seat; tickets are handed out on a first-come, first-served basis.

- **Pavilion at the Old Post Office,** 1100 Pennsylvania Ave. NW (© 202/289-4224). Free concerts by high school and college groups, and sometimes by seasoned musicians, are held year-round, nearly every day at noon, and often on weekdays at 5pm as well.
- **Phillips Collection,** 1600 21st St. NW (© 202/387-2151; www.phillips collection.org). Admission of $5 gains you entry to the gallery's "Artful Evening" jazz concerts, held every Thursday from 5 to 8:30pm in the grand Music Room. Sunday afternoon concerts take place September through May in the Music Room, and are free with the price of museum admission, which is $7.50 for adults.
- **The Smithsonian** (© 202/357-2700). In addition to the Smithsonian's annual **Festival of American Folklife,** held for 2 weeks in late June to early July on the National Mall (see "Outdoor Performances," below, and the "Calendar of Events" in chapter 2 for details), individual Smithsonian museums stage assorted free entertainment year-round—see specific museum listings in chapter 7 and check out their websites.
- **Hotel Tabard Inn,** 1739 N St. NW (© 202/785-1277), and the **Four Seasons Hotel,** 2800 Pennsylvania Ave. NW (© 202/342-0444) are two hotels that provide free entertainment. Every Sunday night, from 7:30 to 10:30pm, in the lounge of the Tabard, bassist Victor Dvoskin, usually accompanied by a guitarist, plays world-class jazz for free. Head to the Garden Terrace Lounge of the Four Seasons most days between 3 and 6:30pm, for live jazz by local musicians. See website, www.dcjazz.com, for other suggestions.
- **Washington National Cathedral,** at Wisconsin and Massachusetts avenues NW (© 202/537-5757). September through July, the cathedral holds organ recitals Sundays at 5pm. Summer Festival ensemble performances take place on various days in June and July, usually at 7:30pm, but sometimes at 5pm or 11am, in the nave of the church. Once a week, year-round, the Cathedral's bell-ringers practice their craft; this event is best appreciated on the grounds of the Cathedral, not inside (see the Cathedral's outdoor performances listing, below).

OUTDOOR PERFORMANCES

Most of Washington's free outdoor performances take place in parks maintained by the **National Park Service,** which provides a complete listing of these events on its website at **www.nps.gov/ncro** (click on "Calendar of Events"). Annual highlights include:

(Many of the following events take place at the Carter Barron Amphitheatre, 4850 Colorado Ave. NW [at 16th St. and Colorado Ave. NW]; for more information about this venue, see the Carter Barron listing under "Indoor Arenas & Outdoor Pavilions.")

- The Shakespeare Theatre (© 202/547-1122) holds its annual Shakespeare Free For All for 2 weeks in June.

- The **National Symphony Orchestra** (© 202/467-4600) usually holds at least two concerts at the Carter Barron during the summer.
- The **Washington Area Music Association** (© 202/783-0360) sponsors at least two free music festivals here each year.
- *The Washington Post*'s "Weekend's Weekend" concert series stages four evenings of diverse musical entertainment—it could be alternative rock one night, and an "island jam" another night.
- The **D.C. Blues Society** (www.dcblues.org) presents its 16th annual D.C. Blues Festival in early September.
- The **National Park Service** (© 202/619-7222 or 202/426-0486) also stages its own series of Carter Barron concerts throughout the summer. They're not free, but are fairly reasonable, given the talent.
- **The National Symphony Orchestra** performs free summer concerts at 8pm on the west side of the Capitol on Memorial Day, July 4, and Labor Day. Seating is on the lawn, so bring a picnic. The music ranges from light classical to country to show tunes of the Gershwin/Rodgers and Hammerstein genre. For further information, call © **202/467-4600.**
- **Fort Dupont Park,** Minnesota Avenue SE at Randle Circle (© **202/690-5185** or 202/619-7222). On this southeast side of town, every Friday and Saturday about 8 or 8:30pm from sometime in July to the end of August, you'll hear renowned Washington blues and jazz artists doing their thing. Bring a blanket and a picnic dinner; arrive early to get a good spot on the lawn. Fort Dupont features both talented local performers and nationally known acts such as Pieces of a Dream, Jean Carne, and Roy Ayers. No tickets are required; admission is free.
- **McPherson Square,** at 15th and I streets NW, and **Farragut Square,** at 17th and K streets NW. The National Park Service (© **202/619-7222**) collaborates with local businesses to offer this series of noontime concerts that take place at two downtown locations, on Wednesday (McPherson Square) and Thursday (Farragut Square), July through August.
- **Military Concerts.** Military bands play all summer long at one of five locations in Washington, D.C.: the **Ellipse,** between 15th and 17th streets NW, south of the White House; the **Marine Barracks,** 8th and I streets SE; the **Navy Memorial Plaza,** 701 Pennsylvania Ave. NW; the **Sylvan Theater,** near 15th Street and Independence Avenue SW, at the southeastern corner of the Washington Monument grounds; and the **U.S. Capitol,** where North, South, and East Capitol Street collide. Performances take place evenings, usually around 8pm, June to Labor Day. For exact times and event details, call the individual branches: the U.S. Army Band, "Pershing's Own" (© **703/696-3399**); the U.S. Navy Band (© **202/433-2525** for a 24-hour recording, or 202/433-6090); the U.S. Marine Band, "The President's Own" (© **202/433-4011** for a 24-hour recording, or 202/433-5809); and the U.S. Air Force Band, "America's International Musical Ambassadors" (© **202/767-5658** for a 24-hour recording, or 202/767-4310). Concerts are free, but reservations may be required for the performance at the Marine Barracks.
- **Smithsonian's Festival of American Folklife,** on the Mall, between 10th and 14th streets NW (© **202/357-2700**). Now in its 38th year, the annual festival highlights the customs and cultures of selected countries and communities within particular regions in this country. The festival lasts for 5 to

10 days, always including July 4th; see "Calendar of Events" for June in chapter 2.

Other outdoor performances around town include these, not found on the National Park Service website:

- **Art Nights on the Mall.** Four Smithsonian museums—the Hirshhorn Museum and Sculpture Garden, the Freer Gallery of Art, the Sackler Gallery, and National Museum of African Art—traditionally stay open until 8pm on Thursdays in summer, and sponsor all sorts of activities between 5 and 8pm, including Latin and jazz music at the Hirshhorn, Asian music and story-telling at the Freer, poetry reading at the Sackler, and African mask-making and music at the National Museum of African Art. All are free, though some events at the Freer may require tickets. Some activities take place inside.

- **Live on Penn.** Saturdays, 4 to 10pm, July to September, an outdoor music festival takes to the street, specifically Pennsylvania Avenue, NW, between 3rd and 6th streets NW. The festival features nationally and locally promi-nent groups, from Violent Femmes, to Everclear, and includes children's activities, cultural exhibits, and local cuisine. The $3 admission benefits the Hoop Dream Scholarship Fund. © **202/969-2979;** www.liveonpenn.com.

- **National Gallery Sculpture Garden,** across 7th Street NW, from the West Wing of the National Gallery of Art, at Constitution Avenue NW (© **202/ 737-4215**). Friday evenings at 5pm, in summer, the sculpture garden and its majestic fountain are the backdrop for live jazz music by Washington's best, like the Brazilian jazz group Origem.

- **National Zoo,** 3001 Connecticut Avenue NW (© **202/673-4989**). Find Lion-Tiger Hill on Thursday evenings at 6:30pm, from late June to early August, and settle in for free "Sunset Serenades," performed by various local musicians.

- **Washington National Cathedral** grounds (see address and phone number above) are a magnificent setting from which to listen to the cathedral's weekly ringing of the bells, at about 12:30pm every Sunday, year-round, fol-lowing the 11am service; this is a carillon performance, in which 53 bells are rung in tuneful patterns. Sit here on a Tuesday evening around 7 or 7:30pm and you will hear a peal bell performance; that is, the ringing of 10 differ-ent bells by 10 different people. (This, too, is a weekly event, year-round.) For information about musical performances, call © **202/537-5757.**

- **Woodrow Wilson Plaza,** Ronald Reagan Building, 1300 Pennsylvania Ave. NW (© **202/312-1300**). Just outside the doors that lead to the DC Visi-tors Center in the Ronald Reagan Building, across from the entrance to the Federal Triangle Metro station, is this plaza that serves perfectly as a stage every weekday in summer through September. A different group performs each day, noon to 1:30pm, everything from mariachi bands to tap dancers to barbershop quartets.

2 The Performing Arts

Washington's performing arts scene has an international reputation. Almost any-thing on Broadway has either been previewed here or will eventually come here. Better yet, D.C. is home to truly excellent and renowned repertory theater troupes, and to fine ballet, opera, and symphony companies. Rock bands, head-liner comedians, and jazz/folk/gospel/R&B/alternative and other musical groups make Washington a must-stop on their tours.

THE TOP THEATERS

Arena Stage   This outpost on the unattractive Washington waterfront is worth seeking out, despite its poor location. (Dine at a downtown restaurant, then drive or take a taxi here; or you can take the Metro, but be careful walking the block or so to the theater.)

Founded by the brilliant Zelda Fichandler in 1950, the Arena Stage is home to one of the oldest acting ensembles in the nation. Several works nurtured here have moved to Broadway, and many graduates have gone on to commercial stardom, including Ned Beatty, James Earl Jones, and Jane Alexander.

Arena presents eight productions annually on two stages: the **Fichandler** (a theater-in-the-round) and the smaller, fan-shaped **Kreeger.** In addition, the Arena houses the **Old Vat,** a space used for new play readings and special productions.

The 2003–04 September-to-June season includes David Auburn's *Proof,* the Lerner & Lowe musical *Camelot,* Bertolt Brecht's *A Man's a Man, Yellowman* by Dael Orlandersmith, and Tennessee Williams's *Orpheus Descending.* The Arena Stage has always championed new plays and playwrights and is committed to producing works from America's diverse cultures, as well as to reinterpreting the works of past masters. 1101 6th St. SW (at Maine Ave.). ✆ **202/488-3300.** www.arena stage.org. Tickets $35–$58; discounts available for students, people with disabilities, groups, and senior citizens. Metro: Waterfront.

John F. Kennedy Center for the Performing Arts   This 33-year-old theater complex strives to be not just the hub of Washington's cultural and entertainment scene, but a performing arts theater for the nation. It is constantly evolving, and right now that evolution involves an immense expansion, which will add two buildings to the 8-acre plaza in front of the center, and better connect the center to the rest of the city. The center lies between the Potomac River and a crisscross of major roadways, which makes it sound like it's easily accessible when, in fact, it is not, for its location actually isolates it from the rest of town. So don't be put off by the unseemly sight of major construction equipment—it's going to be there for quite a while, a decade at least, as the expansion proceeds. The center's performances, meanwhile, continue uninterrupted.

These are top-rated performances by the best ballet, opera, jazz, modern dance, musical, and theater companies in the world. The best costs the most, and you are likely to pay more for a ticket here than at any other theater in D.C.—from $14 for a children's play to more than $280 for a box seat on a Saturday night at the opera, although most ticket prices run in the $50 to $60 range.

Tip: If you want a really good, really cheap seat in the Kennedy Center's Concert Hall, try for a chorister seat. Prices vary widely, but, to give you an idea, the National Symphony Orchestra charges $25 for these seats (orchestra seats go for about $55). Each of the 63 seats is situated right behind the stage and above the orchestra. Call the regular box office number to try and reserve one of these, which are available on a night-by-night basis, that is, you can't book a whole season's worth of chorister seats. Keep in mind, though, that you'll be as much on view as the performing musicians.

The Kennedy Center is committed to being a theater for the people, and toward that end, it continues to stage its **free concert series,** known as "Millennium Stage," which features daily performances by area musicians and sometimes national artists each evening at 6pm in the center's Grand Foyer. (You can check out broadcasts of the nightly performances on the Internet at www. kennedy-center.org/millennium.) During the summer, the Ken-Cen adds Millennium Stage performances every Wednesday at noon on the steps of the Library of Congress's Thomas Jefferson Building. The Friday "Weekend" section of the *Washington Post* lists the free performances scheduled for the coming week; the daily "Style" section lists nightly performances under "Free Events," in the "Guide to the Lively Arts" column. Also call about "pay what you can" performances, scheduled throughout the year on certain days, for certain shows.

The Kennedy Center is actually made up of six different national theaters: the Opera House, the Concert Hall, the Terrace Theater, the Eisenhower Theater, the Theater Lab, and the American Film Institute (AFI) theater. The renovation of the Opera House will be complete by February 2004, when the **Washington Opera** (www.dc-opera.org) returns to perform there. Until then, the company takes the stage at the Daughters of the American Revolution's (DAR) Constitution Hall (see description under "Smaller Auditoriums," below). The 2003–04 schedule includes productions of Verdi's *La Traviata,* Strauss's *Die Fledermas,* Bellini's *Norma,* Puccini's *Manon Lescaut,* and the East Coast premiere of André Previn's first opera, *A Streetcar Named Desire,* based on the play by Tennessee Williams. The Washington Opera's artistic director is Placido Domino, and tickets often sell out before the season begins. The **National Symphony Orchestra** presents concerts in the Concert Hall from September to June.

Among the other productions coming to one of the Kennedy Center stages in the 2003–2004 season are performances by the New York City Ballet Festival, the American Ballet Theatre, and the Dance Theatre of Harlem; the Royal Shakespeare Company's *The Taming of the Shrew;* a new Stephen Sondheim musical, *Bounce;* and *The Producers,* the new Mel Brooks musical. A highlight of the season is the Tennessee Williams Explored Festival, in which the center will stage *A Streetcar Named Desire, Cat on a Hot Tin Roof,* and *The Glass Menagerie,* and an evening of five one-act plays by the playwright, four of them world premieres; this last endeavor, called "Five by Tenn," will be produced by the Shakespeare Theatre, whose artistic director, Michael Kahn, once worked with Williams.

The **Theater Lab** continues by day as Washington's premier stage for children's theater and by night as a cabaret (now in its 17th year) hosting *Shear Madness,* a comedy whodunit (all tickets $34).

These are just a smattering of Kennedy Center offerings. 2700 F St. NW (at New Hampshire Ave. NW and Rock Creek Pkwy). ℰ 800/444-1324 or 202/467-4600 for tickets and information. www.kennedy-center.org. 50% discounts are offered (for select performances) to students, seniors 65 and over, people with permanent disabilities, enlisted military personnel, and persons with fixed low incomes (call ℰ 202/416-8340 for details). Garage parking $12. Metro: Foggy Bottom (though it's a fairly short walk, there's a free shuttle between the station and the Kennedy Center, departing every 15 min. 9:45am–midnight, Mon–Sat, noon–midnight Sun). Bus: 80 from Metro Center.

National Theatre   The luxurious Federal-style National Theatre is the oldest continuously operating theater in Washington (since 1835) and the third oldest in the nation. It's exciting just to see the stage on which Sarah Bernhardt, John Barrymore, Helen Hayes, and so many other notables have performed. The 1,672-seat National is the closest thing Washington has to a Broadway-style playhouse. The 2002–03 season hits included *42nd Street, Chicago,* and *Beauty and the Beast.* The 2003–2004 season was still being negotiated as this book was being researched.

Washington Celebrates Tennessee

If you're a fan of Tennessee Williams, you'll want to know about the astonishing number of Williams productions on stage here, from spring into summer of 2004. See individual listings in this chapter for specific theater information.

At the Kennedy Center   The Kennedy Center is hosting a "Tennessee Williams Explored" Festival, beginning in April. Here's the lineup: **Five by Tenn** (Apr 21–May 9), offers an evening of five one-act plays by Williams, four of the plays world premieres. Directing the plays will be Michael Kahn, the artistic director of The Shakespeare Theatre, here in D.C.; Kahn was also a friend and collaborator of Tennessee Williams. **A Streetcar Named Desire** (Apr 27–May 16), **Cat on a Hot Tin Roof** (June 1–20), and **The Glass Menagerie** (July 6–25), each takes its turn on the Kennedy Center stage. The Washington Opera performs the East Coast premiere of André Previn's first opera, **A Streetcar Named Desire**, based on Williams's play, sung in English, and appearing at the Opera House (May 15, 18, 21, 24, 27, 30, and June 2). Finally, June 11–13, actor Richard Thomas will star in a one-man show, "Letters from Tennessee: A Distant Country," playing Tennessee Williams as revealed through the playwright's letters.

At the Arena Stage   Coincidentally or not, this esteemed repertory theater has chosen to end its 2003–2004 season with yet another Williams play, **Orpheus Descending**, in its Kreeger Theater (May 14–June 27).

One thing that has never flagged at The National is its commitment to offering free public-service programs: Saturday-morning children's theater (puppets, clowns, magicians, dancers, and singers) and Monday-night showcases of local groups and performers September through May, plus free summer films. Call ✆ **202/783-3372** for details. 1321 Pennsylvania Ave. NW. ✆ **800/447-7400**, or 202/628-6161 to charge tickets. www.nationaltheatre.org. Tickets $30–$75; discounts available for students, seniors, military personnel, and people with disabilities. Metro: Metro Center.

Shakespeare Theatre   This is top-level theater, with superb acting. Try and snag tickets to a play here, for the productions are reliably outstanding. Season subscriptions claim many of the seats and the plays almost always sell out, so if you're interested in attending a play here, you'd better buy your tickets now. This internationally renowned classical ensemble company offers five plays, usually three Shakespearean and two modern classics, each September-to-June season. The 2003–04 season includes *Henry IV,* Parts I and II, *A Midsummer Night's Dream, Cyrano de Bergerac,* by Edmond Rostand, and Sheridan's *The Rivals.* The theater is collaborating with the Kennedy Center, during the Center's Tennessee Williams Festival (see the Kennedy Center writeup), to produce an evening of five one-act plays by Williams, four of them world premieres.

The company also offers one free-admission, 2-week run of a Shakespeare production at the Carter Barron Amphitheater in Rock Creek Park. 450 7th St. NW (between D and E sts.). ✆ **202/547-1122**. www.shakespearetheatre.org. Tickets $16–$66, $10 for standing-room tickets sold 1 hr. before sold-out performances; discounts available for students, seniors, and groups. Metro: Archives–Navy Memorial or MCI Center/Gallery Place.

SMALLER THEATERS

Some of Washington's lesser-known theaters are gaining more recognition all the time. Their productions are consistently professional, and sometimes more contemporary and innovative than those you'll find in the more acclaimed theaters. The **Source Theatre Company,** 1835 14th St. NW, between S and T streets (*C* **202/462-1073;** www.sourcetheatre.com), is Washington's major producer of new plays. Joy Zinoman, the artistic director of the **Studio Theatre,** 1333 P St. NW, at 14th Street (*C* **202/332-3300;** www.studiotheatre.org), showcases interesting contemporary plays and nurtures Washington acting talent; the 2002–03 season marked the theater's 25th anniversary. The **Woolly Mammoth Theatre Company,** in the Kennedy Center's Film Theater (*C* **202/393-3939;** www.woollymammoth.net), offers as many as six productions each year, specializing in new, offbeat, and quirky plays. (These are temporary quarters until construction of its new 250-seat state-of-the-art facility, at 7th and D streets NW, in downtown Washington, is complete—scheduled for the fall of 2004.)

In addition, I highly recommend productions staged at the **Folger Shakespeare Library,** 201 E. Capitol St. SE (*C* **202/544-7077;** www.folger.edu). Plays take place in the library's Elizabethan Theatre, which is styled after the inn-yard theater of Shakespeare's time. The theater is intimate and charming, the theater company is remarkably good, and an evening spent here guarantees an absolutely marvelous experience. The 2003–04 season brings to the stage Shakespeare's *All's Well That Ends Well; Melissa Arctic, The Winter's Tale Retold;* and *A Comedy of Errors.* The Elizabethan Theatre is also the setting for musical performances, lectures, readings, and other events.

Finally, there's **Ford's Theatre,** 511 10th St. NW, between E and F streets (*C* **202/347-4833;** www.fordstheatre.org), the actual theater where, on the evening of April 14, 1865, actor John Wilkes Booth shot President Lincoln. Though popular among Washingtonians for its annual holiday performance of Dickens's *A Christmas Carol,* Ford's stages generally mediocre presentations, usually intertwined with American history themes.

INDOOR ARENAS & OUTDOOR PAVILIONS

When Madonna, U2, the Rolling Stones, or the Dixie Chicks come to town, they usually play at one of the huge indoor or outdoor arenas. The 20,600-seat **MCI Center,** 601 F St. NW, where it meets 7th Street (*C* **202/628-3200;** www.mcicenter.com), in the center of downtown, hosts plenty of concerts and also is Washington's premier indoor sports arena (home to the NBA Wizards, the WNBA Mystics, the NHL Capitals, and Georgetown NCAA basketball). Less convenient and smaller is the 10,000-seat **Patriot Center** at George Mason University, 4500 Patriot Circle, Fairfax, VA (*C* **703/993-3000;** www.patriotcenter.com).

Largest of the outdoor venues is the **Robert F. Kennedy Memorial Stadium,** 2400 E. Capitol St. SE (*C* **202/547-9077;** www.dcsportscommission.com), the erstwhile home of the Washington Redskins (they now play at the new FedEx Field stadium in Landover, Maryland). The stadium continues as an outdoor event facility, packing crowds of 55,000-plus into its seats for D.C. United (men's) and Washington Freedom (women's) soccer games, concerts, and all-day music festivals.

The **Nissan Pavilion at Stone Ridge,** 7800 Cellar Door Dr., off Wellington Road in Bristow, VA (*C* **800/455-8999** or 703/754-6400 for concert information; www.nissanpavilion.com), has a capacity of 22,500 seats (10,000 under the roof, the remainder on the lawn), is 25 minutes from the Beltway, and features major acts varying from classical to country. The action is enhanced by giant video screens inside the pavilion and on the lawn.

During the summer, there's quality entertainment almost nightly at the **Merriweather Post Pavilion,** 10475 Little Patuxent Pkwy., just off Route 29 in Columbia, MD (© **301/596-0660;** www.mppconcerts.com), about a 40-minute drive from downtown D.C. There's reserved seating in the open-air pavilion (overhead protection provided in case of rain) and general-admission seating on the lawn (no refunds for rain) to see such performers as Nine Inch Nails, Joni Mitchell, Blink 182, The Cure, No Doubt, Jimmy Buffett, and Britney Spears. If you choose the lawn seating, bring blankets and picnic fare (beverages must be bought on the premises).

My favorite summer setting for music is **Wolf Trap Farm Park for the Performing Arts,** 1551 Trap Rd., Vienna, VA (© **703/255-1860;** www.wolftrap. org). The country's only national park devoted to the performing arts, Wolf Trap, 30 minutes by car from downtown D.C., offers performances by the National Symphony Orchestra (it's their summer home), and has hosted Lucinda Williams, Shawn Colvin, Lyle Lovett, The Temptations, Ani DiFranco, and many others. Performances take place in the 7,000-seat Filene Center, about half of which is under the open sky. You can also buy cheaper lawn seats on the hill, which is sometimes the nicest way to go. If you do, arrive early (the lawn opens 90 min. before the performance) and bring a blanket and a picnic dinner—it's a tradition. Wolf Trap also hosts a number of very popular **festivals.** The park features a daylong Irish music festival in May; the Louisiana Swamp Romp Cajun Festival and a weekend of jazz and blues in June; and the International Children's Festival each September.

The **Carter Barron Amphitheater,** 16th Street and Colorado Avenue NW (© **202/426-0486**), way out 16th Street, is in Rock Creek Park, close to the Maryland border. This is the area's smallest outdoor venue, with 4,250 seats. Summer performances include a range of gospel, blues, and classical entertainment. The shows are usually free, but tickets are required. You can always count on Shakespeare: The **Shakespeare Theatre Free For All** takes place at the Carter Barron usually for 2 weeks in June, Tuesday through Sunday evenings; the free tickets are available the day of performance only, on a first-come, first-served basis (call © **202/334-4790** for details). The 2003 Free For All featured *Hamlet.*

SMALLER AUDITORIUMS

A handful of auditoriums in Washington are really fine places to catch a performance. The smallest, most clublike auditorium is the 350-seat **Barns of Wolf Trap,** 1635 Trap Rd., Vienna, VA (© **703/938-2404**), which is just up the road from Wolf Trap Farm Park (see above). From late fall until May, the schedule features jazz, pop, country, folk, bluegrass, and chamber musicians. This is the summer home of the Wolf Trap Opera Company, which is the only entertainment booked here May through September.

DAR Constitution Hall, on 18th Street NW, between C and D streets (© **202/628-4780;** www.dar.org), is housed within a beautiful turn-of-the-20th-century beaux arts–style building and seats 3,746. Its excellent acoustics have supported an eclectic (and I mean eclectic) group of performers: Sting, the Buena Vista Social Club, John Hiatt, the Count Basie Orchestra, the Los Angeles Philharmonic, Lil Bow Wow, Ray Charles, Trisha Yearwood, The Storkes, and the *O Brother Where Art Thou?* tour.

Fun Fact **Washington Walk of Fame**

If you're going to the Warner Theatre, or are walking by (it's in the heart of downtown), be sure to check out the sidewalk in front of its 13th Street entrance, between E Street and Pennsylvania Avenue NW. Entertainers who have performed here since the theater reopened in 1992 have signed stone "pavers," and these individual blocks, bearing both a signature and a gold star, are on view in the concrete walkway. Look for the signatures of Frank Sinatra, Tony Bennett, Liza Minnelli, Shirley MacLaine, David Copperfield, B. B. King, Mikhail Baryshnikov, Chris Rock, and about 100 others. You'll notice that some performers added their own flourishes: Bonnie Raitt wrote "No Nukes" on hers; Tommy Tune imprinted the soles of his tap shoes in the pavement.

In the heart of happening U Street, the **Lincoln Theatre,** 1215 U St. NW (*C* **202/328-6000;** www.thelincolntheatre.org), was once a movie theater, vaudeville house, and nightclub featuring black stars like Louis Armstrong and Cab Calloway. The theater closed in the 1970s and reopened in 1994 after a renovation restored it to its former elegance. Today the theater books jazz, R&B, gospel, and comedy acts, and events like the D.C. Film Festival.

At the 1,500-seat **Lisner Auditorium,** on the campus of George Washington University, 21st and H streets NW (*C* **202/994-6800;** www.lisner.org), you always feel close to the stage. Bookings sometimes include musical groups like Siouxsie and the Banshees, comedians like "Weird Al" Yankovic, monologist Spalding Gray, and children's entertainers like Raffi, but are mostly cultural shows—everything from a Pakistani rock group to the Washington Revels' annual romp at Christmas.

The **Warner Theatre,** 1299 Pennsylvania Ave. NW, with the entrance on 13th Street, between E and F streets (*C* **202/783-4000;** www.warnertheatre.com), opened in 1924 as the Earle Theatre (a movie/vaudeville palace) and was restored to its original, neoclassical-style appearance in 1992 at a cost of $10 million. It's worth coming by just to see its ornately detailed interior. The 2,000-seat auditorium offers year-round entertainment, alternating dance performances (from Baryshnikov to the Washington Ballet's Christmas performance of *The Nutcracker*) and Broadway/off-Broadway shows (*Cabaret, Lord of the Dance, Godspell*) with headliner entertainment (Sheryl Crow, Margaret Cho, Wynton Marsalis).

3 The Club & Music Scene

If you're looking for a more interactive, tuneful night on the town, Washington offers hip jazz clubs, lively bars, warehouse ballrooms, places where you sit back and listen, places where you can get up and dance, even a roadhouse or two. If you're looking for comic relief, Washington can take care of that, too (the pickings are few but good).

Many nightspots wear multiple hats. For example, the Black Cat is a bar and a dance club, offering food and sometimes poetry readings. So I've listed each nightspot according to the type of music it features. The details are in the description.

The best nightlife districts are Adams-Morgan; the area around U and 14th streets NW, a still-developing district, where it's best to stay on or close to U Street; the 7th Street NW corridor near Chinatown and the MCI Center; and Georgetown. If you don't mind venturing into the suburbs, you should know about Arlington's hot spots (see the "Arlington Row" box on p. 268). As a rule, while club-hopping—even in Georgetown—stick to the major thoroughfares and steer clear of deserted side streets.

The best source of information about what's doing at bars and clubs is *City Paper,* available free at bookstores, movie theaters, drugstores, and other locations.

Washington's clubs and bars tend to keep their own hours; best to call ahead to make sure the place you're headed is open.

COMEDY

In addition to these two comedy venues, the **Warner Theatre** (see "Smaller Auditoriums," above) also features big-name comedians from time to time.

The Capitol Steps *(Moments*   This musical political satire troupe is made up of former Congressional staffers, equal-opportunity spoofers all, who poke endless fun through song and skits at politicians on both sides of the aisle, and at government goings-on in general. You might catch former president Clinton crooning "Livin' Libido Loca," or U.S. Attorney General John Ashcroft bellowing "Glory Glory Paranoia." Washingtonians have been fans since the Steps got started in 1981. Since then, the troupe has performed more than 5,000 shows and released more than 23 albums, including the latest, "Between Iraq and a Hard Place." Shows take place in the Amphitheater, on the concourse level of the Ronald Reagan Building and International Trade Center, at 7:30pm Friday and Saturday. 1300 Pennsylvania Ave. NW (in the Ronald Reagan Bldg.). ℰ **202/408-8736.** www. capsteps.com. Tickets $32. Metro: Federal Triangle.

The Improv   The Improv features top performers on the national comedy club circuit as well as comic plays and one-person shows. *Saturday Night Live* performers David Spade, Chris Rock, and Adam Sandler have all played here, as have comedy bigs Ellen DeGeneres, Jerry Seinfeld, and Robin Williams. Shows are about 1½ hours long and include three comics (an emcee, a feature act, and a headliner). Show times are 8:30pm Sunday through Thursday, 8 and 10:30pm on Friday and Saturday. The best way to snag a good seat is to have dinner here (make reservations), which allows you to enter the club as early as 7pm Sunday through Thursday or after 6:30pm Friday and Saturday. The Friday and Saturday 10:30pm show serves drinks and appetizers only. Dinner entrees (nothing higher than $9.95) include prime rib, sandwiches, and pasta selections. You must be 18 to get in. 1140 Connecticut Ave. NW (between L and M sts.). ℰ **202/296-7008.** www.dcimprov.com. Cover $12 Sun–Thurs, $15 Fri–Sat, plus a 2-drink minimum (waived if you dine). Metro: Farragut North.

POP/ROCK/RAVE/ALTERNATIVE

The Birchmere Music Hall and Bandstand   Worth the cab fare from downtown, if you're a fan of live music by varied, stellar performers, such as Garth Brooks, Jonatha Brooke, Jerry Jeff Walker, Crash Test Dummies, Shawn Colvin, Joe Sample, John Hiatt—I could go on and on. The Birchmere is unique in the area for providing a comfortable and relatively small (500-seat) setting, where you sit and listen to the music (there's not a bad seat in the house) and order food and drinks. The Birchmere got started more than 25 years ago, when it booked mostly country singers. The place has expanded over the years

---

Tips **Metro Takes You There**

Recognizing that Washingtonians are keeping later hours these days, Metro not only keeps its trains running until 3am on weekends, but has also inaugurated special shuttle service to Adams-Morgan (home to lots of nightclubs, but no Metro stations).

Here's what you do: Take the Metro to the Red Line's Woodley Park–Adams-Morgan Station or to the Green Line's U St.–Cardozo Station, and hop on the no. 98 Adams-Morgan–U St. Link Shuttle, which travels through Adams-Morgan, between these two stations, after 6pm daily, except on Saturday, when service starts at 10am. The U Link Shuttle operates every 15 minutes and costs only 35¢ with a transfer from Metrorail, or $1.20 without a transfer.

---

and so has its repertoire; there are still many country and bluegrass artists, but also folk, jazz, rock, gospel, and alternative musicians. The menu tends toward American favorites, such as nachos and burgers; I can recommend the pulled-pork barbecue sandwich and the chili. 3701 Mount Vernon Ave., Alexandria, VA. ℂ 703/549-7500. www.birchmere.com. Ticket prices range from $17–$45. Take a taxi or drive.

Black Cat This comfortable, low-key club draws a black-clad crowd to its concert hall, which features national, international, and local indie and alternative groups. The place is made for dancing, accommodating more than 600 people. Adjoining the hall is the Red Room Bar, a large, funky, red-walled living-roomy lounge with booths, tables, a red-leather sofa, pinball machines, a pool table, and a jukebox stocked with a really eclectic collection. A college crowd collects on weekends, but you can count on seeing a 20- to 30-something bunch here most nights, including members of various bands who like to stop in for a drink. Black Cat also hosts film screenings, poetry readings, and other quiet forms of entertainment in its ground floor room called "Backstage," and serves vegetarian food in its smoke-free cafe. Say hello to owner Dante Ferrando while you're here and to his dad, Bobby, who mans the kitchen. The Red Room Bar is open until 2am Sunday through Thursday, and until 3am Friday and Saturday. Concerts take place 4 or 5 nights a week, beginning at about 8:30pm (call for details). 1811 14th St. NW (between S and T sts.). ℂ 202/667-7960. www.blackcatdc.com. Cover $5–$20 for concerts; no cover in the Red Room Bar. Metro: U St.–Cardozo.

Eighteenth Street Lounge This place maintains its "hot" status. First you have to find it, and then you have to convince the bouncer to let you in. So here's what you need to know: Look for the mattress shop south of Dupont Circle, then look up. "ESL" (as those in the know call it) sits above the shop, and hangs only a tiny plaque at street level to advertise its existence. Wear something exotic and sexy. If you pass inspection, you may be surprised to find yourself in a restored mansion (Teddy Roosevelt once lived here) with fireplaces, high ceilings, and a deck out back. Or maybe you'll just get right out there on the hardwood floors to dance to acid jazz, hip-hop, reggae, or Latin jazz tunes spun by a deejay. 1212 18th St. NW. ℂ 202/466-3922. Cover $10–$20 Tues–Sat. Metro: Dupont Circle or Farragut North.

5 This small, three-level space is a reincarnation of what used to be the Garage, a live-music venue. 5 is a deejay-driven dance club, aiming to capture some of the late-night crowd who are too wired to go home. Open Wednesday through

Sunday nights, with music starting after 10pm. 1214-B 18th St. NW. © 202/331-7123. Cover $5–$15. Metro: Dupont Circle or Farragut North.

Nation   This concert/dance space has separate areas for live music, dance music, and lounging, and a three-tiered outdoor patio. This is primarily a Gen-X mecca (though some performers attract an older crowd). It's also D.C.'s largest club, accommodating about 2,000 people a night. The Pet Shop Boys and Pink are among the groups to have performed here recently. But Nation is best known for its dance parties. Thursday is Goth night for those addicted to psytrance and dark-wave music, black leather and eyeliner. Saturday is given over to a gay dance party called "Velvet." The game room and state-of-the-art lighting/laser/sound systems are a plus. The Nation is in a pretty bad neighborhood, so make sure you have good directions to get there; the building itself is very secure. 1015 Half St. SE (at K St.). © 202/554-1500. www.nationdc.com. Cover $7–$30. Metro: Navy Yard.

9:30 Club   Housed in yet another converted warehouse, this major live-music venue hosts frequent record-company parties and features a wide range of top performers. You might catch Sheryl Crow, Simple Minds, The Clarks, Luna, The Tragically Hip, Lucinda Williams, or even Tony Bennett. It's only open when there's a show on, which is almost every night (but call ahead), and, obviously, the crowd (as many as 1,200) varies with the performer. The sound system is state of the art and the sight lines are excellent. There are four bars: two on the main dance-floor level, one in the upstairs VIP room (anyone is welcome here unless the room is being used for a private party), and another in the distressed-looking cellar. The 9:30 Club is a standup place, literally—there are few seats. 815 V St. NW (at Vermont Ave.). © 202/393-0930. www.930.com. Metro: U St.–Cardozo, 10th St. exit.

Platinum   Housed in a great old building that still has its original marble floor, sweeping staircase, and high ceilings, this nightclub is the exclusive domain of the young and good-looking who like to dance. Music is described as progressive, but it's really just contemporary disco played by deejays. Four levels, three dance floors, a VIP lounge, smoke machines, balconies, high-tech sound systems—it's all here. 915 F St. NW. © 202/393-3555. www.platinumclubdc.com. Cover $10, $15 after midnight Sat. Metro: MCI Center–Gallery Place.

Polly Esther's   This is a three-dance-clubs-in-one emporium with '70s disco music (think the Village People, ABBA, the BeeGees) blaring from the sound system on the "Polly Esther's" dance floor, '80s tunes by artists like Madonna and Prince playing in the "Culture Club," and current radio hits blasting throughout "Club Expo." Decor for each floor matches the music of that era, so, for instance, you'll see such artifacts as a John Travolta memorial and Brady Bunch memorabilia in the Polly Esther's club. Open Thursday through Saturday. 605 12th St. NW. © 202/737-1970. www.pollyesthers.com. Cover $7 Thurs, $8 Fri, $10 Sat. Metro: Metro Center.

State Theatre   This is another club that's located outside the city ("7 minutes from Key Bridge") and not near a Metro station, but it offers reasonably priced live shows featuring great local and national bands (and lots of names from the past, such as Jefferson Starship and Dave Mason). This relatively small hall (holds 800) was once a movie house, and its renovation has endowed it with a superb sound system and good sightlines. The theater has a dance floor, and seats 160 at tables and another 200 theater style in the balcony, with everyone else standing. It's first-come, first-served for the seats, so if you really want one, get here by the time the box office opens at 6:30pm, if not earlier. The State offers a full menu and bar; table dwellers pay an extra $7.50 minimum per person for food. Most people don't mind standing, since the music featured is pretty danceable. Dr. John, Marcia Ball, Beausoleil, The Radiators, and Blame It on Jane are some of the acts you might catch here. 220 N. Washington St., Falls Church, VA. © 703/237-0300. www.thestatetheatre.com. Tickets cost anywhere from $11–$33, depending on the act. Metro: East Falls Church, with a 4-min. cab ride from there.

2:K:9   Not far from the 9:30 Club is this huge and grandiose two-level nightspot with a concrete dance floor, a VIP lounge, two raised cages where women dancers undulate, a bar, and a deejay booth. And that's just the first floor. The second floor features live acts and fake snow-generating machines. If it sounds all too Studio 54-ish, it may be because one of that legendary club's designers had a hand in the design here. Put on your funkiest outfit to dance to hip-hop, techno beats, and international sounds. Open Thursday through Saturday. 2009 8th St. NW. © 202/667-7750. Cover $10–$15 after 9pm. Metro: U St.–Cardozo.

JAZZ & BLUES

A calendar of jazz gigs for these and other clubs is posted at **www.dcjazz.com**, including free performances, such as those at the **Four Seasons Garden Terrace Lounge,** 2800 Pennsylvania Ave. NW (© **202/342-0444**), where a pianist plays jazz standards in the late afternoon.

Blues Alley   Blues Alley, in Georgetown, has been Washington's top jazz club since 1965, featuring such artists as Nancy Wilson, McCoy Tyner, Sonny Rollins, Wynton Marsalis, Rachelle Ferrell, and Maynard Ferguson. There are usually two shows nightly at 8 and 10pm; some performers also do midnight shows on weekends. Reservations are essential (call after noon); since seating is on a first-come, first-served basis, it's best to arrive no later than 7pm and have dinner. Entrees on the steak and Creole seafood menu are in the $17 to $23 range, snacks and sandwiches are $5.25 to $10, and drinks are $5.35 to $9. The decor is classic jazz club: exposed brick walls, beamed ceiling, and small, candlelit tables. Sometimes well-known visiting musicians get up and jam with performers. 1073 Wisconsin Ave. NW (in an alley below M St.). © **202/337-4141.** www.bluesalley.com. Cover $16–$40, plus $7 food or drink minimum, plus $1.75 surcharge. Metro: Foggy Bottom, then take the Georgetown Metro Connection Shuttle.

Bohemian Caverns   Rising from the ashes on the very spot where jazz greats such as Duke Ellington, Billie Holiday, and so many others performed decades ago, Bohemian Caverns hopes to establish that same presence and host today's jazz stars. The club's decor is cavelike, as it was in the '20s. Musicians you might catch here include Shirley Horn, Nap Turner, and Esther Williams. The Caverns is also a restaurant, whose entrees are named after jazz legends and range in price from $7 to $19. You should dress up to come here. 2001 11th St. NW (at U St). © **202/299-0801.** Cover Usually $10–$20. Metro: U St.–Cardozo.

Columbia Station *Value*   This fairly intimate club in Adams-Morgan showcases live blues and jazz nightly. The performers are pretty good, which is amazing, considering there's no cover. Columbia Station is also a bar/restaurant, with the kitchen usually open until midnight, serving pastas, seafood, and Cajun-influenced cuisine. 2325 18th St. NW. © **202/462-6040.** No cover. Metro: U St.–Cardozo or Woodley Park–Zoo–Adams-Morgan and catch the U Link Shuttle.

Madam's Organ Restaurant and Bar *Finds*   This beloved Adams-Morgan hangout fulfills owner Bill Duggan's definition of a good bar: great sounds and

Late-Night Bites

If your stomach is grumbling after the show is over, the dancing has ended, or the bar has closed, you can always get a meal at one of a growing number of late-night or all-night eateries.

In Georgetown, the **Bistro Francais,** 3128 M St. NW (② **202/338-3830**), has been feeding night owls for years; it even draws some of the area's top chefs after their own establishments close. Open until 4am Friday and Saturday, until 3am every other night, the Bistro is thoroughly French, serving steak *frites,* omelets, and pâtés.

On U Street, **Ben's Chili Bowl,** 1213 U St. NW (② **202/667-0909**), serves up chili dogs, turkey subs, and cheese fries until 4am on Friday and Saturday nights.

In Adams-Morgan one all-night dining option is the **Diner,** 2453 18th St. NW (② **202/232-8800**), which serves some typical (eggs and coffee, grilled cheese) and not-so-typical (a grilled fresh salmon club sandwich) diner grub.

Finally, in Dupont Circle, stop in at **Kramerbooks & Afterwords Café,** 1517 Connecticut Ave. NW (② **202/387-1400**), for big servings of everything, from quesadillas to french fries to French toast. The bookstore stays open all night on weekends, and so does its kitchen.

---

sweaty people. The great sounds feature One Night Stand, a jazz group, on Monday; bluesman Ben Andrews on Tuesday; bluegrass with Bob Perilla and the Big Hillbilly Bluegrass Band on Wednesday; and the salsa sounds of Patrick Alban and Noche Latina on Thursday, which is also Ladies' Night. On Friday and Saturday nights, regional blues groups pack the place. The club includes a wide-open bar decorated eclectically with a 150-year-old gilded mirror, stuffed fish and animal heads, and paintings of nudes. The second-floor bar is called Big Daddy's Love Lounge & Pick-Up Joint, which tells you everything you need to know. Other points to note: You can play darts, and redheads pay half-price for drinks. For what it's worth, *Playboy's* May 2000 issue named Madam's Organ one of the 25 best bars in America. Food is served, but I'd eat elsewhere. 2461 18th St. NW. ② 202/667-5370. www.madamsorgan.com. Cover $3–$7. Metro: U St.–Cardozo or Woodley Park–Zoo–Adams-Morgan and catch the Adams-Morgan/U St. Link Shuttle.

Mr. Henry's Capitol Hill   Almost every Friday night, at 8:30pm, Mr. Henry's features a jazz group—maybe the Kevin Cordt Quartet—who play on the second floor of this cozy restaurant. There's no cover, but it's expected that you'll order something off the menu (perhaps a burger or gumbo). Mr. Henry's has been around for at least 30 years and has always attracted a gay and lesbian clientele, though it's a comfortable place for everyone. 601 Pennsylvania Ave. SE. ② 202/ 546-8412. No cover, but $8 minimum food/drink charge. Metro: Eastern Market.

Twins Lounge   In mid-June 2001, Twins moved from its longtime location on the outskirts of town to this much more vital area. This intimate jazz club offers live music nearly every night—it's closed on Monday. On weeknights, you'll hear local artists (open mike on Wed); weekends are reserved for out-of-town acts, such as Bobby Watson, Gil Scott Heron, and James William. Sunday night is a weekly jam session attended by musicians from all over town. The menu features American, Ethiopian, and Caribbean dishes. The age group of the crowd varies. 1344 U St. NW. ℂ 202/234-0072. www.twinsjazz.com. Cover $10–$20. Metro: U St.–Cardozo.

Utopia   Unlike most music bars, the arty New York/SoHo–style Utopia is serious about its restaurant operation. A moderately priced international menu features entrees ranging from lamb couscous to blackened shrimp with Creole cream sauce, not to mention pastas and filet mignon with béarnaise sauce. There's also an interesting wine list and a large selection of beers and single-malt scotches. The setting is cozy and candlelit, with walls used for a changing art gallery show (the bold, colorful paintings in the front room are by Moroccan owner Jamal Sahri). The eclectic crowd here varies with the music, ranging from early 20s to about 35, for the most part, including South Americans and Europeans. There's live music each night it's open, with Thursday always featuring live Brazilian jazz and Wednesday the bluesy jazz singer Pam Bricker. There's no real dance floor, but people find odd spaces to move to the tunes. 1418 U St. NW (at 14th St.). ℂ 202/483-7669. No cover, but $15 per person minimum drink/food charge. Metro: U St.–Cardozo.

INTERNATIONAL SOUNDS

Chi Cha Lounge *Finds*   You can sit around on couches, eat Ecuadoran tapas, and listen to live Latin music, which is featured Sunday through Thursday. Or you can sit around on couches and smoke Arabic tobacco through a 3-foot-high arguileh pipe. Or you can just sit around. This is a popular neighborhood place. 1624 U St. NW. ℂ 202/234-8400 (after 4:30pm). Cover $15 (minimum). Metro: U St.–Cardozo.

Habana Village   This three-story nightclub has a bar/restaurant on the first floor, a bar/dance floor with deejay on the second level, and a live music space on the third floor. Salsa and merengue lessons are given Wednesday through Saturday evenings, $10 per lesson. Otherwise, a deejay or live band plays danceable Latin jazz tunes. 1834 Columbia Rd. NW. ℂ 202/462-6310. Cover $5 Fri–Sat after 9:30pm (no cover for women). Metro: U St.–Cardozo or Woodley Park–Zoo–Adams-Morgan, and catch the Adams-Morgan/U St. Link Shuttle.

Latin Jazz Alley   This Adams-Morgan hot spot is another place to get in on Washington's Latin scene. At the Alley, you can learn to salsa and merengue Wednesday through Saturday nights; each lesson is $5 for beginners, $10 for intermediate dancers. The club features live Brazilian music Thursday nights, 10pm to 1am. Friday and Saturday nights, from about 10pm to 2am, a deejay plays Latin jazz. Dinner is served until midnight. 1721 Columbia Rd. NW, on the 2nd floor of the El Migueleno Cafe. ℂ 202/328-6190. $5–$10 for salsa dance lessons; 2-drink minimum. Metro: U St.–Cardozo or Woodley Park–Zoo–Adams-Morgan and catch the Adams-Morgan/U St. Link Shuttle.

Zanzibar on the Waterfront   One day Washington will get its act together and develop the waterfront neighborhood in which you find Zanzibar. In the meantime, this area is pretty deserted at night, except for a handful of restaurants and Arena Stage. It really doesn't matter, though, because inside the nightclub you're looking out at the Potomac. Yes, this is a club with actual windows. In keeping with current trends, Zanzibar has lots of couches and chairs arranged just so. A Caribbean and African menu is available, and you can dine while listening to both live and deejay music. Open Wednesday through Sunday, Zanzibar offers something different each night, from jazz and blues to oldies. Wednesday is salsa night, with free lessons from 7 to 8pm, though a cover still applies: $5 to get in before 10pm and $10 after An international crowd gathers here to dance or just hang out. 700 Water St. SW. ☎ 202/554-9100. www.zanzibar-otw.com. Cover typically $10 (more for live shows). Metro: Waterfront.

GAY CLUBS

Dupont Circle is the gay hub of Washington, D.C., with at least 10 gay bars within easy walking distance of one another. Here are two from that neighborhood and one located near the White House; also refer back to **Nation** (p. 260), whose Saturday night "Velvet" party is a gay event, and to **Mr. Henry's Capitol Hill** (p. 262), whose live jazz on Friday night pleases every persuasion, though the restaurant itself has long been a popular spot for gays and lesbians.

Apex Twenty-eight years old and still going strong, Apex (used to be called "Badlands") is a favorite dance club for gay men. In addition to the parquet dance floor in the main room, the club has at least six bars throughout the first level. Upstairs is the Annex bar/lounge/pool hall, and a show room where karaoke performers commandeer the mike Friday night. 1415 22nd St. NW, near P St. ☎ 202/296-0505. www.badlandsdc.com. Sometimes a cover of $3–$10, depending on the event. Metro: Dupont Circle.

Hung Jury For the D.C. lesbian insider. Though the address is H Street, you reach this club via an alley off 19th Street. To enter the blue door, you must be a woman or be accompanied by a woman, but Hung Jury welcomes everyone— gays, straights, men, and women. Inside the club is a large dance floor, two bars, a lounge, and a pool table. Open Friday and Saturday nights. 1819 H St. NW. ☎ 202/ 785-8181. Cover $5–$10. Metro: Farragut West.

J.R.'s Bar and Grill This casual and intimate all-male Dupont Circle club draws a crowd that is friendly, upscale, and very attractive. The interior—not that you'll be able to see much of it, because J.R.'s is always sardine-packed—has a 20-foot-high pressed-tin ceiling and exposed brick walls hung with neon beer signs. The big screen over the bar area is used to air music videos, showbiz sing-alongs, and favorite TV shows. Thursday is all-you-can-drink for $8 from 5 to 8pm; at midnight, you get free shots. The balcony, with pool tables, is a little more laid back. Food is served daily, until 5pm Sunday and until 7pm all other days. 1519 17th St. NW (between P and Q sts.). ☎ 202/328-0090. www.jrsdc.com. No cover. Metro: Dupont Circle.

4 The Bar Scene

Washington has a thriving and varied bar scene. But just when you think you know all the hot spots, a spate of new ones pop up. Travel the triangle formed by the intersections of Connecticut Avenue, 18th Street, and M Street, in the Dupont Circle neighborhood, and you'll find the latest bunch. (The triangle is also a nightclub mecca—see the writeups for the Eighteenth Street Lounge and 5, in "The Club & Music Scene" section of this chapter.)

If you want a convivial atmosphere and decent grub, try establishments that are equal parts restaurant and bar. Refer to chapter 6 for details about **Clyde's of Georgetown, Old Ebbitt Grill, Red Sage Border Café,** and **Old Glory Barbecue.**

Bar Rouge Hopping, popping Bar Rouge lies just inside the Hotel Rouge (see chapter 5), but also has its own entrance from the street—you must pass under the watchful eyes of the stone Venuses arrayed in front to reach it. As acid jazz or modern international music pulses throughout the narrow room, a large flat-screen monitor on the back wall of the bar presents evolving visions of flowers blooming, snow falling, and other photographically engineered scenes. The place is full of attitude-swaggering patrons tossing back drinks with names like the Brigitte Bardot Martini. A lucky few have snagged seats on the white leather-cushioned barstools at the deep red mahogany bar. Others lounge on the 20-foot-long tufted banquette and munch on little dishes of scallop ceviche sopapillas, roasted pumpkin ravioli, and other Latin-inspired tastings served by waitresses in patent leather go-go boots and seductive black attire. Bar Rouge aims to be a scene, and succeeds. But be forewarned: If it looks crowded, you'll probably want to go elsewhere. 1315 16th St. NW (at Massachusetts Ave. and Scott Circle). ⓒ 202/232-8000. Metro: Dupont Circle.

Big Hunt This casual and comfy Dupont Circle hangout for the 20- to 30-something crowd bills itself as a "happy hunting ground for humans" (read: meat market). It has a kind of *Raiders of the Lost Ark*/jungle theme. A downstairs room (where music is the loudest) is adorned with exotic travel posters and animal skins; another area has leopard skin-patterned booths under canvas tenting. Amusing murals grace the balcony level, which adjoins a room with pool tables. The candlelit basement is the spot for quiet conversation. The menu offers typical bar food, and the bar offers close to 30 beers on tap, most of them microbrews. An outdoor patio lies off the back pool room.

Note: This place and the Lucky Bar might be the perfect antidotes to their exclusive neighbors down the block, the Eighteenth Street Lounge, Dragonfly, and MCCXXIII. If you're rejected there, forget about it and come here. 1345 Connecticut Ave. NW (between N St. and Dupont Circle). ⓒ 202/785-2333. Metro: Dupont Circle.

Brickskeller *Value* If you like beer and you like choices, head for Brickskeller, which has been around for nearly 40 years and offers about 800 beers from around the world. If you can't make up your mind, ask one of the waiters, who tend to be knowledgeable about the brews. The tavern draws students, college professors, embassy types, and people from the neighborhood. Brickskeller is a series of interconnecting rooms filled with gingham tableclothed tables; upstairs rooms are open only weekend nights. The food is generally okay—and the burgers are more than okay, especially the excellent Brickburger, topped with bacon, salami, onion, and cheese. 1523 22nd St. NW. ⓒ 202/293-1885. No cover. Metro: Dupont Circle or Foggy Bottom.

Cosi Popular from the start, when it was called "XandO" (pronounced "zando"), Cosi by any name is a welcoming place in the morning for a coffee drink, and even more inviting for a cocktail later in the day. Men: You'll see a lot of cute women hanging out here, drawn perhaps by the make-your-own s'mores and other delicious desserts. Cosi also serves sandwiches and soups. The music is loud; the decor a cross between bar and living room. 1350 Connecticut Ave. NW ⓒ 202/296-9341. Metro: Dupont Circle, 19th St. exit. Other locations include those at 1647 20th St. NW, at Connecticut Ave. NW ((ⓒ 202/332-6364), and 301 Pennsylvania Ave. SE ((ⓒ 202/546-3345).

Dragonfly Expect to wait in line to get in here and the other hip clubs along this stretch of Connecticut Avenue. Dragonfly is a club, with music playing, white walls glowing, white-leather chairs beckoning, and people in black vogue-ing. And Dragonfly is a restaurant, with serious aspirations to please sushi-lovers. 1215 Connecticut Ave. NW. ⓒ 202/331-1775. Metro: Dupont Circle or Farragut North.

Value Cheap Eats: Happy Hours to Write Home About

Even the diviest of bars puts out some free nibbles to complement your drink—peanuts or pretzels at the very least. And good-value promotions are increasingly popular at area bars and nightclubs, such as **Whitlow's on Wilson** in Arlington (see the "Arlington Row" box on p. 268), where you can chow down on a half-price burger every Monday night. A step above these are certain fine restaurants and hotels around town that set out gourmet food during happy hour, either for free or an astonishingly low price. Here are three that even Washingtonians may not know about:

In the bar area only, **McCormick & Schmick's,** 1652 K St. NW, at the corner of 17th Street NW (℃ **202/861-2233**), offers a choice of giant burger, fried calamari, quesadillas, fish tacos, and more, for only $1.95 each. The offer is good Monday through Friday from 3:30 to 6:30pm and 10:30pm to midnight. Friendly bartenders make you feel at home as they concoct mixed drinks with juice they squeeze right at the bar (the drinks, alas, are not discounted).

Teaism Penn Quarter, 400 8th St. NW (℃ **202/638-6010**), which is near the MCI Center, the FBI Building, the National Gallery, and nightspots, features happy hour Thursday and Friday from 5:30 to 7:30pm, with free hors d'oeuvres like Thai chicken and Indian curries, Asian noodle salads, sticky white rice, green salad—make a meal of it! Drinks are not discounted, but they are unusual: sakes, Asian beers, gingery margaritas, and the like.

The clubby, mahogany-paneled **Town and Country Lounge,** in the Renaissance Mayflower Hotel, 1127 Connecticut Ave. NW (℃ **202/347-3000**), is the setting weeknights from 5:30 to 7:30pm for complimentary cocktail-hour hors d'oeuvres that change from night to night: slices of roast beef on toasts, chicken/beef fajitas, pastas, and so on. Here, you also have the pleasure of watching the personable bartender Sambonn Lek at work, whether mixing drinks, performing magic tricks, or matchmaking. Drinks are regular price.

The Dubliner   This is your typical old Irish pub, the port you can blow into in any storm, personal or weather-related. It's got the dark-wood paneling and tables, the etched- and stained-glass windows, an Irish-accented staff from time to time, and, most importantly, the Auld Dubliner Amber Ale. You'll probably want to stick to drinks here, but you can grab a burger, grilled chicken sandwich, or roast duck salad; the kitchen is open until 1am. The Dubliner is frequented by Capitol Hill staffers and journalists who cover the Hill. Irish music groups play nightly. In the Phoenix Park Hotel, 520 N. Capitol St. NW, with its own entrance on F St. NW. ℃ 202/737-3773. Metro: Union Station.

ESPN Zone   This is not a date place, unless your date happens to be Anna Kournikova. It's three levels of sports mania, in the form of interactive sports games, a restaurant, 200 televisions throughout the place tuned to sporting events, a bar area, and the most popular attraction, the Screening Room. This last venue offers a giant 16-foot video screen flanked by six 36-inch screens, each showing a different event. Seats with special headphones are arrayed in front of the screen, and you control what you listen to. 555 12th St. NW. © 202/783-3776. www.espnzone.com. Metro: Metro Center.

Fadó   Another Irish pub, but this one is Ireland as theme park. It was designed and built by the Irish Pub Company of Dublin, which shipped everything—the stone for the floors, the etched glass, the milled wood—from Ireland. The pub has separate areas, including an old Irish "bookstore" alcove and a country cottage bar. Authentic Irish food, like potato pancakes, is served with your Guinness. *Fadó,* Gaelic for "long ago," doesn't take reservations, which means that hungry patrons tend to hover over your table waiting for you to finish. 808 7th St. NW. © 202/789-0066. www.fadoirishpub.com. Metro: Gallery Place–Chinatown.

Lucky Bar   Lucky Bar is a good place to kick back and relax. But, in keeping with the times, it also features free salsa dance lessons on Monday night. Sometimes the music is live, but mostly it's courtesy of a deejay. Other times the jukebox plays, but never so loud that you can't carry on a conversation. The bar has a front room overlooking Connecticut Avenue and a back room decorated with good-luck signs, couches, hanging TVs, booths, and a pool table. Lucky Bar is known in the area as a "soccer bar," with its TVs turned to soccer matches going on around the world. 1221 Connecticut Ave. NW. © 202/331-3733. Metro: Dupont Circle or Farragut North.

MCCXXIII   This is about as swank and New York as Washington gets: hipsters lined up at the velvet rope, a dress code (but really an excuse for the doorman to decide whether you measure up for admittance), outrageously high prices (drink and food charges are written in Roman numerals, so some people are taken aback when settling up), a soaring ceiling and opulent interior, beautiful women servers who purr at you, and more beautiful people milling about. 1223 Connecticut Ave. NW. © 202/822-1800. www.1223.com. Cover $10 after 10pm. Metro: Dupont Circle or Farragut North.

Mr. Smith's of Georgetown   Mr. Smith's bills itself as "The Friendliest Saloon in Town," but the truth is that it's so popular among regulars, you're in danger of being ignored if the staff doesn't know you. The bar, which opened about 32 years ago, has a front room with original brick walls, wooden seats, and a long bar, at which you can count on finding pairs of newfound friends telling obscene jokes, loudly. At the end of this room is a large piano around which customers congregate each night to accompany the pianist. An interior light-filled garden room adjoins an outdoor garden area. 3104 M St. NW. © 202/333-3104. www. mrsmiths.com. Metro: Foggy Bottom, then take the Georgetown Metro Connection shuttle.

Nathans   Nathans is in the heart of Georgetown. If you pop in here in midafternoon, it's a quiet place to grab a beer or glass of wine and watch the action on the street. Visit at night, though, and it's a more typical bar scene, crowded with locals, out-of-towners, students, and a sprinkling of couples in from the 'burbs. That's the front room. The back room at Nathans is a civilized, candlelit restaurant serving classic American fare. After 11:30pm on Friday and Saturday, this room turns into a dance hall, playing deejay music and attracting the 20-somethings Friday night, an older crowd Saturday night. 3150 M St. NW (at the corner of Wisconsin Ave.). © 202/338-2600. Metro: Foggy Bottom, then take the Georgetown Metro Connection shuttle.

Politiki and the Pennsylvania Ave. Pourhouse   This welcome addition to the more traditional pubs along this stretch of Capitol Hill has two themes going. Its first floor plays on a Pittsburgh theme (honoring the owner's roots),

Arlington Row

As unlikely as it seems, one of the hottest spots for Washington nightlife is a stretch of suburban street in Arlington, Virginia. I'm talking about a section of Wilson Boulevard in the Clarendon neighborhood, roughly between Highland and Danville streets. For years, people referred to this area as "Little Vietnam," for the many Vietnamese cafes and grocery stores that have flourished here. Now some are calling it "the new Adams-Morgan," as some pretty good nightclubs and several well-reviewed restaurants have joined the still-strong Vietnamese presence. So take the Metro to the Clarendon stop and walk down Wilson, or drive up Wilson from Key Bridge, turn left on Edgewood Road or another side street, and park on the street. Then walk to these spots, all of which serve food:

The smallest of the bunch, **Galaxy Hut,** 2711 Wilson Blvd. (© **703/525-8646;** www.galaxyhut.com), is a comfortable bar with far-out art on the walls and a patio in the alley. Look for live alternative rock most nights. No cover.

At **IOTA,** 2832 Wilson Blvd. (© **703/522-8340;** iotaclubandcafe.com), up-and-coming local bands take the stage nightly in a setting with minimal decor (cement floor, exposed brick walls, and a wood-beamed ceiling); there's a patio in back. There's live music nightly. If there's a cover, it's usually $8 to $15.

Whitlow's on Wilson, 2854 Wilson Blvd. (© **703/276-9693;** www.whitlows.com), is the biggest spot on the block, spreading throughout four rooms, the first showcasing the music (usually blues, with anything from surfer music to rock thrown in). The place has the appearance of a diner, from Formica table–booths to a soda fountain, and serves retro diner food. (Mon half-price burger nights are a good deal.) The other rooms hold coin-operated pool tables, dartboards, and air hockey. Cover is usually $3 to $5 Thursday through Saturday after 9pm.

Clarendon Grill, 1101 N. Highland St. (© **703/524-7455;** www.cgrill.com), wins a best decor award for its construction theme: murals of construction workers, building materials displayed under the glass-covered bar, and so forth. Music is a mix of modern rock, jazz, and reggae. Cover is $3 to $5 Wednesday through Saturday.

Now, get in your car, hop the Metro, or get out your rambling shoes to visit one other place, about a mile south of this stretch of Wilson:

Rhodeside Grill, 1836 Wilson Blvd. (© **703/243-0145;** www.rhodesidegrill.com), 3 blocks from the Courthouse Metro stop, is a well-liked American restaurant on its first floor. The rec-room-like bar downstairs features excellent live bands playing roots rock, jazz funk, Latin percussion, country rock, reggae—you name it. Cover averages $5 or more Thursday through Saturday starting at 9:30pm.

displaying Steeler and Penguin paraphernalia, and drawing Iron City drafts from its tap and pierogis from the kitchen. Downstairs is a tiki bar: Think Scorpion Bowl and piña colada drinks, pupu platters, and hula dancer figurines. The basement has pool tables, a bar, and a lounge area (behind beaded curtains); the street level has booths and a bar; and the top floor occasionally features live music, dance lessons, and a promised Don Ho night. Now's your chance to wear your Hawaiian shirt. 319 Pennsylvania Ave. SE. ℂ 202/546-1001. Metro: Capitol South.

Post Pub *(Value)*   This joint fits into the "comfortable shoe" category. Situated across from the offices of the *Washington Post*, the pub gets busy at lunch, grows quiet in the afternoon, and picks up again in the evening. Post Pub has two rooms furnished with old-fashioned black banquettes, faux wood paneling, mirrored beer insignias, jukeboxes, cigarette machines, and a long bar with tall stools. There are different happy-hour specials every night, like the 5 to 9pm Friday "Anything Absolut," which offers drinks made with Absolut vodka for $2.75 each. The food is homey and inexpensive (under $10) fare like onion rings, sandwiches, and chicken parmigiana. 1422 L St. NW (between Vermont and 15th sts.). ℂ 202/628-2111. Metro: McPherson Square.

Spy Lounge   You enter this cool bar through the Felix Restaurant and Lounge (see chapter 6 for a review), and that's because Alan Popowsky owns them both. The Spy attempts a modern European feel, with metal stools and white walls, and builds upon a spy theme, showing scenes from James Bond movies continually on its TV screens. Popowsky keeps the place from getting too crowded, or riffraffy, by allowing only a certain number of people in at a time (and only those who are dressed attractively). 2406 18th St. NW. ℂ 202/483-3549. Metro: U St.–Cardozo or Woodley Park–Zoo–Adams-Morgan, and catch the Adams-Morgan/U St. Link Shuttle.

Toka Café   Toka is small, underground, and upscale, affecting a hip New York look, with its sleek decor of white walls and brushed steel accents, aluminum bar stools and glass-topped bar. Toka pursues a NYC ambience, too, requiring no dress code, but catering to a crowd that can afford its pricey cocktails, like the $9 signature drink, the "Tokatini" (orange vodka and Cointreau), and who enjoy bites of fancy food, such as crab croquettes or grape leaves stuffed with duck confit. (Toka is both a restaurant and bar.) Patrons overwhelmed the small space when Toka first opened in 2002; like Topaz and Rouge (see write-ups in this section), Toka works best when it's not crowded. 1140 19th St. NW. ℂ 202/429-8652. Metro: Dupont Circle or Farragut North.

The Tombs   Housed in a converted 19th-century Federal-style home, the Tombs, which opened in 1962, is a favorite hangout for students and faculty of nearby Georgetown University. (Bill Clinton came here during his college years.) They tend to congregate at the central bar and surrounding tables, while local residents head for "the Sweeps," the room that lies down a few steps and has red-leather banquettes.

Directly below the upscale 1789 restaurant, the Tombs benefits from 1789 chef Riz Lacoste's supervision. The menu offers burgers, sandwiches, and salads, as well as more serious fare. 1226 36th St. NW. ℂ 202/337-6668. Cover sometimes on Tues or Sun nights, never more than $5. Metro: Foggy Bottom, then take the Georgetown Metro Connection shuttle into Georgetown.

Topaz Bar   This is Bar Rouge's sister (they are owned and managed by the same companies) and also lies within a hotel, the Topaz. The decor here emphasizes cool sensuality, hence the Philippe Starck bar stools, blue velvet settees, zebra-patterned ottomans, and leopard-print rugs. A lighting scheme fades into and out of colors: blue to pink to black, and so on. Everyone here is drinking the Blue Nirvana, a combo of champagne, vodka, and a touch of blueberry liqueur—a concoction that tends to turn your tongue blue, by the way. The Topaz Bar serves small plates of delicious Asian-inspired tastes, like shrimp and pork dumplings and stir-fry of sea scallops. 1733 N St. NW. © 202/393-3000. Metro: Dupont Circle or Farragut North.

Tryst This is the most relaxed of Washington's lounge bars. The room is surprisingly large for Adams-Morgan, and it's jam-packed with worn armchairs and couches, which are usually occupied, no matter what time of day. People come here to have coffee or a drink, get a bite to eat, read a book, meet a friend. The place feels almost like a student lounge on a college campus, only alcohol is served. A bonus: Tryst offers free wireless Internet service. 2459 18th St. NW. © 202/ 232-5500. www.trystdc.com. Metro: U St.–Cardozo or Woodley Park–Zoo–Adams-Morgan and catch the Adams-Morgan/U St. Link Shuttle.

Tune Inn *Finds* Capitol Hill has a number of bars that qualify as institutions, but the Tune Inn is probably the most popular. Capitol Hill staffers and their bosses, apparently at ease in dive surroundings, have been coming here for cheap beer and greasy burgers since it opened in 1955. (All the longtime Capitol Hillers know that Friday is crab cake day at the Tune Inn, and they all show up.) 33½ Pennsylvania Ave. SE. © 202/543-2725. Metro: Capitol South.

10

Side Trips from Washington, D.C.

Just across the Potomac River from Washington are Old Town Alexandria, a smaller, less crowded version of Georgetown, and Mount Vernon, George Washington's plantation. It's easy enough—and recommended—to tour these historic areas, if you have the time.

Old Town Alexandria is a mere 8 miles from the capital, and Mount Vernon is 8 miles beyond Alexandria. At Mount Vernon, you'll be able to tour our first president's exquisite estate and gardens, as you learn fascinating facts about the man/soldier/hero/statesman.

In Old Town Alexandria, you'll discover a charming waterfront village full of historic attractions, good restaurants and shops, lively bars and nightclubs, and streets for strolling.

But don't expect to find these spots any less crowded than the capital's attractions; their unique appeal, suburban locations, and proximity to downtown make them popular to local tourists and out-of-towners, alike.

If you'd like to explore farther afield, consider picking up a copy of *Frommer's Virginia* or *Frommer's Maryland & Delaware.*

1 Mount Vernon

Only 16 miles south of the capital, George Washington's Southern plantation dates from a 1674 land grant to the president's great-grandfather.

ESSENTIALS

GETTING THERE If you're going by car, take any of the bridges over the Potomac River into Virginia and follow the signs pointing the way to National Airport/Mount Vernon/George Washington Memorial Parkway. You travel south on the George Washington Memorial Parkway, the river always to your left, passing by National Airport on your right, continuing through Old Town Alexandria, where the parkway is renamed "Washington Street," and heading 8 miles farther, until you reach the large circle that fronts Mount Vernon.

You might also take a bus or boat to Mount Vernon. These bus and boat tour prices include the price of admission to Mount Vernon.

Gray Line Buses (© 202/289-1995; www.graylinedc.com) go to Mount Vernon daily (except Christmas, Thanksgiving, and New Year's Day), leaving from the bus's terminal at Union Station at 8:30am and returning by 1:30pm. The cost is $30 per adult and $15 per child age 3 through 11. From mid-June through October, Gray Line operates a second tour to Mount Vernon, leaving Union Station at 2pm. Ticket prices are the same. Gray Line often offers other tours, so call for further information.

The Spirit of Washington Cruises' (© 202/554-8000; www.spiritcruises.com) *Potomac Spirit* leaves from Pier 4 (6th and Water streets SW; 3 blocks from the

---

(Fun Fact **The George Washington Memorial Parkway**

Though few people realize it, the George Washington Memorial Parkway is actually a national park. The first section was completed in 1932 to honor the bicentennial of George Washington's birth. The parkway follows the Potomac River, running from Mount Vernon, past Old Town and the nation's capital, ending at Great Falls, Virginia. Today, the parkway is a major commuter route leading into and out of the city. Even the most impatient driver, however, can't help but notice the beautiful scenery and views of the Jefferson and Lincoln memorials and the Washington Monument that you pass along the way.

Green line Metro's Waterfront Station) every day except Monday, from mid-March to mid-October at 8:30am, returning by 3pm; cost is $32 per adult, $22 per child (ages 6–11; free for children under 6). The Potomac Riverboat Company's (© **703/684-0580** or 703/548-9000; www.potomacriverboatco.com) *Miss Christin* operates Tuesday through Sunday May through August (weekends only Apr and Sept–Oct), departing at 11am for Mount Vernon from the pier adjacent to the Torpedo Factory, at the bottom of King Street in Old Town Alexandria, and costing $27 per adult, $15 per child (ages 6–10; free for children under 6). Arrive 30 minutes ahead of time at the pier, to secure a place on the boat. The trip takes 50 minutes each way. The boat departs Mount Vernon at 4pm to return to Old Town.

See the section on "Organized Tours," in chapter 7 for further details about other touring options.

If you're in the mood for exercise in a pleasant setting, rent a **bike** (see the box called "Biking to Old Town Alexandria & Mount Vernon" on p. 279 for rental locations and other information).

Finally, it is possible to take **public transportation** to Mount Vernon by riding the Metro to the Yellow Line's Huntington Station and proceeding to the lower level, where you catch the Fairfax Connector bus (no. 101) to Mount Vernon. The connector bus is a 20-minute ride and costs 50¢. Call © **703/339-7200** for schedule information.

TOURING THE ESTATE

Mount Vernon Estate and Gardens   If it's beautiful out, and you have the time, you could easily spend half a day or more soaking in the life and times of George Washington at Mount Vernon. The centerpiece of a visit to this 500-acre estate is a tour through 14 rooms of the mansion, whose oldest part dates from the 1740s. The plantation was passed down from Washington's great-grandfather, who acquired the land in 1674, eventually to George in 1754. Washington proceeded over the next 45 years to expand and fashion the home to his liking, though the American Revolution and his years as president kept Washington away from his beloved estate much of the time.

What you see today is a remarkable restoration of the mansion, displaying many original furnishings and objects used by the Washington family. The rooms have been repainted in the original colors favored by George and Martha. There's no formal guided tour, but attendants stationed throughout the house and grounds provide brief orientations and answer questions; when there's no line, a walk-through takes about 20 minutes. You can also rent an audio tour for

$4 that provides a 40-minute plantation overview narration. Maps of the property are available at the entrance, including an adventure map for children.

But don't stop there. After leaving the house, you can tour the outbuildings: the kitchen, slave quarters, storeroom, smokehouse, overseer's quarters, coach house, and stables. A 4-acre exhibit area called "George Washington, Pioneer Farmer" includes a replica of Washington's 16-sided barn and fields of crops that he grew (corn, wheat, oats, and so forth). Docents in period costumes demonstrate 18th-century farming methods. At its peak, Mount Vernon was an 8,000-acre working farm, reminding us that, more than anything, Washington considered himself first and foremost a farmer.

A museum on the property exhibits Washington memorabilia, and details of the restoration are explained in the museum's annex; there's also a gift shop. You'll want to walk around the grounds (especially in nice weather) and see the wharf (and take a 30-min. narrated excursion on the Potomac, offered three times a day, seasonally, Tues–Sun, $8 per person), the slave burial ground, the greenhouse, the lawns and gardens, and the tomb containing George and Martha Washington's sarcophagi (24 other family members are also interred here). Public memorial services are held at the estate every year on the third Monday in February, the date commemorating Washington's birthday; admission is free that day. (This is also the site's busiest day, with an average of 17,000 people descending upon the place.)

Mount Vernon belongs to the Mount Vernon Ladies' Association, which purchased the estate for $200,000 in 1858, from John Augustine Washington, great-grand-nephew of the first president. Without the group's purchase, the estate might have crumbled and disappeared, for neither the federal government nor the Commonwealth of Virginia had wanted to buy the property when it was earlier offered for sale.

Today more than a million people tour the property annually. The best time to visit is off-season; during the heavy tourist months (especially in spring), avoid weekends and holidays if possible, and arrive early year-round to beat the crowds.

Southern end of the George Washington Memorial Pkwy. (mailing address: P.O. Box 110, Mount Vernon, VA 22121). (℃ **703/780-2000.** www.mountvernon.org. Admission $11 adults (50¢ discount for seniors), $5 children 6–11, free for children under 6. Apr–Aug daily 8am–5pm; Mar and Sept–Oct daily 9am–5pm; Nov–Feb daily 9am–4pm.

DINING & SHOPPING

Mount Vernon's comprehensive **gift shop** offers a wide range of books, children's toys, holiday items, Mount Vernon private-labeled food and wine, and Mount Vernon licensed furnishings.

A **Food Court** features indoor and outdoor seating and a menu of baked goods, deli sandwiches, coffee, grilled items, Pizza Hut pizza, and Mrs. Fields cookies. You can't **picnic** on the grounds of Mount Vernon, but you can drive a mile north on the parkway to Riverside Park, where there are tables and a lawn overlooking the Potomac.

Meanwhile, the Mount Vernon Inn restaurant is still the option I'd recommend.

Tips Special Activities at Mount Vernon

There's an ongoing schedule of events at Mount Vernon, especially in summer. These might include tours focusing on 18th-century gardens, slave life, colonial crafts, or archaeology; and, for children, hands-on history programs and treasure hunts. Call to find out whether anything is on during your visit.

Mount Vernon Inn AMERICAN TRADITIONAL   Lunch or dinner at the inn is an intrinsic part of the Mount Vernon experience. It's a quaint and charming colonial-style restaurant, complete with period furnishings and three working fireplaces. The waiters are all in 18th-century costumes. Be sure to begin your meal with the homemade peanut and chestnut soup (usually on the lunch menu). Lunch entrees range from colonial turkey "pye" (a sort of Early American quiche served in a crock with garden vegetables and a puffed pastry top) to a pulled pork barbecue sandwich. There's a full bar, and premium wines are offered by the glass. At dinner, tablecloths and candlelight make this a more elegant setting. Choose from soups (perhaps broccoli cheddar) and salads, entrees such as Maryland crab cakes or roast venison with peppercorn sauce, homemade breads, and dessert (like whiskey cake or English trifle).

Near the entrance to Mount Vernon Estate and Gardens. 🕐 **703/780-0011.** Reservations recommended for dinner. Lunch main courses $5.50–$8.50; dinner main courses $13–$24; fixed-price dinner $15. AE, DISC, MC, V. Daily 11am–3:30pm; Mon–Sat 5–9pm.

2 Alexandria

Old Town Alexandria is about 8 miles south of Washington.

Founded by a group of Scottish tobacco merchants, the seaport town of Alexandria was born in 1749 when a 60-acre tract of land was auctioned off in half-acre lots. Colonists came from miles around, in ramshackle wagons and stately carriages, in sloops, brigantines, and lesser craft, to bid on land that would be "commodious for trade and navigation and tend greatly to the ease and advantage of the frontier inhabitants." The auction took place in Market Square (still intact today), and the surveyor's assistant was a capable lad of 17 named George Washington. (Market Square, by the way, is the site of the oldest continually operating farmers' market in the country; go there on a Sat between 5 and 9:30am and you'll be participating in a 254-year-old tradition.)

Today, the original 60 acres of lots in George Washington's hometown (also Robert E. Lee's) are the heart of Old Town, a multimillion-dollar urban renewal historic district. Many Alexandria streets still bear their original colonial names (King, Queen, Prince, Princess, Royal—you get the drift), while others, like Jefferson, Franklin, Lee, Patrick, and Henry, are obviously post-Revolutionary.

In this "mother lode of Americana," the past is being restored in an ongoing archaeological and historical research program. And though the present can be seen in the abundance of shops, boutiques, art galleries, and restaurants that capitalize on the tourist traffic, it's still easy to imagine yourself in colonial times by listening for the rumbling of horse-drawn vehicles over cobblestone (portions of Prince and Oronoco streets are still paved with cobblestone); dining on Sally Lunn bread and other 18th-century grub in the centuries-old Gadsby's Tavern; and learning about the lives of the nation's forefathers during walking tours that take you in and out of their houses.

ESSENTIALS
GETTING THERE   If you're driving, take the Arlington Memorial or the 14th Street Bridge to the George Washington Memorial Parkway south, which becomes Washington Street in Old Town Alexandria. Washington Street intersects with King Street, Alexandria's main thoroughfare. Turn left from Washington Street onto one of the streets before or after King Street (southbound left turns are not permitted from Washington St. onto King St.) and you'll be heading toward the waterfront and the heart of Old Town. If you turn right from Washington Street

Old Town Alexandria

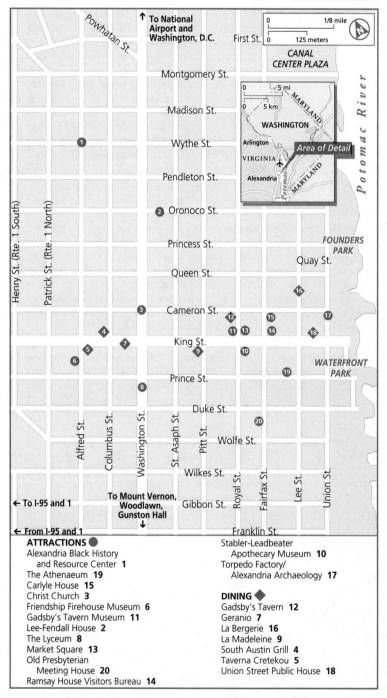

To National Airport and Washington, D.C.

First St.

CANAL CENTER PLAZA

Potomac River

Montgomery St.

Madison St.

Wythe St.

Pendleton St.

Oronoco St.

Princess St.

FOUNDERS PARK

Quay St.

Queen St.

Cameron St.

King St.

WATERFRONT PARK

Prince St.

Duke St.

Wolfe St.

Wilkes St.

To Mount Vernon, Woodlawn, Gunston Hall

Gibbon St.

← To I-95 and 1

← From I-95 and 1

Franklin St.

Henry St. (Rte. 1 South)
Patrick St. (Rte. 1 North)
Alfred St.
Columbus St.
Washington St.
St. Asaph St.
Pitt St.
Royal St.
Fairfax St.
Lee St.
Union St.

Powhatan St.

WASHINGTON

MARYLAND

Arlington

VIRGINIA

Alexandria

MARYLAND

Area of Detail

5 mi
5 km

ATTRACTIONS

Alexandria Black History and Resource Center **1**
The Athenaeum **19**
Carlyle House **15**
Christ Church **3**
Friendship Firehouse Museum **6**
Gadsby's Tavern Museum **11**
Lee-Fendall House **2**
The Lyceum **8**
Market Square **13**
Old Presbyterian Meeting House **20**
Ramsay House Visitors Bureau **14**

Stabler-Leadbeater Apothecary Museum **10**
Torpedo Factory/ Alexandria Archaeology **17**

DINING

Gadsby's Tavern **12**
Geranio **7**
La Bergerie **16**
La Madeleine **9**
South Austin Grill **4**
Taverna Cretekou **5**
Union Street Public House **18**

onto King Street, you'll find an avenue of shops and restaurants. You can obtain a free parking permit from the Visitors Center (see below), or park at meters or in garages. The town is compact, so you won't need a car once you arrive.

The easiest way to make the trip may be the Metro's Yellow and Blue lines to the King Street station. From the King Street station, you can catch an eastbound AT2, AT5, or AT7 blue-and-gold DASH bus (*C* **703/370-DASH**), marked either "Old Town" or "Braddock Metro," which will take you up King Street. Ask to be dropped at the corner of Fairfax and King streets, which will put you right across the street from Ramsay House, the visitor center. The fare is $1 most of the time, but free weekends, from Friday evening through Sunday night. Or you can walk into Old Town, although it's about a mile from the station into the center of Old Town.

VISITOR INFORMATION The **Alexandria Convention and Visitors Association,** located at Ramsay House Visitors Center, 221 King St., at Fairfax Street (*C* **800/388-9119** or 703/838-4200; www.funside.com), is open daily from 9am to 5pm (closed Jan 1, Thanksgiving, and Dec 25). Here you can obtain a map/self-guided walking tour and brochures about the area; learn about special events that might be scheduled during your visit and get tickets for them; and receive answers to any questions you might have about accommodations, restaurants, sights, or shopping. The center supplies materials in five languages.

If you come by car, get a free 1-day parking permit here for any 2-hour meter for up to 24 hours; when you park, put money in the meter to cover yourself until you post your permit. The permit can be renewed for a 2nd day.

ORGANIZED TOURS Though it's easy to see Alexandria on your own by putting yourself in the hands of colonial-attired guides at individual attractions, you might consider taking a comprehensive walking tour. The Visitors Center offers 1½-hour architectural and history tours, leaving from the Visitors Center garden, weather permitting, at 10:30am every day but Sunday, when it leaves at 1:30pm. The tour costs $10 per person (free for age 6 and under) and you pay the guide when you arrive at the Visitors Center.

Doorways to Old Virginia (*C* **703/548-0100**) conducts "Lanterns, Lights—Ghosts and Graveyard Tours," March through November (again, weather permitting) at 7:30 and 9pm Friday and Saturday, 7:30pm only on Sunday. This 1-hour tour departs from Ramsay House and costs $6 for adults, $4 for children ages 7 to 12, free for children under 7. You purchase tickets from the guide.

CITY LAYOUT Old Town is very small and laid out in an easy grid. At the center is the intersection of Washington Street and King Street. Streets change from North to South when they cross King Street. For example, North Alfred Street is the part of Alfred north of King Street. Guess where South Alfred Street is.

SPECIAL EVENTS

Two organizations publish helpful calendars of key Alexandria events: the **Alexandria Convention and Visitors Association** (*C* **800/388-9119** or 703/838-4200; www.funside.com), which covers Alexandria at large; and the City of Alexandria's **Office of Historic Alexandria** (*C* **703/838-4554;** www.ci.alexandria.va.us then "Tourism and History," then "Historic Events Calendar"), which focuses on the historic sights. You can call and ask them to mail you information, or you can access their separate and continually updated websites. Event highlights include:

January The **birthdays of Confederate General Robert E. Lee and his father,** Revolutionary War Colonel "Light Horse Harry" Lee, are celebrated together at

Value Patriot Pass & Block Tickets

Money-saving tickets are on sale at the **Ramsay House Visitors Center.** A **Patriot Pass ticket,** costing $28 for an adult, $16 for children ages 11 to 17, admits you to the Carlyle House, Gadsby's Tavern Museum, Lee-Fendall House, and the Stabler-Leadbeater Apothecary. It also reserves your place on a guided walking tour of Old Town, as well as a ride aboard the *Admiral Tilp* riverboat that cruises the Potomac River along the Alexandria waterfront. The Patriot Pass can save you about $7 per adult and $8 per child. Unfortunately, it can be hard to coordinate the timed tours of the historic sights and the scheduled departures of the walking tour and boat excursion within the framework of a single day. The Patriot ticket makes the most sense if you're staying more than 1 day. Also available are regular Old Town Pass tickets, which include everything that the Patriot ticket does, except for the walking tour; tickets are $18 for adults and $8 for children.

If you're here just for the day, you can still save money by buying a **block ticket** for admission to Gadsby's Tavern Museum, the Carlyle House, and the Stabler-Leadbeater Apothecary Shop. The ticket, which can also be purchased at any of the buildings, costs $9 for adults, $5 for children ages 11 to 17, free for children under 11. The savings come to about $1.50 per adult, $1 per child.

---

the Lee-Fendall House the third Sunday of the month. The party features period music, refreshments, and house tours. Admission in 2003 was $5 per adult, $2 for children 11 to 17, and free for children under 11.

February   Alexandria celebrates **George Washington's Birthday,** on Presidents' Weekend, which precedes the federal holiday, usually the third Monday in February. Festivities typically include a colonial costume or black-tie banquet, followed by a ball at Gadsby's Tavern, a 10-kilometer race, special tours, a Revolutionary War encampment at Fort Ward Park (complete with uniformed troops engaging in skirmishes), the nation's largest George Washington Birthday Parade (50,000–75,000 people attend each year), and 18th-century comic opera performances. Most events, such as the parade and historical reenactments, are free. The Birthnight Ball at Gadsby's Tavern requires tickets, which cost $75 per person in 2003.

March   On the first Saturday in March, King Street is the site of a popular **St. Patrick's Day Parade.**

April   Alexandria celebrates **Historic Garden Week in Virginia** with tours of privately owned local historic homes and gardens the third Saturday of the month. Call the Visitors Center (© **703/838-4200**) in early 2004 for more information about tickets and admission prices for the tour.

June   The **Red Cross Waterfront Festival,** the second weekend in June, honors Alexandria's historic importance as a seaport and the vitality of its Potomac shoreline today with a display of historic tall ships, ship tours, boat rides and races, nautical art exhibits, waterfront walking tours, fireworks, children's games, an arts and crafts show, food booths, and entertainment. Admission is charged.

July   Alexandria's birthday (its 255th in 2004) is celebrated with a concert performance by the Alexandria Symphony Orchestra, fireworks, birthday cake, and other festivities. The Saturday following the Fourth of July. All events are free.

September   This year is the 62nd Annual Tour of Historic Alexandria Homes, which takes you to some of the city's most beautifully restored and decorated private homes. Third Saturday in September. Tickets and information from the Visitors Center.

October   October is Arts Month in Alexandria, and celebrations include the **Alexandria Arts Safari,** which takes place on the first Saturday in October and features archaeological and arts tours, and interactive events. Torpedo Factory. Free.

Halloween Walking Tours take place toward the end of October. A lantern-carrying guide in 18th-century costume describes Alexandria's ghosts, graveyards, legends, myths, and folklore as you tour the town and graveyards. Call the visitor center for information.

November   There's a **Christmas Tree Lighting** in Market Square the Friday after Thanksgiving; the ceremony, which includes choir singing, puppet shows, dance performances, and an appearance by Santa and his elves, begins at 7pm. The night the tree is lit, thousands of tiny lights adorning King Street trees also go on.

December   Holiday festivities continue with the **Annual Scottish Christmas Walk** on the first Saturday in December. Activities include kilted bagpipers, Highland dancers, a parade of Scottish clans (with horses and dogs), caroling, fashion shows, storytelling, booths (selling crafts, antiques, food, hot mulled punch, heather, fresh wreaths, and holly), and children's games. Admission is charged for some events.

The **Historic Alexandria Candlelight Tour,** the second week in December, visits seasonally decorated historic Alexandria homes and an 18th-century tavern. There is colonial dancing, string quartets, madrigal and opera singers, and refreshments, too. Purchase tickets at the Ramsay House Visitors Center.

There are so many holiday-season activities that the Visitors Association issues a special brochure about them each year. Pick one up to learn about decorations, workshops, walking tours, tree lightings, concerts, bazaars, bake sales, craft fairs, and much more.

WHAT TO SEE & DO

Colonial and post-Revolutionary buildings are Old Town Alexandria's main attractions. My favorites are the Carlyle House and Gadsby's Tavern Museum, but they are all worth a visit.

Except for the Alexandria Black History and Resource Center, whose closest Metro stop is the Braddock Street station, and Fort Ward, to which you should drive or take a taxi, these sites are most easily accessible via the King Street Metro station, combined with a ride on the DASH bus to the center of Old Town.

Old Town has hundreds of charming boutiques, antiques stores, and gift shops selling everything from souvenir T-shirts to 18th-century reproductions. Some of the most interesting are at the sites, but most are clustered on King and Cameron streets and their connecting cross streets. A guide to antiques stores is available at the Visitors Center. Also see chapter 8, which includes some Alexandria shops.

Alexandria Black History Resource Center   In a 1940s building that originally housed the black community's first public library, the center exhibits historical objects, photographs, documents, and memorabilia relating to black citizens of Alexandria from the 18th century forward. In addition to the permanent collection, the museum presents rotating exhibits and other activities. If

Moments **Biking to Old Town Alexandria & Mount Vernon**

One of the nicest ways to see Washington is on a bike ride in Virginia. Rent a bike at Fletcher's Boat House or some other location listed under "Outdoor Activities" in chapter 7, then hop on the pathway that runs along the Potomac River, heading toward the monuments and the Arlington Memorial Bridge. In Washington, this is the Rock Creek Park Trail; once you cross Memorial Bridge (near the Lincoln Memorial) into Virginia, the name changes to the Mount Vernon Trail, which, as it sounds, is a straight shot to Mount Vernon.

As you tool along, you have a breathtaking view of the Potomac and of Washington's grand landmarks: the Kennedy Center, Washington Monument, Lincoln Memorial, Jefferson Memorial, the National Cathedral off in one direction, and the Capitol off in the other.

Of course, this mode of transportation is also a great way to see Old Town Alexandria and Mount Vernon, too. The trail carries you past Reagan National Airport, via two pedestrian bridges that take you safely through the airport's roadway system. Continue on to Old Town, where you really should dismount for a walk around, a tour of some of the historic properties listed in this chapter, or take in some refreshment from one of the restaurants, before you proceed to Mount Vernon. The section from Memorial Bridge to Mount Vernon is about 19 miles in all.

you're interested in further studies, check out the center's Watson Reading Room. A half hour is really enough time to spend at the center.

The center is actually on the outskirts of Old Town, and not in the best neighborhood. From here, it makes sense to walk, rather than to take the Metro or even a taxi, into Old Town. Have a staff person point you in the direction of Washington Street, where you will turn right and be only 2 blocks from the Lee-Fendall House, at Oronoco and Washington streets (see below).

638 N. Alfred St. (at Wythe St.). © **703/838-4356.** http://oha.ci.Alexandria.va.us/bhrc. Free admission (donations accepted). Tues–Sat 10am–4pm; Sun 1–5pm. Metro: Braddock Rd. From the station, walk across the parking lot and bear right until you reach the corner of West and Wythe sts., where you'll proceed 5 blocks east along Wythe until you reach the center.

The Athenaeum   This grand building, with its Greek Revival architecture-style, stands out among the narrow old townhouses on the cobblestone street. Built in 1851, the Athenaeum has been many things: the Bank of the Old Dominion, where Robert E. Lee kept his money prior to the Civil War; a commissary for the Union Army during the Civil War; a church; a triage center where wounded Union soldiers were treated; and a medicine warehouse. Now the hall serves as an art gallery and performance space for the Northern Virginia Fine Arts Association. So pop by to admire the Athenaeum's imposing exterior, including the four soaring Doric columns, and its interior hall: 24-foot-high ceilings, enormous windows, and whatever contemporary art is on display. Won't take you more than 20 minutes, tops.

201 Prince St. (at South Lee St.). © **703/548-0035.** www.Alexandria-athenaeum.org. Free admission (donations accepted). Wed–Fri 11am–3pm; Sat 1–3pm; Sun 1–4pm.

Carlyle House   One of Virginia's most architecturally impressive 18th-century homes, Carlyle House also figured prominently in American history. In 1753, Scottish merchant John Carlyle completed the mansion for his bride, Sarah Fairfax of Belvoir, a daughter of one of Virginia's most prominent families. It was designed in the style of a Scottish/English manor house and lavishly furnished. Carlyle, a successful merchant, had the means to import the best furnishings and appointments available abroad for his new Alexandria home.

When it was built, Carlyle House was a waterfront property with its own wharf. A social and political center, the house was visited by the great men of the day, including George Washington. But its most important moment in history occurred in April 1755, when Maj. Gen. Edward Braddock, commander-in-chief of His Majesty's forces in North America, met with five colonial governors here and asked them to tax colonists to finance a campaign against the French and Indians. Colonial legislatures refused to comply, one of the first instances of serious friction between America and Britain. Nevertheless, Braddock made Carlyle House his headquarters during the campaign, and Carlyle was less than impressed with him. He called the general "a man of weak understanding . . . very indolent . . . a slave to his passions, women and wine . . . as great an Epicure as could be in his eating, tho a brave man." Possibly these were the reasons his unfinanced campaign met with disaster. Braddock received, as Carlyle described it, "a most remarkable drubbing."

Tours are given on the hour and half hour and take about 40 minutes; allow another 10 or 15 minutes if you plan to tour the tiered garden of brick walks and boxed parterres. Two of the original rooms, the large parlor and the adjacent study, have survived intact; the former, where Braddock met the governors, still retains its original fine woodwork, paneling, and pediments. The house is furnished in period pieces; however, only a few of Carlyle's possessions remain. In an upstairs room, an architecture exhibit depicts 18th-century construction methods with hand-hewn beams and hand-wrought nails.

121 N. Fairfax St. (between Cameron and King sts.). ℂ 703/549-2997. www.carlylehouse.org. Admission $4 adults, $2 children 11–17, free for children under 11; or buy a block ticket. Tues–Sat 10am–4:30pm; Sun noon–4:30pm. Winter hours 10am–4pm.

Christ Church   This sturdy redbrick Georgian-style church would be an important national landmark even if its two most distinguished members had not been Washington and Lee. It has been in continuous use since 1773.

There have, of course, been many changes over the years. The bell tower, church bell, galleries, and organ were added by the early 1800s, the "wine-glass" pulpit in 1891. But much of what was changed later has since been restored to its earlier state. The pristine white interior with wood moldings and gold trim is colonially correct. For the most part, the original structure remains, including the hand-blown glass in the windows. The town has grown up around the building that was once known as the "Church in the Woods."

Christ Church has had its historic moments. Washington and other early church members fomented revolution in the churchyard, and Robert E. Lee met here with Richmond representatives to discuss assuming command of Virginia's military forces at the beginning of the Civil War. You can sit in the pew where George and Martha sat with her two Custis grandchildren, or in the Lee family pew.

It's traditional for U.S. presidents to attend a service here on a Sunday close to Washington's birthday and sit in his pew. One of the most memorable of these visits took place shortly after Pearl Harbor, when Franklin Delano Roosevelt

> **Tips Planning Note**
>
> Many Alexandria attractions are closed on Monday.

attended services with Winston Churchill on the World Day of Prayer for Peace, January 1, 1942.

Of course, you're invited to attend a service (Sun at 8, 9, and 11:15am and 5pm; Wed at 7:15am, 12:05, and 6:15pm). There's no admission, but donations are appreciated. A guide gives brief lectures to visitors. A gift shop is open mornings, Tuesday through Saturday and the first and third Sunday. Twenty minutes should do it here.

118 N. Washington St. (at Cameron St.). ℂ **703/549-1450.** www.historicchristchurch.org. Suggested donation $5 adults, $3 children. Mon–Sat 9am–4pm; Sun 2–4pm. Closed all federal holidays.

Fort Ward Museum & Historic Site *(Kids*   A short drive from Old Town is a 45-acre museum and park that transport you to Alexandria during the Civil War. The action here centers, as it did in the early 1860s, on an actual Union fort that Lincoln ordered erected. It was part of a system of Civil War forts called the "Defenses of Washington." About 90% of the fort's earthwork walls are preserved, and the Northwest Bastion has been restored with six mounted guns (originally there were 36). A model of 19th-century military engineering, the fort was never attacked by Confederate forces. Self-guided tours begin at the Fort Ward ceremonial gate.

Visitors can explore the fort and replicas of the ceremonial entrance gate and an officer's hut. There's a museum of Civil War artifacts on the premises where changing exhibits focus on subjects such as Union arms and equipment, medical care of the wounded, and local war history.

There are picnic areas with barbecue grills in the park surrounding the fort. Living-history presentations take place throughout the year. This is a good stop if you have young children, in which case you could spend an hour or two here (especially if you bring a picnic).

4301 W. Braddock Rd. (between Rte. 7 and N. Van Dorn St.). ℂ **703/838-4848.** www.fortward.org. Free admission. Park open daily 9am to sunset; museum Tues–Sat 9am–4pm; Sun noon–5pm. Donations welcome. Call for information regarding special holiday closings. From Old Town, follow King St. west, go right on Kenwood Ave., then left on West Braddock Rd.; continue for ¾ mile to the entrance on the right.

Friendship Firehouse   Alexandria's first firefighting organization, the Friendship Fire Company, was established in 1774. In the early days, the company met in taverns and kept its firefighting equipment in a member's barn. Its present Italianate-style brick building dates from 1855; it was erected after an earlier building was, ironically, destroyed by fire. Local tradition holds that George Washington was involved with the firehouse as a founding member, active firefighter, and purchaser of its first fire engine, although research does not confirm these stories. The museum displays an 1851 fire engine, and old hoses, buckets, and other firefighting apparatus. This is a tiny place, which you can easily "do" in 20 minutes.

107 S. Alfred St. (between King and Prince sts.). ℂ **703/838-3891.** http://oha.ci.Alexandria.va.us/friendship. Free admission. Fri–Sat 10am–4pm; Sun 1–4pm.

Gadsby's Tavern Museum   Alexandria was at the crossroads of 18th-century America, and its social center was Gadsby's Tavern, which consisted of two buildings (one Georgian, one Federal) dating from around 1785 and 1792, respectively. Innkeeper John Gadsby combined them to create "a gentleman's tavern," which he operated from 1796 to 1808; it was considered one of the finest in the country. George Washington was a frequent dinner guest; he and Martha danced in the second-floor ballroom, and it was here that Washington celebrated his last birthday. The tavern also welcomed Thomas Jefferson, James Madison, and the Marquis de Lafayette, the French soldier and statesman who served in the American army under Washington during the Revolutionary War and remained close to Washington. It was the scene of lavish parties, theatrical performances, small circuses, government meetings, and concerts. Itinerant merchants used the tavern to display their wares, and traveling doctors and dentists treated a hapless clientele (these were rudimentary professions in the 18th century) on the premises.

The rooms have been restored to their 18th-century appearance. On the 30-minute tour, you'll get a good look at the Tap Room, a small dining room; the Assembly Room, the ballroom; typical bedrooms; and the underground icehouse, which was filled each winter from the icy river. Tours depart 15 minutes before and after the hour. Inquire about living-history programs, such as "Gadsby's Time Travels," geared toward children, and "Candlelight Tours," which takes you through the museum in the evening, and may include music and entertainment along the way. Cap off the experience with a meal at the restored colonial-style restaurant (see "Dining," below).

134 N. Royal St. (at Cameron St.). ✆ **703/838-4242**. www.gadsbystavern.org. Admission $4 adults, $2 children 11–17, free for children under 11; or buy a block ticket. Tours Apr–Oct Tues–Sat 10am–5pm, Sun–Mon 1–5pm; Nov–Mar Wed–Sat 11am–4pm, Sun 1–4pm. Closed most federal holidays.

Lee-Fendall House Museum   This handsome Greek Revival–style house is a veritable Lee family museum of furniture, heirlooms, and documents. "Light Horse Harry" Lee never actually lived here, though he was a frequent visitor, as was his good friend George Washington. He did own the original lot, but sold it to Philip Richard Fendall (himself a Lee on his mother's side), who built the house in 1785. Fendall married three Lee wives, including Harry's first mother-in-law, and, later, Harry's sister.

Thirty-seven Lees occupied the house over a period of 118 years (1785–1903), and it was from this house that Harry wrote Alexandria's farewell address to George Washington, delivered when he passed through town on his way to assume the presidency. (Harry also wrote and delivered, but not at this house, the famous funeral oration to Washington that contained the words: "First in war, first in peace, and first in the hearts of his countrymen.") During the Civil War, the house was seized and used as a Union hospital.

Thirty-minute guided tours interpret the 1850s era of the home and provide insight into Victorian family life. You'll also see the colonial garden with its magnolia and chestnut trees, roses, and boxwood-lined paths. Much of the interior woodwork and glass is original.

614 Oronoco St. (at Washington St.). ✆ **703/548-1789**. www.leefendallhouse.org. Admission $4 adults, $2 children 11–17, free for children under 11. Tues–Sat 10am–4pm; Sun 1–4pm. Tours on the hour 10am–3pm. Call ahead to make sure the museum is open, since it often closes for special events. Closed Thanksgiving and mid-Dec to Feb.

The Lyceum   This Greek Revival building houses a museum depicting Alexandria's history from the 17th through the 20th century. It features changing exhibits and an ongoing series of lectures, concerts, and educational programs.

You can obtain maps and brochures about Virginia state attractions, especially Alexandria attractions. The knowledgeable staff will be happy to answer questions. But even without its many attractions, the brick and stucco Lyceum merits a visit. Built in 1839, it was designed in the Doric temple style to serve as a lecture, meeting, and concert hall. It was an important center of Alexandria's cultural life until the Civil War, when Union forces appropriated it for use as a hospital. After the war it became a private residence, and still later it was subdivided for office space. In 1969, however, the city council's use of eminent domain prevented the Lyceum from being demolished in favor of a parking lot. Allow about 20 minutes here.

201 S. Washington St. (off Prince St.). ℂ 703/838-4994. www.alexandriahistory.org. Free admission. Mon–Sat 10am–5pm; Sun 1–5pm. Closed Jan 1, Thanksgiving, and Dec 25.

Old Presbyterian Meeting House   Presbyterian congregations have worshipped in Virginia since the Rev. Alexander Whittaker converted Pocahontas in Jamestown in 1614. This brick church was built by Scottish pioneers in 1775. Although it wasn't George Washington's church, the Meeting House bell tolled continuously for 4 days after his death in December 1799, and memorial services were preached from the pulpit here by Presbyterian, Episcopal, and Methodist ministers. According to the Alexandria paper of the day, "The walking being bad to the Episcopal church the funeral sermon of George Washington will be preached at the Presbyterian Meeting House." Two months later, on Washington's birthday, Alexandria citizens marched from Market Square to the church to pay their respects.

Many famous Alexandrians are buried in the church graveyard, including John and Sarah Carlyle, Dr. James Craik (the surgeon who treated—some say killed—Washington, dressed Lafayette's wounds at Brandywine, and ministered to the dying Braddock at Monongahela), and William Hunter Jr., founder of the St. Andrew's Society of Scottish descendants, to whom bagpipers pay homage on the first Saturday of December. It is also the site of a Tomb of an Unknown Revolutionary War Soldier. Dr. James Muir, minister between 1789 and 1820, lies beneath the sanctuary in his gown and bands.

The original Meeting House was gutted by a lightning fire in 1835, but parishioners restored it in the style of the day a few years later. The present bell, said to be recast from the metal of the old one, was hung in a newly constructed belfry in 1843, and a new organ was installed in 1849. The Meeting House closed its doors in 1889, and for 60 years it was virtually abandoned. But in 1949 it was reborn as a living Presbyterian U.S.A. church, and today the Old Meeting House looks much as it did following its first restoration. The original parsonage, or manse, is still intact. There's no guided tour, but there is a recorded narrative in the graveyard. Allow 20 minutes for touring.

321 S. Fairfax St. (between Duke and Wolfe sts.). ℂ 703/549-6670. www.opmh.org. Free admission, but you must obtain a key from the office to tour the church. Sun services at 8:30 and 11am, except in summer, when 1 service is held at 10am.

Stabler-Leadbeater Apothecary Museum   When its doors closed in 1933, this landmark drugstore was the second oldest in continuous operation in America. Run for five generations by the same Quaker family (beginning in 1792), the store counted Robert E. Lee (who purchased the paint for Arlington House here), George Mason, Henry Clay, John C. Calhoun, and George Washington among its famous patrons. Gothic Revival decorative elements and Victorian-style doors were added in the 1840s. Today the apothecary looks much as it did in colonial times, its shelves lined with original handblown gold-leaf–labeled bottles (actually the most valuable collection of antique medicinal bottles in the country), old scales stamped with the royal crown, patent medicines, and equipment for bloodletting.

The clock on the rear wall, the porcelain-handled mahogany drawers, and two mortars and pestles all date from about 1790. Among the shop's documentary records is this 1802 order from Mount Vernon: "Mrs. Washington desires Mr. Stabler to send by the bearer a quart bottle of his best Castor Oil and the bill for it."

A 5-minute audio tour will guide you around the displays. The adjoining gift shop uses its proceeds to maintain the apothecary. Allow 15 minutes.

105–107 S. Fairfax St. (near King St.). ℂ 703/836-3713. Admission $2.50 adults, $2 children 11–17, free for children under 11; or buy a block ticket. Mon–Sat 10am–4pm; Sun 1–5pm. Closed major holidays.

Torpedo Factory   This block-long, three-story building was built in 1918 as a torpedo shell-case factory, but now accommodates some 160 professional artists and craftspeople who create and sell their own works on the premises. Here you can see artists at work in their studios: potters, painters, printmakers, photographers, sculptors, and jewelers, as well as those who create stained-glass windows and fiber art.

On permanent display are exhibits on Alexandria history provided by Alexandria Archaeology (ℂ 703/838-4399; www.alexandriaarchaeology.org), which is headquartered here and engages in extensive city research. A volunteer or staff member is on hand to answer questions. Art lovers could end up browsing for an hour or two.

105 N. Union St. (between King and Cameron sts. on the waterfront). ℂ 703/838-4565. www.torpedo factory.org. Free admission. Daily 10am–5pm; archaeology exhibit area Tues–Fri 10am–3pm, Sat 10am–5pm, Sun 1–5pm. Closed Easter, July 4, Thanksgiving, Dec 25, and Jan 1.

ACCOMMODATIONS

It is simply not possible to find inexpensive lodging within, or close by, Old Town Alexandria. In fact, Historic Old Town proper has only one hotel inside its boundaries. That one, the **Holiday Inn Select Old Town,** 480 King St. (ℂ **800/368-5047** or 703/549-6080; www.oldtownhis.com), and another just outside the Historic District, **Morrison House,** 116 S. Alfred St. (ℂ **866/834-6628** or 703/838-8000; www.morrisonhouse.com), are the two I'd recommend, if you're interested in staying overnight on this side of the Potomac. Expect to pay for their fine accommodations.

Rates at the Holiday Inn range from $150 (a special rate for employees of the government or military) to $269; suites start at $400. Rooms feature 18th-century–style furnishings; king, queen, or double beds; and sitting areas. Amenities at this hotel include complimentary continental breakfast on weekdays, bike rentals, a fitness center, and an indoor pool. Ask about discounts for AAA, AARP, government, and any other groups to which you may belong.

Morrison House is an elegant small hotel recently inducted as a member into the elite Relais & Châteaux. The hotel has only 45 rooms, each appointed in high style with canopied four-poster beds, mahogany armoires, decorative fireplaces, and the like. Rates start at $175 for the smallest room off-season, and at $349 for a deluxe room in-season. Morrison House is known for its restaurant, **Elysium,** which presents award-winning contemporary American cuisine.

For other recommendations, check the **Alexandria Convention and Visitors Association** website, **www.funside.com**, where you can book an online reservation and also read about various promotions that hotels are offering.

DINING

There are so many fine restaurants in Alexandria that Washingtonians often drive over just to dine here and stroll the cobblestone streets.

Gadsby's Tavern COLONIAL AMERICAN   George Washington often came here to dine and dance, and this is where he reviewed his troops for the last time. Gadsby's Tavern tends toward the touristy, but it does evoke the 18th century authentically, with period music, wood-plank floors, hurricane-lamp wall sconces, and a rendition of a Hogarth painting over the fireplace (one of several).

Servers are dressed in traditional colonial attire. A strolling violinist entertains Tuesday and Wednesday nights, an "18th-century gentleman" regales guests with song and tells the news of the day (200 years ago, on the day you are there). When the weather's nice, you can dine in a flagstone courtyard edged with flower beds.

The fare is adequate. It's all homemade, including the sweet Sally Lunn bread, which is baked daily. You might start with soup from the stockpot served with homemade sourdough crackers, followed by baked ham and cheese pie (a sort of Early American quiche), hot roast turkey with giblet gravy and bread-and-sage stuffing on Sally Lunn bread, or George Washington's favorite: slow-roasted crisp duckling served with fruit dressing and Madeira sauce. For dessert, try the English trifle or creamy buttermilk-custard pie with a hint of lemon. Colonial "coolers" are also available: scuppernong, Wench's Punch, and such. The Sunday brunch menu adds such items as thick slices of toast dipped in a batter of rum and spices, with sausage, hash browns, and hot cinnamon syrup. And a desserts and libations menu highlights such favorites as Scottish apple gingerbread and bourbon apple pie, along with a wide selection of beverages.

138 N. Royal St. (at Cameron St.). ✆ **703/548-1288**. Reservations recommended at dinner. Lunch/brunch items $8–$15; dinner main courses $15–$25. Half-price portions available on some items for children 12 and under. AE, DC, MC, V. Mon–Sat 11:30am–3pm; Sun 11am–3pm; daily 5:30–10pm.

La Madeleine *Kids* FRENCH CAFE   It may be part of a self-service chain, but this place is charming nonetheless. Its French country interior has a beamed ceiling, bare oak floors, a wood-burning stove, and maple hutches displaying crockery and pewter mugs. Its range of affordable menu items makes this a good choice for families with finicky eaters in tow.

Come in the morning for fresh-baked croissants, Danish, scones, muffins, and brioches, or a heartier bacon-and-eggs plate. Throughout the day, there are delicious salads (such as roasted vegetables and rigatoni), sandwiches (including a traditional croque monsieur), and hot dishes ranging from quiche and pizza to rotisserie chicken with a Caesar salad. After 5pm, additional choices include pastas and specials such as beef bourguignonne and salmon in dill-cream sauce, both served with a crispy potato galette and sautéed broccoli. Conclude with a yummy fruit tart or chocolate, vanilla, and praline triple-layer cheesecake with graham-cracker crust. Wine and beer are served.

500 King St. (at S. Pitt St.). ✆ **703/739-2854**. www.lamadeleine.com. Reservations not accepted. Breakfast main courses $3.30–$6.50; lunch and dinner main courses $5–$10. AE, DISC, MC, V. Sun–Thurs 7am–10pm; Fri–Sat 7am–11pm.

South Austin Grill SOUTHERN/SOUTHWESTERN   One of six Austin Grills in the area, this one offers the same menu, music, and ambience as other links in the chain. See p. 155 for a review of the Glover Park location.

801 King St. (at S. Columbus St.). ✆ **703/684-8969**. www.austingrill.com. Reservations not accepted. Main courses $8–$17. AE, DC, DISC, MC, V. Mon 11:30am–10:30pm; Tues–Thurs 11:30am–11pm; Fri 11:30am–midnight; Sat 11am–midnight; Sun 11am–10:30pm.

Taverna Cretekou ✿ GREEK   There aren't many truly Greek (as opposed to Mediterranean or Middle Eastern) restaurants in the Washington area, and this is undeniably the best. The Taverna has been open for 30 years, and is only gaining in popularity, for its traditional dishes of spanakopita and moussaka, as well as contemporary items, such as grilled red snapper with oregano and lemon, or rainbow trout stuffed with spinach and feta. The ouzo flows and, on Thursday nights, Greek music and dancing breaks out, usually ending up with diners and waiters joining the musicians.

818 King St. (at Alfred St.). ⓒ 703/548-8688. www.tavernacretekou.com. Reservations recommended. Lunch and dinner items $11–$18; Sun brunch $16. AE, DISC, MC, V. Tues–Fri 11:30am–2:30pm and 5–10pm; Sat noon–11pm; Sun brunch 11am–3pm and dinner 5–9:30pm.

Union Street Public House AMERICAN/SEAFOOD You might have to wait in line to be seated, but the line usually moves fast, since the restaurant has lots of pubby rooms. The laid-back atmosphere and comfortable decor make this a natural stop for families, groups, informal dates, and anyone who's just hopped off the bike trail to Mount Vernon. Window seats upstairs are coveted for their views of King Street. Downstairs rooms tend to emphasize the *pub* in public house—this is where singles mingle. The menu offers burgers, po' boys, oysters, fried calamari, salads, and so on.

121 S. Union St. ⓒ 703/548-1785. www.usphalexandria.com. Reservations accepted for groups of 8 or more, except on Fri–Sat nights. Main courses $7–$20. AE, DISC, MC, V. Mon–Thurs 11:30am–10:30pm; Fri–Sat 11:30am–11:30pm; Sun 11am–10:30pm.

WORTH A SPLURGE

Geranio 𝒢 REGIONAL ITALIAN Many folks think this is the best restaurant in Old Town. After a dinner in front of the log fire, a fine bottle of Chianti, an appetizer of potted duck with garlic confit and olive oil crostini (or maybe the lobster risotto), entree of grilled salmon with pancetta and red-wine sauce (or maybe the osso buco), followed by dessert of tiramisu (or maybe lemon parfait), you might agree. Excellent service.

722 King St. (between Washington and Columbus sts.). ⓒ 703/548-0088. www.geranio.net. Reservations recommended. Lunch items $8–$17; dinner main courses $12–$26. AE, DC, DISC, MC, V. Mon–Fri 11:30am–2:30pm; Mon–Sat 6–10:30pm; Sun 5:30–9:30pm.

La Bergerie 𝒢 CLASSIC FRENCH This restaurant has been here forever and is ever popular, even though its longtime owners sold La Bergerie in 2002. Waiters are tuxedoed and entrees are updated traditional: escargots sprinkled with hazelnuts, smoky foie gras, lobster bisque with lobster and its coral, tournedos of beef with wild mushrooms and béarnaise sauce. The restaurant is known for its soufflés and apple tart, which you must request when you order your entrees. You'll want to dress up here.

218 N. Lee St. ⓒ 703/683-1007. www.labergerie.com. Reservations required. Lunch main courses $13–$17; dinner main courses $17–$29. AE, DC, DISC, MC, V. Mon–Sat 11:30am–2:30pm and 5:30–10:30pm; Sun 5–10pm.

Appendix A:
Washington, D.C., in Depth

Two hundred and fourteen years ago, the world wondered why America had chosen this swampy locale as its capital. It took its first hundred years for Washington to evolve from bumpkin backwater status to an international hub of power, diplomacy, and beauty. Today, Washington, D.C., fully commands center stage.

And people from all over the world do come to see D.C. Tourism contributes to the bustle of this city that serves as the seat of the nation's government, as well as home to more than 572,000 people, scores of vibrant neighborhoods, countless historic landmarks and other tourist attractions, a thriving cultural and arts scene, many beautiful parks, and loads of terrific restaurants. The capital is the centerpiece of a metropolitan region that extends into the suburbs of Virginia and Maryland. This Greater Washington area has a population of 5.5 million people, making it one of the most rapidly expanding metropolitan areas, as well as the fastest growing job base, in the nation.

Just a few short years ago, Washington wasn't so attractive; visitors came to tour federal buildings, like the Capitol, the White House, and the Smithsonian museums, but stayed away from the downtown and nontouristy areas. The city's revitalization in the past few years is largely due to Mayor Anthony A. Williams (handily re-elected in 2002), his city council, and Congresswoman Eleanor Holmes Norton, whose herculean efforts to revive the economy and provide better services around the city have encouraged developers and entrepreneurs to invest here. Their success has led Congress to contemplate handing over more control of the District to the District itself. Since D.C. is not a state, Congress oversees the city's budget and legislation. Residents elect a mayor and council, who govern the nonfederal responsibilities of the city, but Congress's micromanagement of these local issues tends to impede planning and progress. Residents also elect a delegate to Congress (Norton is the current representative), who introduces legislation and votes in committees, but who cannot vote on the House floor. This unique situation, in which residents of the District pay federal income taxes but don't have a vote in Congress, is increasingly a matter of local concern—you may notice D.C. license plates bearing the inscription "Taxation without Representation." Congresswoman Norton and others have begun to push for D.C.'s statehood or, at the very least, a true vote in Congress. For more information about the history, politics, and local lore of the city of Washington, check out the website, www.dc.gov, which provides a lot of good information in itself, but also links you to many other helpful sources.

Whether or not Washington eventually wins voting rights and statehood, its dual roles as nation's capital and independent city have always been and will ever be intertwined with American history, as the following section makes clear.

History 101

A WANDERING CONGRESS It all began in 1783, when 250 Revolutionary War soldiers, understandably angered because Congress was ignoring their petitions for back pay, stormed the temporary capitol in Philadelphia to demand justice. The citizens of Philadelphia sympathized with the soldiers and ignored congressional pleas for protection; as the soldiers rioted outside, lawmakers huddled inside the State House behind locked doors. When the soldiers finally calmed down and returned to their barracks, Congress decided it would be prudent to move itself to Princeton. Lawmakers also decided they needed a capital city whose business was government and the protection thereof.

This decision to relocate was not a new one. Congress had been so nomadic during its first decade that when a statue of George Washington was commissioned in 1783, satirist Francis Hopkinson suggested putting it on wheels so that it could follow the government around. Before permanently settling in Washington, Congress convened in New York, Baltimore, Philadelphia, Lancaster, Princeton, Annapolis, York, and Trenton.

A DEAL MADE OVER DINNER When Congress proposed that a city be designed and built for the sole purpose of housing the government of the new nation, fresh difficulties arose. There was a general feeling that wherever the capital might be built, a great commercial center would blossom; therefore, many cities vied for the honor. Then, too, northerners were strongly opposed to a southern capital—and vice versa. Finally, after 7 years of bickering, New Yorker Alexander Hamilton and Virginian Thomas Jefferson worked out a compromise over dinner one night in New York. The North would support a southern site for the capital in return for the South's assumption of debts

Dateline

- **1608** Capt. John Smith sails up Potomac River from Jamestown; for the next 100 years, Irish-Scottish settlers colonize the area.
- **1783** Continental Congress proposes new "Federal Town"; both North and South vie for it.
- **1790** A compromise is reached: If the South pays off the North's Revolutionary War debts, the new capital will be situated in its region.
- **1791** French engineer Pierre Charles L'Enfant designs the capital city but is fired within a year.
- **1792** Cornerstone is laid for Executive Mansion.
- **1793** Construction begins on the Capitol.
- **1800** First wing of the Capitol completed; Congress moves from Philadelphia; Pres. John Adams moves into Executive Mansion.
- **1801** Library of Congress established.
- **1812** War with England.
- **1814** British burn Washington.
- **1817** Executive Mansion rebuilt, its charred walls painted white; becomes known as White House.
- **1822** Population reaches 33,000.
- **1829** Smithsonian Institution founded for the "increase and diffusion of knowledge."
- **1861** Civil War; Washington becomes North's major supply depot.
- **1865** Capitol dome completed; Lee surrenders to Grant on April 8; Lincoln assassinated at Ford's Theatre on April 14.
- **1871** Alexander "Boss" Shepherd turns Washington into a showplace, using many of L'Enfant's plans.
- **1900** Population reaches about 300,000.
- **1901** McMillan Commission plans development of Mall from Capitol to Lincoln Memorial.
- **1907** Union Station opens, largest train station in country.
- **1912** Cherry trees, a gift from Japan, planted in Tidal Basin.
- **1914** World War I begins.
- **1922** Lincoln Memorial completed.

incurred by the northern states during the Revolutionary War. As a further sop to the North, it was agreed that the seat of government would remain in Philadelphia through 1800 to allow suitable time for surveying, purchasing land, and constructing government buildings.

ENTER L'ENFANT TERRIBLE An act passed in 1790 specified a site "not exceeding 10 miles square" to be located on the Potomac. President George Washington, an experienced surveyor charged with selecting the exact site, chose a part of the Potomac Valley where the river becomes tidal and is joined by the Anacostia. Maryland gladly provided 69¼ square miles and Virginia 30¾ square miles for the new Federal District. (In 1846, Virginia's territorial contribution was returned to the state.) The District today covers about 67 square miles.

President Washington hired French military engineer Pierre Charles L'Enfant to lay out the federal city. It has since been said that "it would have been hard to find a man better qualified artistically and less fitted by temperament" for the job. L'Enfant arrived in 1791 and immediately declared Jenkins Hill (today Capitol Hill) "a pedestal waiting for a monument." He surveyed every inch of the designated Federal District and began creating his vision by selecting dominant sites for major buildings. He designed 160-foot-wide avenues radiating from squares and circles centered on monumental sculptures and fountains. The Capitol, the "presidential palace," and an equestrian statue—the last to be erected where the Washington Monument stands today—were to be the city's focal points. Pennsylvania Avenue would be the major thoroughfare, and the Mall was conceived as a bustling ceremonial avenue of embassies and other distinguished buildings.

L'Enfant's plan dismayed landowners who had been promised $66.66

1941 First plane lands at National Airport; United States declares war on Japan.

1943 Pantheon-inspired Jefferson Memorial and Pentagon completed.

1960 Population declines for first time, from 800,000 to 764,000.

1963 More than 200,000 March on Washington, hear Martin Luther King Jr.'s "I Have a Dream" speech supporting civil rights.

1971 John F. Kennedy Center for Performing Arts opens.

1976 Metro, city's first subway system, opens in time for bicentennial.

1982 Vietnam Veterans Memorial erected in Constitution Gardens.

1993 U.S. Holocaust Memorial Museum opens near Mall.

1994 Marion Barry is elected to a fourth term as mayor after serving time in prison.

1995 Korean War Veterans Memorial is dedicated; Pennsylvania Avenue closed to vehicular traffic in front of the White House on security grounds.

1997 Federal government offers aid package to save D.C. from bankruptcy; Franklin Delano Roosevelt Memorial is dedicated.

1998 White House beset by sex scandal; In December, the House of Representatives impeaches the president.

1999 Washington, D.C., inaugurates Mayor Anthony Williams; In February, the Senate acquits the president.

2001 While thousands protest, Pres. George W. Bush takes office in January after the most controversial election in modern U.S. history; In September, 180 people die when terrorists hijack a commercial airliner and crash it into the Pentagon.

2002 The city recovers from the aftermath of September 11, 2001, terrorist attacks, rebuilds the destroyed section of the Pentagon, and imposes tighter security at federal buildings and airports. An elusive pair of snipers terrorizes the D.C. area, killing 10 people and wounding 3, before capture in October. D.C. Mayor Anthony Williams wins re-election.

continues

per acre for land donated for buildings, while land for avenues was to be donated free; of the 6,661 acres to be included in the boundaries of the federal city, about half would comprise avenues and the 2-mile-long Mall.

■ **2003** The U.S. invades Iraq. D.C.'s own City Museum of Washington opens, to tell the story of Washington, from a nonfederal perspective.

A more personable man might have won over the reluctant landowners and commissioners, inspiring them with his dreams and his passion, but L'Enfant exhibited only a peevish and condescending secretiveness that alienated one and all. A year after he had been hired, L'Enfant was fired. Congress offered him $2,500 compensation for his year of work, and James Monroe urged him to accept a professorship at West Point. Insulted, he spurned all offers, suing the government for $95,500 instead. He lost and died a pauper in 1825. In 1909, in belated recognition of his services, his remains were brought to Arlington National Cemetery. Some 118 years after he had conceived it, his vision of the federal city finally had become a reality.

HOME NOT-SO-SWEET HOME   In 1800, government officials (106 representatives and 32 senators) arrived according to schedule, ready to settle into their new home. What they found bore little resemblance to a city. "One might take a ride of several hours within the precincts without meeting with a single individual to disturb one's meditation," commented one early resident. Pennsylvania Avenue was a mosquito-infested swamp, and there were fewer than 400 habitable houses. Disgruntled Secretary of the Treasury Oliver Wolcott wrote his wife, "I do not perceive how the members of Congress can possibly secure lodgings, unless they will consent to live like Scholars in a college or Monks in a monastery." The solution was a boom in boardinghouses.

Abigail Adams was dismayed at the condition of her new home, the presidential mansion. The damp caused her rheumatism to act up, the main stairs had not yet been constructed, not a single room was finished, and there were not even enough logs for all the fireplaces. And since there was "not the least fence, yard, or other convenience," she hung the presidential laundry in the unfinished East Room. To attend presidential affairs or to visit one another, Washington's early citizens had to drive through mud and slush, their vehicles often becoming embedded in bogs and gullies—not a pleasant state of affairs, but one that would continue for many decades.

There were many difficulties in building the capital. Money, as always, was in short supply, as were materials and labor, with the result that the home of the world's most enlightened democracy was built largely by slaves. And always, in the background, there was talk of abandoning the city and starting over somewhere else.

REDCOATS REDUX   Then came the War of 1812. At first, fighting centered on Canada and the West—both too far away to affect daily life in the capital. (In the early 1800s, it was a 33-hr. ride from Washington, D.C., to Philadelphia—if you made good time.) In May 1813, the flamboyant British Rear Admiral Cockburn sent word to the Executive Mansion that "he would make his bow" in the Madisons' drawing room shortly. On August 23, 1814, alarming news reached the capital: The British had landed troops in Maryland. On August 24, James Madison was at the front, most of the populace had fled, and Dolley Madison created a legend by refusing to leave the president's mansion without Gilbert Stuart's famous portrait of George Washington. As the

British neared her gates, she calmly wrote a blow-by-blow description to her sister:

"Our kind friend, Mr. Carroll, has come to hasten my departure, and is in a very bad humour with me because I insist on waiting until the large picture of General Washington is secured, and it requires to be unscrewed from the wall. This process was found too tedious for these perilous moments; I have ordered the frame to be broken, and the canvas taken out; it is done . . . And now, dear sister, I must leave this house, or the retreating army will make me a prisoner in it, by filling up the road I am directed to take."

When the British arrived early that evening, they found dinner set up on the table (Dolley had hoped for the best until the end), and, according to some accounts, ate it before torching the mansion. They also burned the Capitol, the Library of Congress, and newly built ships and naval stores. A thunderstorm later that night saved the city from total destruction, while a tornado the next day added to the damage but daunted the British troops.

It seemed that the new capital was doomed. Margaret Bayard Smith, wife of the owner of the influential *National Intelligencer,* privately lamented, "I do not suppose the Government will ever return to Washington. All those whose property was invested in that place, will be reduced to general poverty . . . The consternation about us is general. The despondency still greater." But the *Intelligencer* was among the printed voices speaking out against even a temporary move. Editorials warned that it would be a "treacherous breach of faith" with those who had "laid out fortunes in the purchase of property in and about the city." To move the capital would be "kissing the rod an enemy has wielded."

Washingtonian pride rallied and the city was saved once again. Still, it was a close call; Congress came within nine votes of abandoning the place!

In 1815, leading citizens erected a brick building in which Congress could meet in relative comfort until the Capitol was restored. The Treaty of Ghent, establishing peace with Great Britain, was ratified at Octagon House, where the Madisons were temporarily ensconced. And Thomas Jefferson replaced the destroyed contents of the Library of Congress with his own books. Confidence was restored and the city began to prosper. When the Madisons moved into the rebuilt presidential mansion, its exterior had been painted gleaming white to cover the charred walls. From then on, it would be known as the White House.

THE CITY OF MAGNIFICENT INTENTIONS   Between the War of 1812 and the Civil War, few people evinced any great enthusiasm for Washington. European visitors in particular looked at the capital and found it wanting. It was still a provincial backwater, with Pennsylvania Avenue and the Mall remaining muddy messes inhabited by pigs, goats, cows, and geese. Many were repelled by the slave auctions openly taking place in the backyard of the White House. The best that could be said—though nobody said it—was that the young capital was picturesque. Meriwether Lewis kept the bears he captured during his 4,000-mile expedition up the Missouri in cages on the president's lawn. Native American chiefs in full regalia were often seen negotiating with the white man's government. Matching them in visual splendor were magnificently attired European court visitors.

The only foreigner who praised Washington was Lafayette, who visited in 1825 and was feted with lavish balls and dinners throughout his stay. Charles Dickens gave the city the raspberry in 1842:

"It is sometimes called the City of Magnificent Distances, but it might with greater propriety be termed the City of Magnificent Intentions . . . Spacious avenues, that begin in nothing and lead nowhere; streets, miles long, that only want houses, roads, and inhabitants; public buildings that need but a public to be complete; and ornaments of great thoroughfares, which only lack great thoroughfares to ornament—are its leading features."

Tobacco chewing and sloppy senatorial spitting particularly appalled him:

"Both houses are handsomely carpeted, but the state to which these carpets are reduced by the universal disregard of the spittoon with which every honorable member is accommodated, and the extraordinary improvements on the pattern which are squirted and dabbled upon it in every direction, do not admit of being described. I will merely observe, that I strongly recommend all strangers not to look at the floor; and if they happen to drop anything . . . not to pick it up with an ungloved hand on any account."

But Dickens's critique was mild when compared with Anthony Trollope's, who declared Washington in 1860 "as melancholy and miserable a town as the mind of man can conceive."

A NATION DIVIDED   During the Civil War, the capital became an armed camp. It was the principal supply depot for the Union Army and an important medical center. Parks became campgrounds, churches became hospitals, and forts ringed the town. The population doubled from 60,000 to 120,000, including about 40,000 former slaves who streamed into the city seeking federal protection. More than 3,000 soldiers slept in the Capitol building, and a bakery was set up in the basement. The streets were filled with the wounded, and Walt Whitman became a familiar figure, making daily rounds to comfort the ailing soldiers. In spite of everything, Lincoln insisted that work on the incomplete Capitol be continued. "If people see the Capitol going on, it is a sign we intend the Union shall go on," he said. When the giant dome was finished in 1863 and a 35-star flag was flown overhead, Capitol Hill's field battery fired a 35-gun salute, honoring the Union's then 35 states.

There was joy in Washington and an 800-gun salute in April 1865, when news of the fall of the Confederacy reached the capital. The joy was short-lived, however. Five days after Appomattox, President Lincoln was shot at Ford's Theatre while attending a performance of *Our American Cousin.* Black replaced the festive tricolored draperies decorating the town, and Washington went into mourning.

The war had enlarged the city's population while doing nothing to improve its facilities. Agrarian, uneducated ex-slaves stayed on, and poverty, unemployment, and disease were rampant. A red-light district remained, the parks were trodden bare, and tenement slums mushroomed within a stone's throw of the Capitol.

LED BY A SHEPHERD   Whereas L'Enfant had been aloof and introverted, his glorious vision was not forgotten, finally being implemented 70 years later by Alexander "Boss" Shepherd, a swashbuckling and friendly man. A real estate speculator who had made his money in a plumbing firm, Shepherd shouldered a musket in the Union Army and became one of Gen. Ulysses S. Grant's closest intimates. When Grant became president, he wanted to appoint Shepherd governor, but blue-blooded opposition ran too high. Washington high society considered him a parvenu and feared his ambitions for civic leadership. In response, Grant named the more popular Henry D. Cooke (a secret Shepherd ally) governor and appointed Shepherd vice president of the Board of Public Works. No one was fooled. Shepherd made all the governor's decisions, and a joke went around the capital: "Why is the new governor like a sheep? Because he is led by A. Shepherd." He became the official governor in 1873.

Shepherd vowed that his "comprehensive plan of improvement" would make the city a showplace. But an engineer he wasn't—occasionally, newly paved streets had to be torn up because he had forgotten to install sewers. But he was a first-rate politician who knew how to accomplish his goals. He began by hiring an army of laborers and starting them on projects all over town. Congress would have had to halt work on half-finished sidewalks, streets, and sewers throughout the District in order to stop him. It would have been a mess. The press liked and supported the colorful Shepherd; however, people forced out of their homes because they couldn't pay the high assessments for improvements hated him. Between 1871 and 1874, he established parks, paved and lighted the streets, installed sewers, filled in sewage-laden Tiber Creek, and planted more than 50,000 trees. He left the city bankrupt—more than $20 million in debt. But he got the job done.

L'ENFANT REBORN   Through the end of the 19th century, Washington continued to make great aesthetic strides. The Washington Monument, long a truncated obelisk and major eyesore, was finally dedicated in 1885. Pennsylvania Avenue was becoming the ceremonial thoroughfare L'Enfant had envisioned, and important buildings were completed one after another. Shepherd had done a great deal, but much was still left undone. In 1887, L'Enfant's "Plan for the City of Washington" was resurrected. In 1900, Michigan Senator James McMillan—a retired railroad mogul with architectural and engineering knowledge—determined to complete the job L'Enfant had started a century earlier. A tireless lobbyist for government-sponsored municipal improvements, he persuaded his colleagues to appoint an advisory committee to create "the city beautiful." At his personal expense, McMillan sent this illustrious committee—landscapist Frederick Law Olmsted (designer of New York's Central Park), sculptor Augustus Saint-Gaudens, and noted architects Daniel Burnham and Charles McKim—to Europe for 7 weeks to study the landscaping and architecture of that continent's great capitals. Assembled at last was a group that combined L'Enfant's artistic genius and Shepherd's political savvy.

"Make no little plans," counseled Burnham. "They have no magic to stir men's blood, and probably themselves will not be realized. Make big plans, aim high in hope and work, remembering that a noble and logical diagram once recorded will never die, but long after we are gone will be a living thing, asserting itself with ever growing insistency."

The committee's big plans—almost all of which were accomplished—included the development of a complete park system, selection of sites for government buildings, and the designing of the Lincoln Memorial, the Arlington Memorial Bridge, and the Reflecting Pool (the last inspired by Versailles). They also got to work on improving the Mall; their first step was to remove the tracks, train sheds, and stone depot constructed there by the Baltimore and Potomac Railroad. In return, Congress authorized money to build the monumental Union Station, whose design was inspired by Rome's Baths of Diocletian.

Throughout the McMillan Commission years, the House was under the hostile leadership of Speaker "Uncle Joe" Cannon of Illinois, who, among other things, swore he would "never let a memorial to Abraham Lincoln be erected in that goddamned swamp" (West Potomac Park). Cannon caused some problems and delays, but on the whole the committee's prestigious membership added weight to their usually accepted recommendations. McMillan, however, did not live to see most of his dreams accomplished. He died in 1902.

By the 20th century, Washington was no longer an object of ridicule. The capital was coming into its own as a finely designed city of sweeping vistas studded with green parks and grand architecture. Congress's 1899 mandate limiting building heights in downtown Washington ensured the prominence of landmarks in the landscape. As the century progressed, the city seamlessly incorporated additional architectural marvels, including the Library of Congress, Union Station, and the Corcoran Gallery, which were all built around the turn of the century; several more Smithsonian museums and the Lincoln Memorial were completed in 1922. A Commission of Fine Arts was appointed in 1910 by President Taft to create monuments and fountains, and, thanks to Mrs. Taft, the famous cherry trees presented to the United States by the Japanese in 1912 were planted in the Tidal Basin.

During the Great Depression in the 1930s, FDR's Works Progress Administration (WPA) put the unemployed to work erecting public buildings and artists to work beautifying them. By the 1930s, too, increasing numbers of automobiles—nearly 200,000—were traversing Washington's wide avenues, joining the electric streetcars that had been in use since about 1890.

Washington's population, meanwhile, continued to grow, spurred by the influx of workers remaining after each of the world wars. In 1950, the city's population reached a zenith of more than 800,000 residents, an estimated 60% of whom were black. At the same time that Washington was establishing itself as a global power, the city was gaining renown among African Americans as a hub of black culture, education, and identity. From the 1920s to the 1960s, Washington drew the likes of Cab Calloway, Duke Ellington, and Pearl Bailey, who performed at speakeasies and theaters along a stretch of U Street called the Black Broadway. (The reincarnated "New U," as it is dubbed, now attracts buppies, yuppies, and restless youth to its nightclubs and bars.) Howard University, created in 1867, distinguished itself as the nation's most comprehensive center for the higher education of blacks. And when the Civil Rights movement gained momentum throughout the country in the 1960s and 1970s, Washington's large black presence (nearly 75% of the city's overall population) and activist spirit were instrumental in furthering the cause.

On August 28, 1963, black and white Washingtonians joined the ranks of the more than 200,000 who "Marched on Washington" to ensure passage of the Civil Rights Act. It was at this event that Rev. Martin Luther King Jr. delivered his stirring "I Have a Dream" speech at the Lincoln Memorial, where 41 years earlier, during the memorial's dedication ceremony, black officials were required to stand and watch from across the road, segregated from the whites. When King was assassinated on April 4, 1968, rioting erupted here as it did in many cities around the country.

Ever since, black and white Washingtonians have continued to thrash out race relations in a city whose population has stabilized at 572,000, about 60% of which now is African American, including the city's mayor and congressional representative. Mayor Anthony A. Williams, who handily won re-election to a second term in 2002, and Congresswoman Eleanor Holmes Norton, who is now in her seventh term in office, continue to focus their efforts on improving the city, each fighting tirelessly for their constituency.

Washington, the federal city, proceeds apace, adding more jewels to its crown. In 1989, renovation of the city's magnificent Union Station was completed. Architect Daniel Burnham also designed the palatial City Post Office Building, which, in 1993, became part of the Smithsonian complex as the National Postal Museum.

The same year saw the opening of the U.S. Holocaust Memorial Museum, adjoining the Mall. In 1995, the Korean War Veterans Memorial was dedicated. Washington's fourth presidential monument—and the first in more than half a century—was dedicated in May 1997, to honor Franklin Delano Roosevelt; it is the first memorial in Washington designed to be totally wheelchair accessible. The Women in Military Service Memorial, next to Arlington Cemetery, was inaugurated in October 1997, followed, in June 1998, by a Civil War memorial recognizing the efforts of African-American soldiers who fought for the Union.

The year 2003 saw the opening of a huge, new convention center, a City Museum of Washington (across the street from the convention center), and the National Air and Space Museum's large auxiliary building, the Steven F. Udvar-Hazy Center, at the Washington–Dulles International Airport. Coming in 2004: the opening of the Smithsonian's National Museum of the American Indian, and the dedication of the National World War II Memorial, both on the National Mall.

If the city's optimism about its prosperity and growth was profoundly shaken by the terrorist attacks of September 11, 2001, it has been largely restored in the years since. The economy continues to rebound, and tourists are returning to Washington. Today, as always, the capital of the United States gladly welcomes to town visitors from around the world.

Appendix B:
Useful Toll-Free Numbers
& Websites

AIRLINES

Air Canada
© 888/247-2262
www.aircanada.ca

Airtran Airlines
© 800/247-8726
www.airtran.com

American Airlines
© 800/433-7300
www.aa.com

American Trans Air
© 800/435-9282
www.ata.com

British Airways
© 800/247-9297
© 0345/222-111 or 0845/77-333-77
  in Britain
www.british-airways.com

Continental Airlines
© 800/525-0280
www.continental.com

Delta Air Lines
© 800/221-1212
www.delta.com

Frontier Airlines
© 800/432-1359
www.frontierairlines.com

JetBlue
© 800/538-2583
www.jetblue.com

Midwest Express
© 800/452-2022
www.midwestexpress.com

Northwest Airlines
© 800/225-2525
www.nwa.com

Southwest Airlines
© 800/435-9792
www.southwest.com

United Airlines
© 800/241-6522
www.united.com

US Airways
© 800/428-4322
www.usairways.com

Virgin Atlantic Airways
© 800/862-8621 in continental U.S.
© 0293/747-747 in Britain
www.virgin-atlantic.com

CAR-RENTAL AGENCIES

Alamo
© 800/227-8367
www.goalamo.com

Avis
© 800/331-1212 in continental U.S.
© 800/TRY-AVIS in Canada
www.avis.com

Budget
© 800/527-0700
www.budget.com

Dollar
© 800/800-4000
www.dollar.com

Enterprise
© 800/325-8007
www.enterprise.com

Hertz
© 800/654-3131
www.hertz.com

National
© 800/CAR-RENT
www.nationalcar.com

Rent-A-Wreck
✆ 800/535-1391
www.rentawreck.com

Thrifty
✆ 800/367-2277
www.thrifty.com

MAJOR HOTEL & MOTEL CHAINS

Best Western International
✆ 800/528-1234
www.bestwestern.com

Clarion Hotels
✆ 800/CLARION
www.clarionhotel.com
or www.hotelchoice.com

Comfort Inns
✆ 800/228-5150
www.hotelchoice.com

Courtyard by Marriott
✆ 800/321-2211
www.courtyard.com
or www.marriott.com

Days Inn
✆ 800/325-2525
www.daysinn.com

Doubletree Hotels
✆ 800/222-TREE
www.doubletree.com

Econo Lodges
✆ 800/55-ECONO
www.hotelchoice.com

Fairfield Inn by Marriott
✆ 800/228-2800
www.marriott.com

Hampton Inn
✆ 800/HAMPTON
www.hampton-inn.com

Hilton Hotels
✆ 800/HILTONS
www.hilton.com

Holiday Inn
✆ 800/HOLIDAY
www.basshotels.com

Howard Johnson
✆ 800/654-2000
www.hojo.com

Hyatt Hotels & Resorts
✆ 800/228-9000
www.hyatt.com

ITT Sheraton
✆ 800/325-3535
www.starwood.com

Marriott Hotels
✆ 800/228-9290
www.marriott.com

Motel 6
✆ 800/4-MOTEL-6
www.motel6.com

Quality Inns
✆ 800/228-5151
www.hotelchoice.com

Radisson Hotels International
✆ 800/333-3333
www.radisson.com

Ramada Inns
✆ 800/2-RAMADA
www.ramada.com

Red Carpet Inns
✆ 800/251-1962
www.reservahost.com

Red Lion Hotels & Inns
✆ 800/547-8010
www.hilton.com

Red Roof Inns
✆ 800/843-7663
www.redroof.com

Residence Inn by Marriott
✆ 800/331-3131
www.marriott.com

Rodeway Inns
✆ 800/228-2000
www.hotelchoice.com

Super 8 Motels
✆ 800/800-8000
www.super8.com

Travelodge
✆ 800/255-3050
www.travelodge.com

Wyndham Hotels and Resorts
✆ 800/822-4200 in continental U.S. and Canada
www.wyndham.com

Index

See also Accommodations and Restaurant indexes, below.

FROMMER'S® COMPLETE TRAVEL GUIDES

Alaska
Alaska Cruises & Ports of Call
Amsterdam
Argentina & Chile
Arizona
Atlanta
Australia
Austria
Bahamas
Barcelona, Madrid & Seville
Beijing
Belgium, Holland & Luxembourg
Bermuda
Boston
Brazil
British Columbia & the Canadian
  Rockies
Brussels & Bruges
Budapest & the Best of Hungary
California
Canada
Cancún, Cozumel & the Yucatán
Cape Cod, Nantucket & Martha's
  Vineyard
Caribbean
Caribbean Cruises & Ports of Call
Caribbean Ports of Call
Carolinas & Georgia
Chicago
China
Colorado
Costa Rica
Cuba
Denmark
Denver, Boulder & Colorado Springs
England
Europe
European Cruises & Ports of Call

Florida
France
Germany
Great Britain
Greece
Greek Islands
Hawaii
Hong Kong
Honolulu, Waikiki & Oahu
Ireland
Israel
Italy
Jamaica
Japan
Las Vegas
London
Los Angeles
Maryland & Delaware
Maui
Mexico
Montana & Wyoming
Montréal & Québec City
Munich & the Bavarian Alps
Nashville & Memphis
New England
New Mexico
New Orleans
New York City
New Zealand
Northern Italy
Norway
Nova Scotia, New Brunswick &
  Prince Edward Island
Oregon
Paris
Peru
Philadelphia & the Amish Country
Portugal

Prague & the Best of the Czech
  Republic
Provence & the Riviera
Puerto Rico
Rome
San Antonio & Austin
San Diego
San Francisco
Santa Fe, Taos & Albuquerque
Scandinavia
Scotland
Seattle & Portland
Shanghai
Sicily
Singapore & Malaysia
South Africa
South America
South Florida
South Pacific
Southeast Asia
Spain
Sweden
Switzerland
Texas
Thailand
Tokyo
Toronto
Tuscany & Umbria
USA
Utah
Vancouver & Victoria
Vermont, New Hampshire & Maine
Vienna & the Danube Valley
Virgin Islands
Virginia
Walt Disney World® & Orlando
Washington, D.C.
Washington State

FROMMER'S® DOLLAR-A-DAY GUIDES

Australia from $50 a Day
California from $70 a Day
England from $75 a Day
Europe from $70 a Day
Florida from $70 a Day
Hawaii from $80 a Day

Ireland from $60 a Day
Italy from $70 a Day
London from $85 a Day
New York from $90 a Day
Paris from $80 a Day

San Francisco from $70 a Day
Washington, D.C. from $80 a Day
Portable London from $85 a Day
Portable New York City from $90
  a Day

FROMMER'S® PORTABLE GUIDES

Acapulco, Ixtapa & Zihuatanejo
Amsterdam
Aruba
Australia's Great Barrier Reef
Bahamas
Berlin
Big Island of Hawaii
Boston
California Wine Country
Cancún
Cayman Islands
Charleston
Chicago
Disneyland®
Dublin
Florence

Frankfurt
Hong Kong
Houston
Las Vegas
Las Vegas for Non-Gamblers
London
Los Angeles
Los Cabos & Baja
Maine Coast
Maui
Miami
Nantucket & Martha's Vineyard
New Orleans
New York City
Paris
Phoenix & Scottsdale

Portland
Puerto Rico
Puerto Vallarta, Manzanillo &
  Guadalajara
Rio de Janeiro
San Diego
San Francisco
Savannah
Seattle
Sydney
Tampa & St. Petersburg
Vancouver
Venice
Virgin Islands
Washington, D.C.

FROMMER'S® NATIONAL PARK GUIDES

Banff & Jasper
Family Vacations in the National
  Parks

Grand Canyon
National Parks of the American West
Rocky Mountain

Yellowstone & Grand Teton
Yosemite & Sequoia/Kings Canyon
Zion & Bryce Canyon

FROMMER'S® MEMORABLE WALKS

Chicago	New York	San Francisco
London	Paris	

FROMMER'S® WITH KIDS GUIDES

Chicago	Ottawa	Vancouver
Las Vegas	San Francisco	Washington, D.C.
New York City	Toronto	

SUZY GERSHMAN'S BORN TO SHOP GUIDES

Born to Shop: France	Born to Shop: Italy	Born to Shop: New York
Born to Shop: Hong Kong,	Born to Shop: London	Born to Shop: Paris
Shanghai & Beijing		

FROMMER'S® IRREVERENT GUIDES

Amsterdam	Los Angeles	San Francisco
Boston	Manhattan	Seattle & Portland
Chicago	New Orleans	Vancouver
Las Vegas	Paris	Walt Disney World®
London	Rome	Washington, D.C.

FROMMER'S® BEST-LOVED DRIVING TOURS

Britain	Germany	Northern Italy
California	Ireland	Scotland
Florida	Italy	Spain
France	New England	Tuscany & Umbria

HANGING OUT™ GUIDES

Hanging Out in England	Hanging Out in France	Hanging Out in Italy
Hanging Out in Europe	Hanging Out in Ireland	Hanging Out in Spain

THE UNOFFICIAL GUIDES®

Bed & Breakfasts and Country	Southwest & South Central	Mexio's Best Beach Resorts
Inns in:	Plains	Mid-Atlantic with Kids
California	U.S.A.	Mini Las Vegas
Great Lakes States	Beyond Disney	Mini-Mickey
Mid-Atlantic	Branson, Missouri	New England & New York with
New England	California with Kids	Kids
Northwest	Central Italy	New Orleans
Rockies	Chicago	New York City
Southeast	Cruises	Paris
Southwest	Disneyland®	San Francisco
Best RV & Tent Campgrounds in:	Florida with Kids	Skiing & Snowboarding in the West
California & the West	Golf Vacations in the Eastern U.S.	Southeast with Kids
Florida & the Southeast	Great Smoky & Blue Ridge Region	Walt Disney World®
Great Lakes States	Inside Disney	Walt Disney World® for
Mid-Atlantic	Hawaii	Grown-ups
Northeast	Las Vegas	Walt Disney World® with Kids
Northwest & Central Plains	London	Washington, D.C.
	Maui	World's Best Diving Vacations

SPECIAL-INTEREST TITLES

Frommer's Adventure Guide to Australia &	Frommer's France's Best Bed & Breakfasts and
New Zealand	Country Inns
Frommer's Adventure Guide to Central America	Frommer's Gay & Lesbian Europe
Frommer's Adventure Guide to India & Pakistan	Frommer's Italy's Best Bed & Breakfasts and
Frommer's Adventure Guide to South America	Country Inns
Frommer's Adventure Guide to Southeast Asia	Frommer's Road Atlas Britain
Frommer's Adventure Guide to Southern Africa	Frommer's Road Atlas Europe
Frommer's Britain's Best Bed & Breakfasts and	Frommer's Road Atlas France
Country Inns	The New York Times' Guide to Unforgettable
Frommer's Caribbean Hideaways	Weekends
Frommer's Exploring America by RV	Places Rated Almanac
Frommer's Fly Safe, Fly Smart	Retirement Places Rated
	Rome Past & Present

Booked aisle seat.

Reserved room with a view.

With a queen – no, make that a king-size bed.

With Travelocity, you can book your flights and hotels together, so you can get even better deals than if you booked them separately. You'll save time and money without compromising the quality of your trip. Choose your airline seat, search for alternate airports, pick your hotel room type, even choose the neighborhood you'd like to stay in.

Travelocity

Visit www.travelocity.com or call 1-888-TRAVELOCITY

Fly.
Sleep.
Save.

Now you can book your flights and
hotels together, so you can get even better deals
than if you booked them separately.

Travelocity
Visit www.travelocity.com
or call 1-888-TRAVELOCITY